CW01676702

More HOW TO DRAW MANGA

Vol. 4

Mastering Bishoujo Characters

MORE HOW TO DRAW MANGA Vol. 4: Mastering Bishoujo Characters
by Hikaru Hayashi, Rio Yagizawa/ Go Office

Copyright © 2003 Hikaru Hayashi, Rio Yagizawa/ Go Office
Copyright © 2003 Graphic-sha Publishing Co., Ltd.

This book was first designed and published by Graphic-sha Publishing Co., Ltd. in Japan in 2003.
This English edition was published by Graphic-sha Publishing Co., Ltd. in Japan in 2004.

Artwork and Production:	Kazuaki Morita, Tetsudo Degawa, Hiroko Shioda, Akira Gokita, Kozue Onishi, Kento Shimazaki, Mayumi Tomaru, Yasuo Matsumoto, Mikako Hayashi, Aki Kuraoka, Rio Yagizawa
Production Assistant:	Takumi Takahashi, Kozue Onishi, Haruki Takahashi, Chiyako Shirakawa
Production Support:	Julie Asakura, Kento Shimazaki
Cover Artwork:	Kazuaki Morita
English Main Title Logo Design:	Hideyuki Amemura
Composition and Text:	Hikaru Hayashi, Rio Yagizawa (Go Office)
Article Contributor :	Yoshihiro Yonezawa
Composition and Scenario:	Hikaru Hayashi, Rio Yagizawa/ Go Office
Costume Supervisor:	Kimiko Morimoto
English Edition Layout:	Shinichi Ishioka
English Translation Management:	Língua fránca, Inc. (an3y-skmt@asahi-net.or.jp)
Planning Editor:	Motofumi Nakanishi (Graphic-sha Publishing Co., Ltd.)

Foreign Language Edition Project Coordinator: Kumiko Sakamoto (Graphic-sha Publishing Co., Ltd.)

All rights reserved. No part of this publication may be reproduced or used in any form or by any means - graphic, electronic, or mechanical, including photocopying, recording, taping, or information storage and retrieval systems - without written permission of the publisher and the copyright holders.

Distributor:
Japan Publications Trading Co., Ltd.
1-2-1 Sarugaku-cho, Chiyoda-ku, Tokyo, 101-0064
Telephone: +81(0)3-3292-3751 Fax: +81(0)3-3292-0410
E-mail: jpt@jptco.co.jp
URL: http://www.jptco.co.jp/

First printing: September 2004

ISBN 4-7661-1485-X
Printed and bound in China

More HOW TO DRAW MANGA

Vol. 4

Mastering Bishoujo Characters

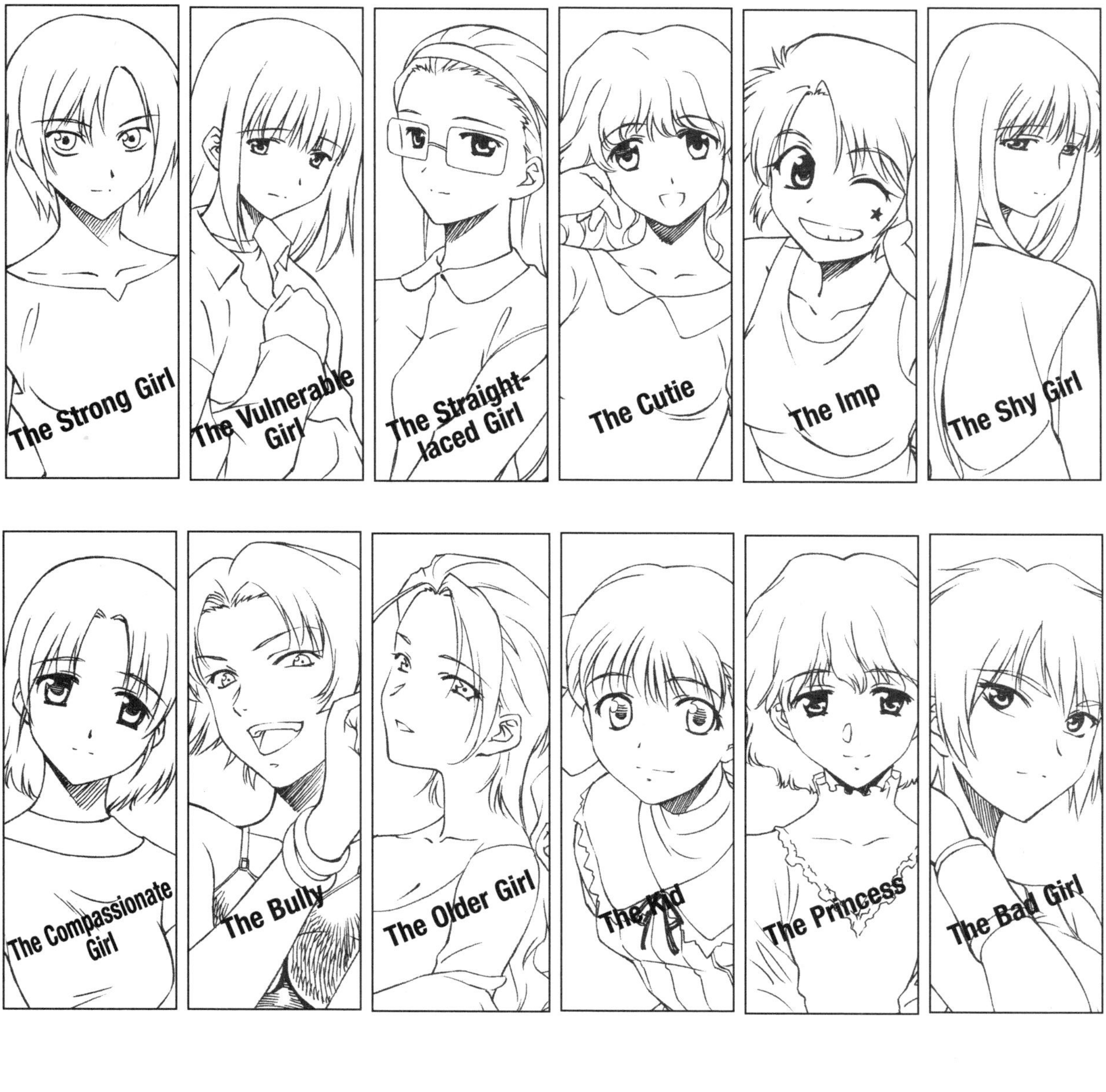

Table of Contents

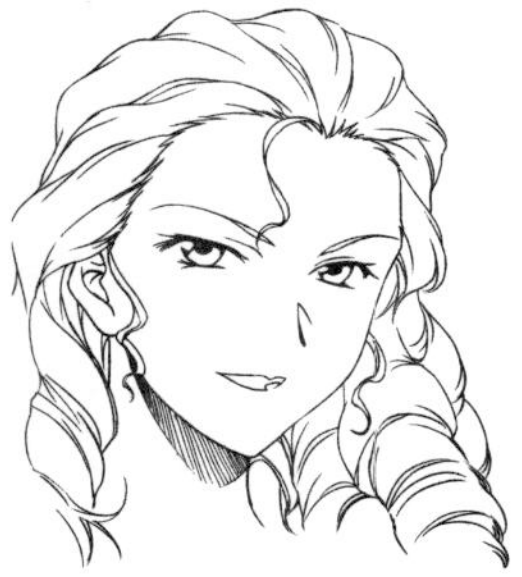

Chapter 1
Twelve Character Types

Chapter 1 Twelve Character Types 7
Using Impressions to Portray the Twelve Character Types 8
Key Points in Distinguishing the Twelve Character Types 10
01: The Strong Girl 12
02: The Vulnerable Girl 16
03: The Straight-laced Girl 20
04: The Cutie 24
05: The Imp 28
06: The Shy Gir 32
07: The Compassionate Girl 36
08: The Bully 40
09: The Older Girl 44
10: The Kid 48
11: The Princess 52
12: The Bad Girl 56
Height Distinctions 60
Three Categories: Average (the Standard), Tall, and Short
Height Portrayal Samples
Selecting Costumes That Match the Character 64
Concealing Fashions
Body Conscious and Revealing Outfits
Intermediate Fashions
Uniform Portrayal 66
Uniforms with Blazers
Sailor Suits
Tricks to Designing Uniforms for the Twelve Character Types 72
Key Design Points
Blazer-Style Uniforms
Jacket-Style Uniform
Sailor Suits
Dress-Style Uniforms
Uniforms with Sweaters
Techniques in Character Image Design 78

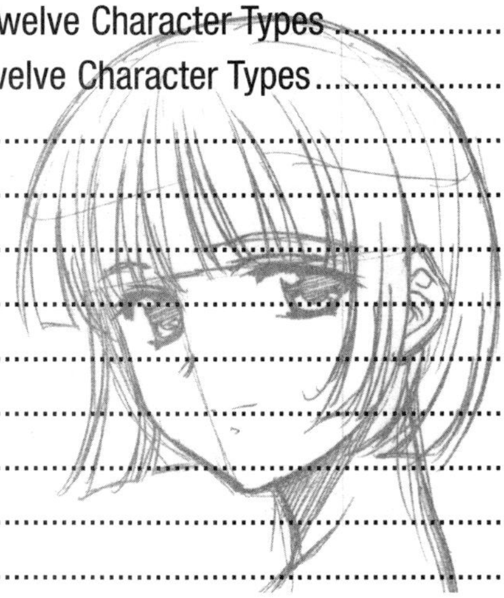

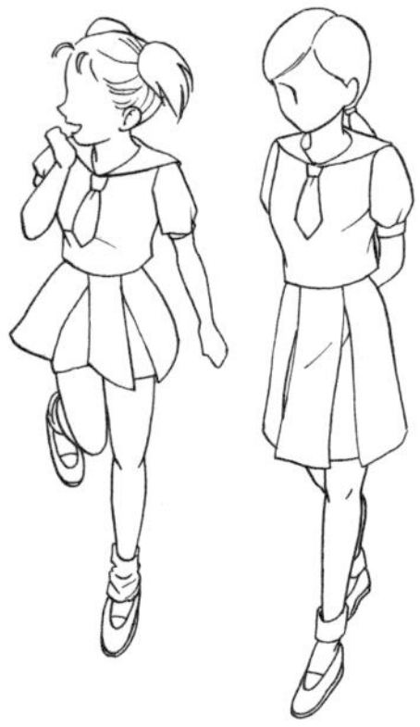

Chapter 2
Making the Figure Move 81

The Fundamentals of Character Movements 82
- Front View
- 3/4 View
- Side View

Walking Scenes 88
- When Walking Scenes Appear in *Manga*
- The Fundamentals of Walking
- Differences in Pace
- Using Bust Shots to Portray Walking
- Rear View/Leaving
- Scenes of Going to/Leaving School (Overhead Shots)
- Style of Walking as Indication of Emotional State

Drawing Characters Entering through Doors 102
- Portraying a Closing Door

Popular Relaxed, Conversational Poses 106
- Leaning against a Wall While Standing Use a curved line for the waist.
- Sitting Near a Wall
- Crouching
- Sitting against a Wall Chatting

Hand Gestures in Conversation Scenes 116

Running, Leaping, Falling Three Basic Action Poses 120
1. Breaking into a Run; Running 120
2. Jumping (Leaping) 122
3. Falling 124

Figures and Cars
—Using Facial Expressions and Body Language to Portray Driving 126

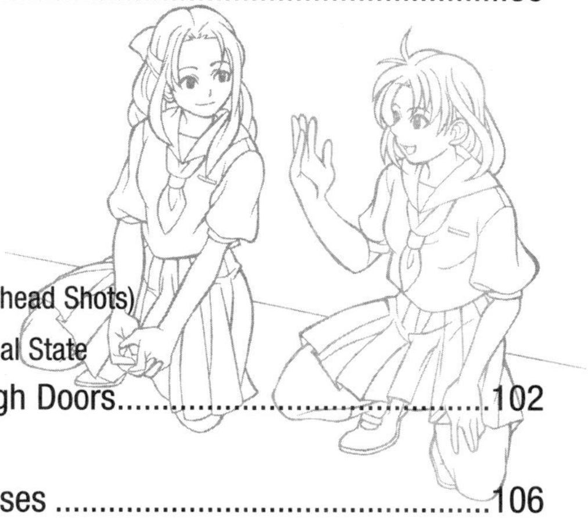

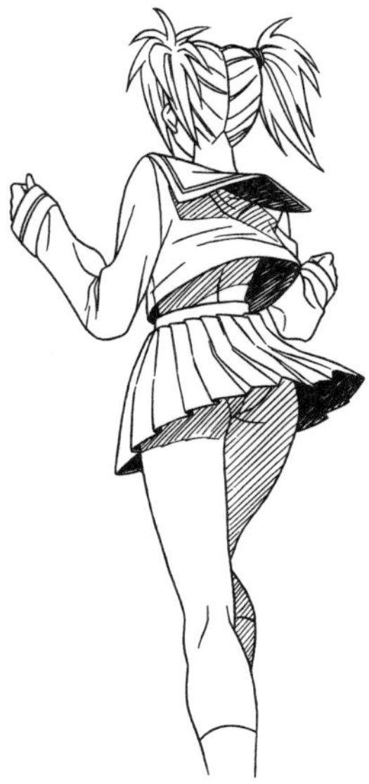

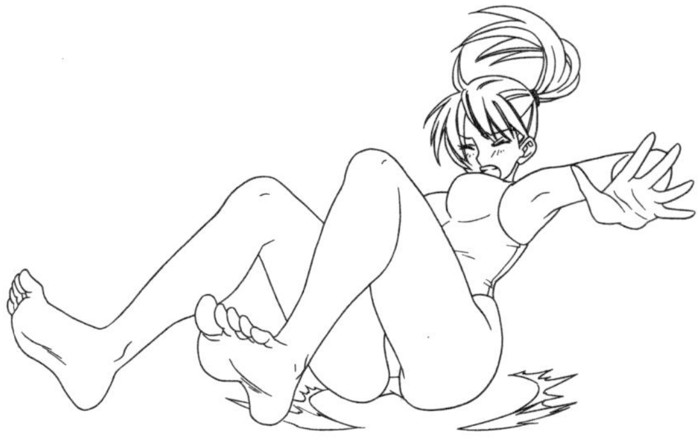

Forward

Characters with contradictory personalities are vital. For example, at first glance, the character may appear vulnerable, but really she is spirited and scrappy. Or, maybe she gives a strong first impression, but in actuality she is a coward to the extreme and pessimistic.

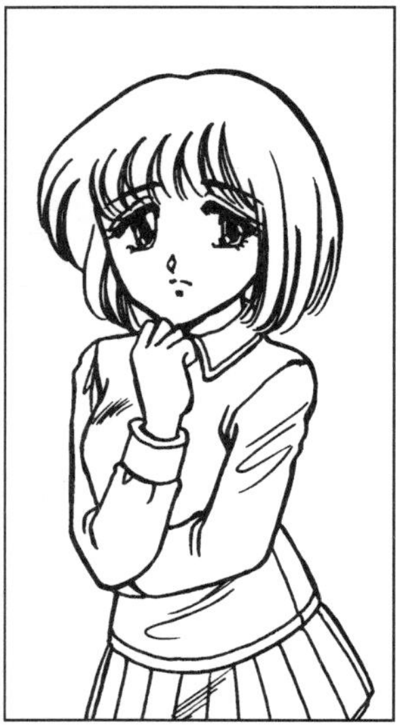

She seems delicate.

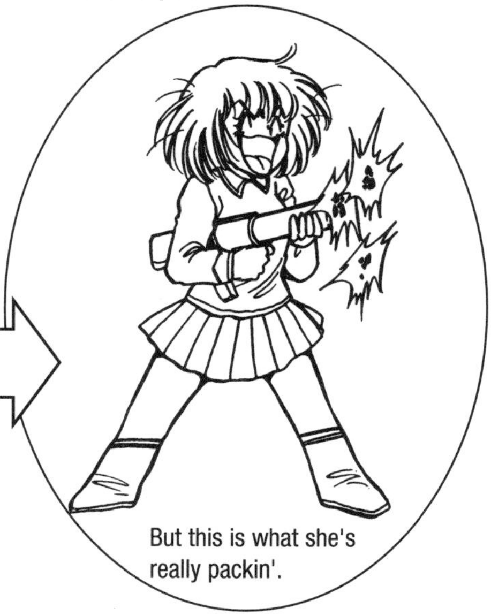

But this is what she's really packin'.

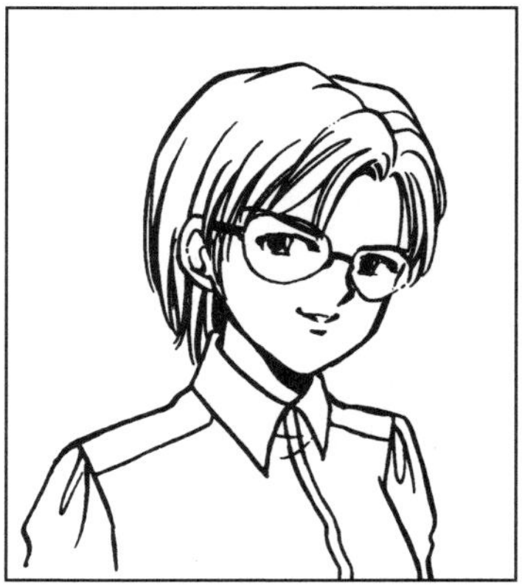

She seems bright.

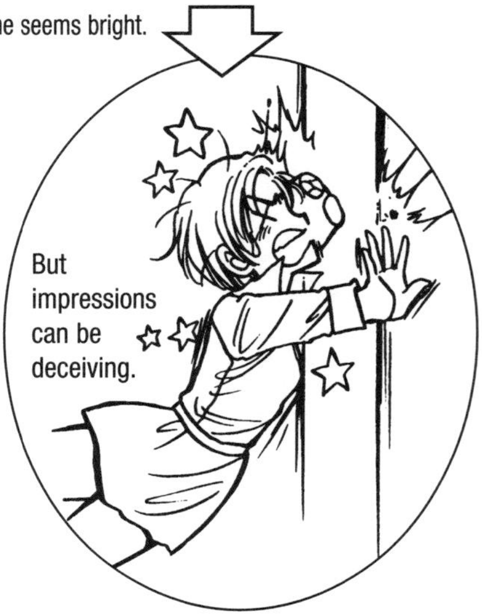

But impressions can be deceiving.

The reader must be given a first impression of a character—that she is vulnerable or straight-laced. This will allow you to furnish the character with an unexpected side or a contradictory personality, thus making her memorable, striking, and individualistic.

Make an effort to master techniques in project a character's personality at a glance.

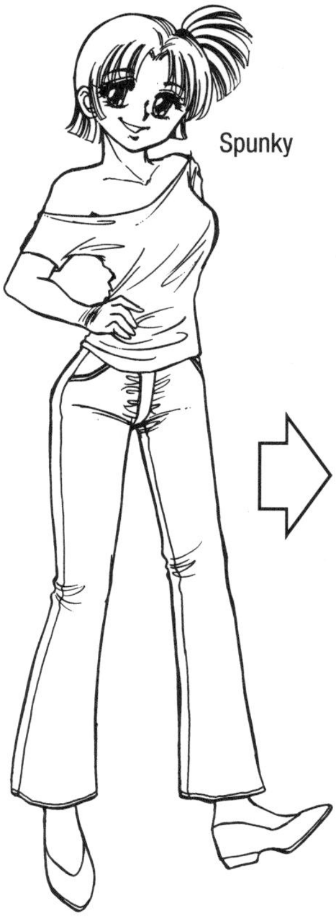

Spunky

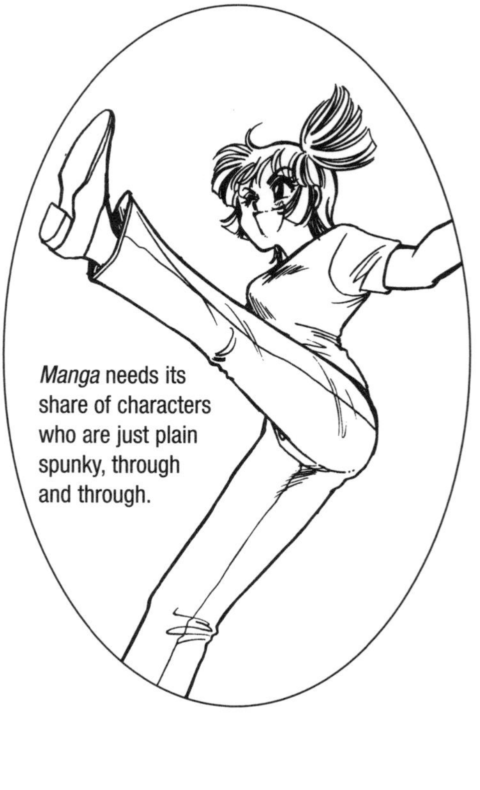

Manga needs its share of characters who are just plain spunky, through and through.

Chapter 1

Twelve Character Types

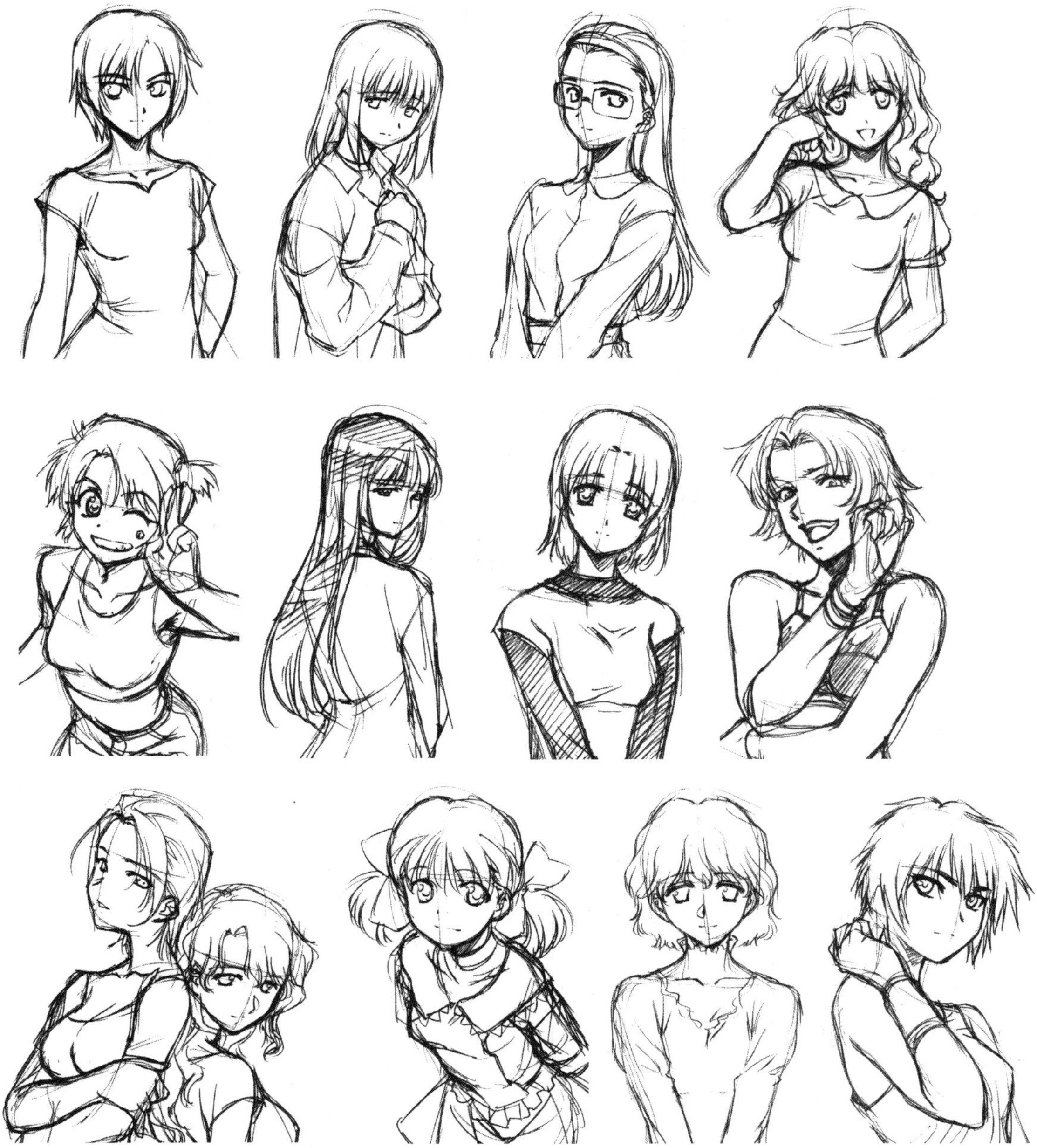

Using Impressions to Portray the Twelve Character Types

There are twelve stereotypical female characters that appear in *manga*. Exaggerate the shape of their eyes, the size of the mouths, their hairstyles, heights, and clothing to project the desired image (i.e. exploit preconceived notions).

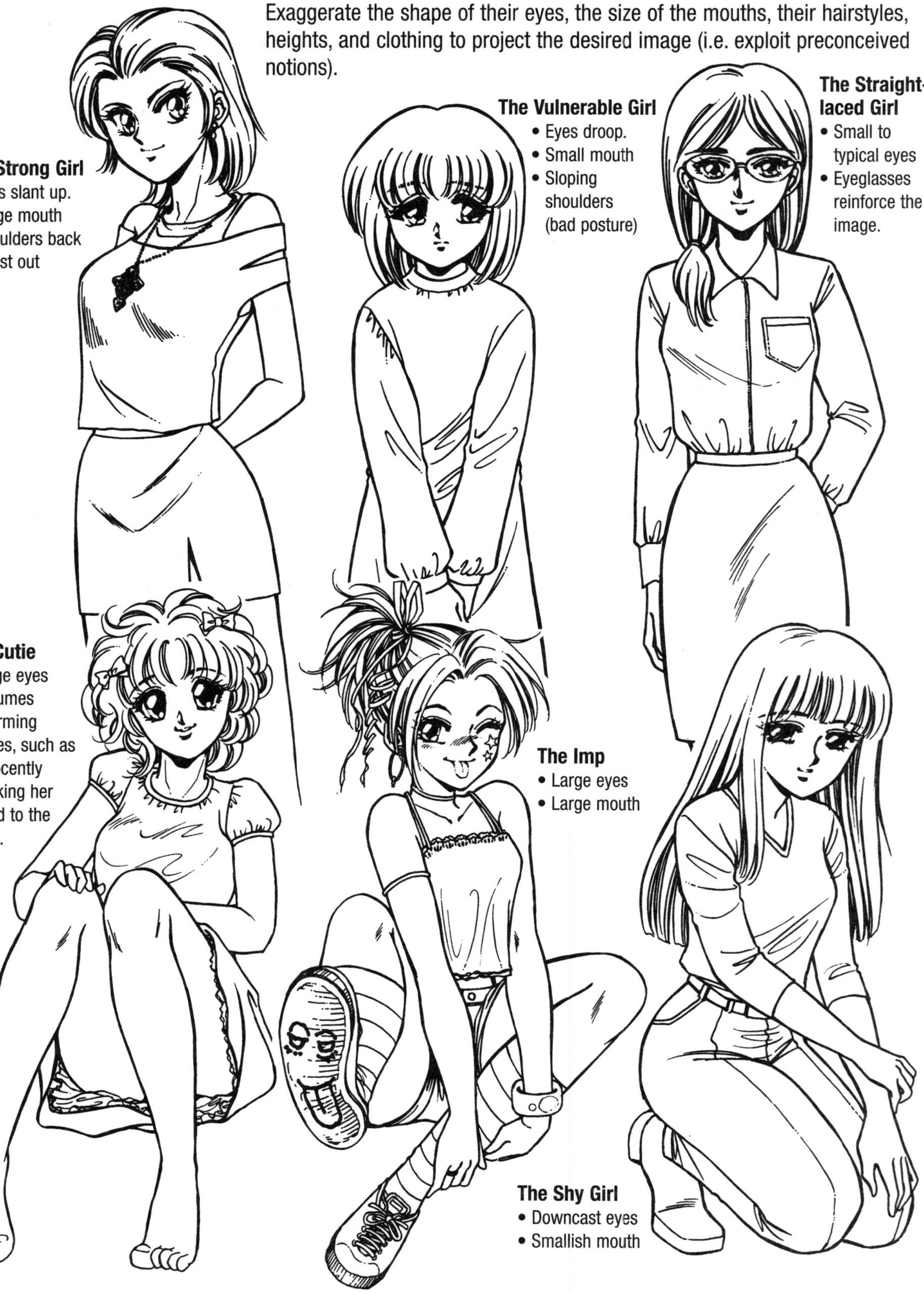

The Strong Girl
- Eyes slant up.
- Large mouth
- Shoulders back
- Chest out

The Vulnerable Girl
- Eyes droop.
- Small mouth
- Sloping shoulders (bad posture)

The Straight-laced Girl
- Small to typical eyes
- Eyeglasses reinforce the image.

The Cutie
- Large eyes
- Assumes charming poses, such as innocently cocking her head to the side.

The Imp
- Large eyes
- Large mouth

The Shy Girl
- Downcast eyes
- Smallish mouth

Enlarging the mouth creates a more vivacious and aggressive impression, while making the mouth small reinforces the impression of being quiet or passive.

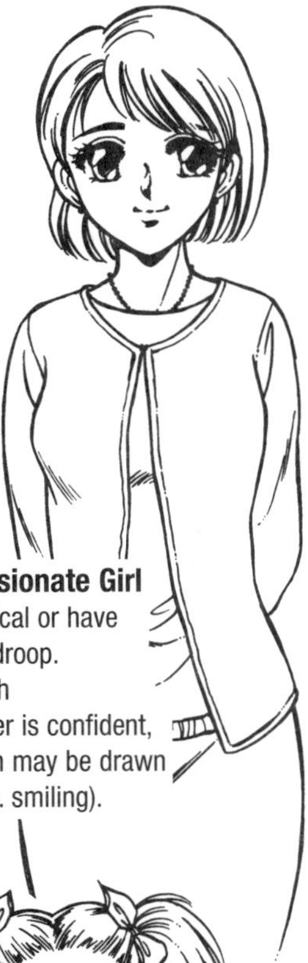

The Compassionate Girl
- Eyes are typical or have a moderate droop.
- Typical mouth
- This character is confident, so her mouth may be drawn upturned (i.e. smiling).

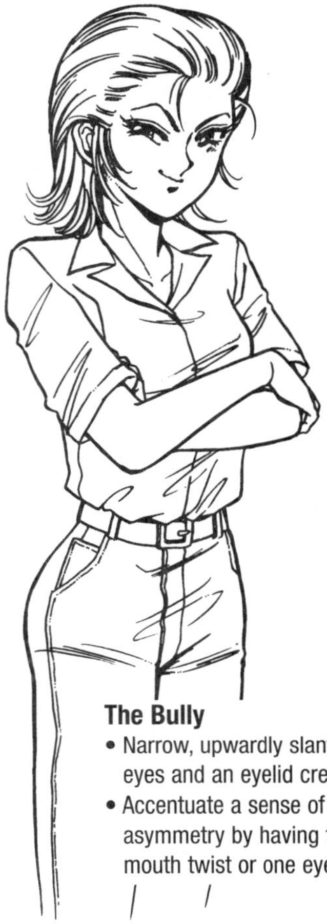

The Bully
- Narrow, upwardly slanted eyes and an eyelid crease
- Accentuate a sense of asymmetry by having the mouth twist or one eye squint

The Older Girl
- Small eyes
- Hint of lipstick on the mouth and other cosmetic effects are recommended.

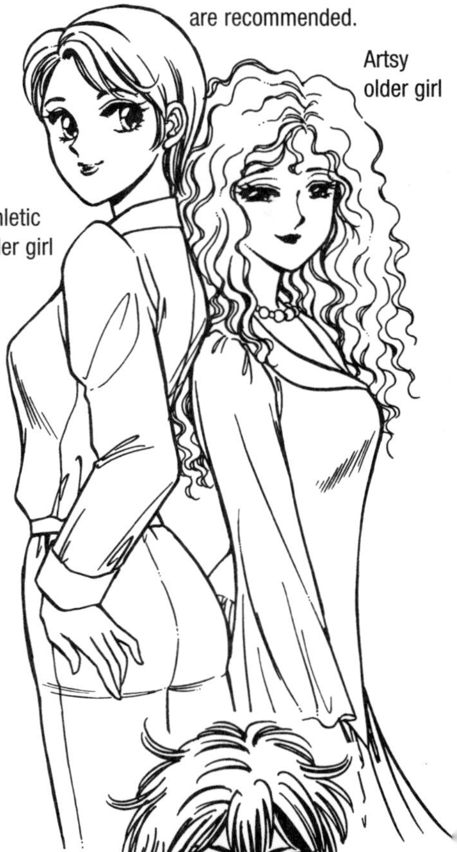

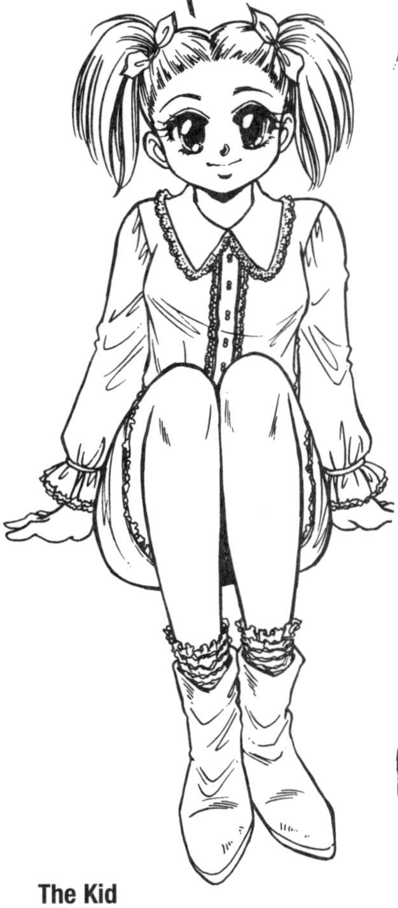

The Kid
- Large eyes and mouth
- Short hair or pigtails evokes a childlike feel.

The Princess
- Large pupils and irises and moderately drooped eyes create the impression of being gentle and well-bred.

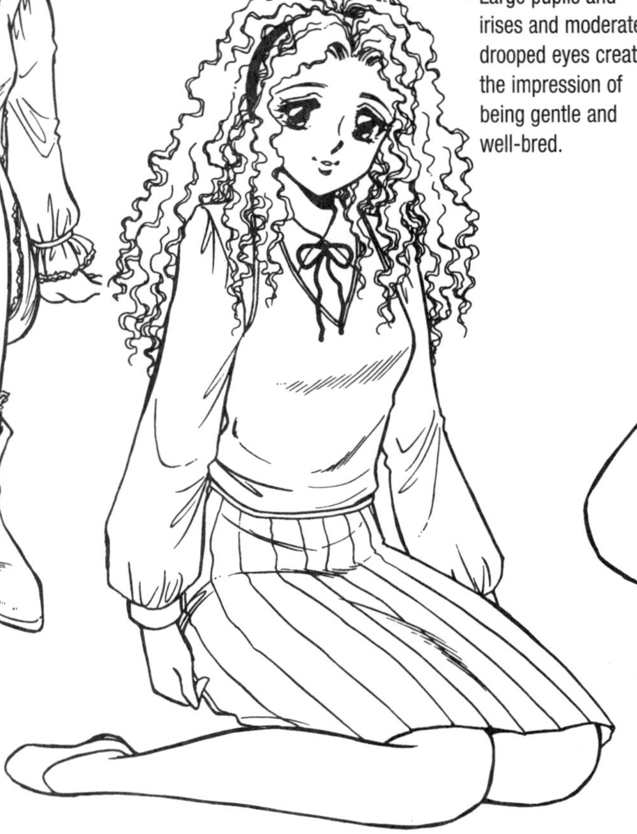

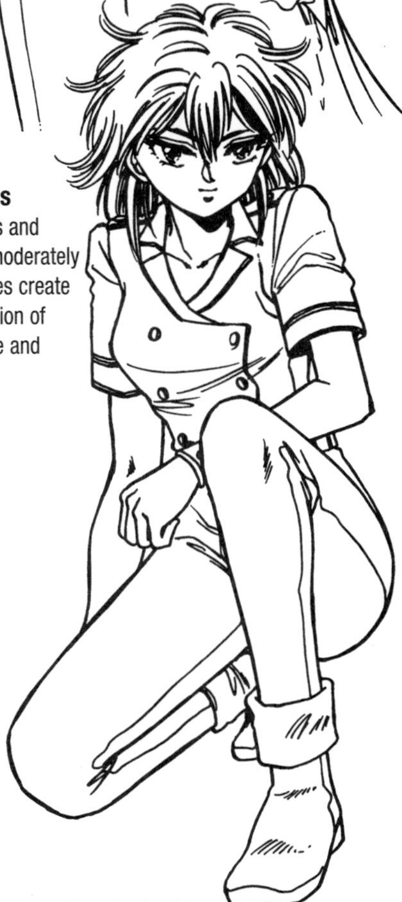

The Bad Girl
- Generally drawn with moderately upward slanting eyes
- Tousled hair evokes the impression of an unruly personality.

Key Points in Distinguishing the Twelve Character Types: Contrasting the Eyes, Mouth, and Hair

The Strong Girl vs. The Vulnerable Girl

E.g. Strong vs. Timid

The twelve character types consist of six pairs of opposites. Contrasting the distinguishing features of each pair will allow you to portray them readily.

The Strong Girl has upward slanting eyes. The eyebrows arc up as well.

The eyebrows should be clearly delineated.

A large mouth reinforces the idea of a vivacious personality.

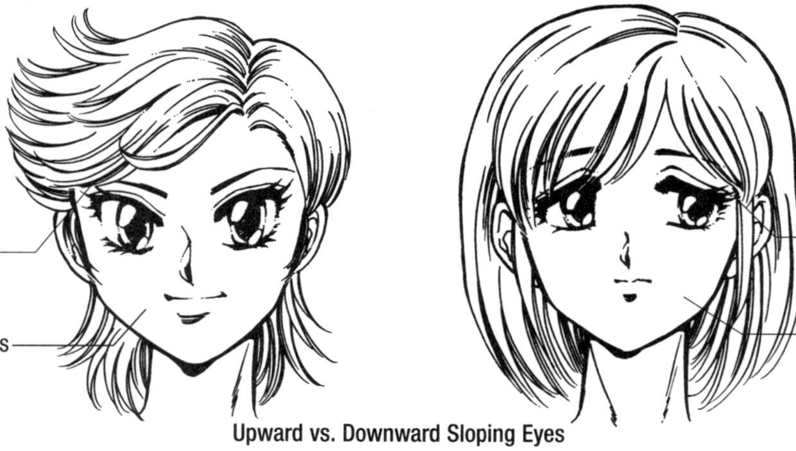

Vulnerable types have droopy eyes and eyebrows.

Eyelid fold

Smallish mouth

Upward vs. Downward Sloping Eyes

The Straight-laced Girl vs. The Cutie

E.g. The Math Wiz vs. The Bubblehead

The Straight-laced Girl has typical eyes, eyebrows, and mouth.

Eyeglasses are effective.

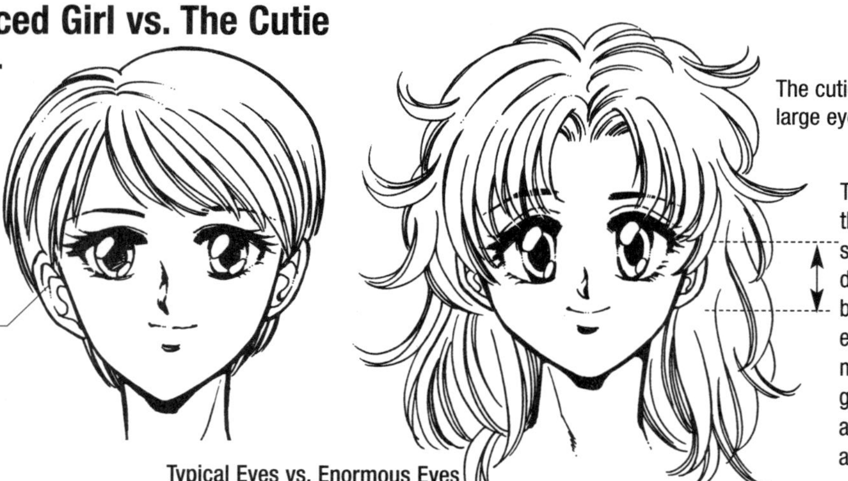

The cutie has large eyes.

The larger the eyes, the shorter the distance between the eyes and the mouth, generating a childlike appearance.

Typical Eyes vs. Enormous Eyes

The Zany Girl vs. The Reserved Girl

Eg. Loud vs. Quiet

Since you want the zany girl to project an atypical personality, draw her hair messy and unkempt, even when giving her a traditional cut.

A large mouth suggests a perky personality.

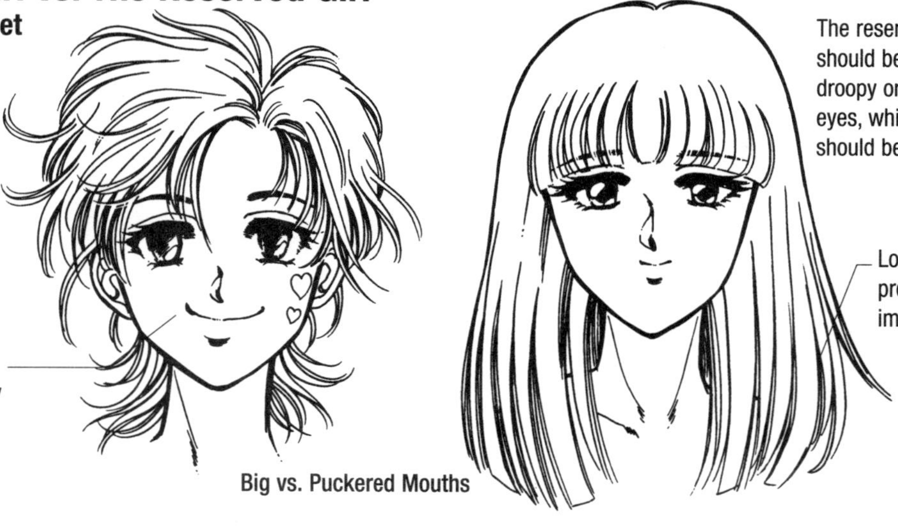

The reserved girl should be given droopy or squinting eyes, while the mouth should be small.

Long hair projects a gentle impression.

Big vs. Puckered Mouths

The Compassionate Girl vs. The Bully
E.g. Perpetually Tranquil vs. Ornery

The Compassionate Girl has a "roundish" look. Keep a round image in mind when drawing the face, pupils/irises, and lips.

Droopy or moderately droopy eyes are customary elements used to project a gentle image.

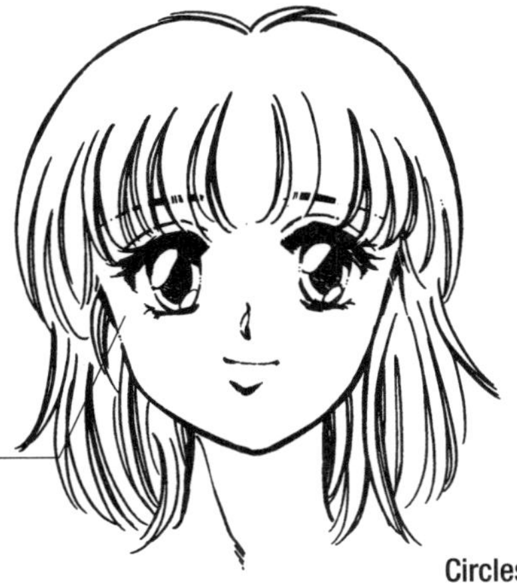

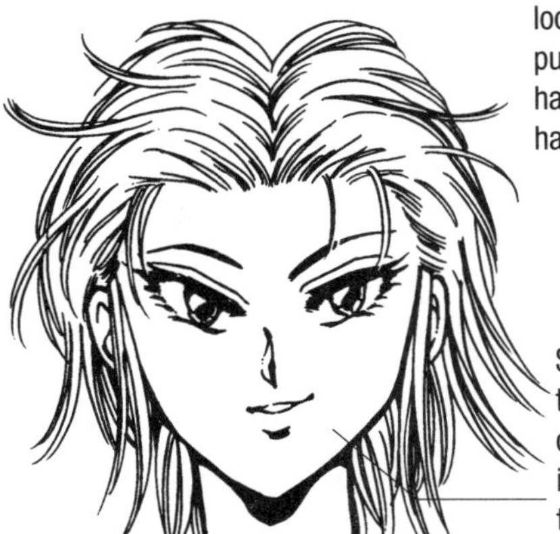

The Bully has a triangular or squarish look to her. The face, pupils/irises, eyes, jaw, hair, etc. all should have an angular feel.

Show the mouth twisting upward or other such idiosyncratic technique rather than using simple curved or straight lines.

Circles vs. Triangles

The Older Girl vs. The Kid
E.g. Adult vs. Child

There are two types of older girls. Accentuating the eyelashes and adding suggestion of lipstick evokes a mature atmosphere.

Downward sloping, almond-shaped eyes and long hair suggest a gentle older girl.

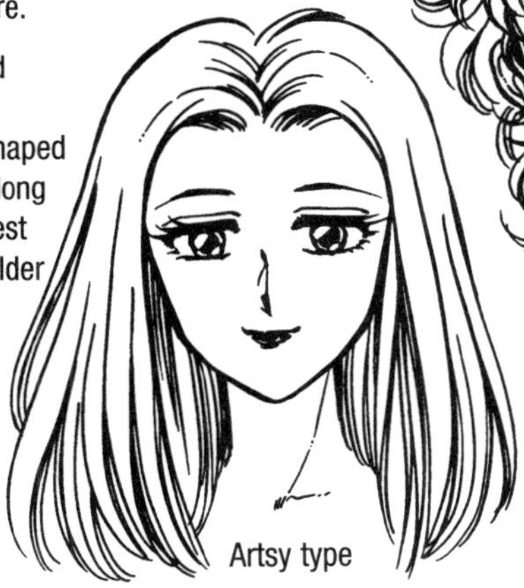

Artsy type

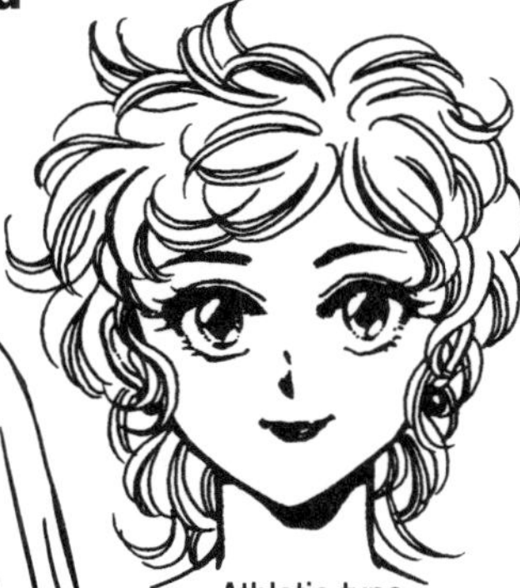

Athletic type

Bright, wide-open eyes and short hair suggest an active older girl.

For the kid, use big pupils/irises and eyebrows to accentuate the eyes, making them look wide open, thus generating rascally atmosphere.

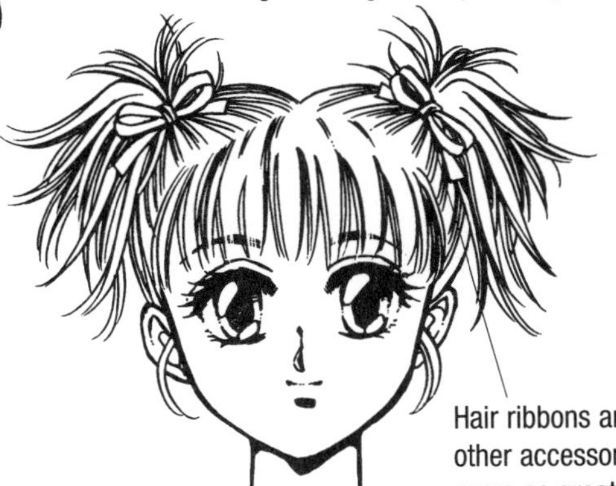

Hair ribbons and other accessories serve as great accent points.

Made-up vs. Unmade Faces

The Princess vs. The Bad Girl
E.g. Raised in a Hothouse vs. Wild off the Vine

Use droopy eyes and large pupils/irises for the Princess to create the air of gentle breeding.

Use fancy, wavy or curly, long hairstyles that would be impractical for typical lifestyles.

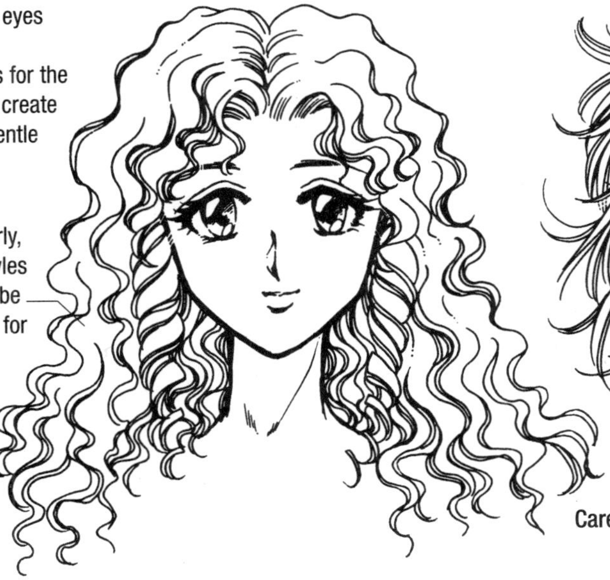

Give the Bad Girl upward slanting eyes, small pupils/irises, and a pointed jaw to generate a "tough" impression.

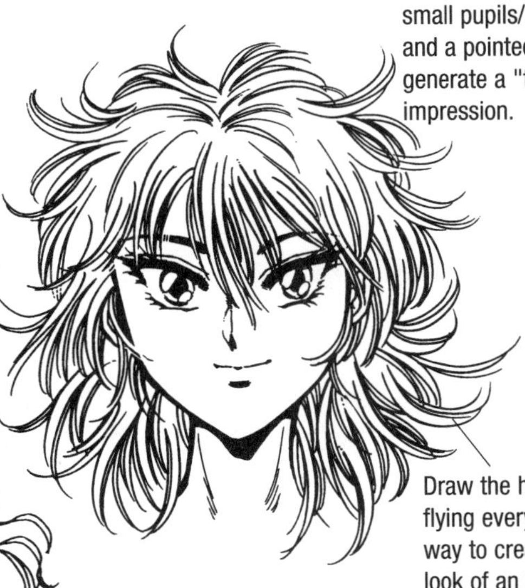

Draw the hair flying every which way to create the look of an unruly desperado.

Carefully Coiffed vs. Disheveled Hair

01 The Strong Girl

This character has a dynamic personality. Upward tilting eyes are the key to expressing her vitality.

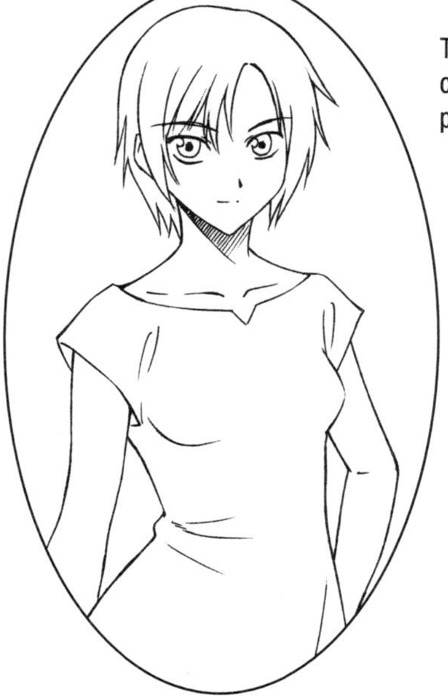

Thick eyebrows help convey a strong personality or will.

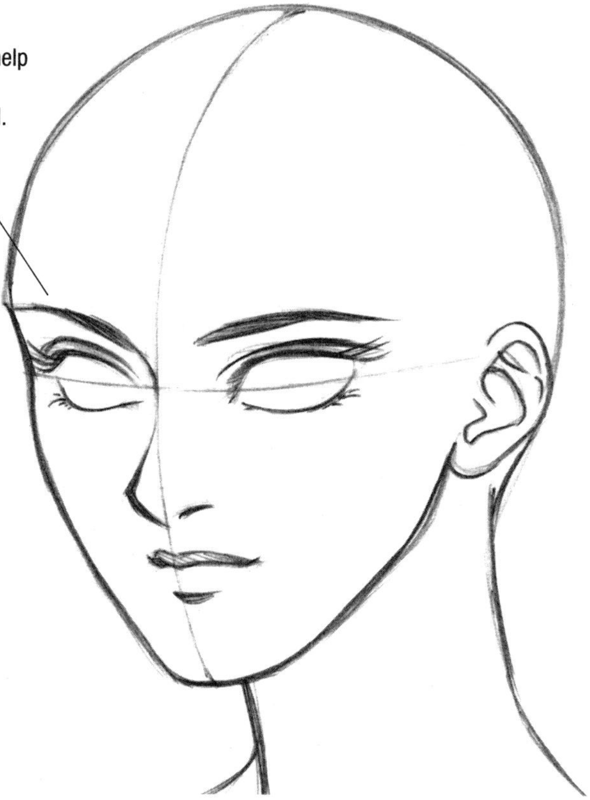

Basic Points

- The Strong Girl should exude confidence.
- She should appear dignified.
- She often has a combative spunkiness to her.

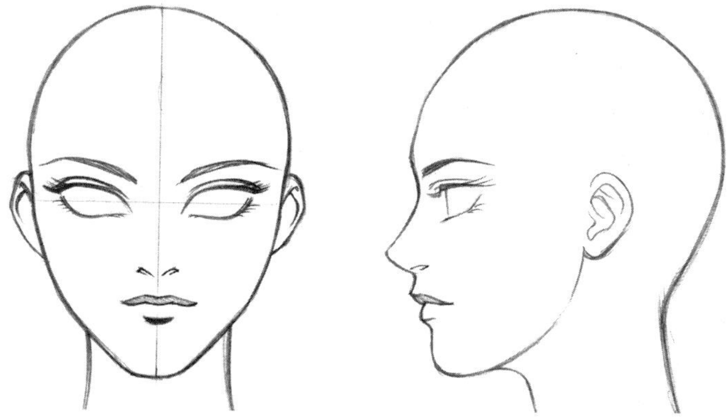

Two Basic Types of Upward Slanted Eyes

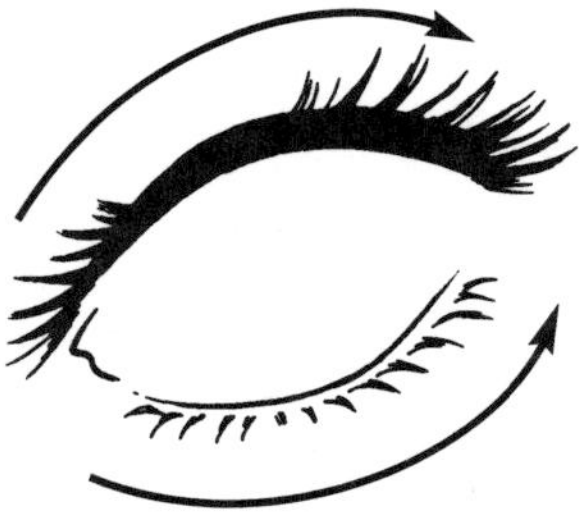

Almond-shaped

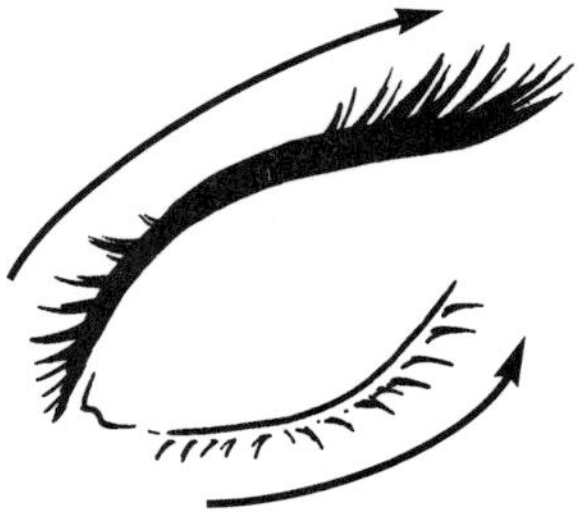

The corner of the eye slopes upward.

The key is to draw the lower eyelid tilting upward as well.

Piercing gazes are often drawn using upward tilting eyes. However, please note that they are not the same thing.

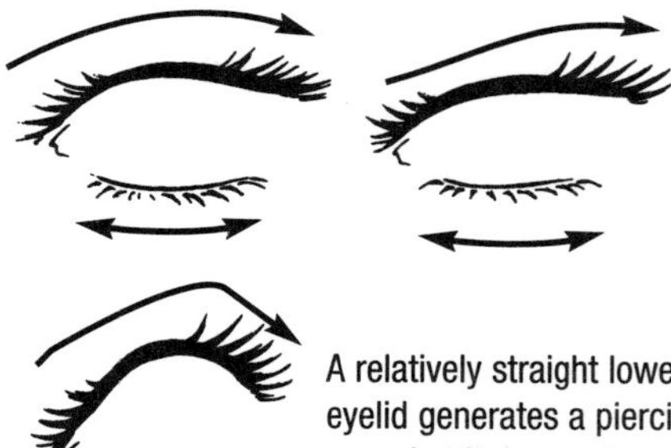

A relatively straight lower eyelid generates a piercing gaze, but it does not create an upward sloping eye.

Key Variation Points Modify the character by changing the mouth's size.

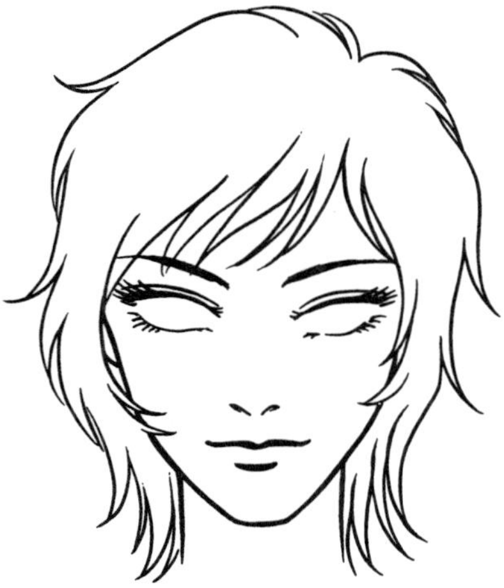

Large mouth

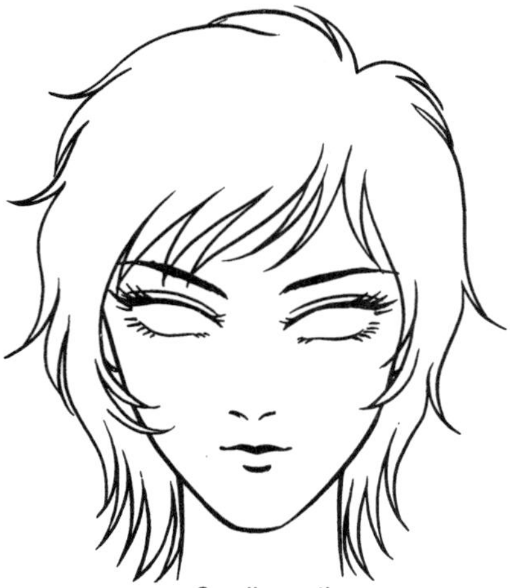

Small mouth

Not good

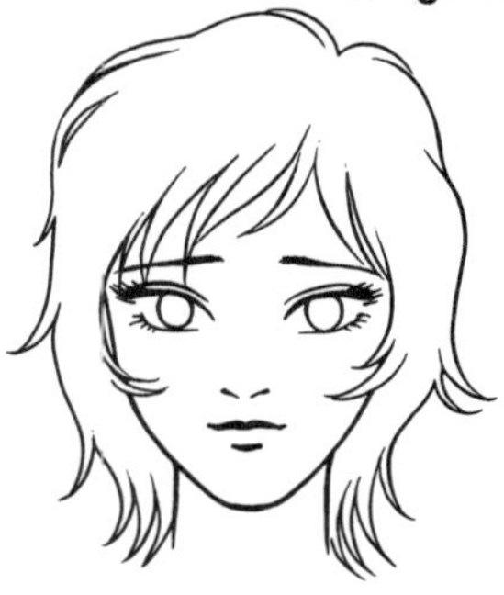

From a design perspective, I recommend that artists avoid drawing roof-shaped eyebrows, rising at the middle and slanting down. (Such eyebrows are used to portray specific emotional states.)

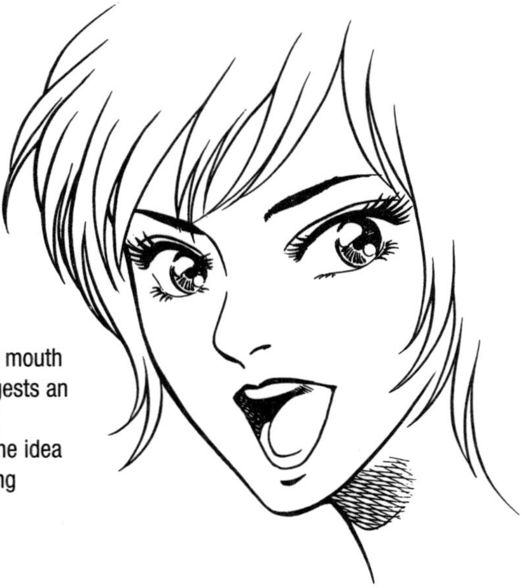

Showing the mouth opened suggests an active talker, reinforcing the idea of an outgoing personality.

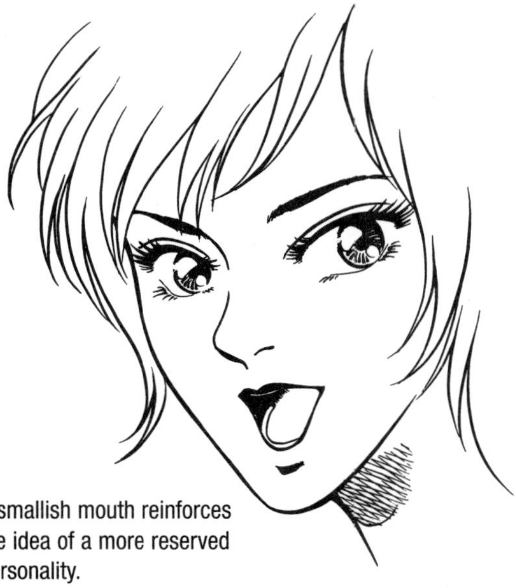

A smallish mouth reinforces the idea of a more reserved personality.

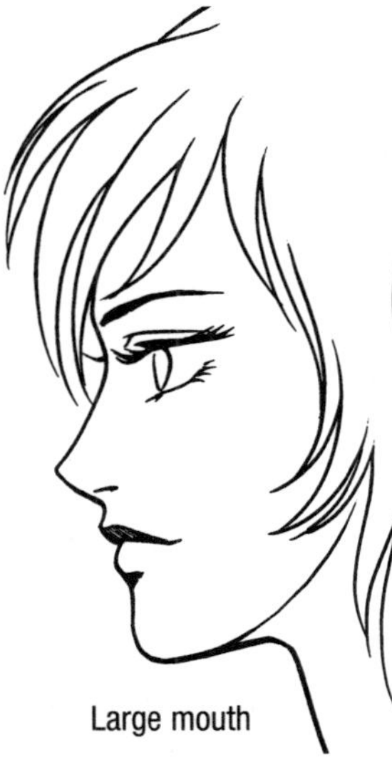

Large mouth

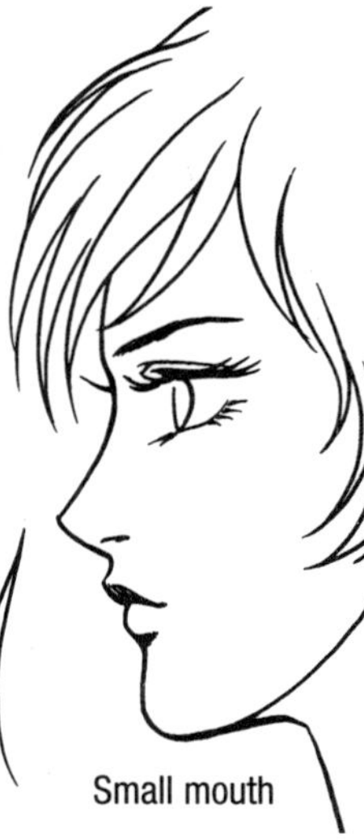

Small mouth

Drawing thick eyebrows creates the air of a strong character.

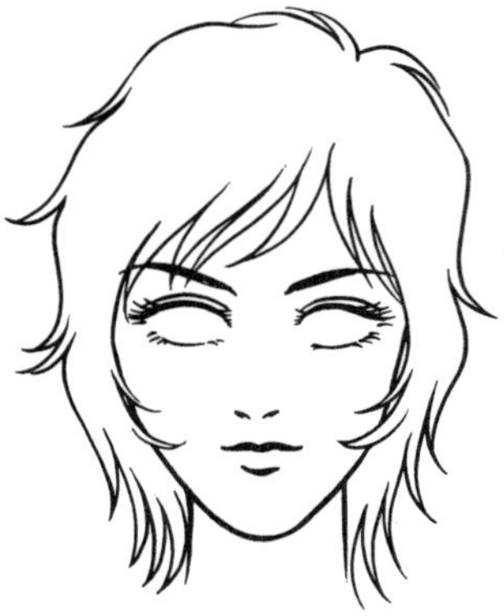

Typical eyes

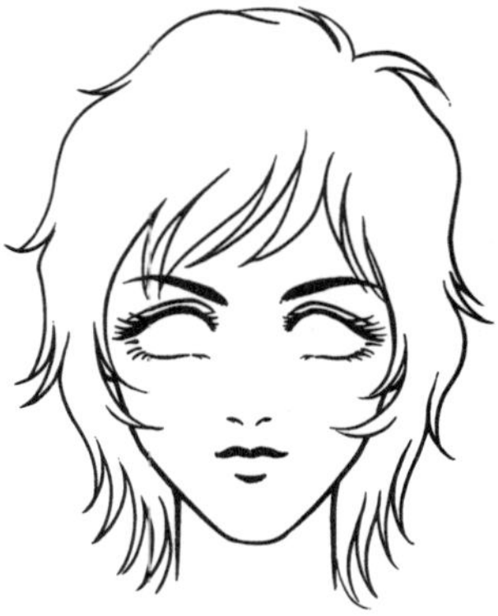

Downward sloping eyes

Full Figure

Strong personalities are also generally thought to be extroverted and open. Draw this girl standing proudly with her shoulders back and chest out (full of confidence).

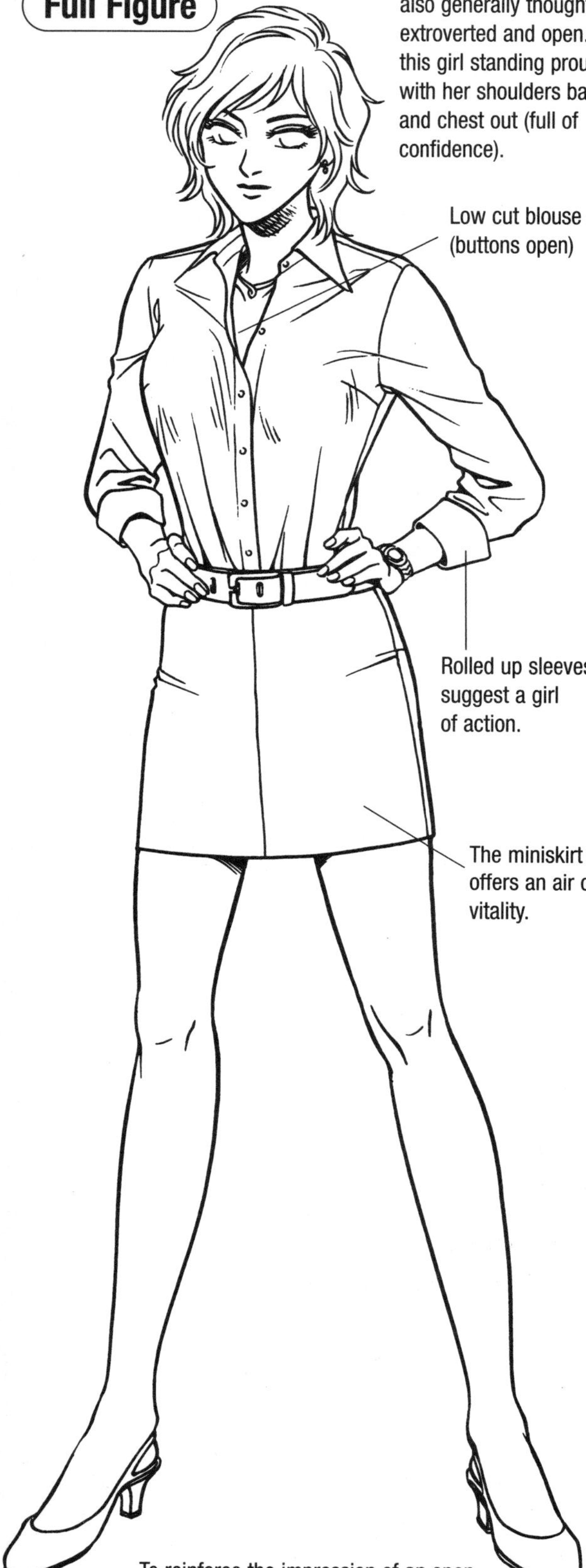

To reinforce the impression of an open, confident nature, select fashions that emphasize her figure and her legs.

• Square Shoulders

Good

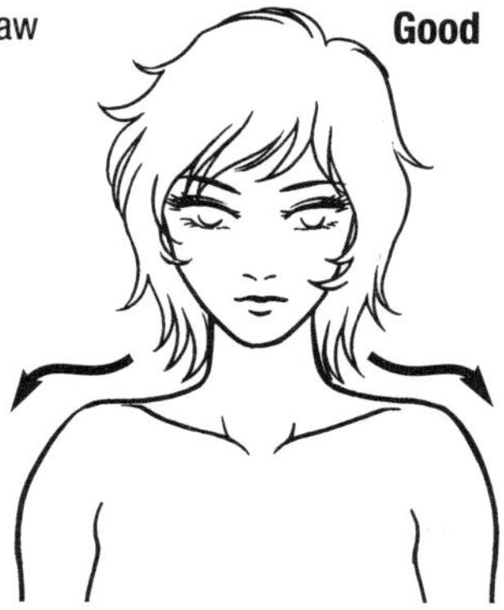

Square shoulders help suggest a puffed-out chest—a proud posture.

Not good

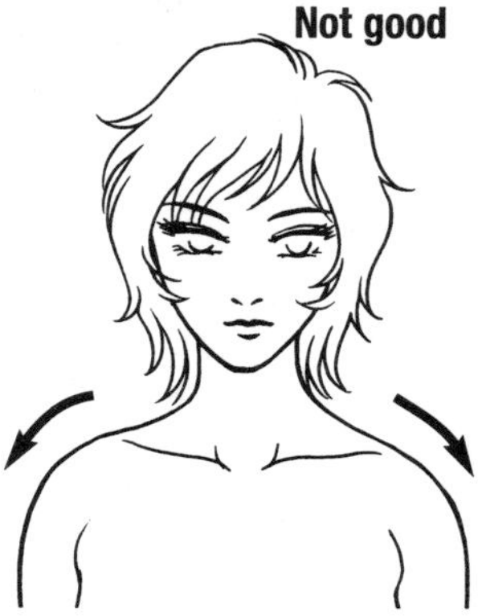

Rounded shoulders project a gentle atmosphere, offering a more vulnerable impression.

• Torsion

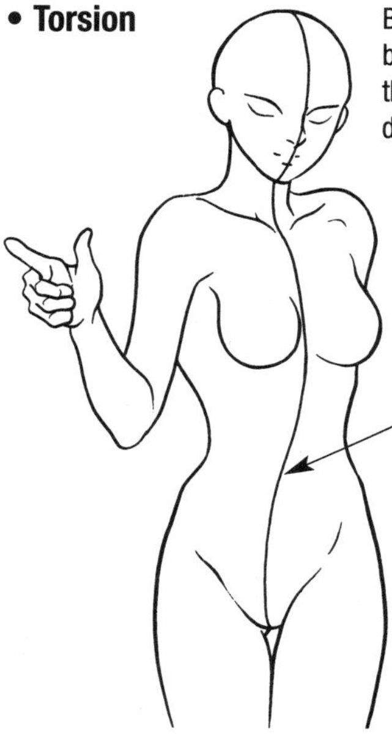

Both upper bodies face the same direction.

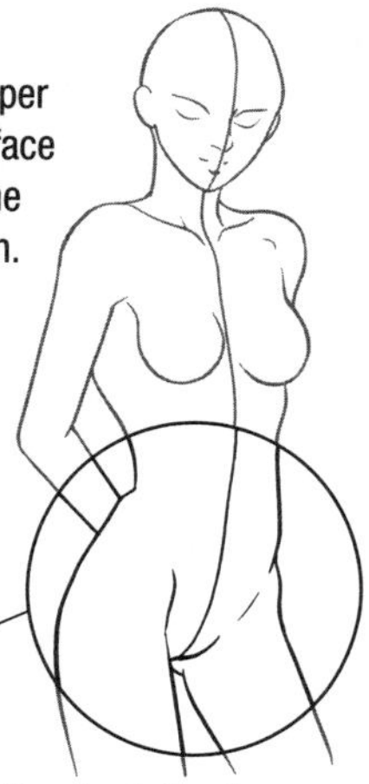

Standard standing pose

Adjusting the direction of the lower body creates a twisted pose. This creates a feel of movement, emphasizing the character's dynamic nature.

• Thrust-out Chest

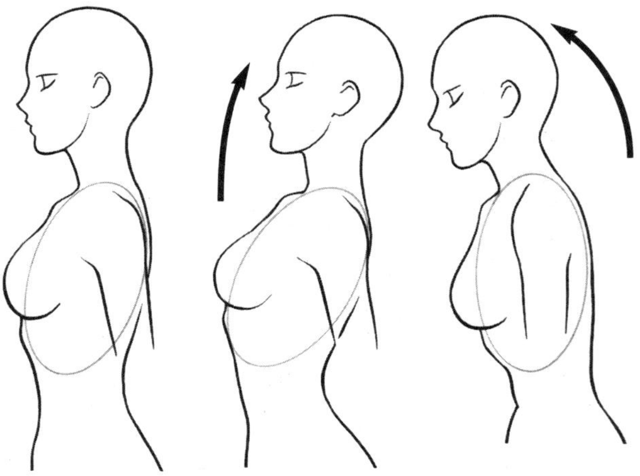

Typical posture

Raising the chin slightly generates an overly confident, haughty air.

Rounding the back and tilting the body forward creates a menacing pose.

Standard Fashions

Since the Strong Girl has an outgoing, dynamic image, draw her primarily in comfortable clothing—casual and sporty clothing.

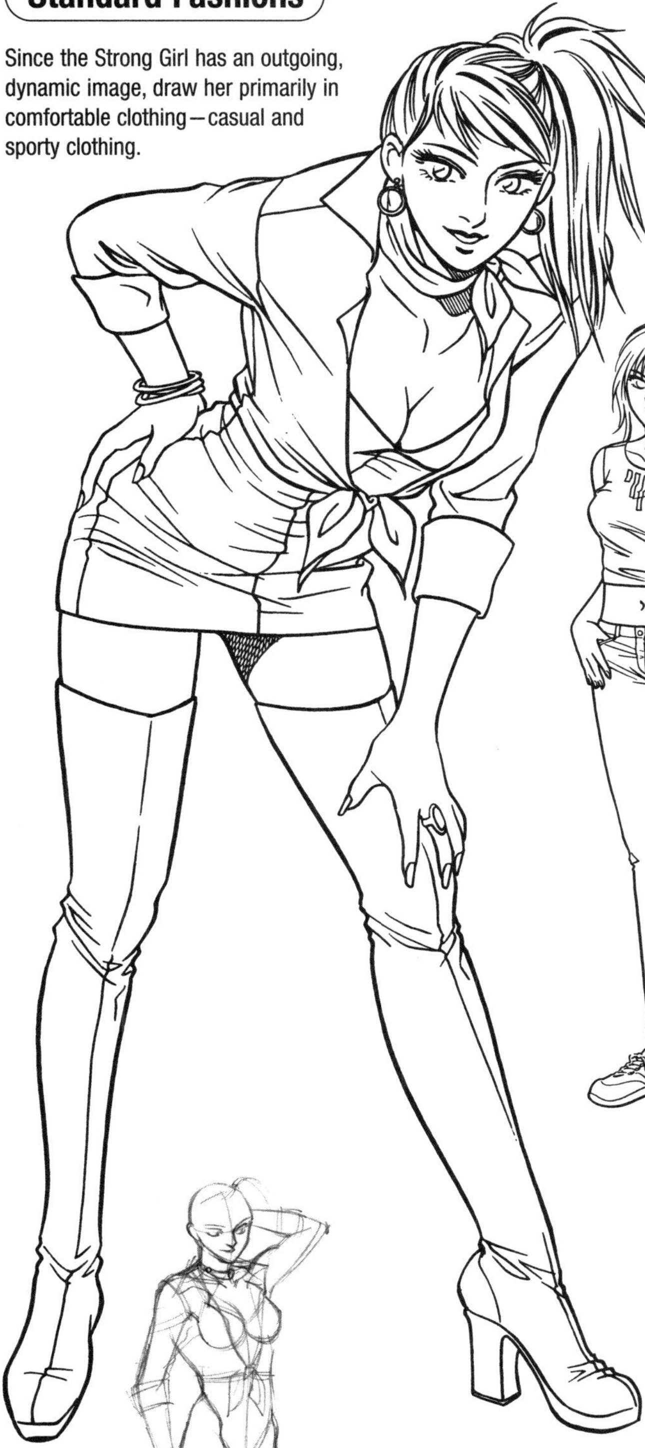

Strong characters often dress in somewhat provocative clothing, such as designs exposing the navel, etc.

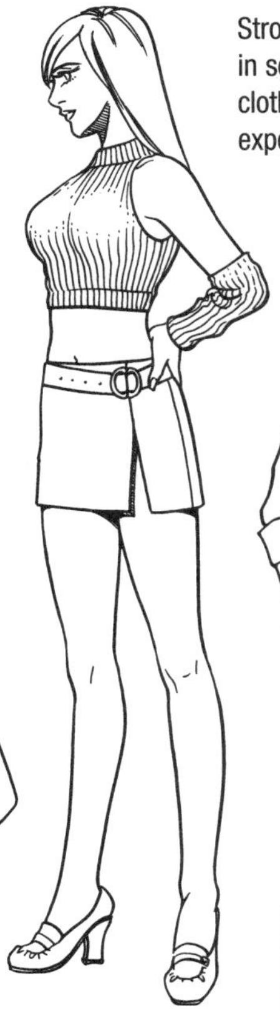

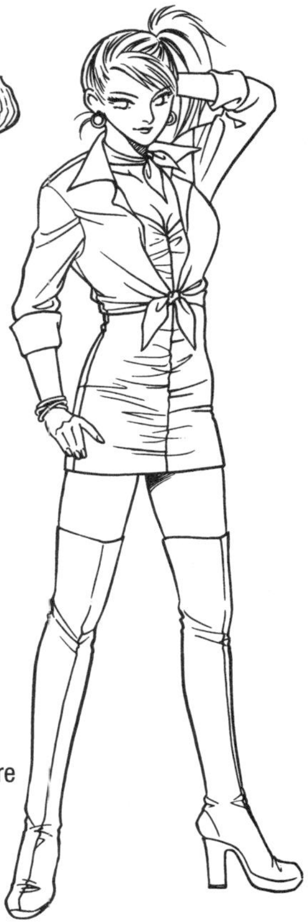

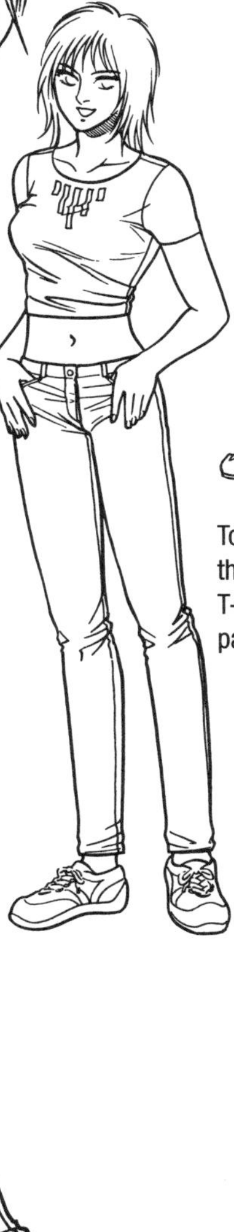

Tomboyish yet sexy are the key words here: T-shirts, tank tops, pants, miniskirts, etc.

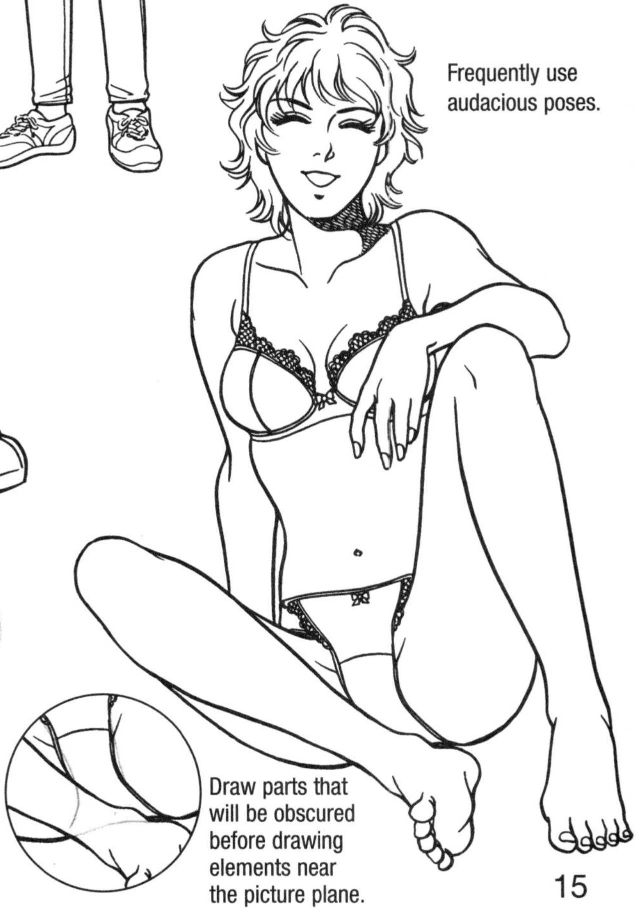

Frequently use audacious poses.

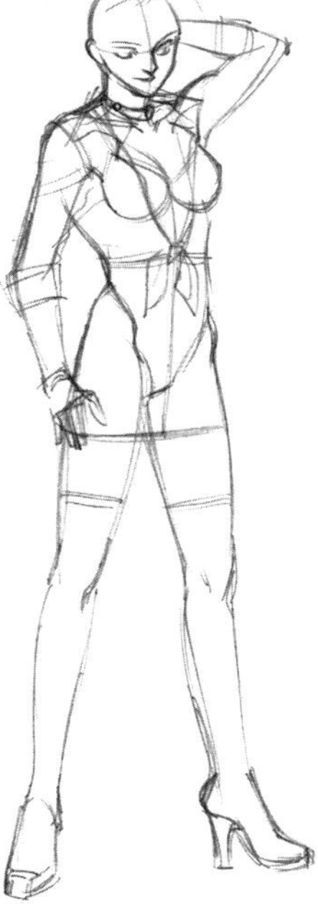

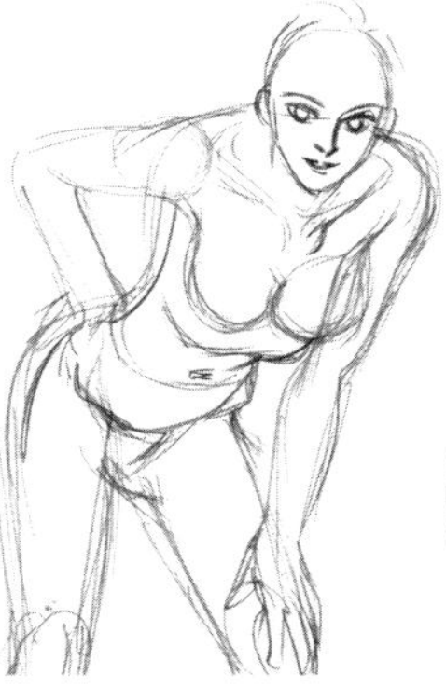

Draw parts that will be obscured before drawing elements near the picture plane.

02 The Vulnerable Girl

The vulnerable girl has a passive personality. This character is usually drawn with smallish eyes and mouth, using drooping eyes as a foundation.

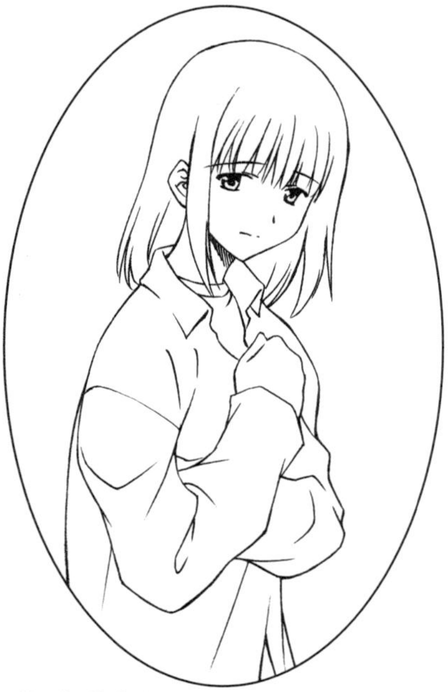

Basic Points
- Overall hunched posture
- Downcast eyes
- Using smallish eyes and mouth will generate a passive atmosphere.

Use roof-shaped, downward sloping eyebrows.

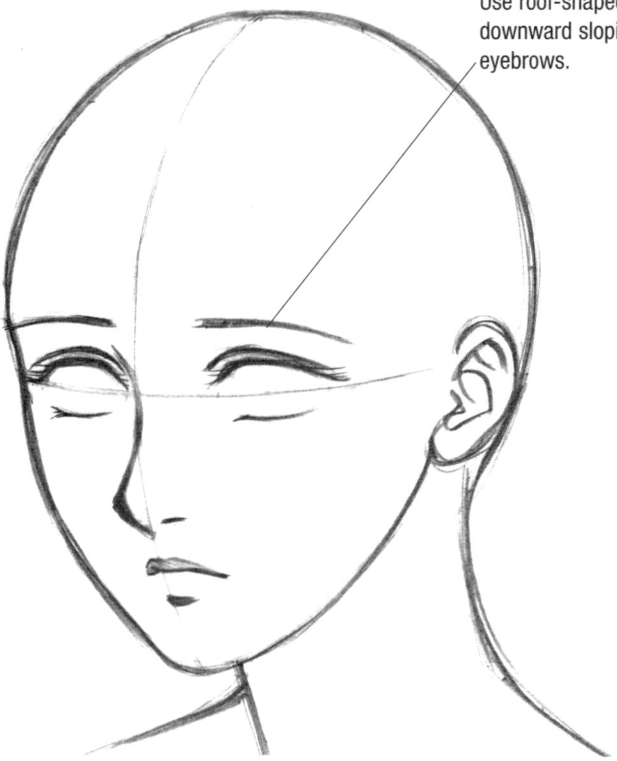

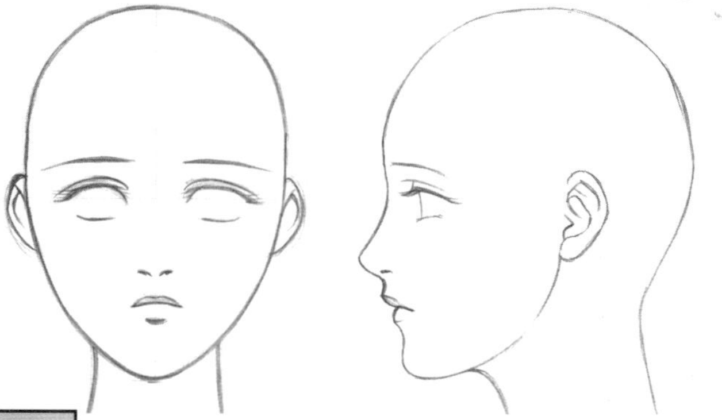

A hunched posture is essential to generating a vulnerable atmosphere.

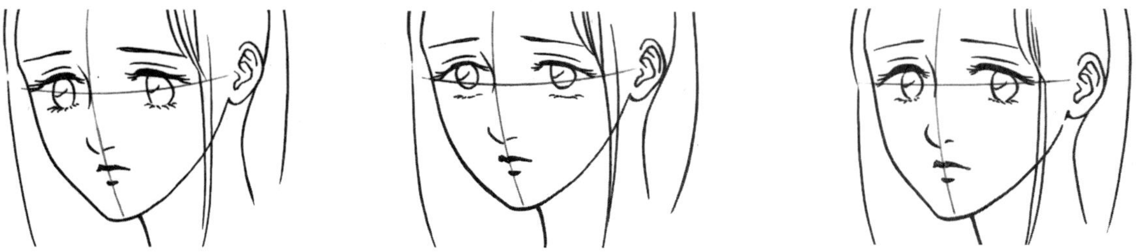

Downcast eyes

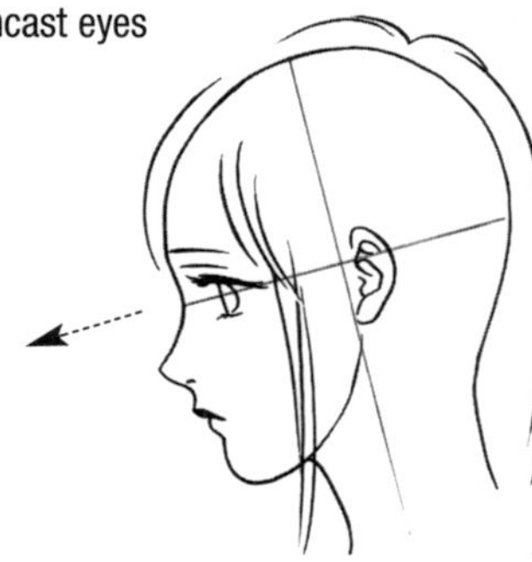

The white of the eye to the sides and underneath the pupils/irises should be visible when she looks at another character.

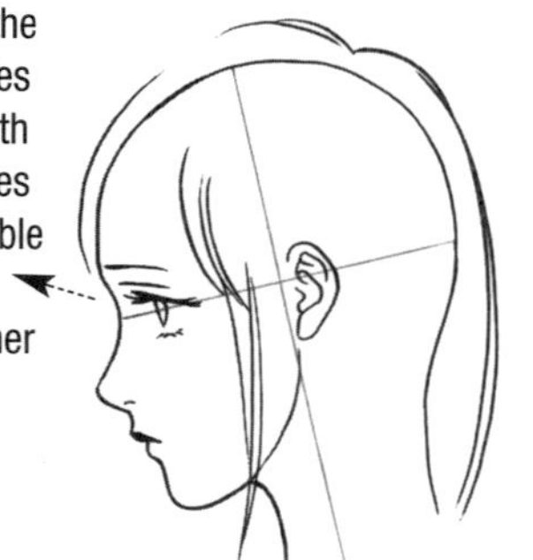

The eyes should be slightly downcast even when looking directly at the reader.

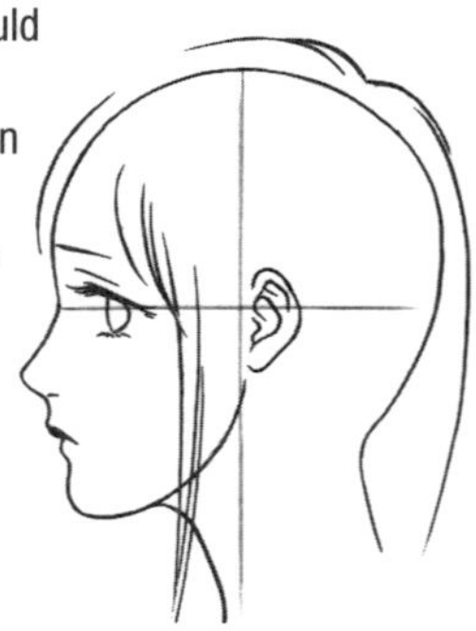

Key Variation Points Draw small eyes and eyelid folds.

Not good

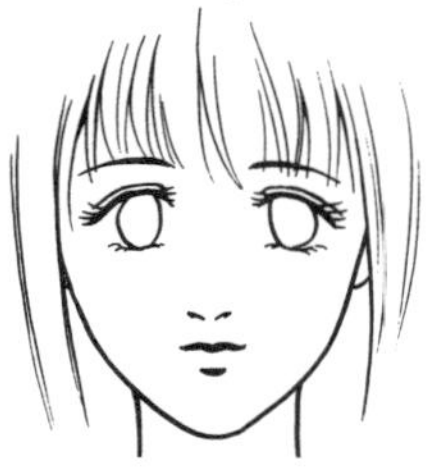

Typical, downward sloping eyes: This turns the character into your basic, typical "cutie."

Acceptable

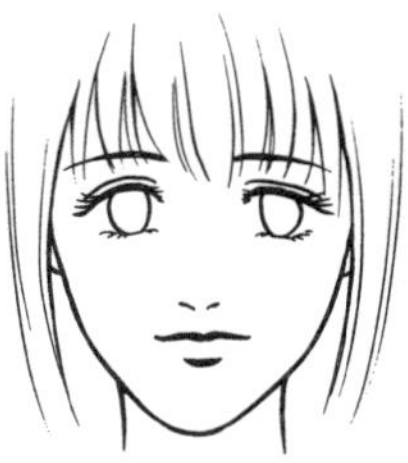

Giving her a large mouth reinforces a friendly or spunky impression.

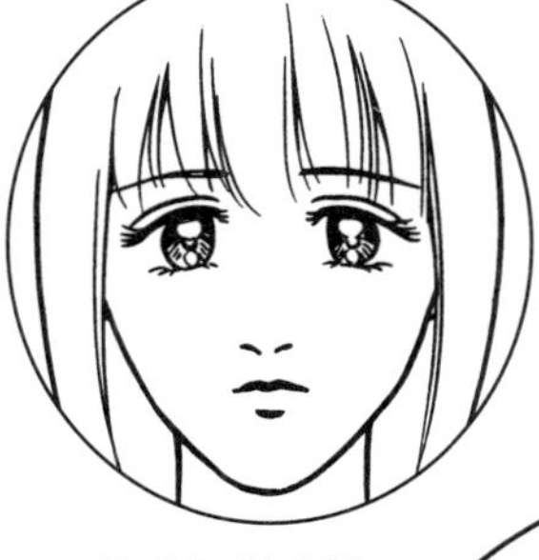

Eyelid with fold

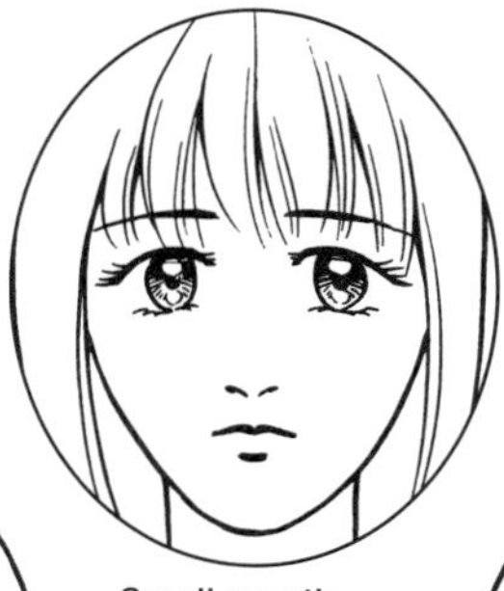

Small mouth

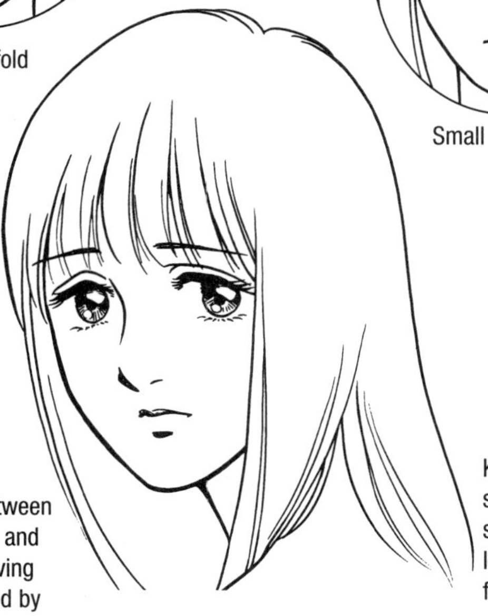

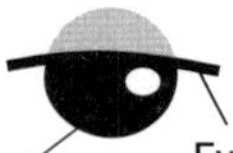

Widen the gap between the eyelid contour and fold line while halving the space occupied by the iris.

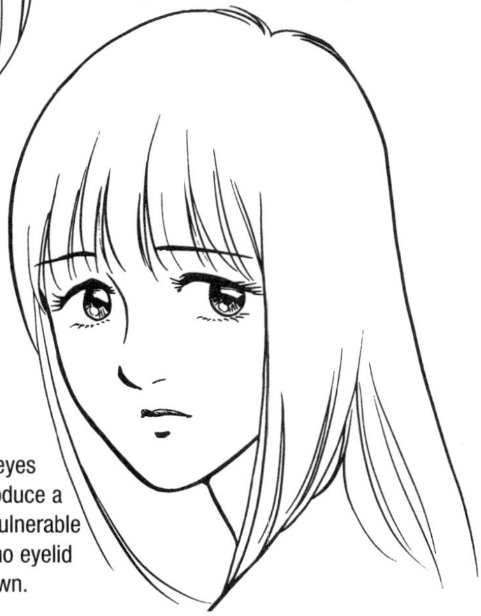

Keeping the eyes small will produce a satisfyingly vulnerable look even if no eyelid folds are drawn.

Using Hair to Portray a Character's Mood

Silhouette Effects

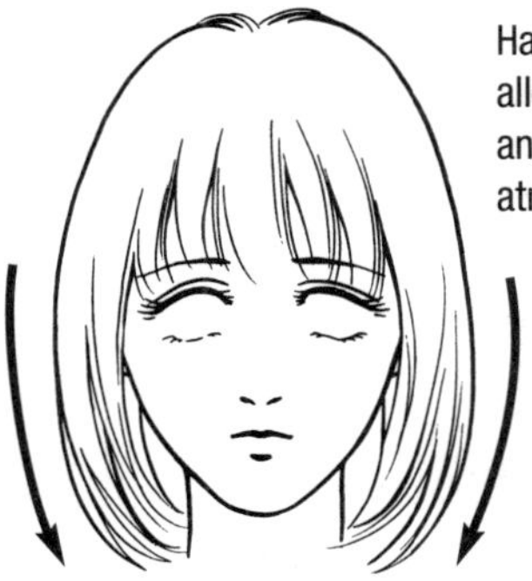

Hair curling inward allows you to suggest an introverted mood or atmosphere.

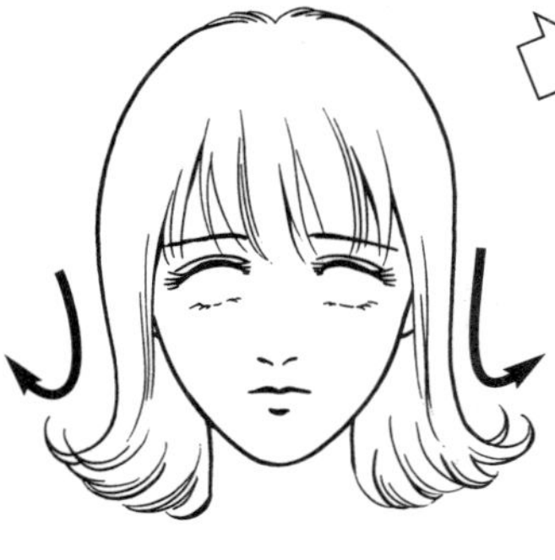

Showing the hair flipping outward creates a cheerful mood even on timid characters with downward sloping and/or small eyes.

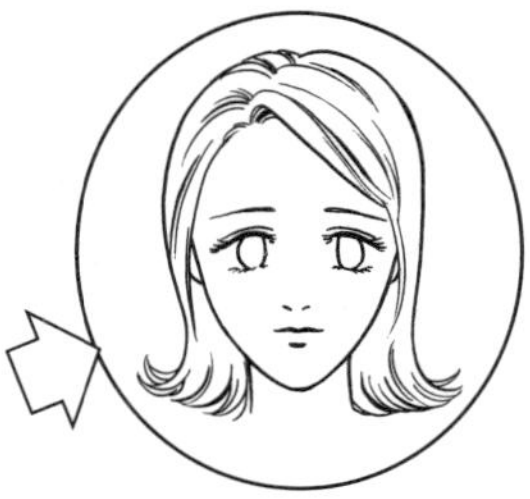

Exposing the forehead suggests a cheerful, friendly personality.

Bangs

The forehead hidden suggests an introverted character.

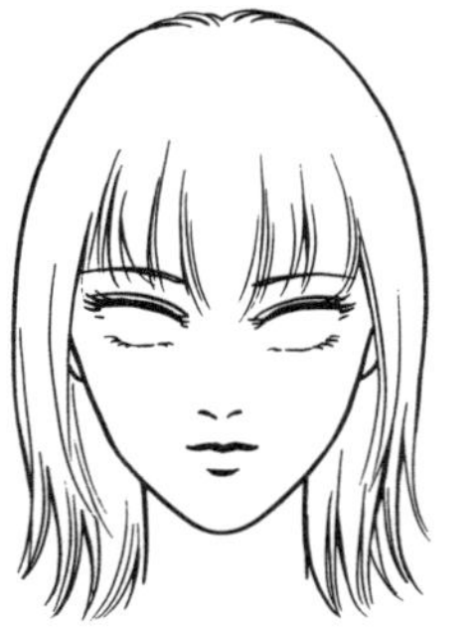

Using the hair to hide the forehead projects a dark, mysterious impression even when paired with upward slanting eyes on extroverted characters.

The forehead exposed suggests an outgoing character.

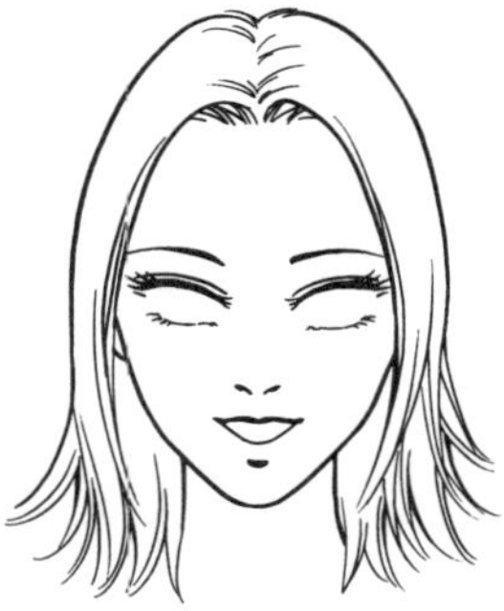

No bangs underscores the sense of vivaciousness projected by characters with upward slanting eyes.

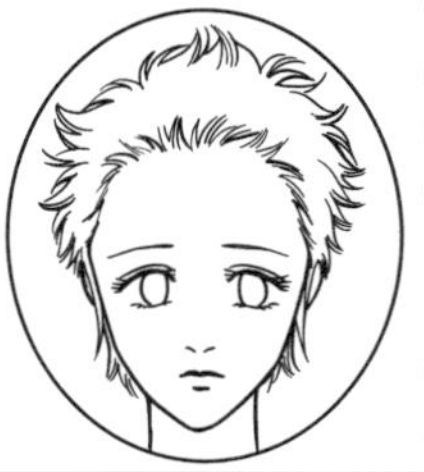

Vulnerable characters with droopy eyes are not suited to hairstyles with the forehead exposed. Rather than using this look with a timid personality, use it to express when a regular character feels despondent or apprehensive.

Full Figure

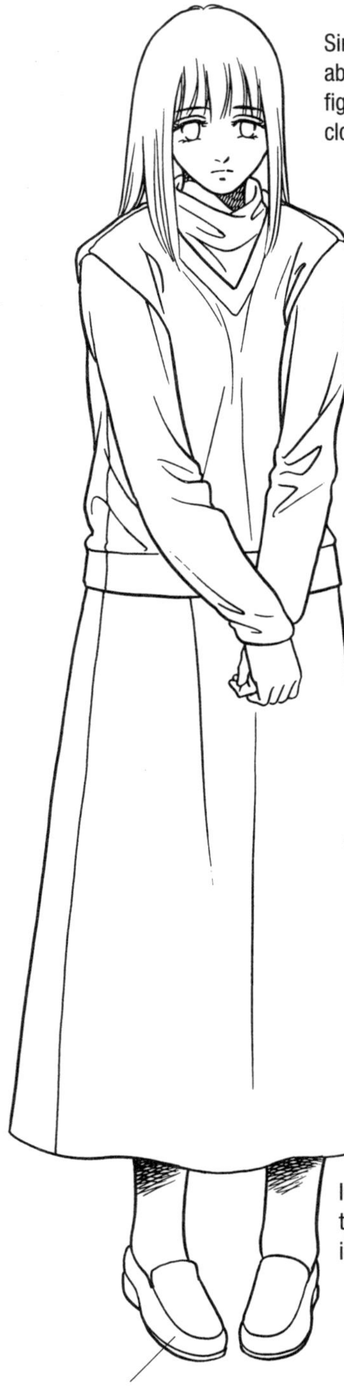

The character's reticent, introverted personality reflects in her appearance. Since her emotional state is supposed to be directed inward, give extra care to the direction of her hair and her stance. This character does not outwardly display either her emotional state or her body. Since she often lacks confidence, show her hunching forward with the shoulders rounded.

• Rounded Shoulders and Bad Posture Are Key Points.

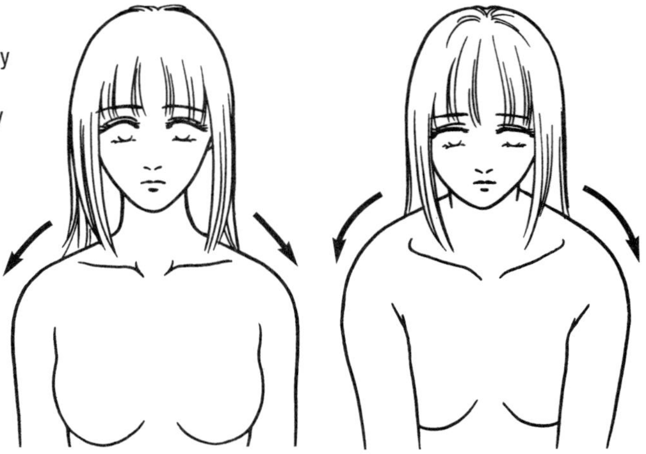

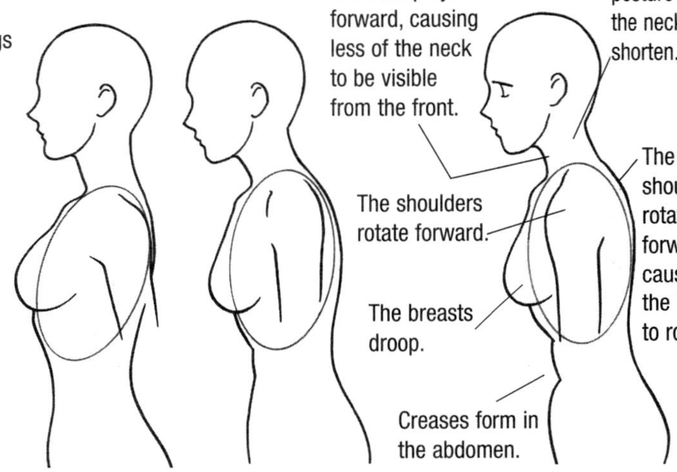

Here, a normal posture is distorted as timidity is reflected in the character's body.

• Speaking over the Shoulder

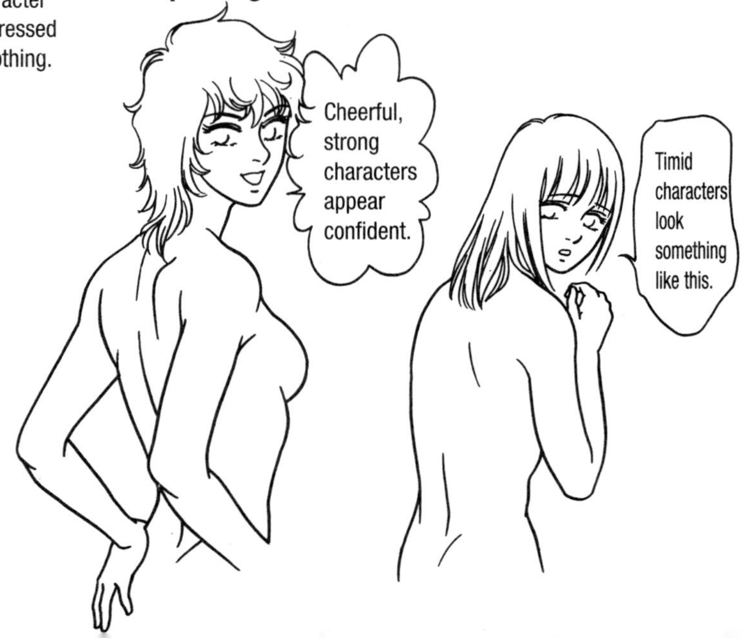

Standard Fashions

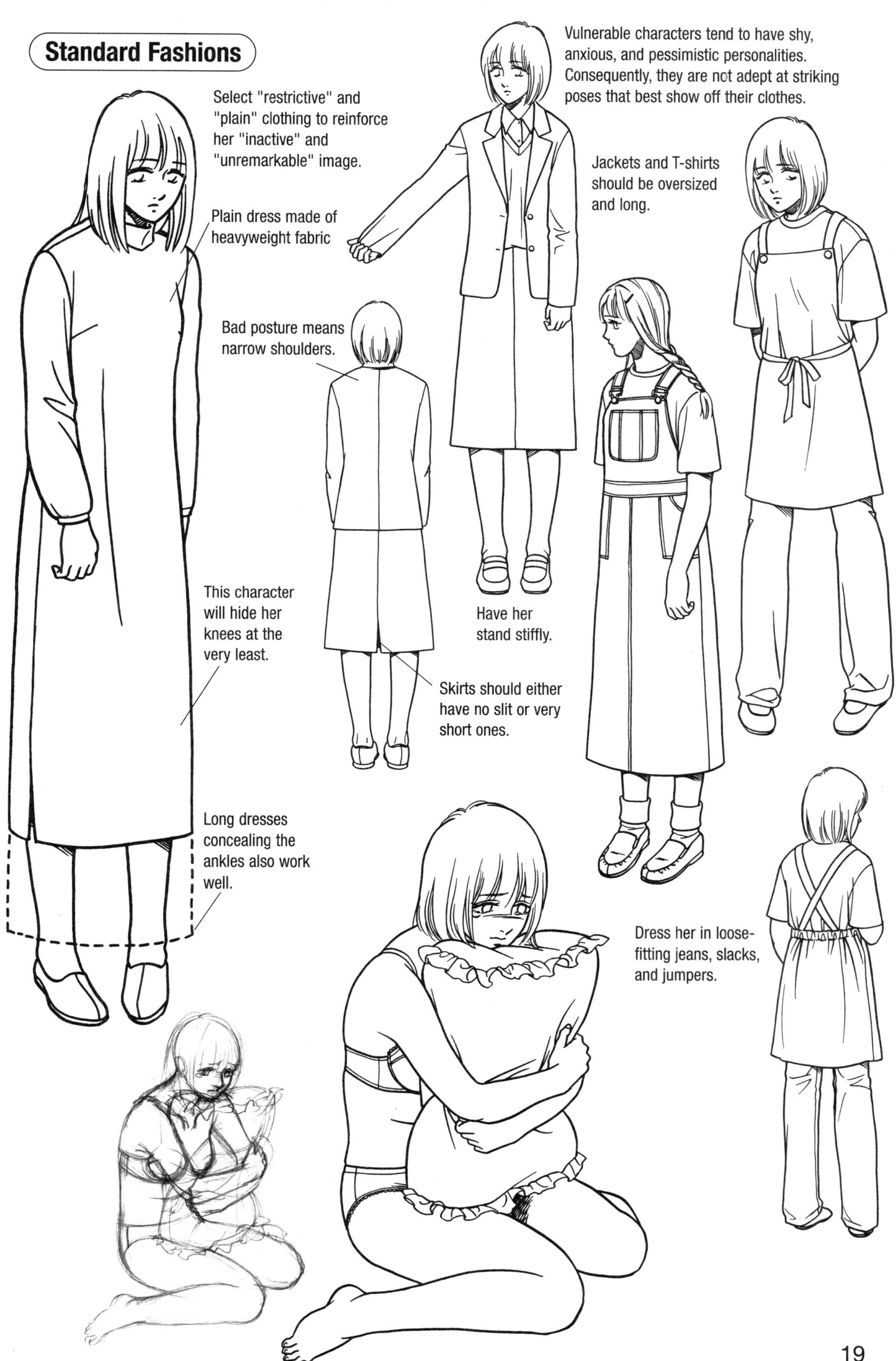

03 The Straight-laced Girl

Almond-shaped eyes and eyeglasses are key.

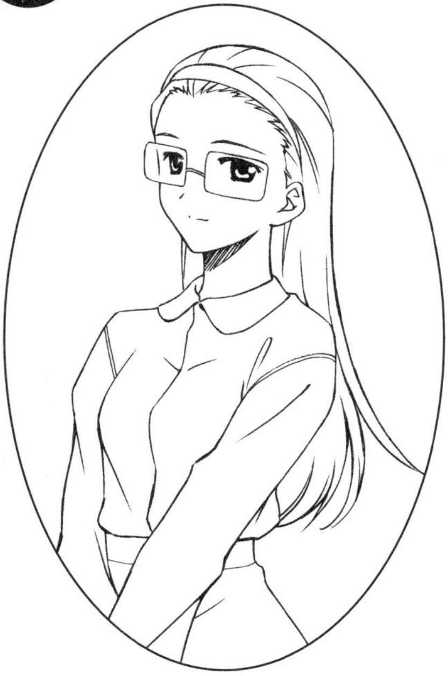

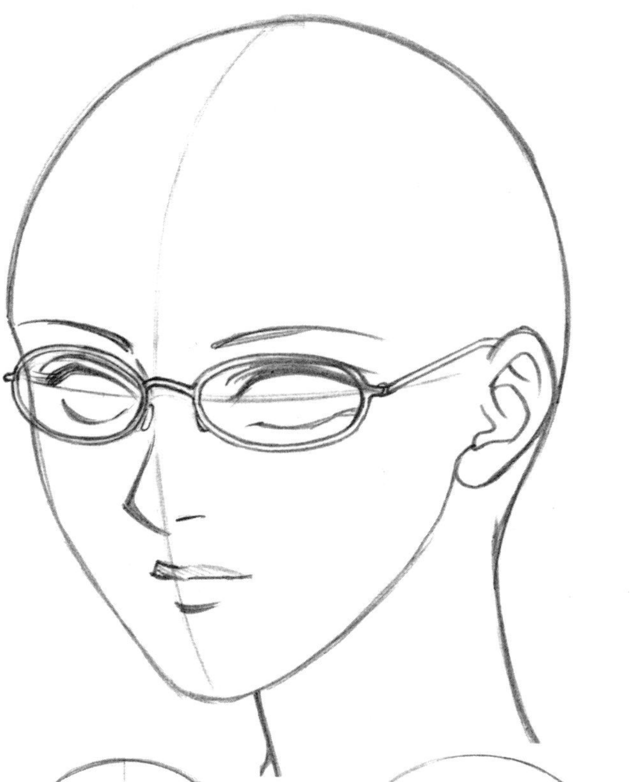

Basic Points

- Prim and proper air
- Has a strong sense of time and place (i.e. understands how she should behave under given circumstances; is able to appropriately judge a situation and possesses proper common sense and social etiquette).
- Keep her appearance plain.

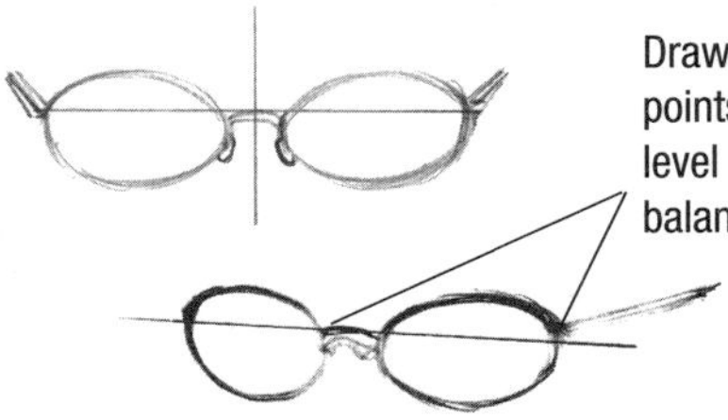

Draw these two points at the same level to obtain visual balance.

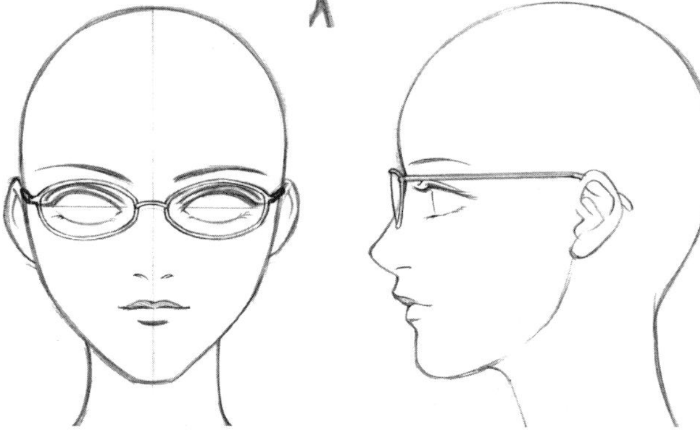

Three Basic Eye Types

Typical Eye (Almond-shaped)

Downward Sloped Eye

Upward Sloped Eye

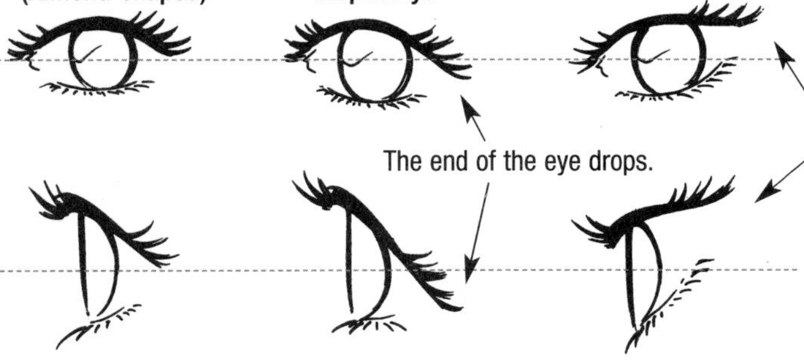

The end of the eye drops.

Drawing the eye's end higher than its center creates an upward sloping eye or a glaring eye.

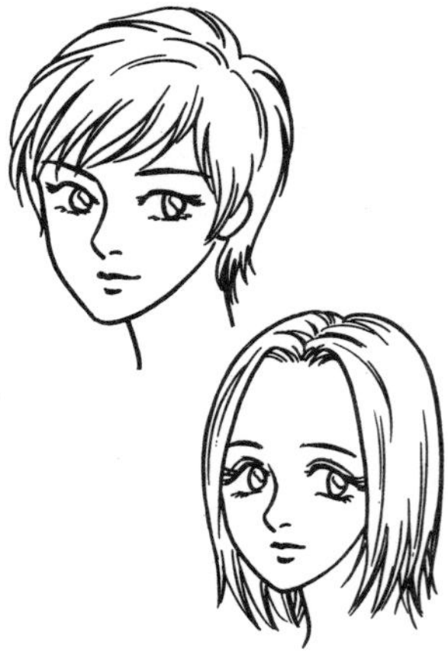

Eye with Large Pupil and Iris

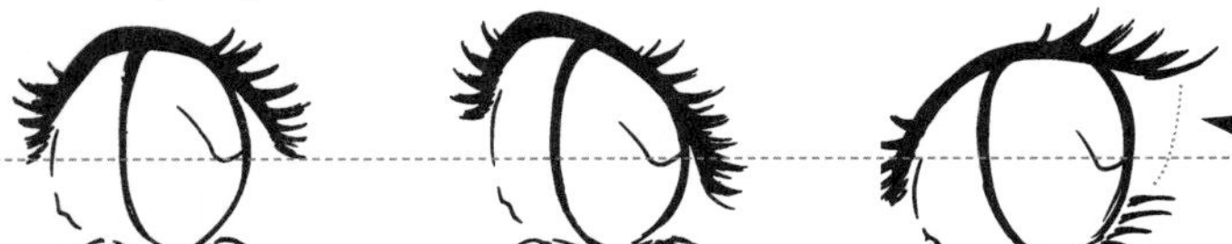

Maintain an awareness of all the eye's contour lines, even those omitted from the final rendition.

Typical eyes and downward sloping (droopy) eyes can appear similar, so modify the hairstyle or give the face big eyes to distinguish between character types.

Key Variation Points Hair, Eyeglasses, Mode of Dress

Stylish-Prim ◄• • • • • • • • • Straight-laced • • • • • • • • ► Ultra Straight-laced

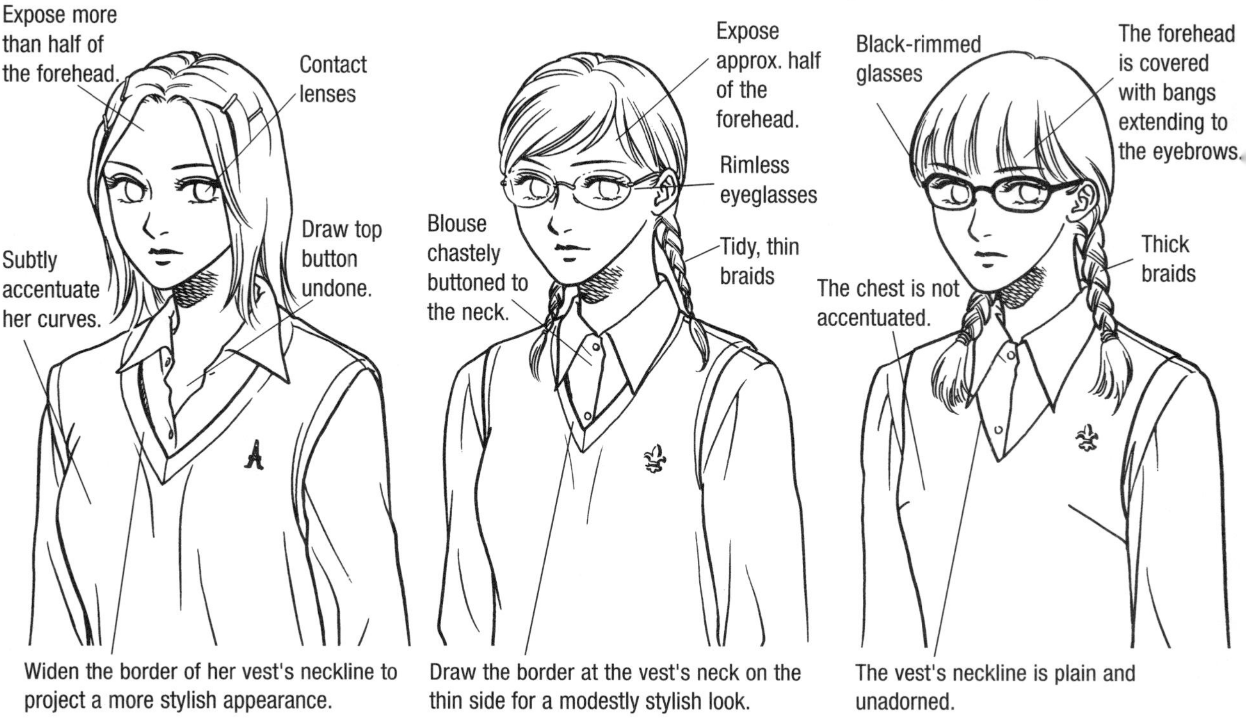

Straight-laced Look: Rimless Eyeglasses

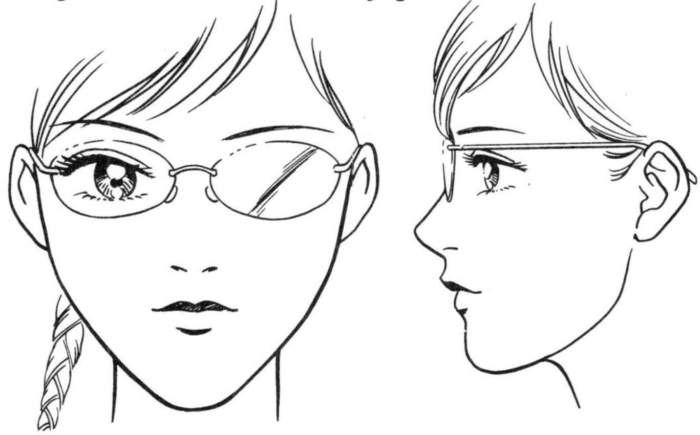

Ultra Straight-laced Look: (Black) Rimmed Glasses

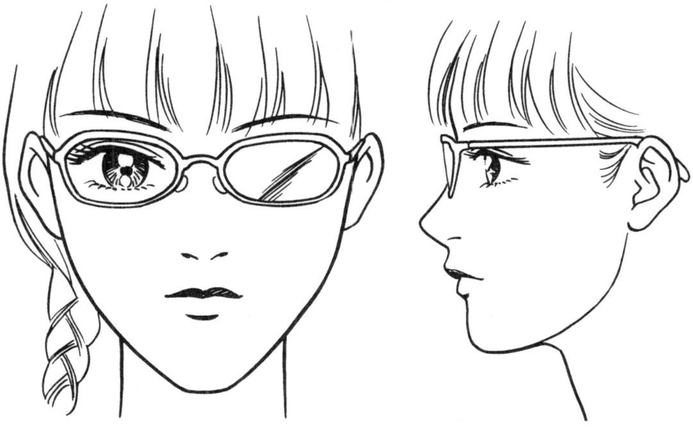

Large irises give the impression of a typical, simple, honest girl.

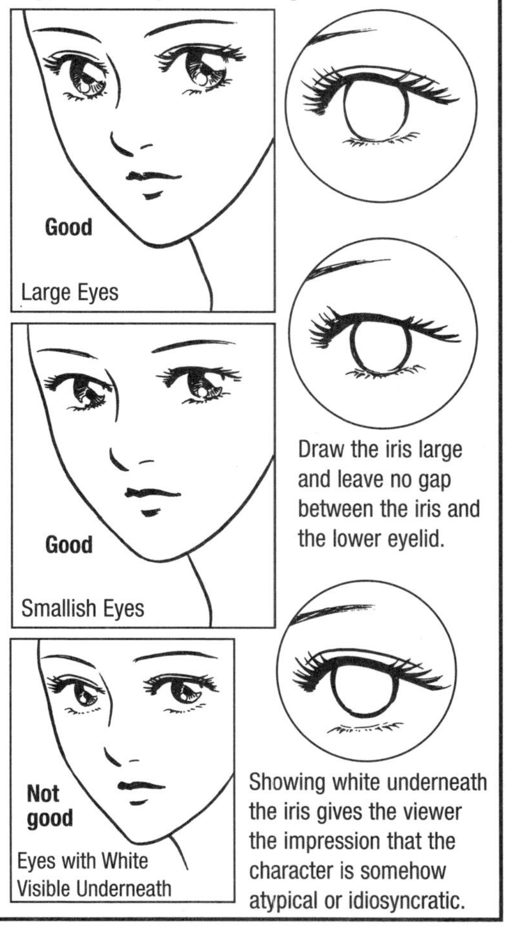

Full Figure

The Straight-laced Girl is formal, prim, and proper. Her outfits and outer appearance should come across as lack-luster.

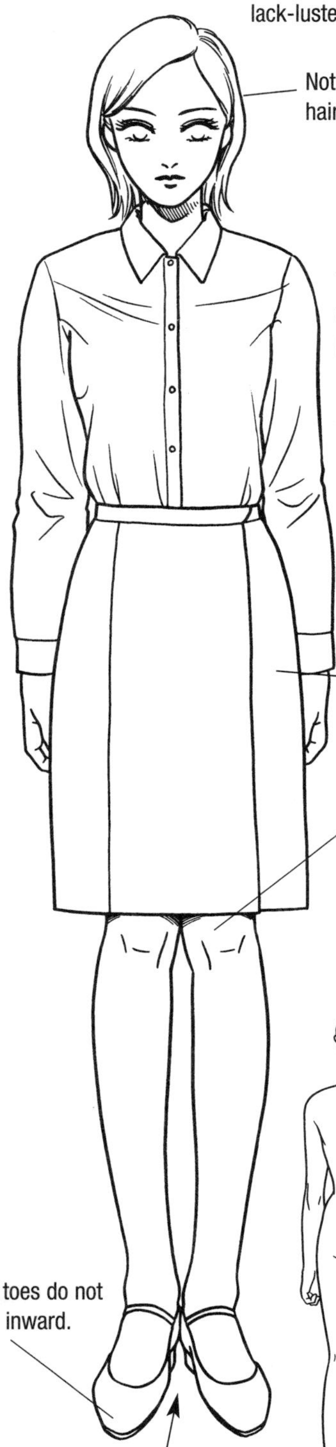

Not overly ostentatious hairstyle

The figure's overall appearance should be plain.

Above-the-knee skirt length

The skirt's length is approx. knee-length. Exposing the knee generates an active look, while covering the knee produces a meek and mild atmosphere.

The toes do not turn inward.

The heels touch giving the impression of standing primly and properly.

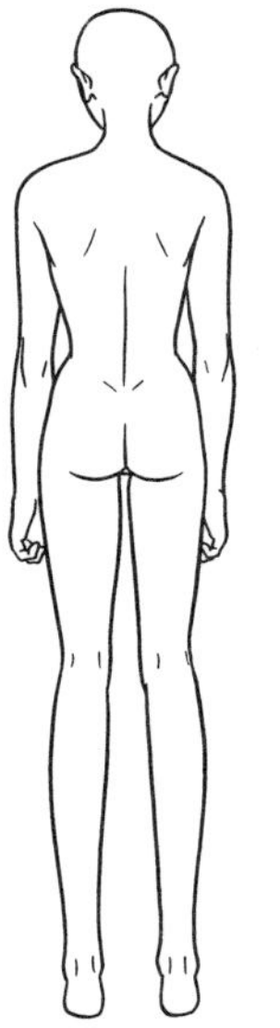

A figure standing bolt upright is often used when a character is unaware that she is being viewed.

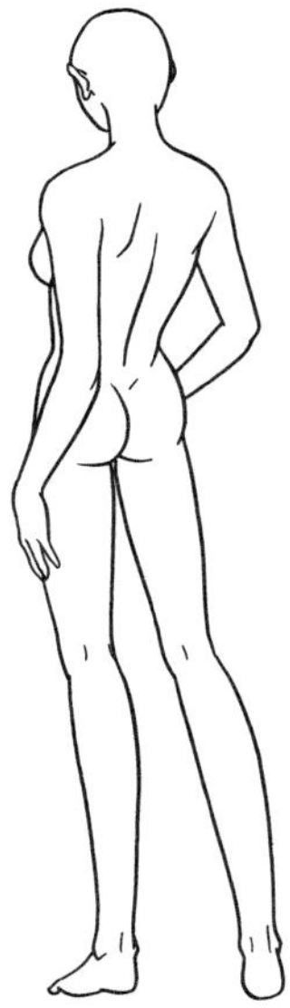

Twisting poses are often used when the character is conscious of being viewed by another or when wanting another to look at her.

• Draw a Squarish Upper Body.

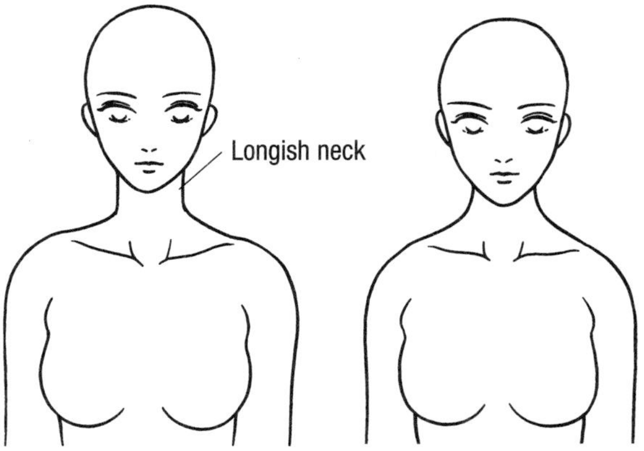

Longish neck

Square or slightly rounded shoulders give the impression of an overly serious personality. Thickening the muscles will create an athletic appearance.

Create a slouched posture by shortening the neck and accentuating the roundness of the shoulders. This will produce a roundish look overall, leading to a "sweet" image.

• Stiff Poses

Poses focusing on this character's prim and proper qualities result in masculine stances.

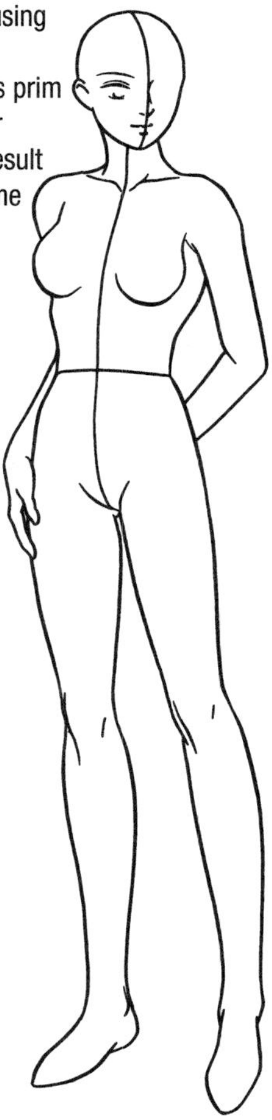

Postures straighten out when the character is not particularly attempting to make herself fetching. The upper body and lower body face the same direction.

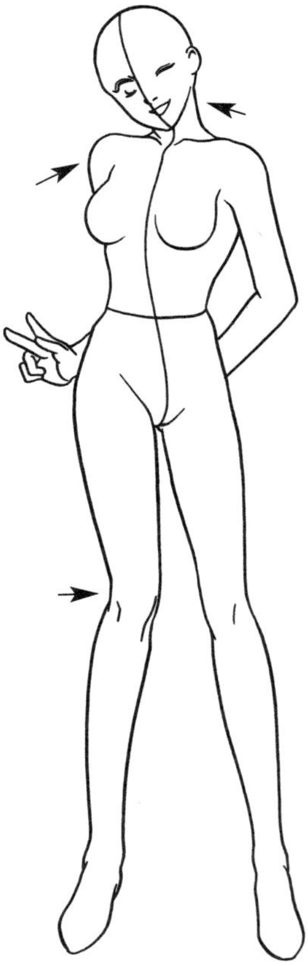

In this pose, the character is trying to look girlish or cute. The tilting of the neck, twisting of the shoulders, and placement of the feet all add to her awareness of her appearance.

Standard Fashions

Dress the Straight-laced Girl in typical or plain fashions. Take a look at school uniforms or secretary fashions for reference. Blouses, jackets, knee-length skirts, and slacks are all popular elements.

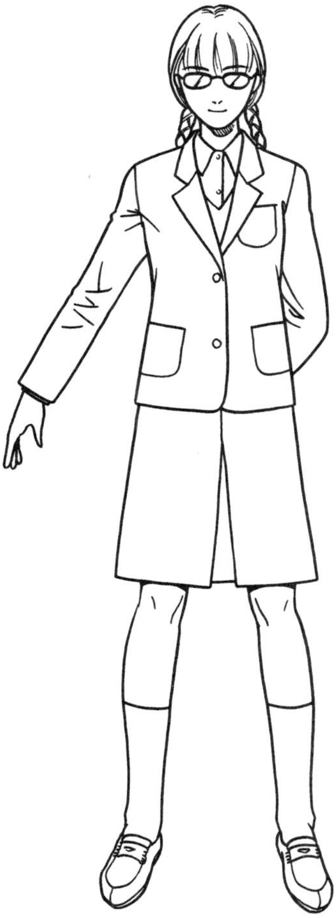

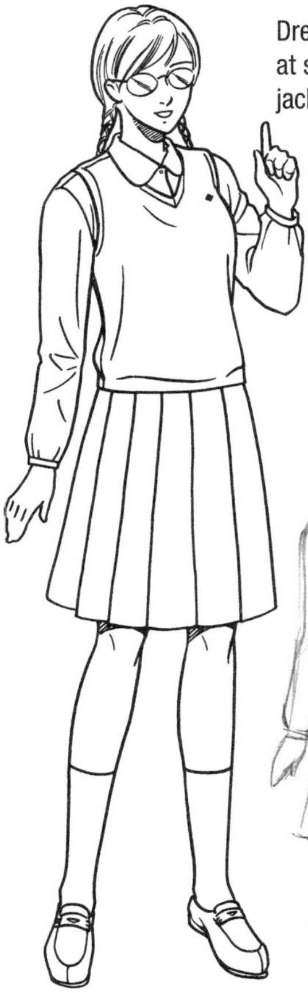

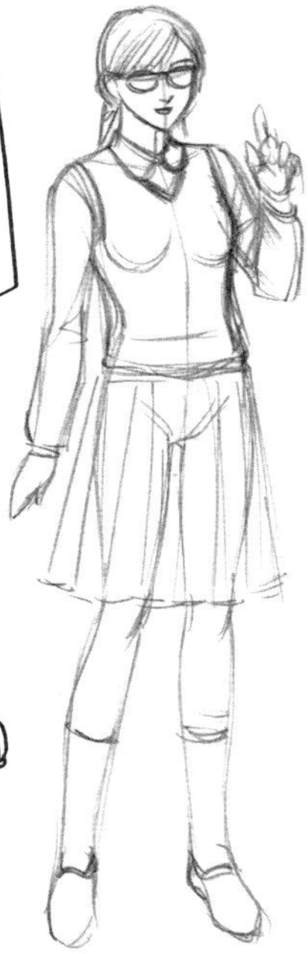

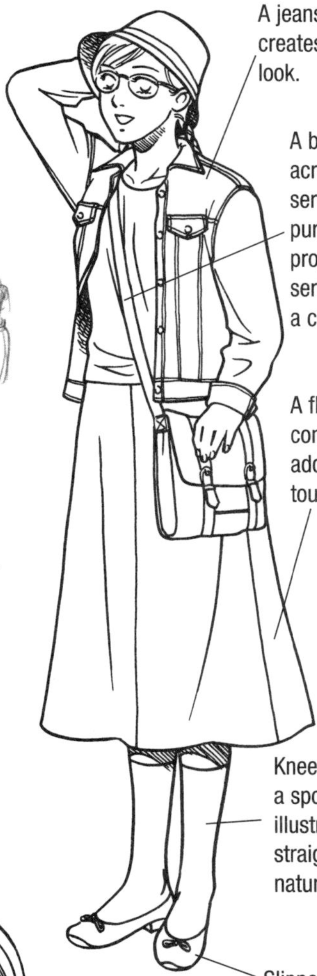

A jeans jacket creates a casual look.

A bag worn across the body serves the dual purpose of projecting a serious as well as a cute look.

A flared skirt is a common way of adding a girlish touch.

Knee-highs affect a sporty air while illustrating her straight-laced nature.

Slippers

Shortening the skirt length gives the character a more stylish appearance.

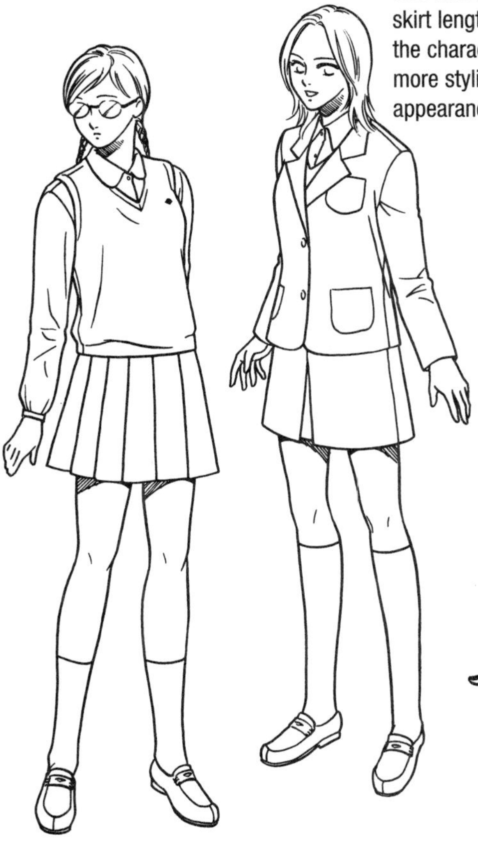

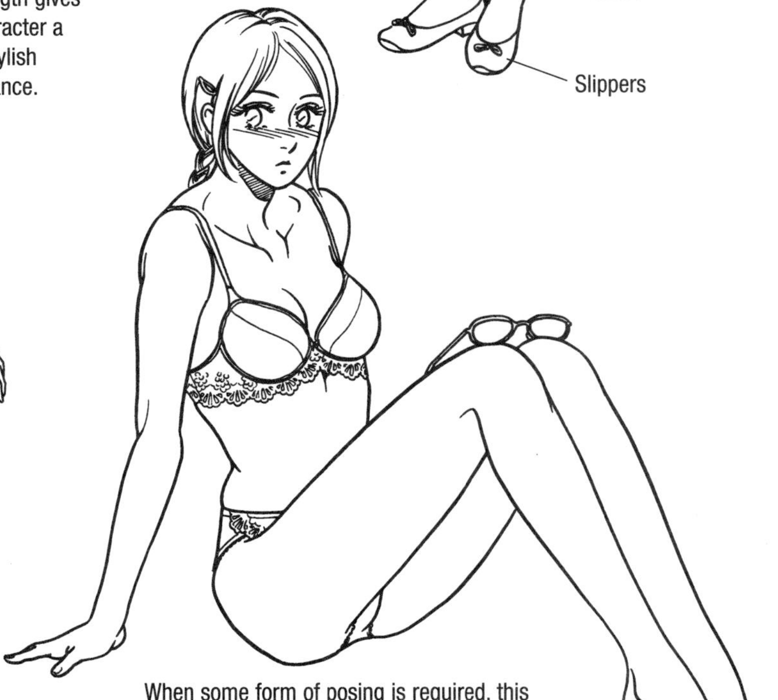

When some form of posing is required, this serious character should be able to comply to a certain extent.

04 The Cutie

The Cutie usually falls into two categories: the energetic cutie and the gentle cutie. Both of them are commonly drawn with large, drooping eyes.

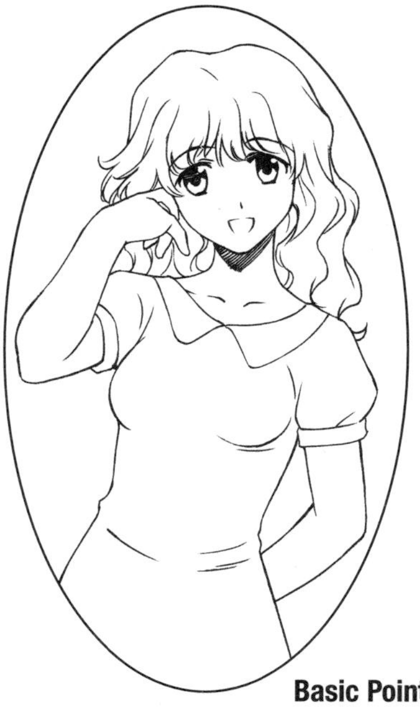

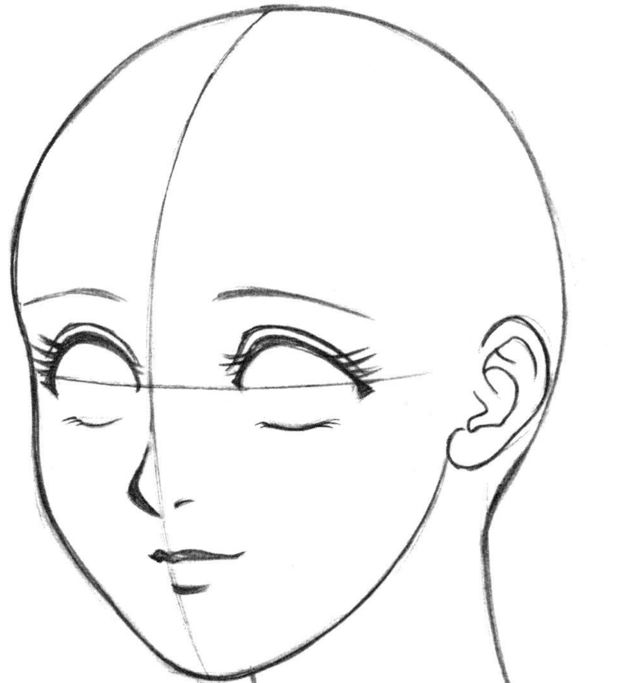

Use a roundish face.

Basic Points

Energetic Cutie:

- She tends to present herself as girlish and delightful in her gestures and poses.
- Vivacious

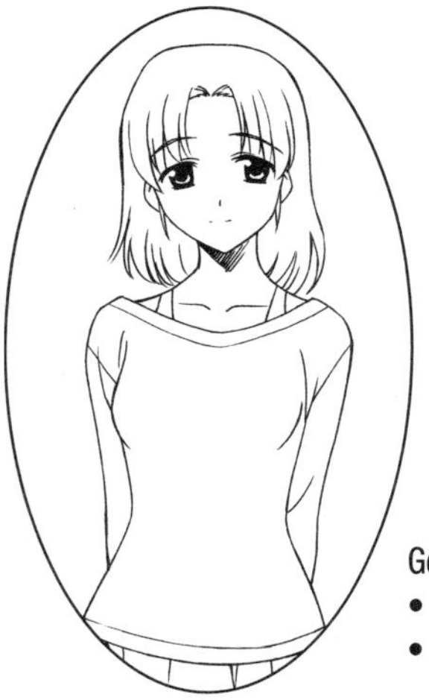

Gentle Cutie

- Easygoing
- Charmingly air-headed

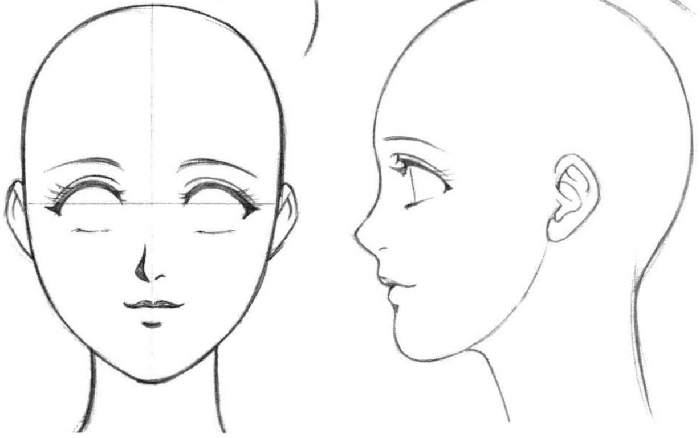

Three Points for Consideration When Drawing the Cutie

The Eyes' Size

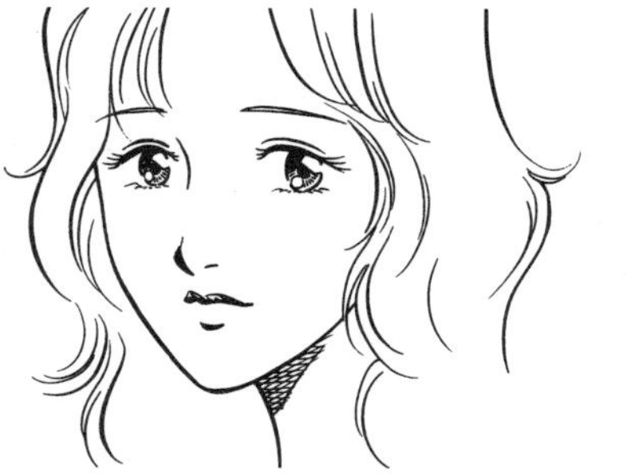

Smallish eyes, even downward sloping eyes, underscore a mature and gentle atmosphere, generating a look that diverges from our target: "cute."

The Face's Shape

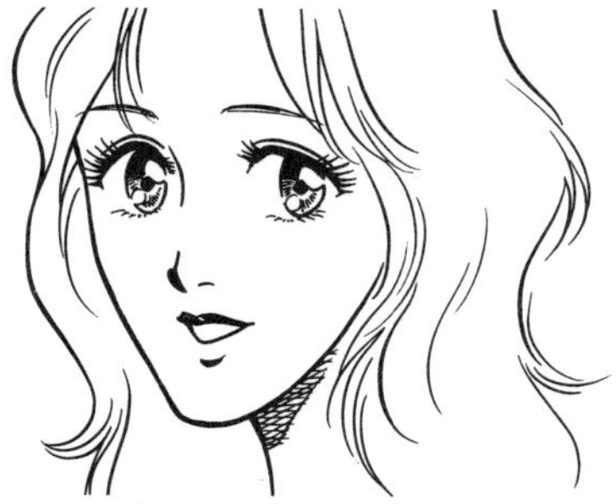

A narrow jaw and long face create an "older girl" look, even if paired with large eyes.

The Nose's Size

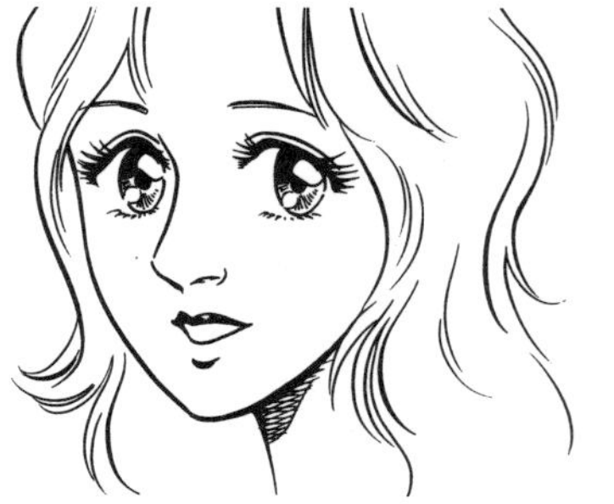

Overemphasizing the bridge of the nose or drawing the nose too large will make your character appear more ethnically Caucasian.

Key Variation Points Modify the character by changing the hairstyle and mouth's size.

Small Mouth

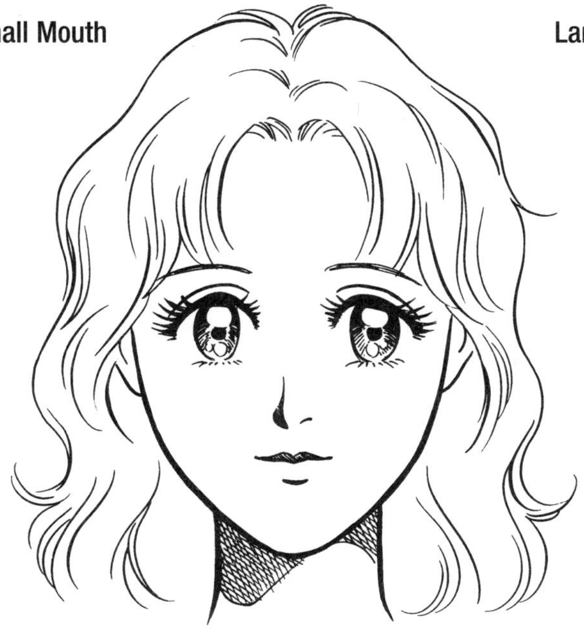

A small mouth produces a more elegant tone or rich girl/princess-type atmosphere.

Large Mouth

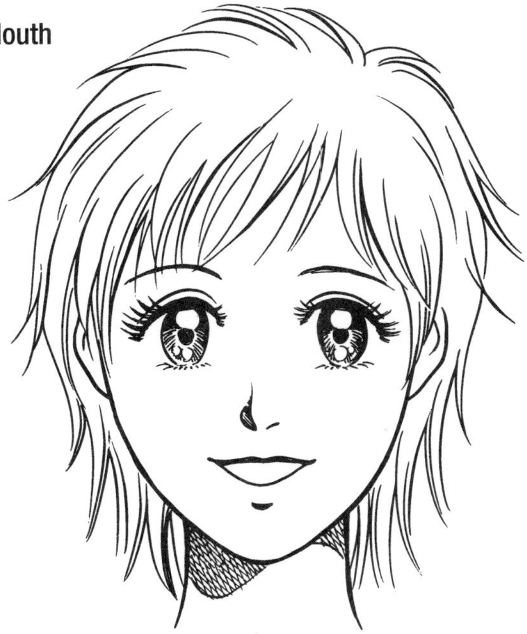

A large mouth allows you to create a spunky mood or tomboyish look.

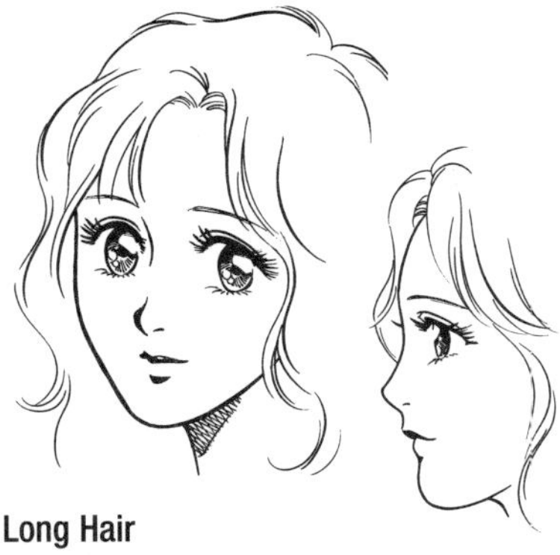

Long Hair
Long hair tends to make a character appear more "princess-ish." Crossed eyes with big irises result in the stereotypical "cutie" look.

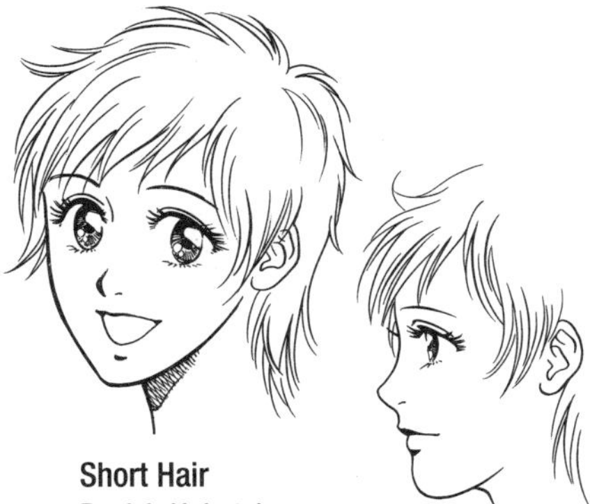

Short Hair
Boyish Hairstyle

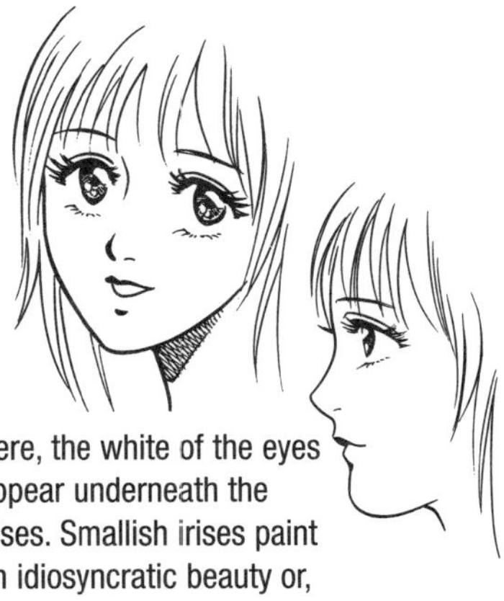

Here, the white of the eyes appear underneath the irises. Smallish irises paint an idiosyncratic beauty or, conversely, a perfectly average character.

Fixed Gazes Give Poses Charm

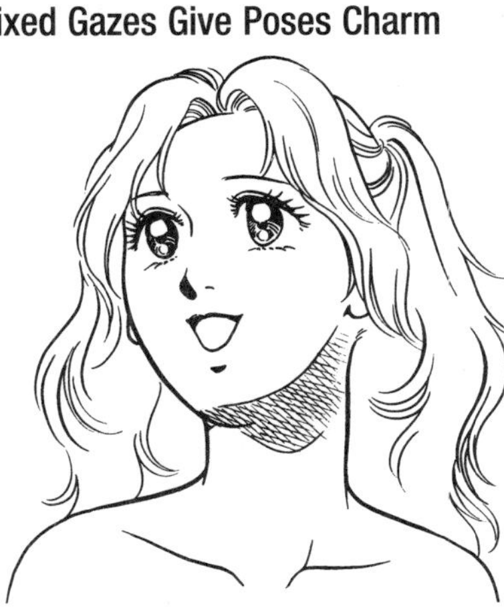

Angled face looking up

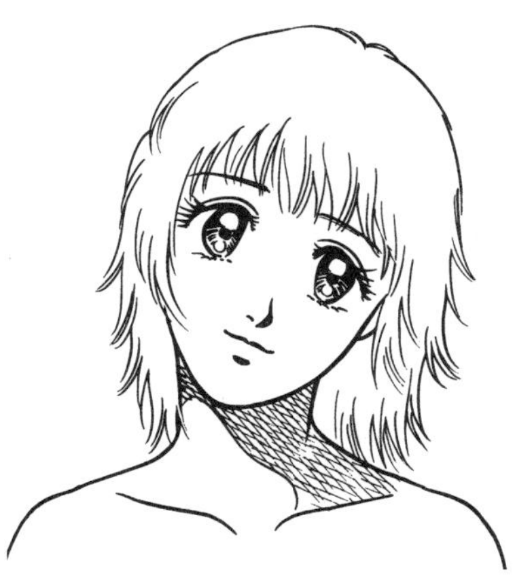

Gazing with head cocked slightly to the side

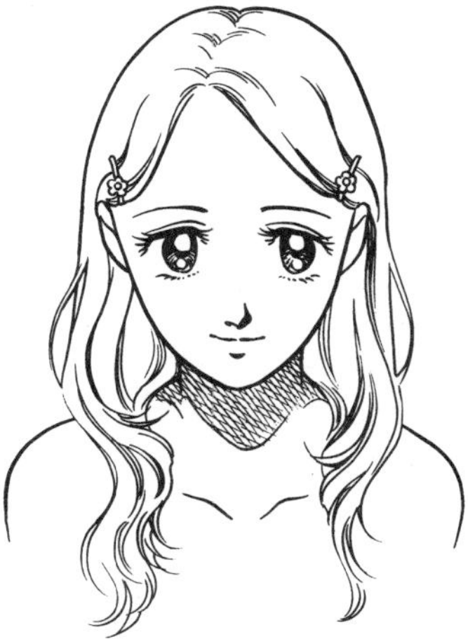

Looking up with chin pulled down

Full Figure

The key to a cutie character lies in her liveliness of her movements. Even in an innocent standing pose, she displays consciousness of her appeal in the angle of her neck and in the twisting of her shoulders and waist. Consequently, when drawing this character, take care to draw poses suggesting constant awareness of being seen by others.

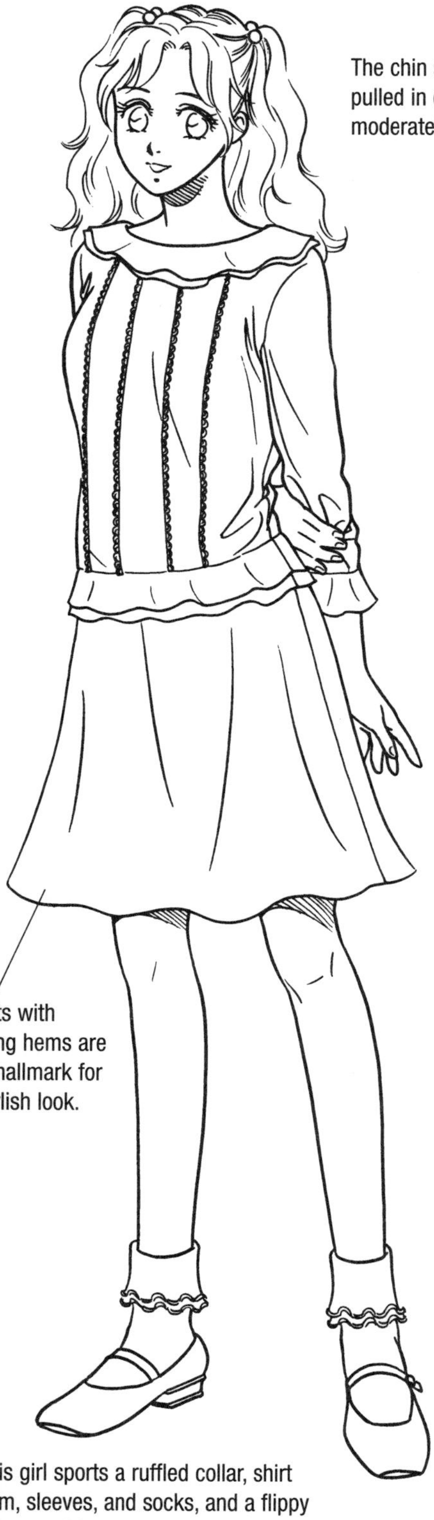

Skirts with flaring hems are the hallmark for a girlish look.

This girl sports a ruffled collar, shirt hem, sleeves, and socks, and a flippy skirt matching her hair's waves, producing a cohesive girlish image. Lace and ruffles work effectively in creating a "cute" look.

The chin should be pulled in or seen from a moderately low angle.

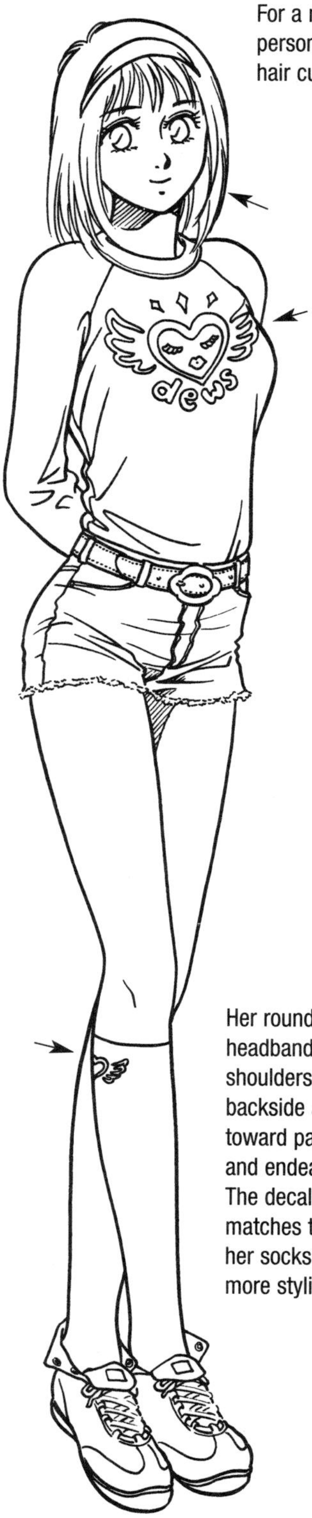

For a more reserved personality, show the hair curling inward.

Her round face, the headband's arc, her shoulders, chest, and backside all work toward painting a round and endearing image. The decal on her chest matches the ones on her socks, offering a more stylish look.

• Pay Attention to Posture

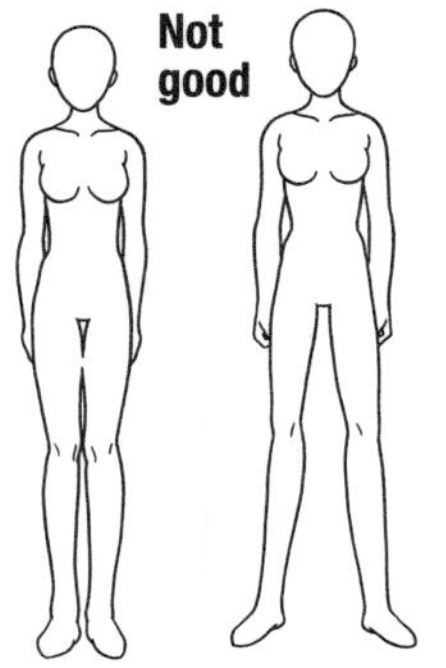

Having her standing stiffly, whether it be with her legs together or spread, does not look cute.

• Cute Postures

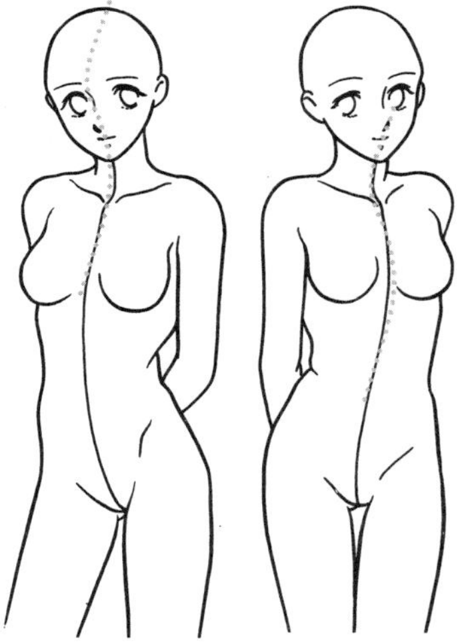

Contraposition (S-curve) poses are intended to show off a girl to her most charming.

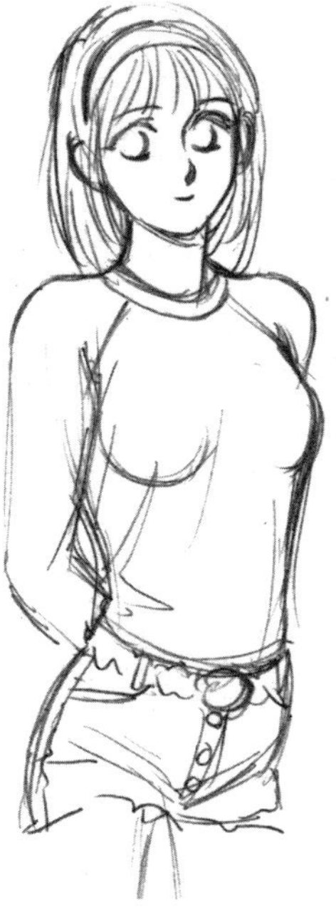

Standard Fashions

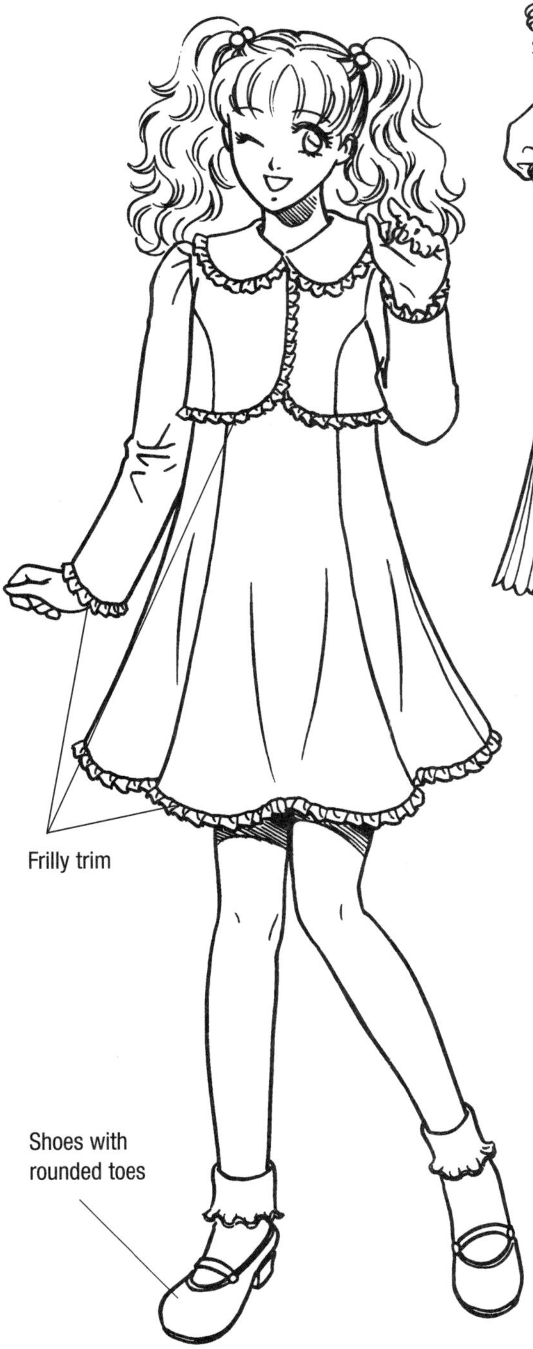

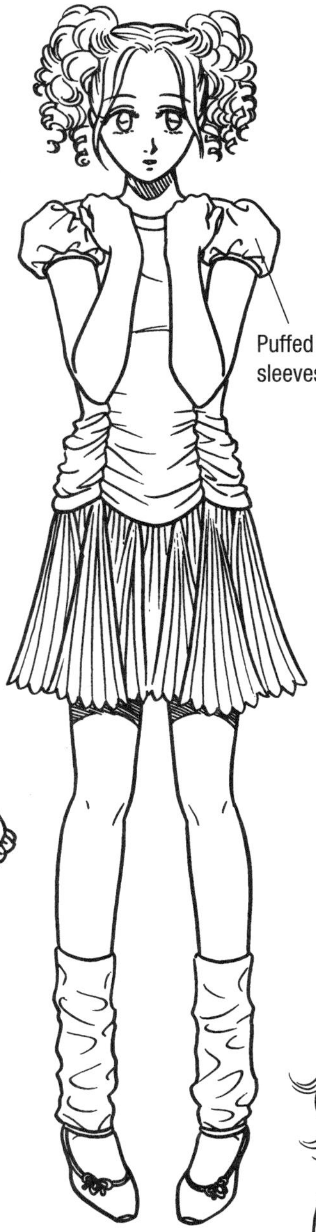

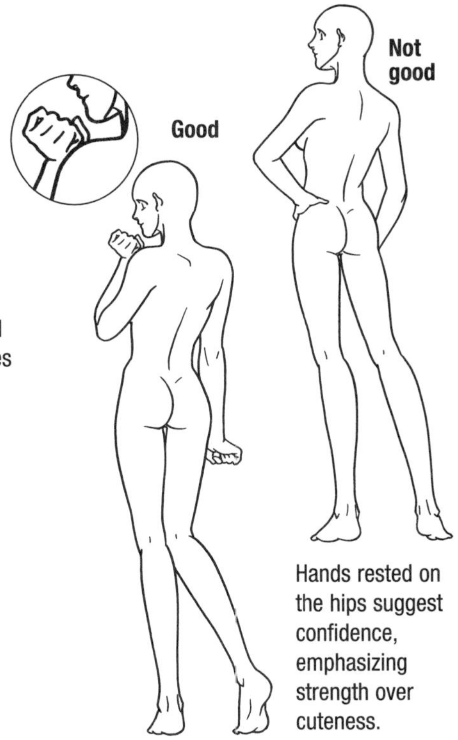

Hands rested on the hips suggest confidence, emphasizing strength over cuteness.

Showing the cutie bringing her knees together or holding her hand close to her face is also effective.

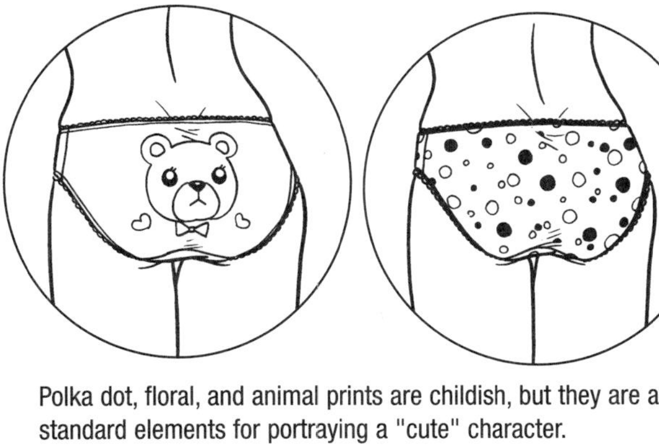

Polka dot, floral, and animal prints are childish, but they are also standard elements for portraying a "cute" character.

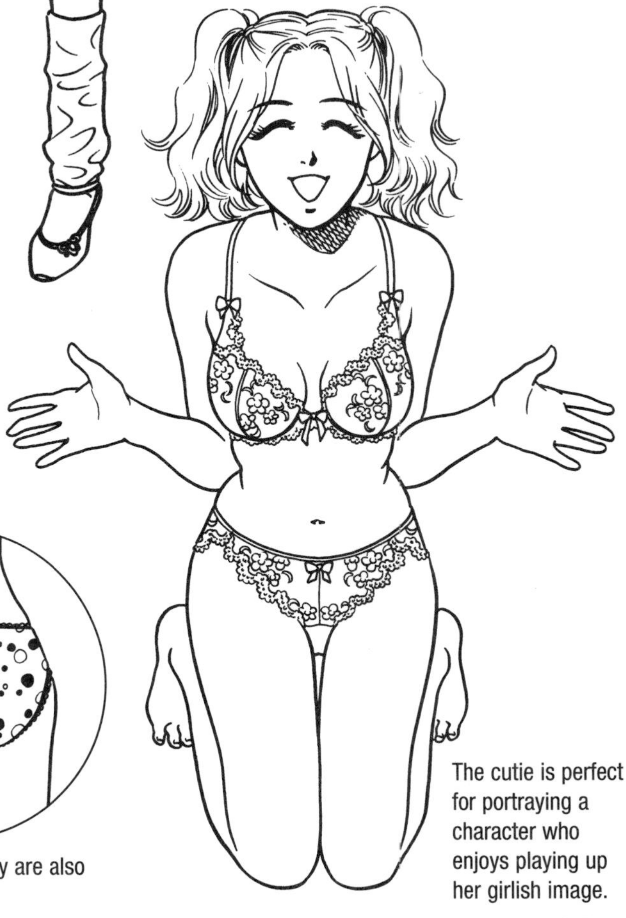

The cutie is perfect for portraying a character who enjoys playing up her girlish image.

05 The Imp

The Imp is energetic and ready for action. Her key features are a large mouth and large, laughing eyes.

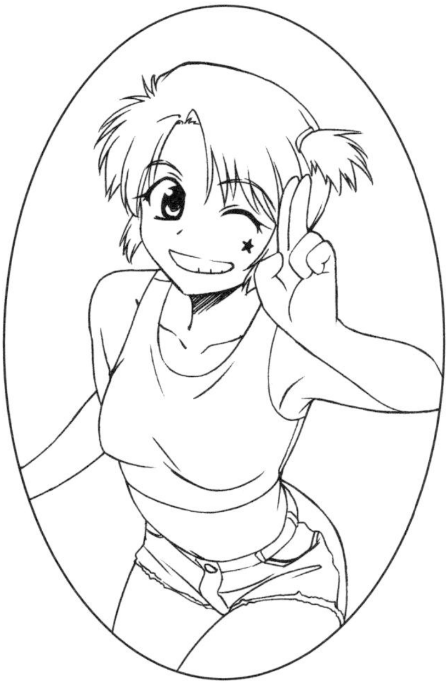

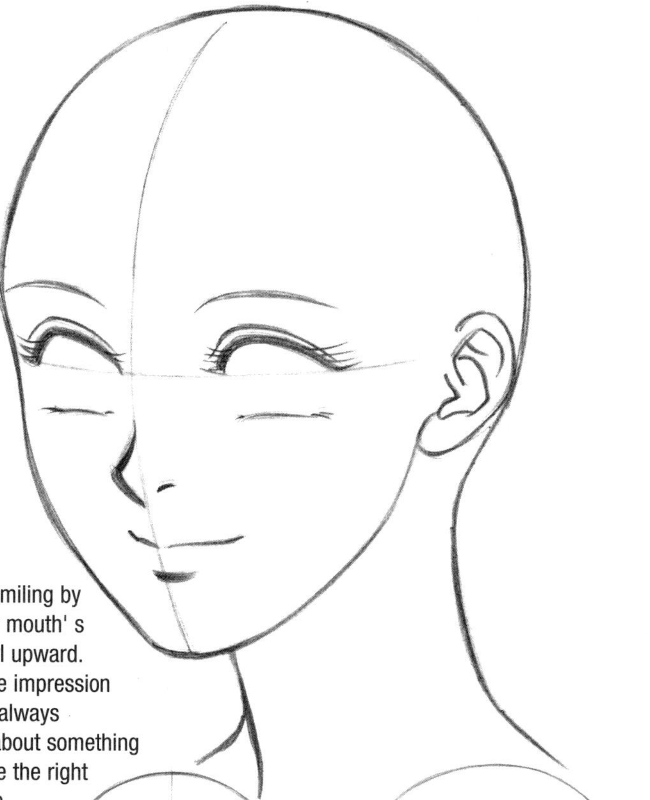

Show her smiling by making her mouth' s corners curl upward. Creating the impression that she is always scheming about something will produce the right atmosphere.

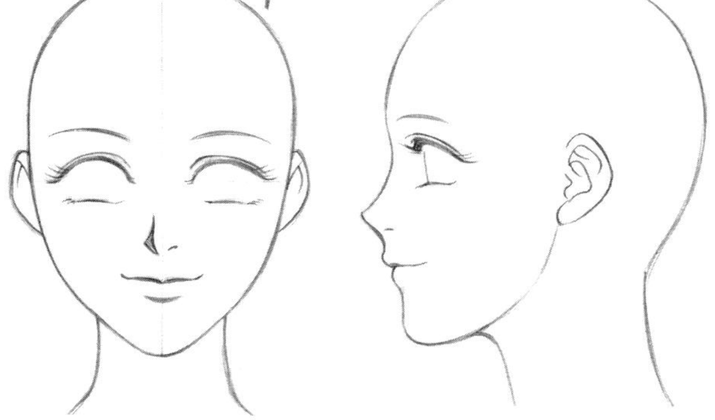

Basic Points

- Active character
- Show this character engaging in conspicuous poses that the others do not engage in, such as winking, sticking out her tongue, or moving or gesturing wildly.

Laughing Eyes

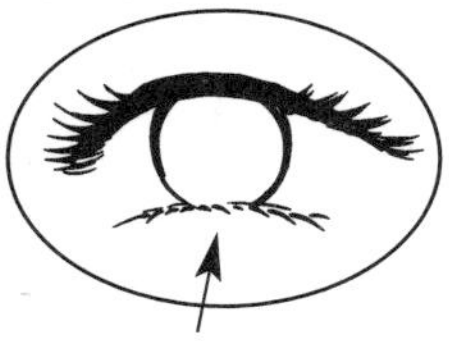

The lower eyelid also takes an upward arc.

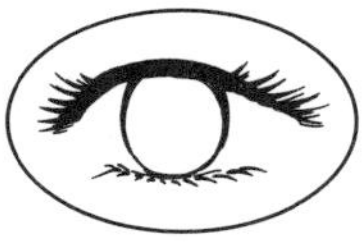

Ref. Fig.: Typical Eye

Key Points in Emphasizing Eccentricity

Distinguish her from other characters by thickening her eyebrows, darkening her lower eyelid contour, and drawing her mouth wide open.

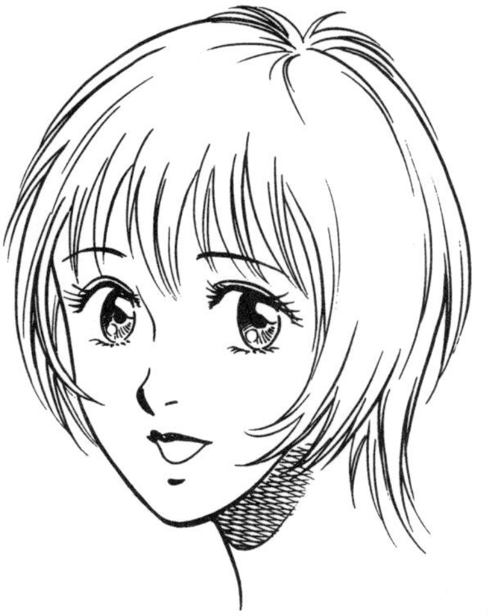

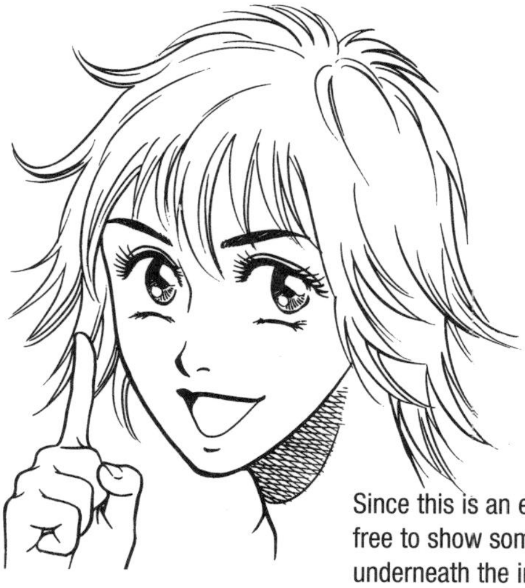

Since this is an eccentric character, feel free to show some white of the eye underneath the iris.

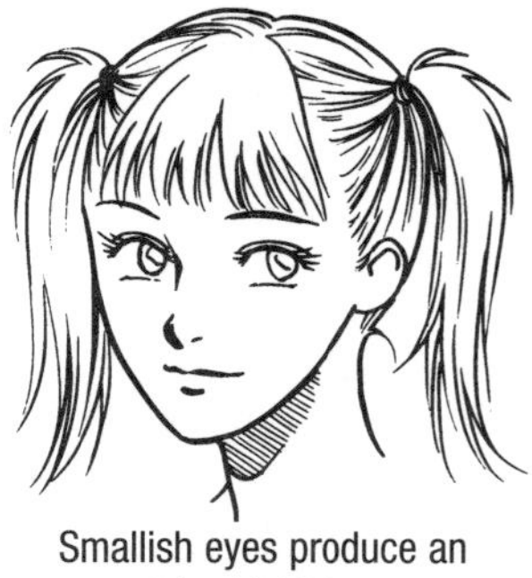

Smallish eyes produce an eccentric sidekick character.

Key Variation Points

Use the Hair to Reinforce the Imp's Bright, Cheerful, Vivacious Image.

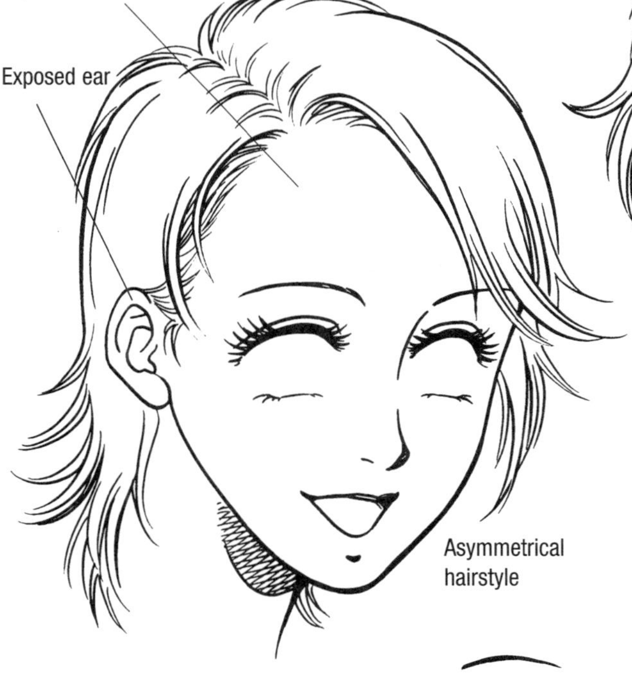

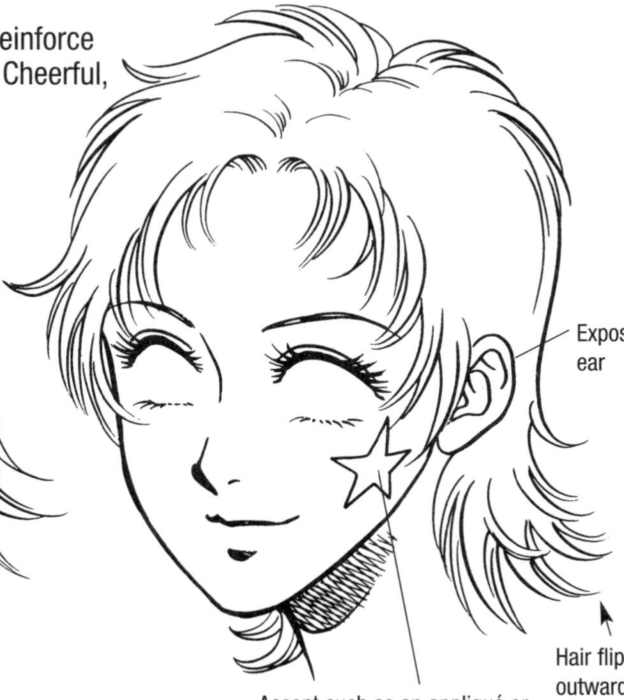

There is a wide variety of potential face appliqués. Show her wearing an appliqué or using makeup to create her own design.

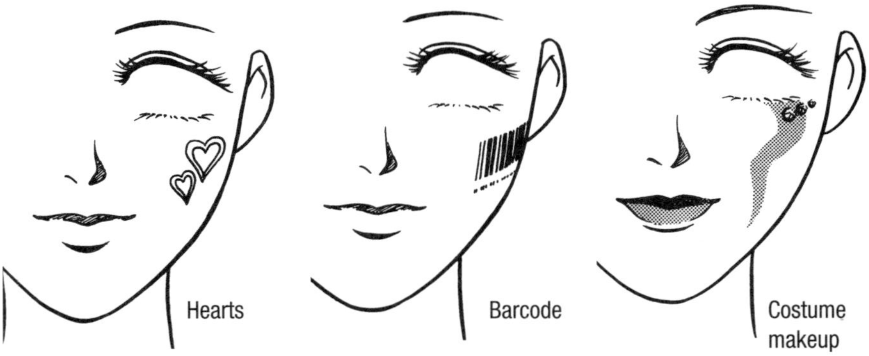

Short Hair: Basic to an Active Look

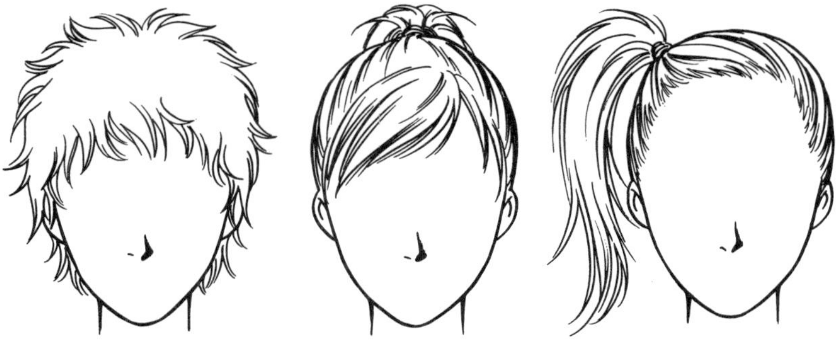

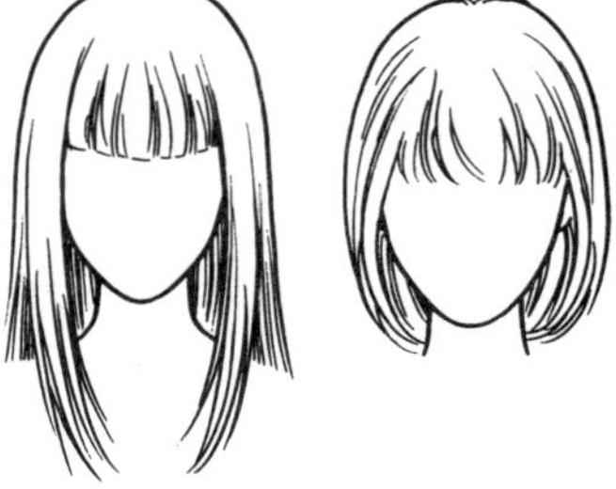

Evenly trimmed bangs or hair curling underneath suggest an introverted personality.

The trick is to leave the ears exposed.

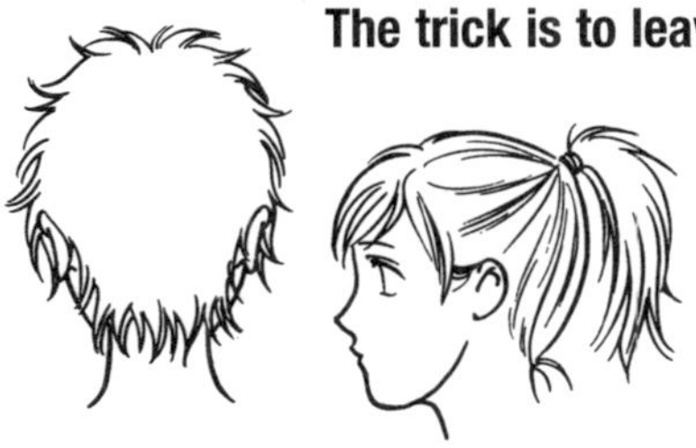

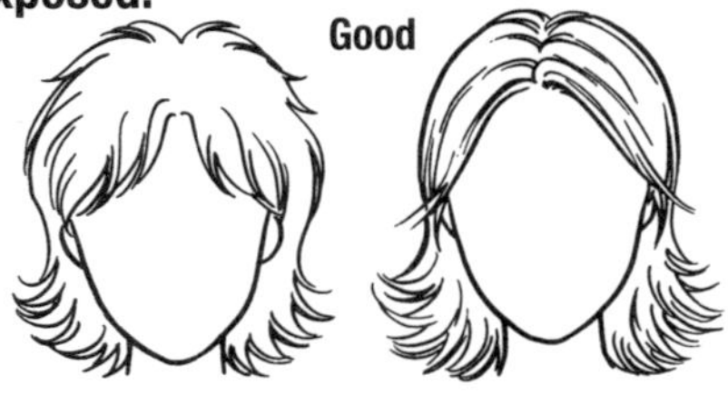

Bouncy styles with hair flipping outward help to project an extroverted image.

Full Figure

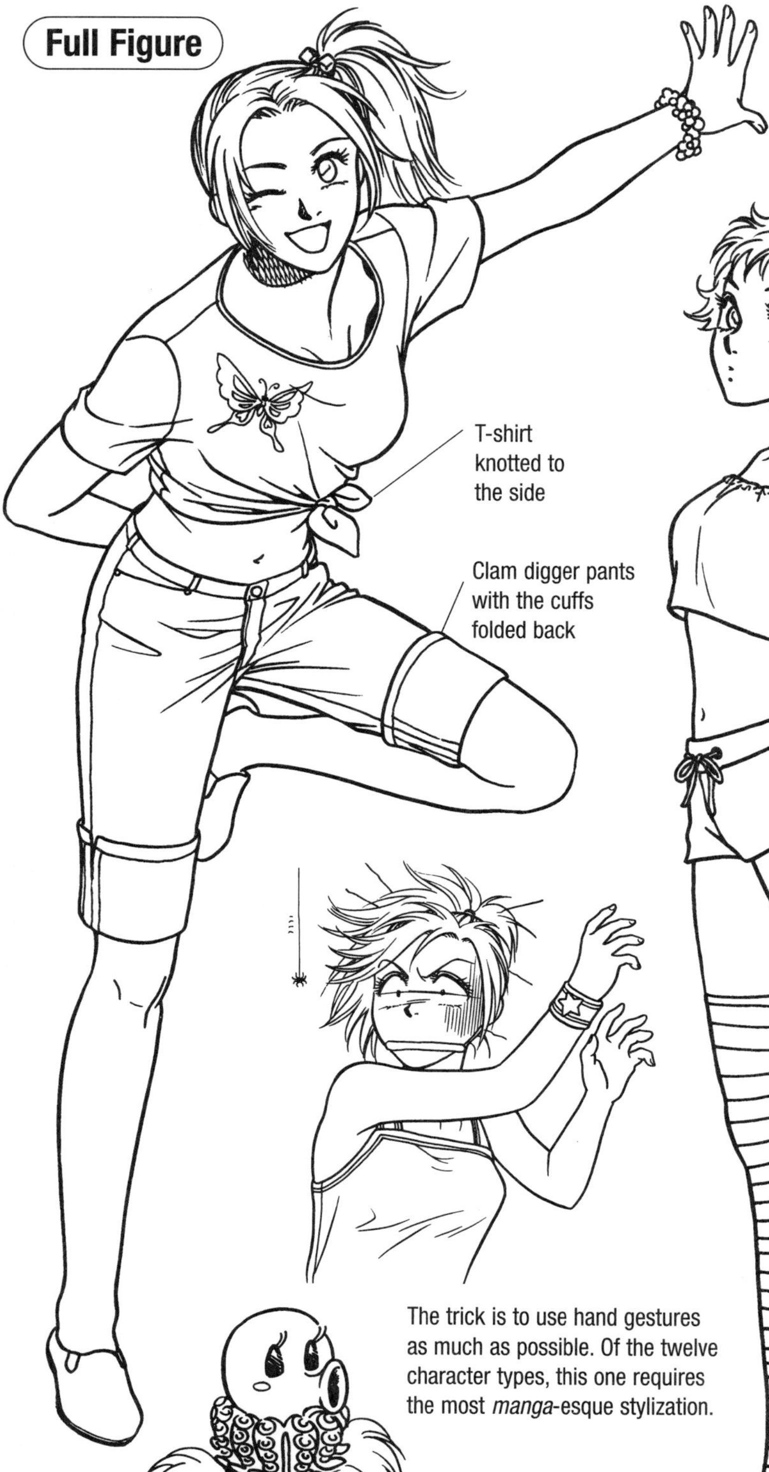

• Energetic Dynamism

Represent this girl as a strongly eccentric character. If she is supposed just to stand at a 3/4 view, she will undoubtedly stand on her toes or do something else contrary to what she was asked. The Imp also tends to fiddle with perfectly average clothing articles, wearing them in her own idiosyncratic way.

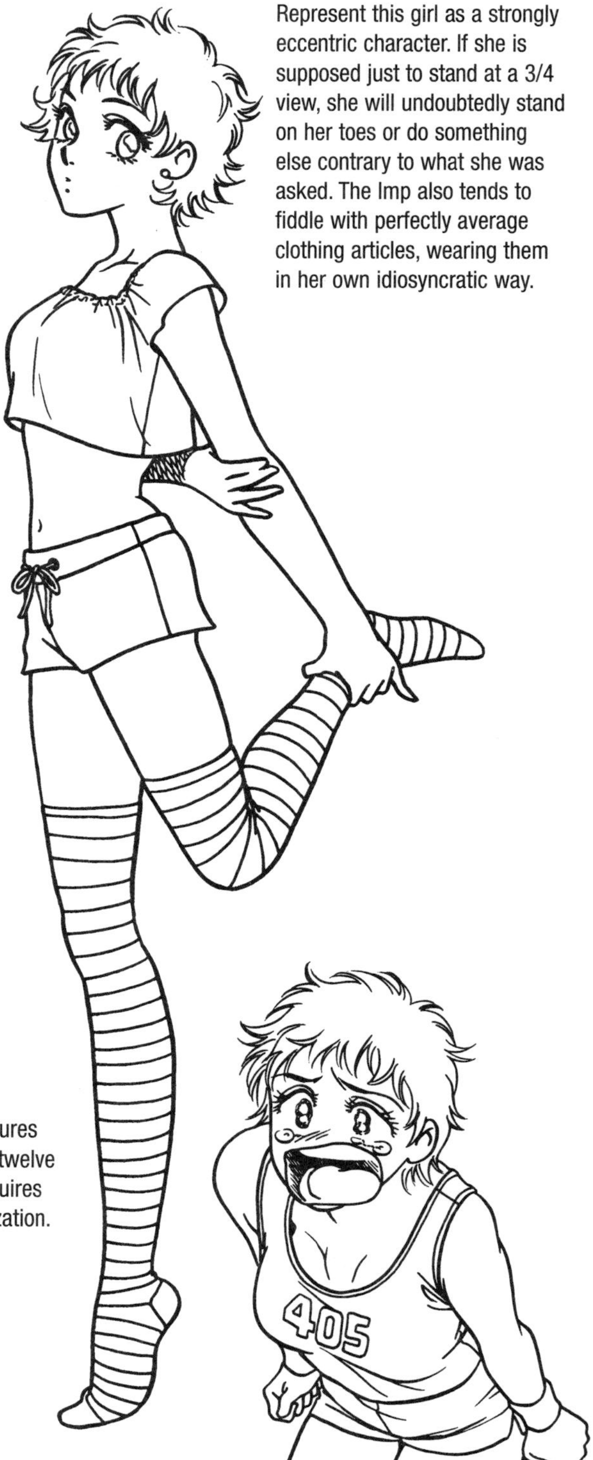

The trick is to use hand gestures as much as possible. Of the twelve character types, this one requires the most *manga*-esque stylization.

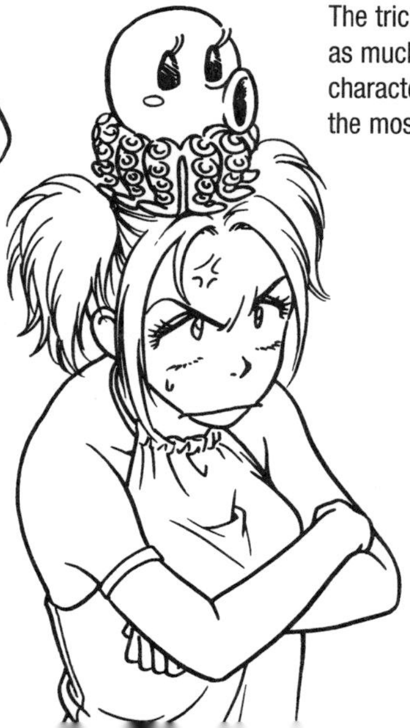

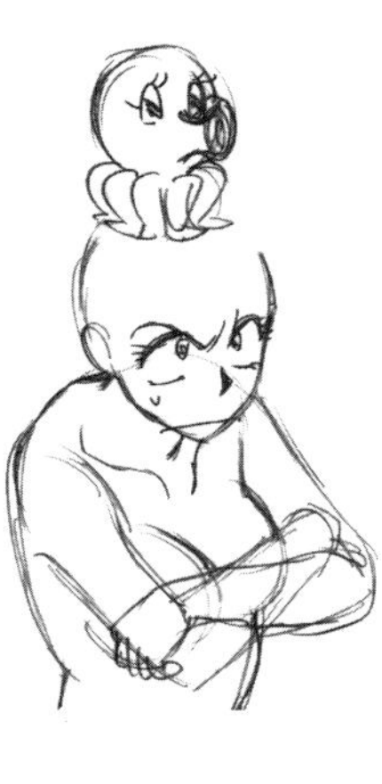

Try to show the Imp losing control in her facial expressions or throwing her entire self into flamboyant body language.

Standard Fashions

Dress the Imp primarily in comfortable, casual wear. The Imp is not the vampish type, which should be illustrated in her body language.

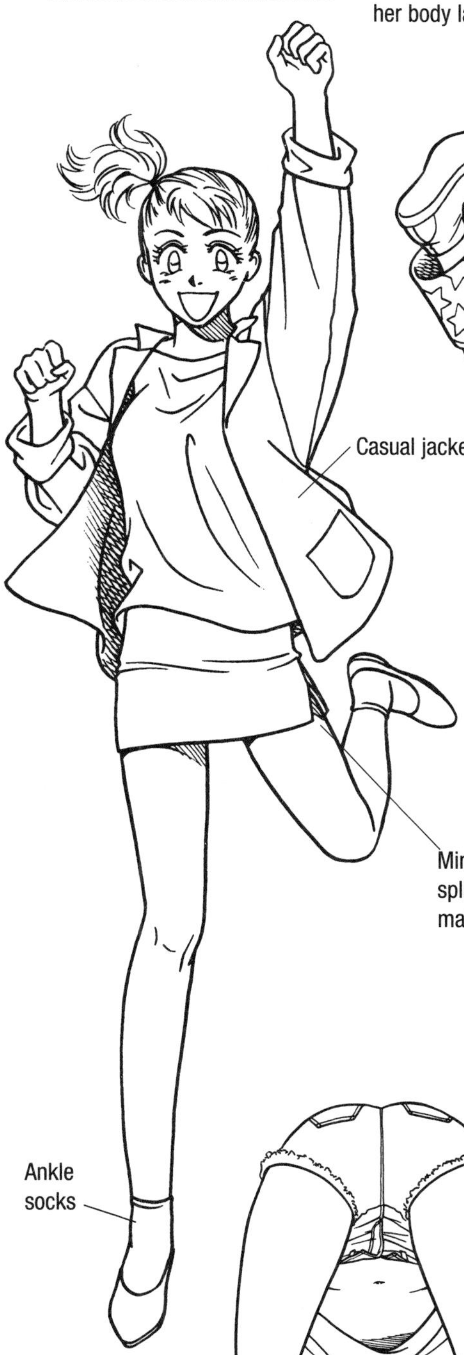

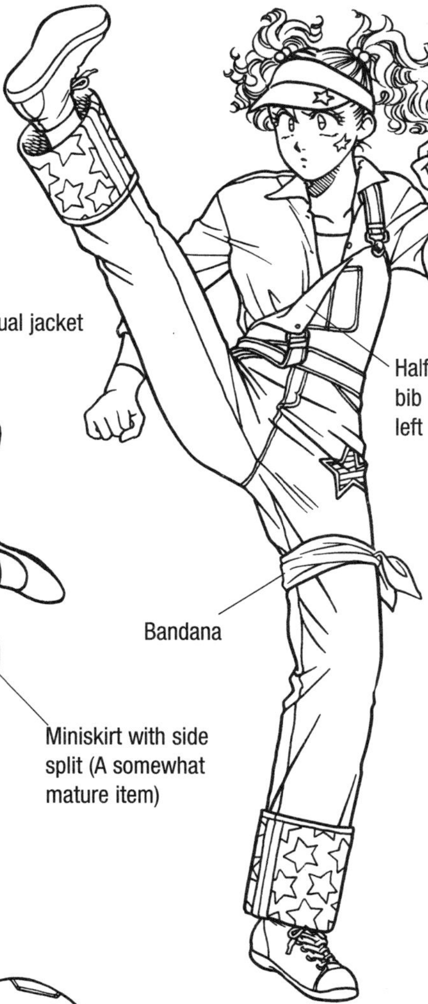

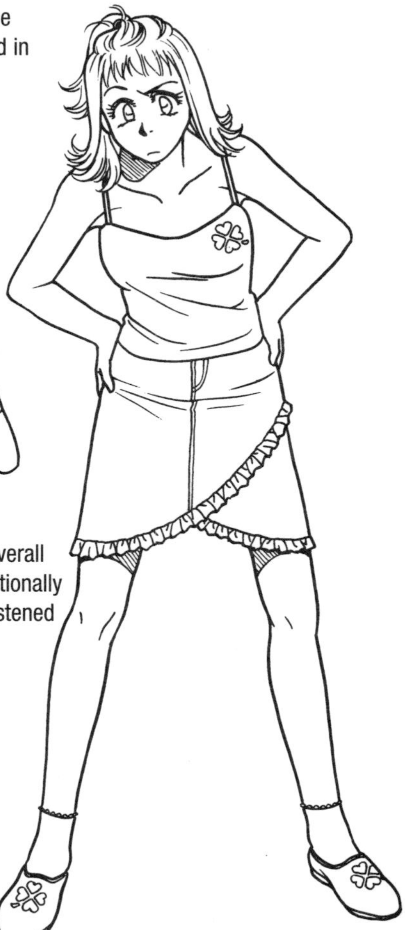

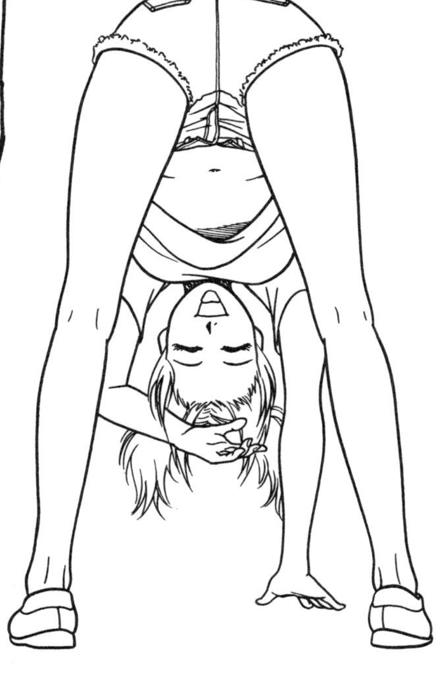

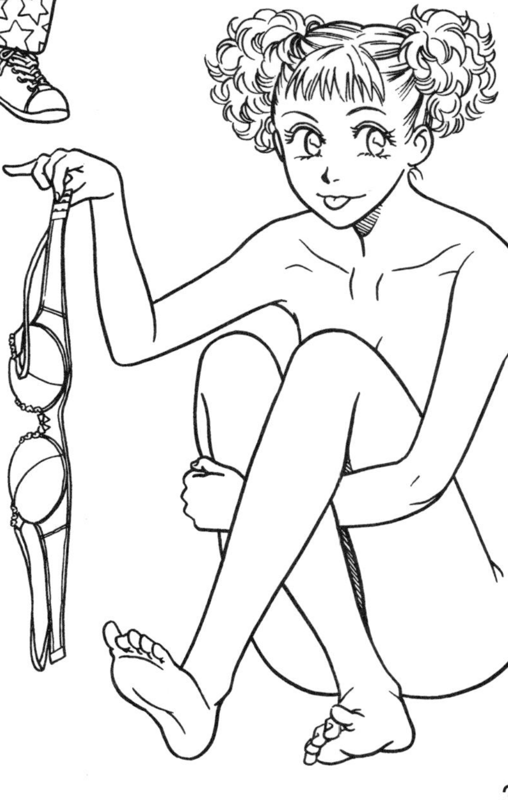

06 The Shy Girl

The Shy Girl is a passive personality. Almond-shaped eyes, a lowered gaze, and long hair are key.

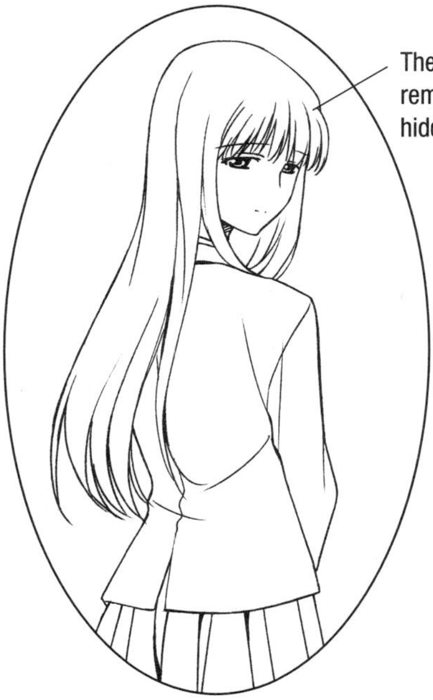

The forehead should remain predominately hidden.

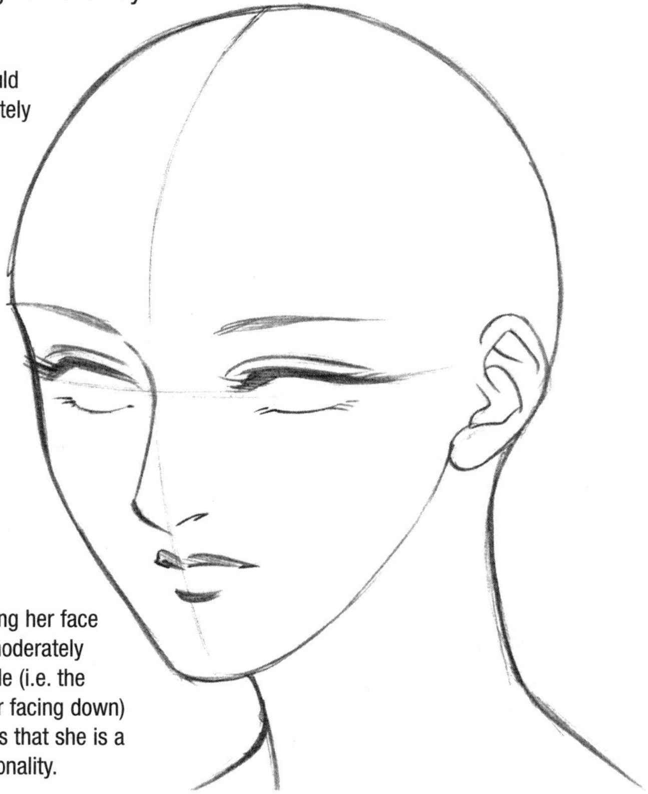

Composing her face from a moderately high angle (i.e. the character facing down) reinforces that she is a shy personality.

Basic Points
- Smallish mouth
- Narrow face
- Longish, thin neck

Not good **Not good**

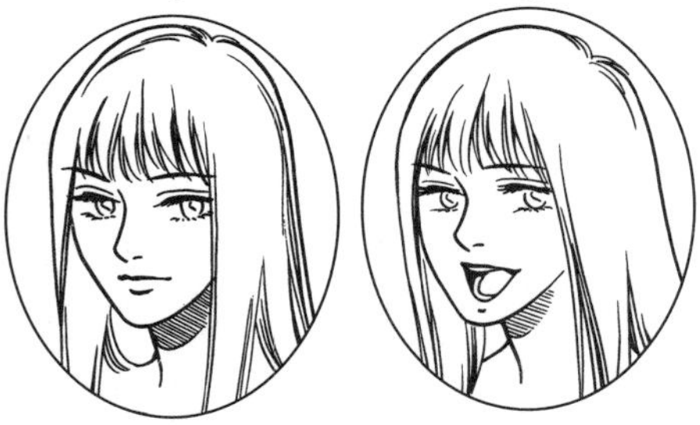

A large mouth will cause the character to lose her quiet image. The same holds true for showing her mouth open.

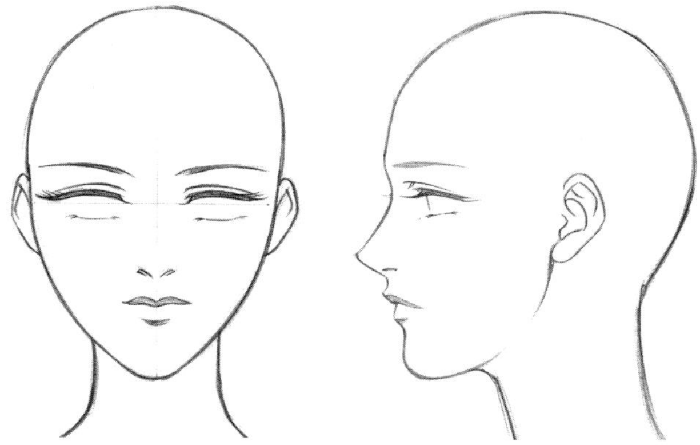

Downcast Eyes Are Half the Size of Open Eyes

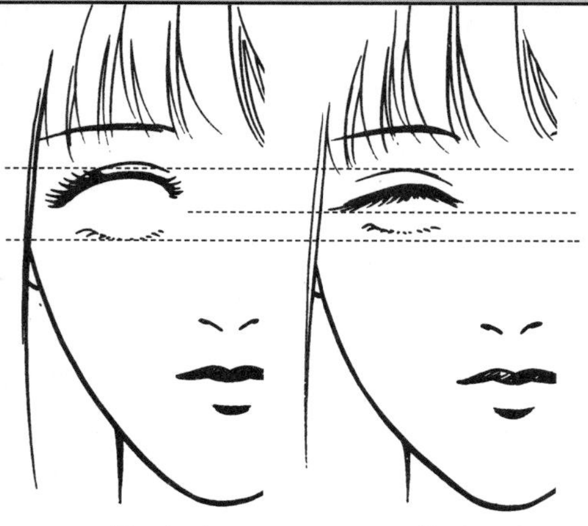

Standard eye Downcast eye

Making a Standard Eye Gaze Downcast

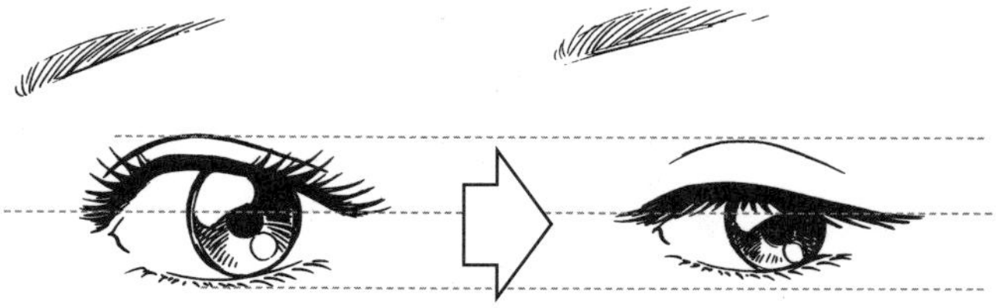

Making an Almond-shaped Eye Downcast

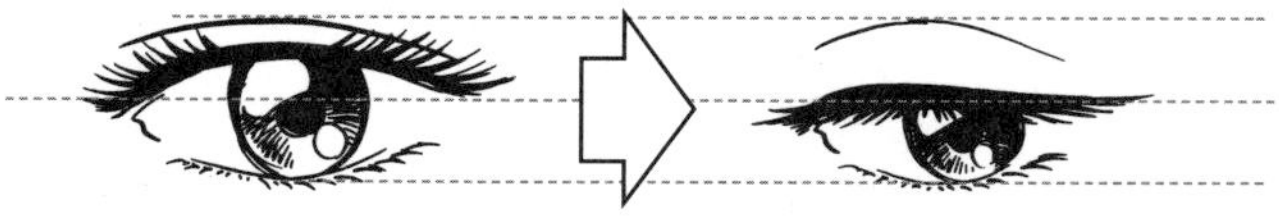

Key Variation Points

Standard Eyes and Downward and Upward Slanting Eyes

Regardless of eye shape, the Shy Girl's eyes are always downcast and with eyelid folds. Her hairstyle should cover her forehead.

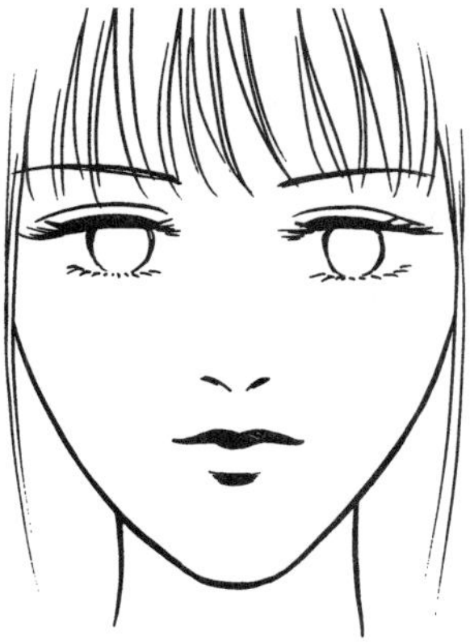

Standard eyes: Standard look

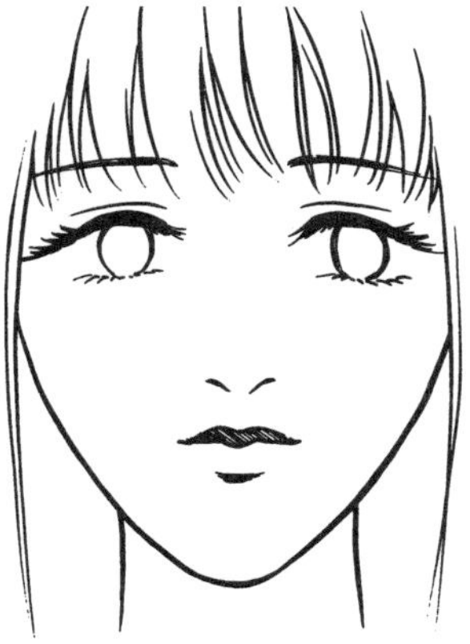

Droopy eyes: Reinforce a gentle atmosphere

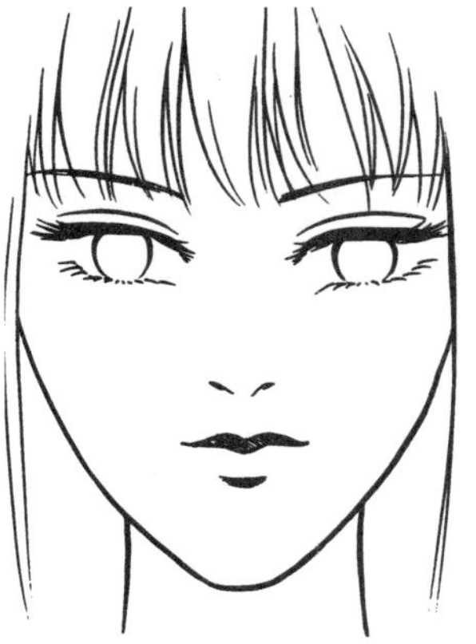

Upward slanting eyes: Offers a subtly stronger impression.

The Critical Eyelid Fold

Not good

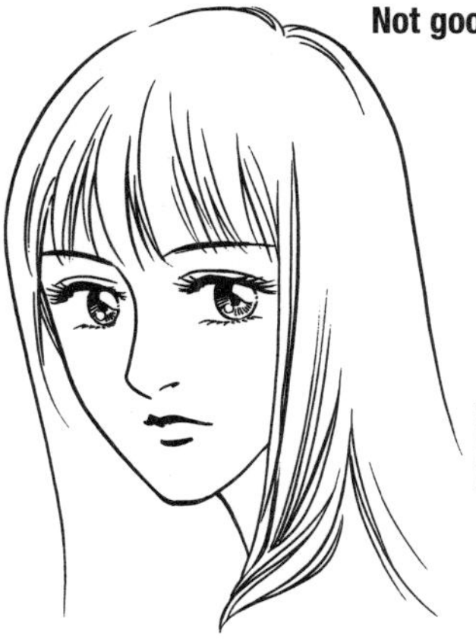

Moderately narrowed eyes

The trick to drawing downcast eyes is the eyelid fold.

Good

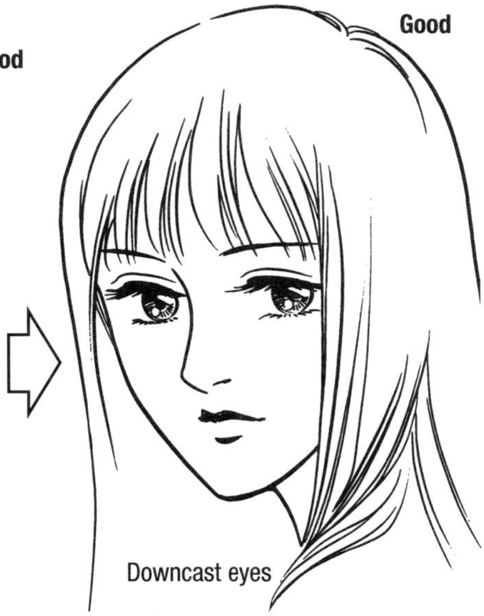

Downcast eyes

Portrayal Tip

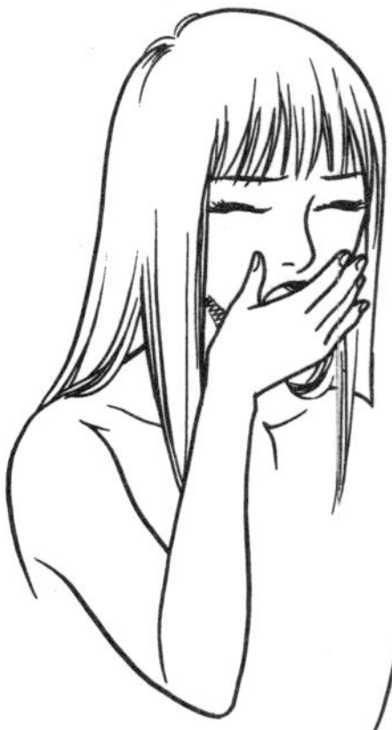

Have the character use her hand to cover her mouth when yawning or laughing.

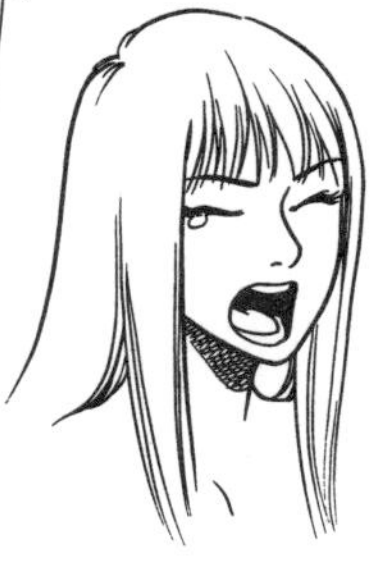

Drawing the mouth open will destroy the character's image.

Standard Shy Girl Look: Straight Hair Down to the Back

Good

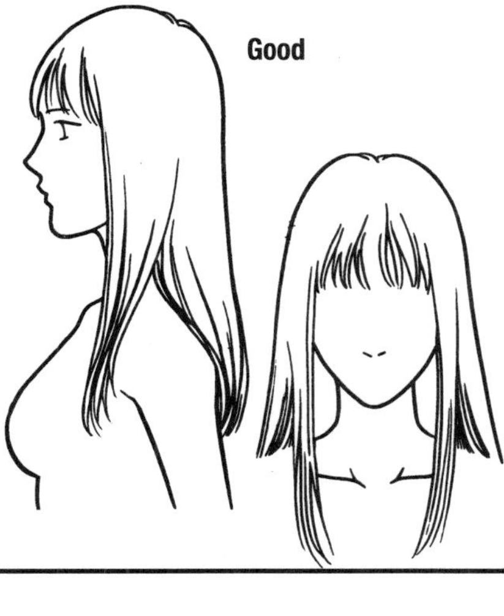

Acceptable

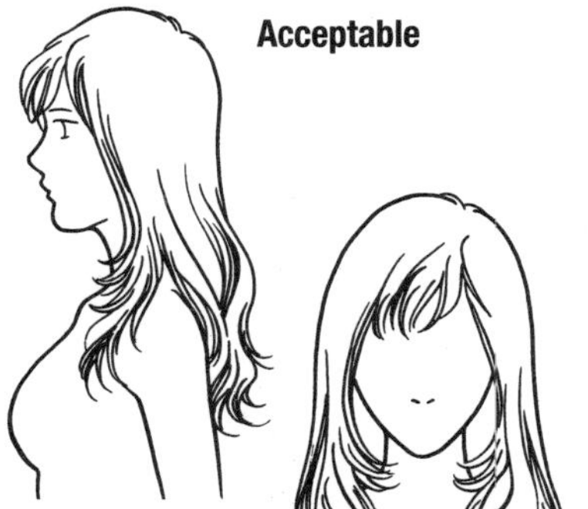

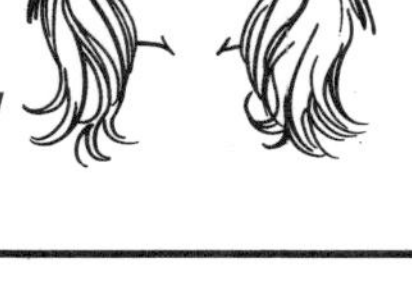

Long, wavy hair may also be worn by the Shy Girl, provided that her forehead is covered.

Not good

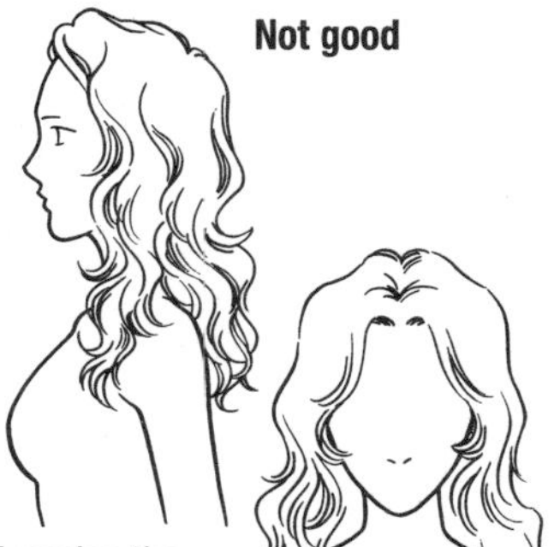

Exposing the forehead will undermine the character's image.

Full Figure

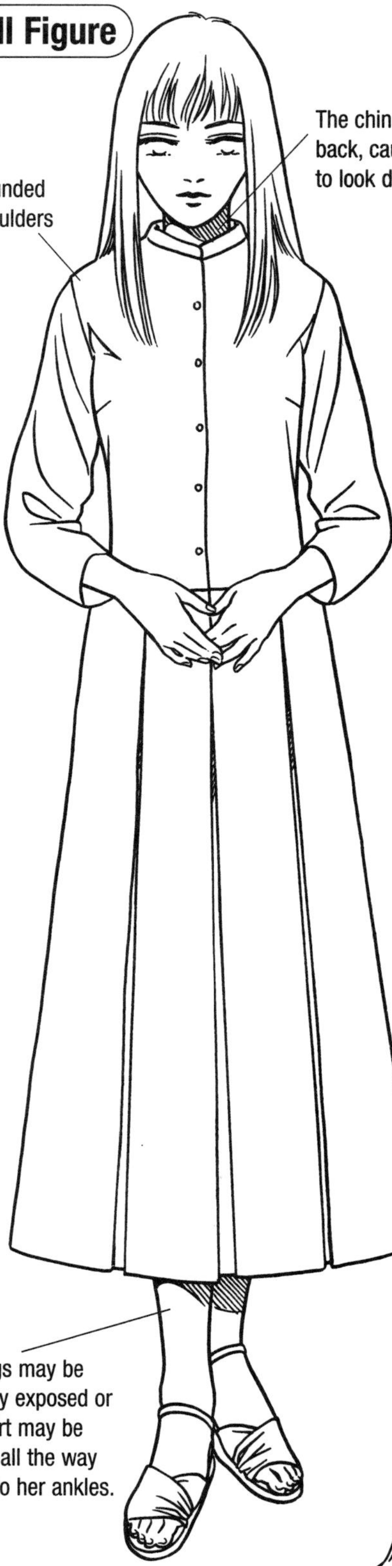

This character does not spend much effort making herself look pretty or drawing attention to her figure. To reinforce her quiet, gentle image, dress her in long skirts that emphasize concealment rather than comfort.

• Slim Build for the Shy Girl

The Shy Girl's neck is longer and slenderer than that of a typical character. Maintain an image of slimness when drawing her torso as well.

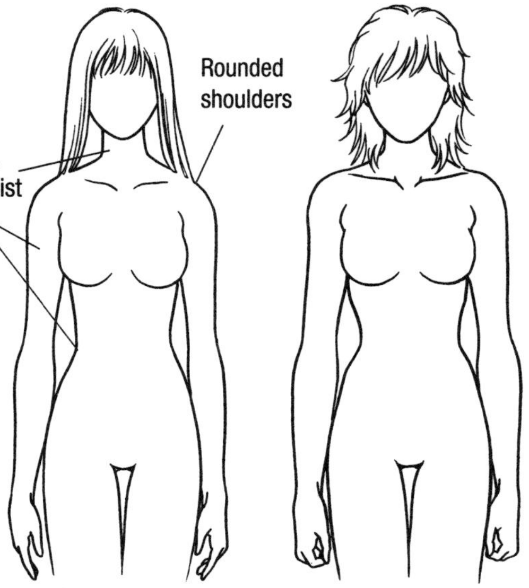

• Pulled-in Chin

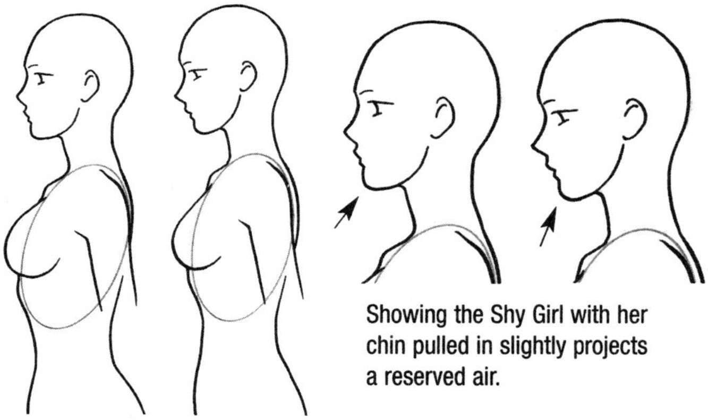

Showing the Shy Girl with her chin pulled in slightly projects a reserved air.

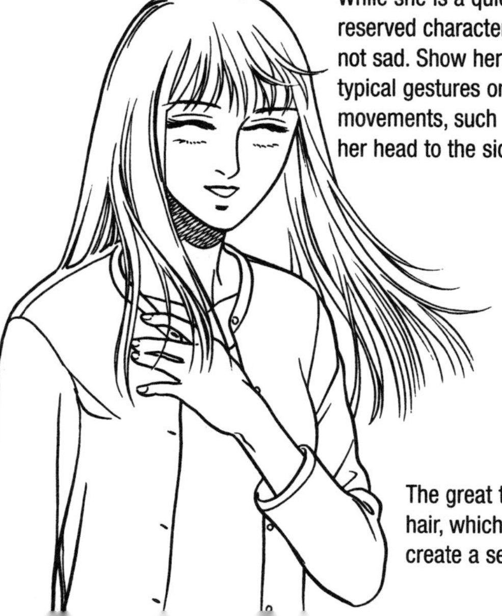

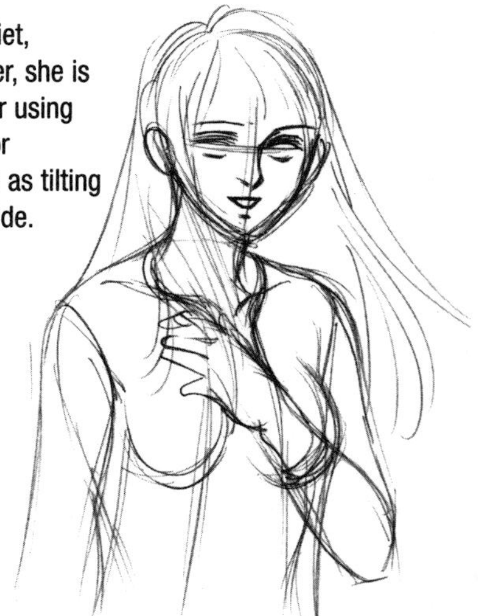

While she is a quiet, reserved character, she is not sad. Show her using typical gestures or movements, such as tilting her head to the side.

The great thing about the Shy Girl is her long hair, which makes it easy for the artist to create a sense of movement.

Standard Fashions

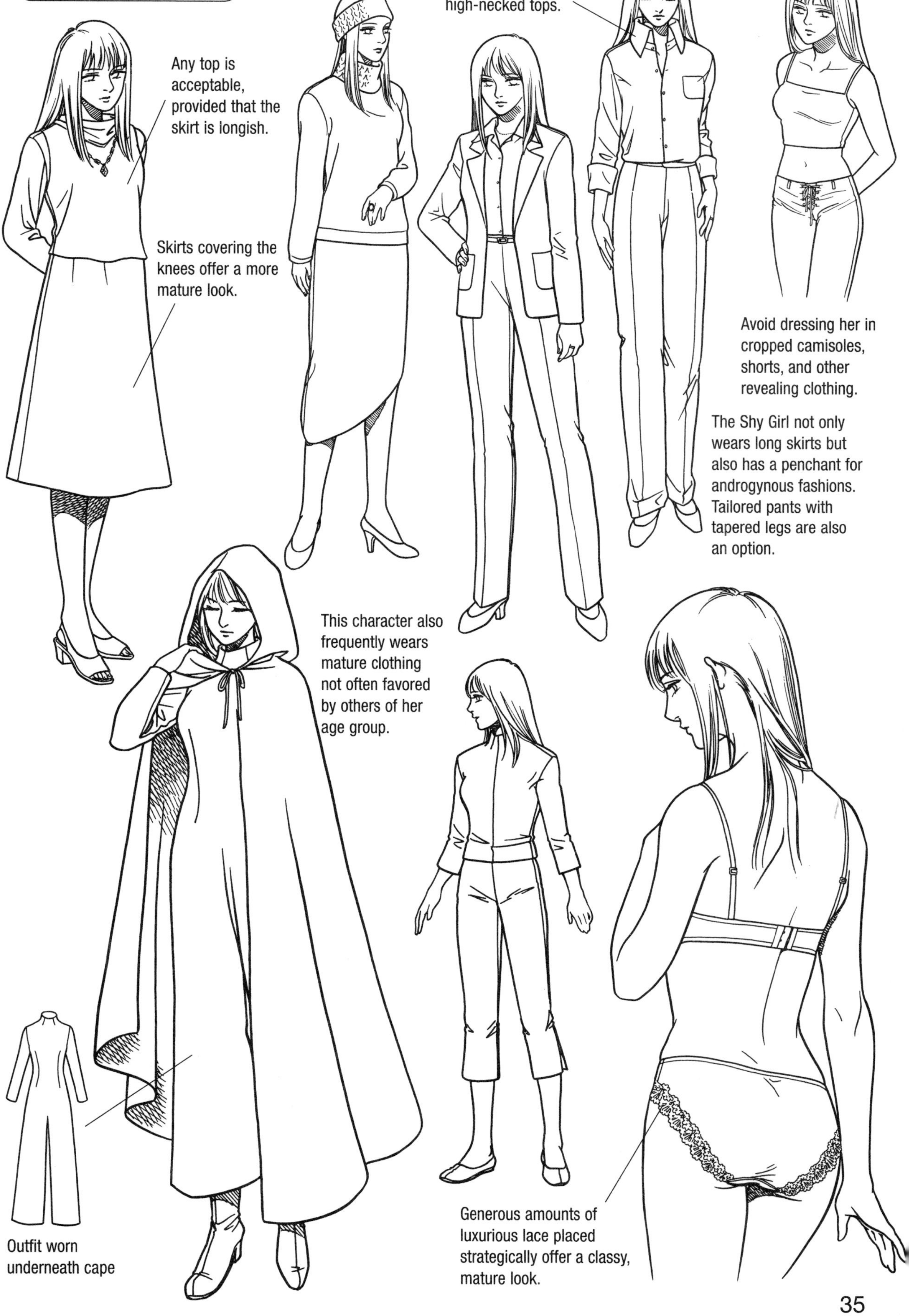

07 The Compassionate Girl

This girl is fundamentally a character of action. Key elements are her droopy eyes, eyelid folds, roof-shaped eyebrows, and a soft smile.

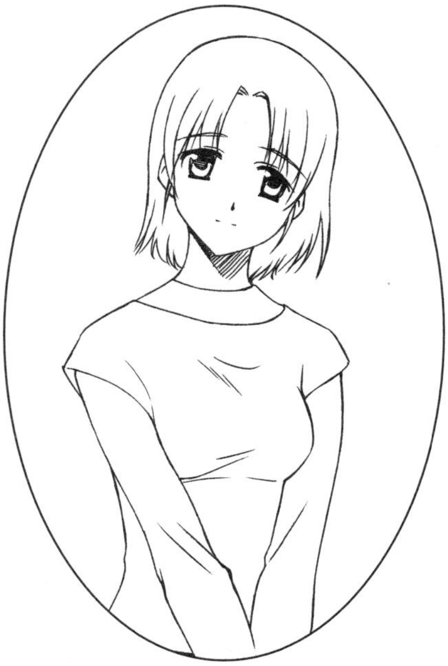

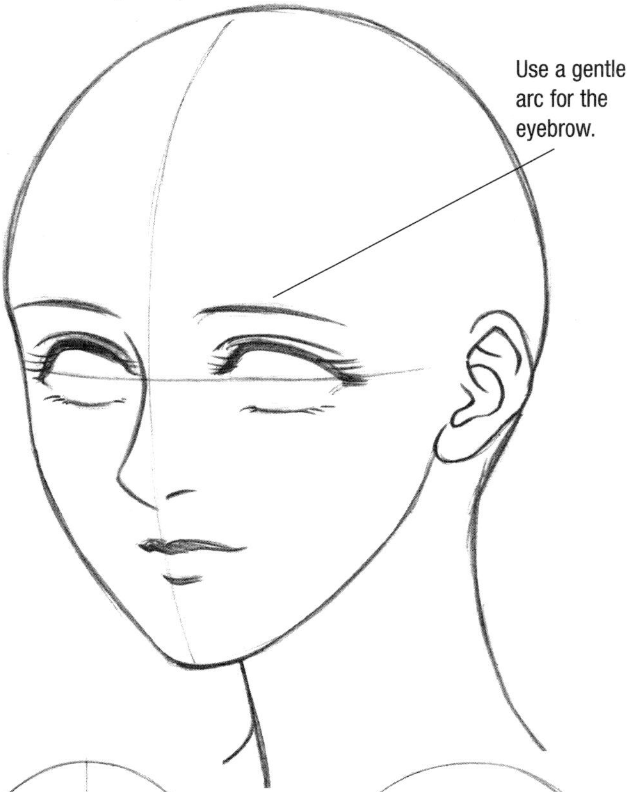

Basic Points

- Direct gaze
- Gentle eyes
- She is like a receptacle at her essence—accepting rather than laying blame.
- She has subconscious confidence, giving her a calm demeanor.

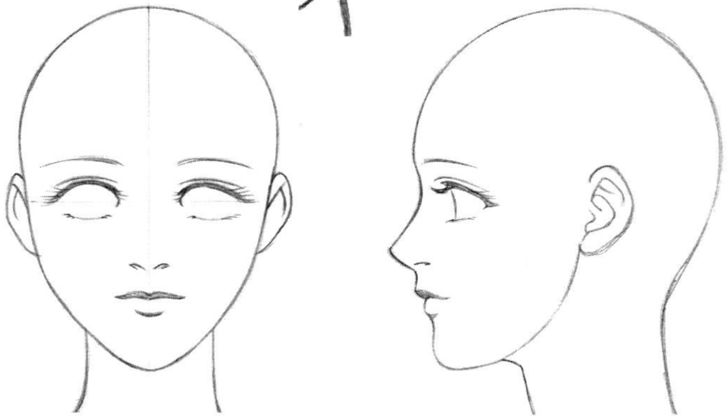

The Gaze Is Vital

Good

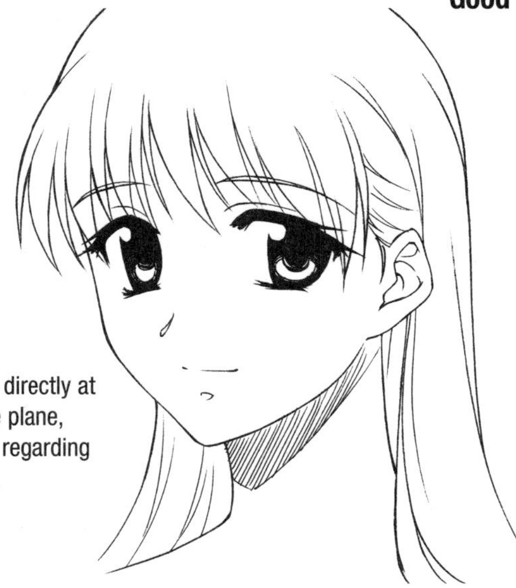

She gazes directly at the picture plane, seemingly regarding the reader.

Acceptable

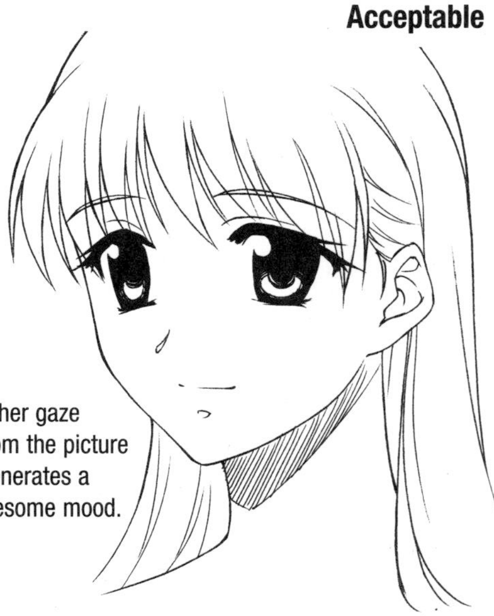

Shifting her gaze away from the picture plane generates a sad, lonesome mood.

Key Variation Points — Modify the character by changing the hair.

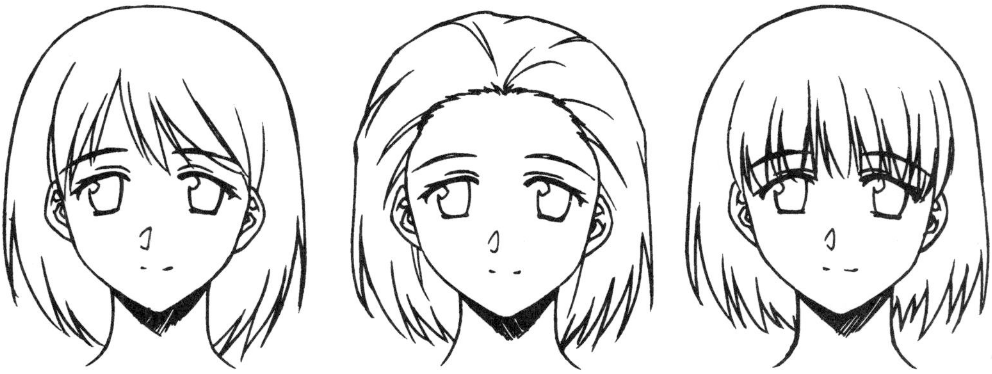

This character is normally shown with droopy eyes and an eyelid fold. Key features are her gently arcing eyebrows sloping softly upward toward the center of the brow.

The Compassionate Girl may have bangs or may have her forehead exposed.

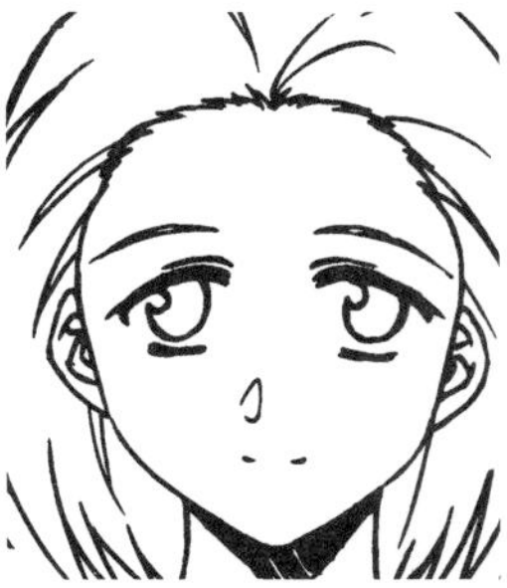

Showing the white underneath her irises may make her seem cold and indifferent.

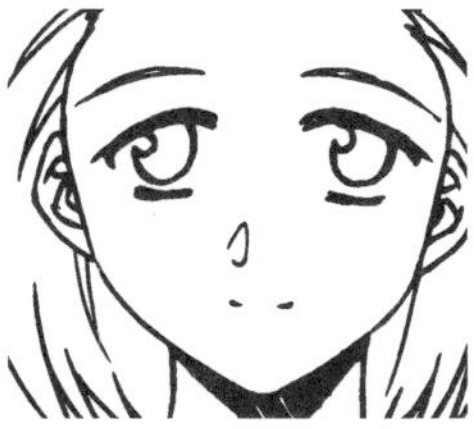

She still retains her gentle atmosphere without the eyelid fold, but she appears more strong-willed.

Using Eyes and Eyebrows to Distinguish between Different Droopy-Eyed Character Types

The Straight-laced Girl | **The Cutie** | **The Vulnerable Girl** | **The Shy Girl** | **The Compassionate Girl**

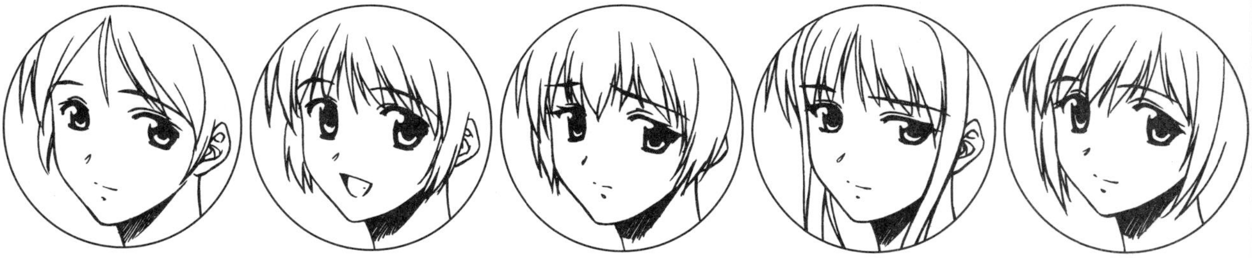

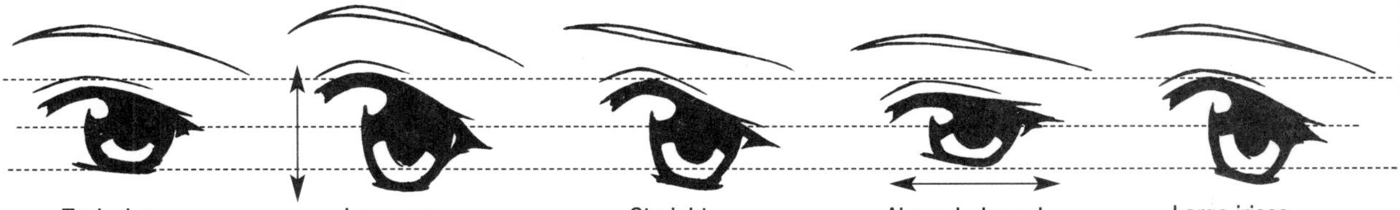

Typical eye | Large eye (More height) | Straight eyebrows | Almond-shaped eyes (Long eyes) | Large irises

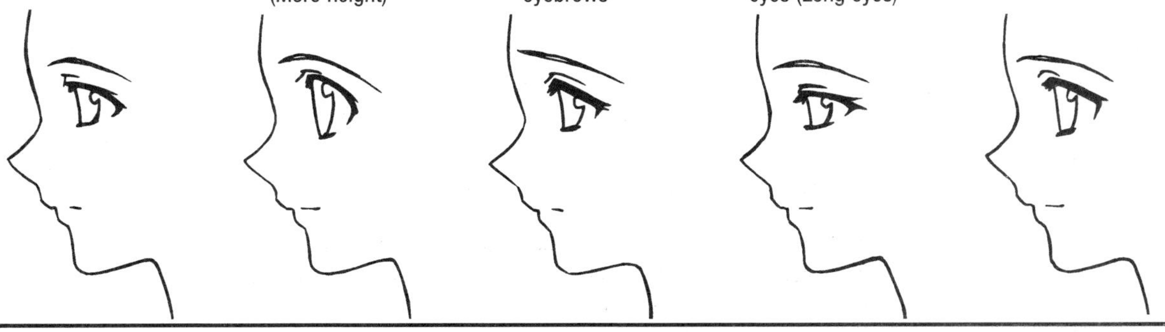

Full Figure

Use round shapes for gentle characters.

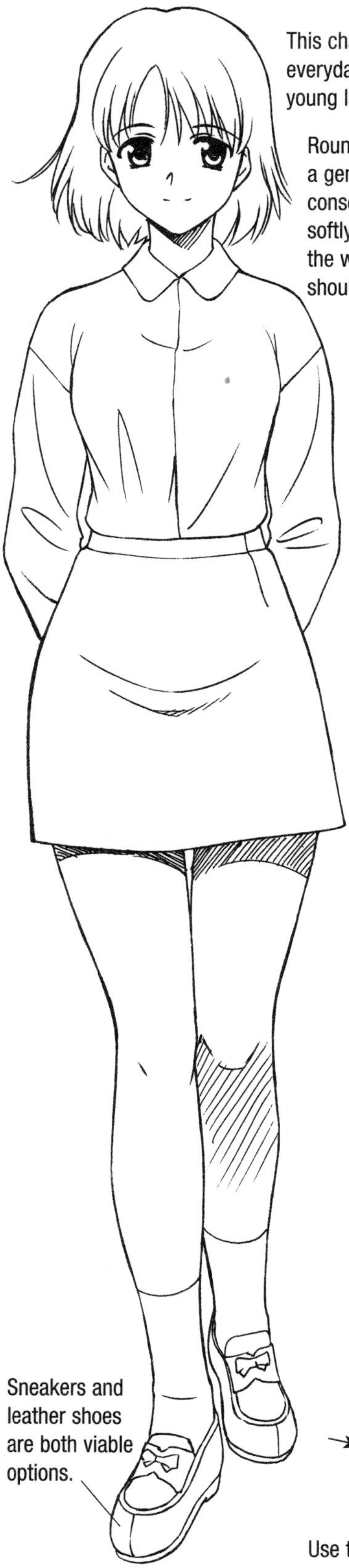

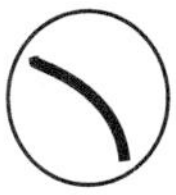

• Contrast between the Compassionate Girl's Build and an Athletic Build

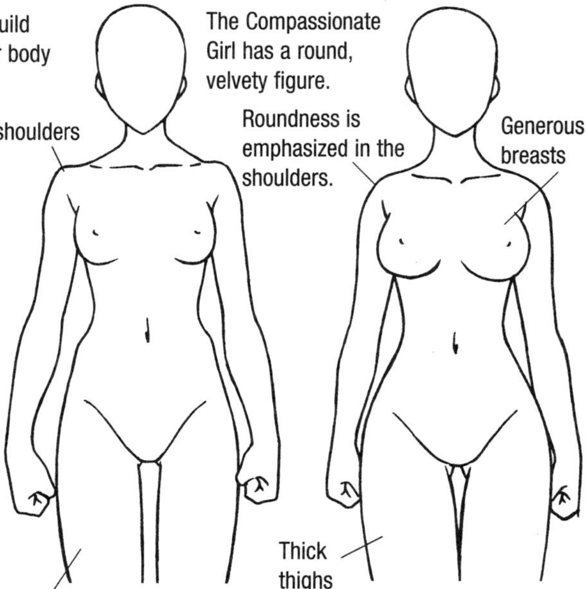

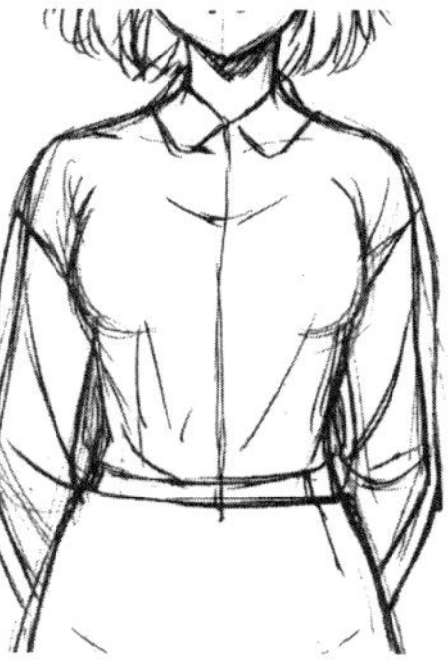

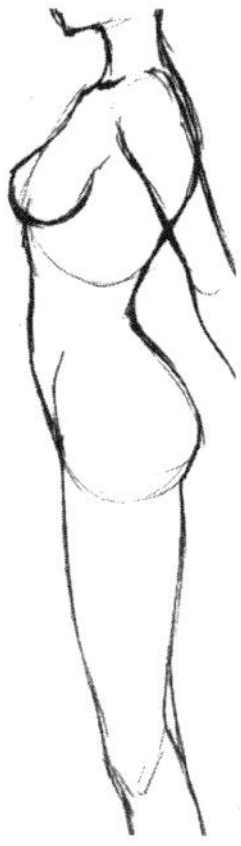

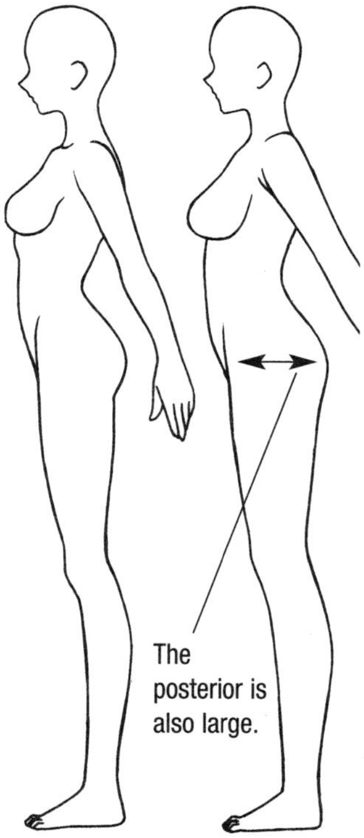

• Fleshy Build

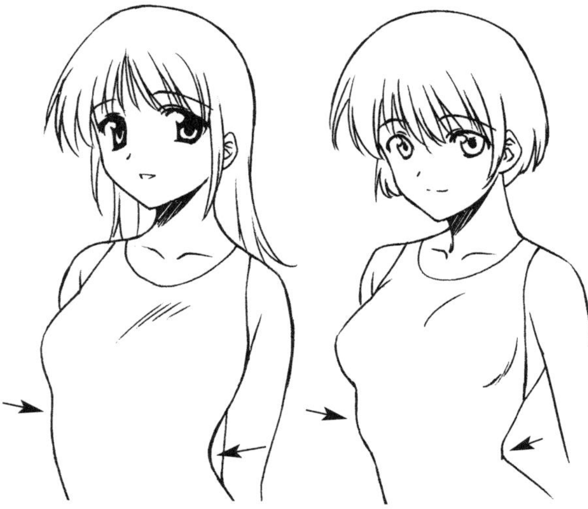

Use this character type when seeking to design a character imbued with feminine tenderness. The chest should be round. Use uncomplicated strokes to define the curves underneath the breasts and the waist.

This is a typical character featuring emphasized curves, which are highlighted by the contours underneath the breasts and in the waist.

Standard Fashions

Polo shirts and sweaters lend themselves to creating a soft, round look.

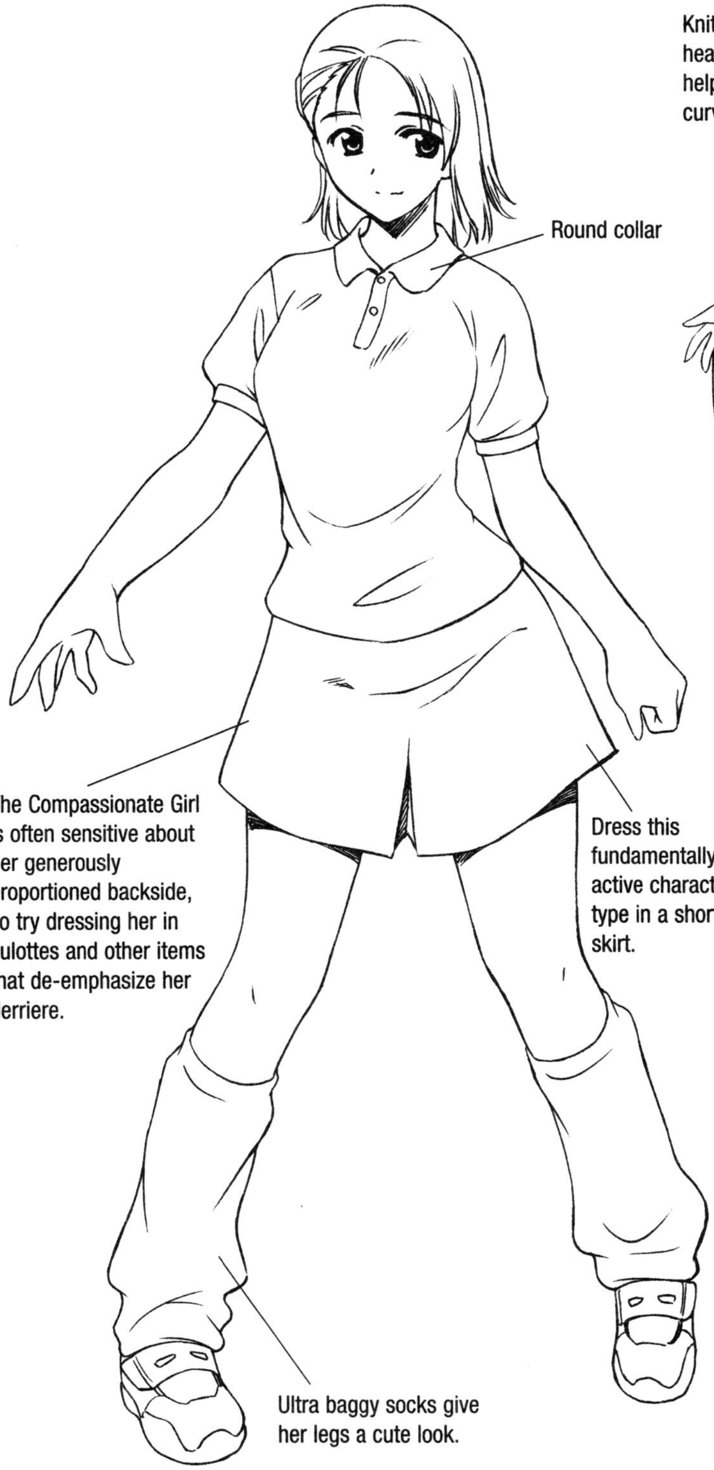

Round collar

The Compassionate Girl is often sensitive about her generously proportioned backside, so try dressing her in culottes and other items that de-emphasize her derriere.

Dress this fundamentally active character type in a short skirt.

Ultra baggy socks give her legs a cute look.

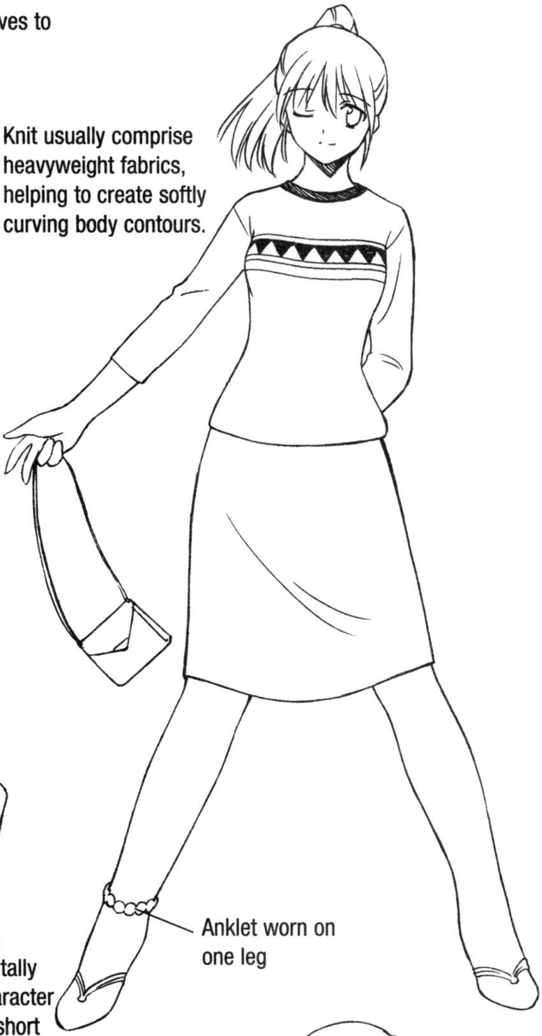

Knit usually comprise heavyweight fabrics, helping to create softly curving body contours.

Anklet worn on one leg

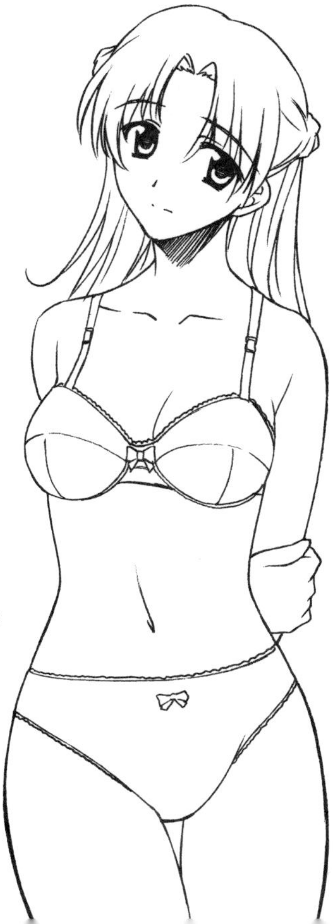

Plain undergarments, like the conventional full-cup bra and large, white briefs, project a conservative, gentle impression.

08 The Bully

The Bully is a dynamic character. Her trademark features are narrow, upward slanting eyes and a large, curling mouth.

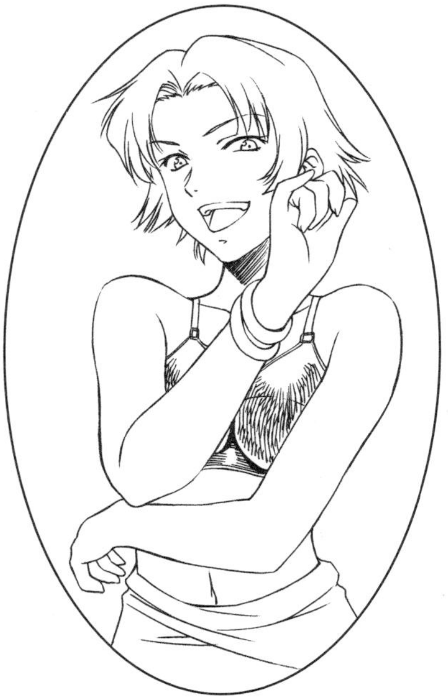

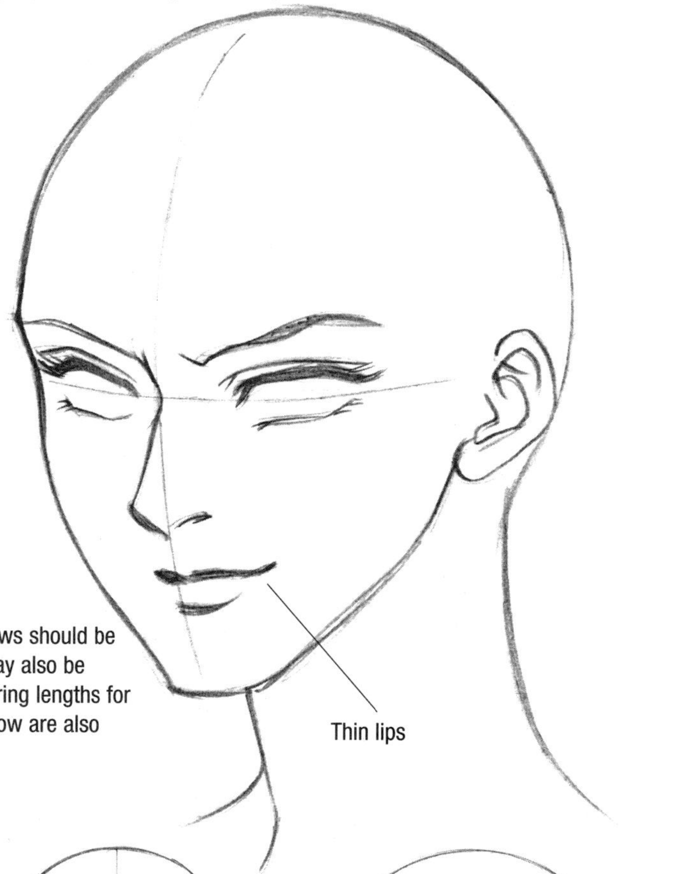

The eyebrows should be thin and may also be short. Differing lengths for each eyebrow are also acceptable.

Basic Points

- Draw asymmetrical eyes, mouth, and eyebrows.
- Give her a pointed, angular look in her hair, clothing, and figure.
- Exposing her forehead creates an outgoing look, while concealing her forehead makes her appear sinister.
- Give characters with aggressive personalities angular jaws and shoulders.

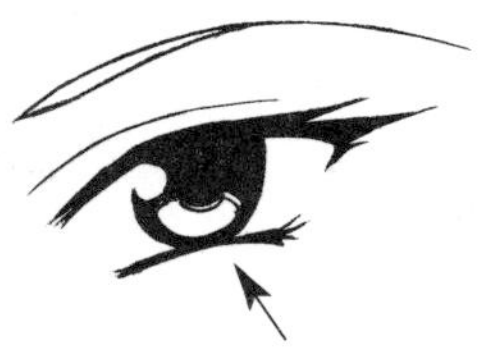

An upward arcing lower lid is the sign of a menacing personality.

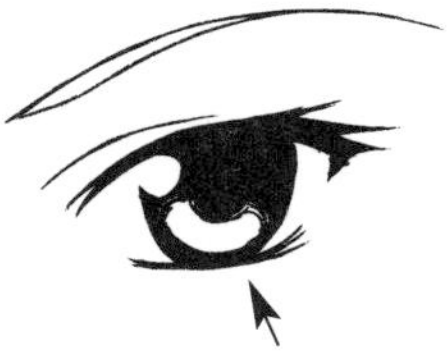

Ref. Fig.: Note that the lower lid curves downward on the typical eye.

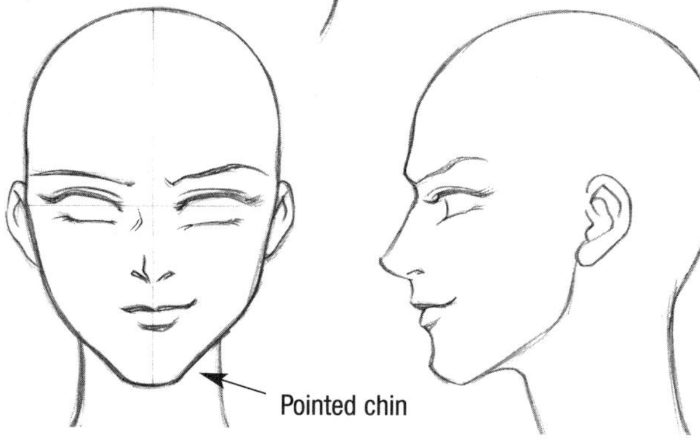

Asymmetrical Features Indicate a Mean Disposition.

Standard lips are symmetrical.

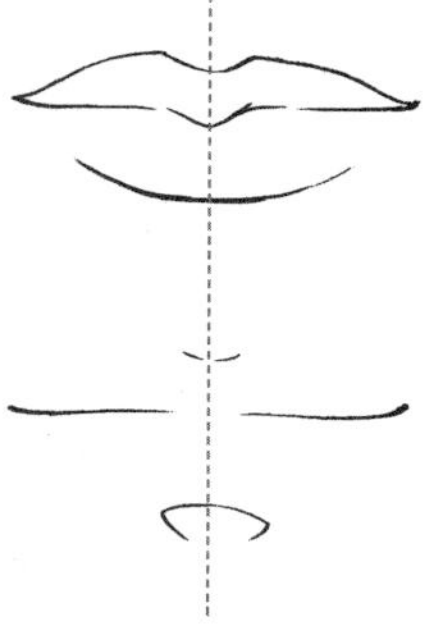

Curling lips are asymmetrical.

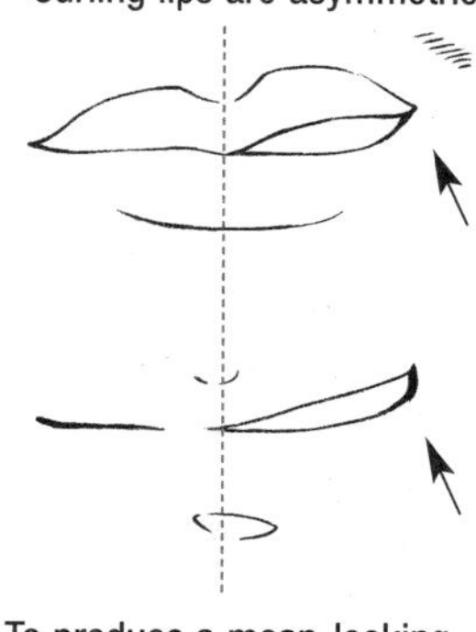

To produce a mean-looking mouth, show one of the corners curling up.

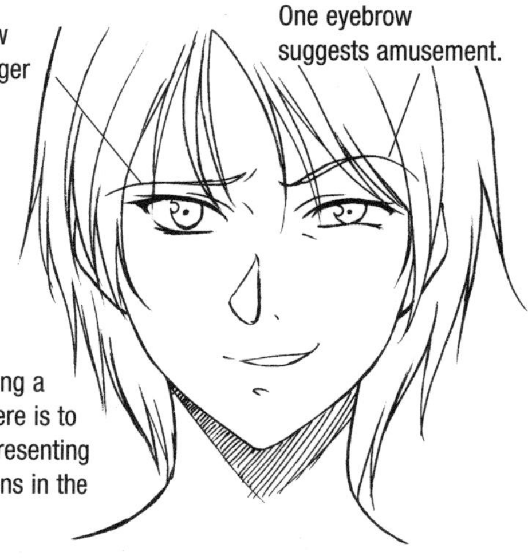

The trick to creating a "mean" atmosphere is to mix elements representing conflicting emotions in the facial features.

Key Variation Points Modify the character by changing the eyes' and irises' sizes.

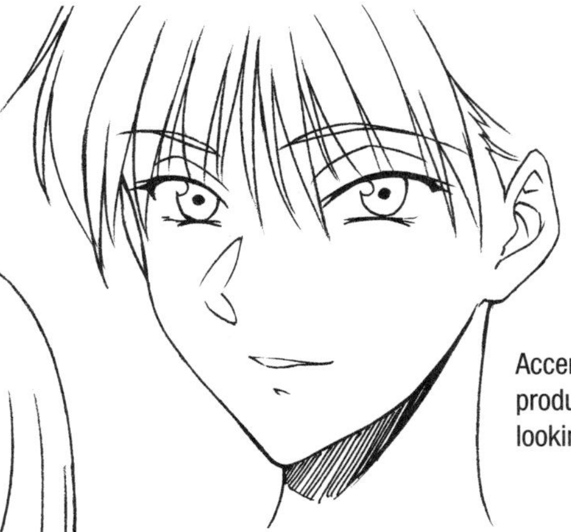

Accentuating the eyelid fold produces an eccentric-looking character.

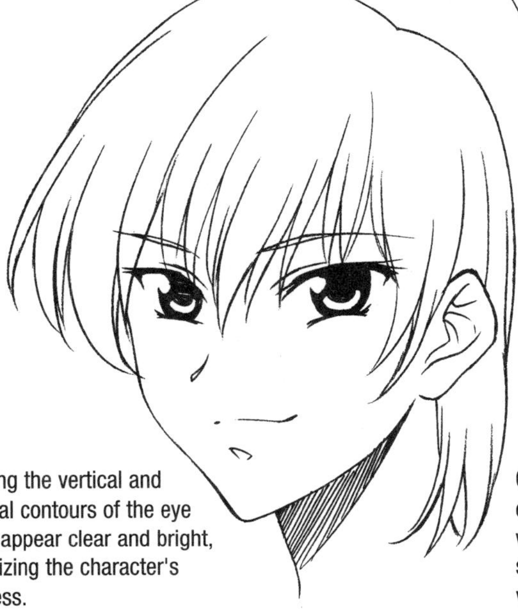

Darkening the vertical and horizontal contours of the eye make it appear clear and bright, emphasizing the character's willfulness.

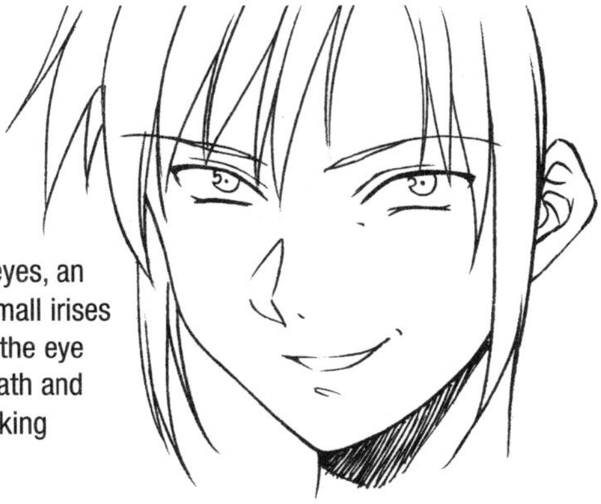

Give her narrow eyes, an eyelid fold, and small irises with the white of the eye showing underneath and voilá! A mean-looking character results.

Use of the Eyelid's Curve

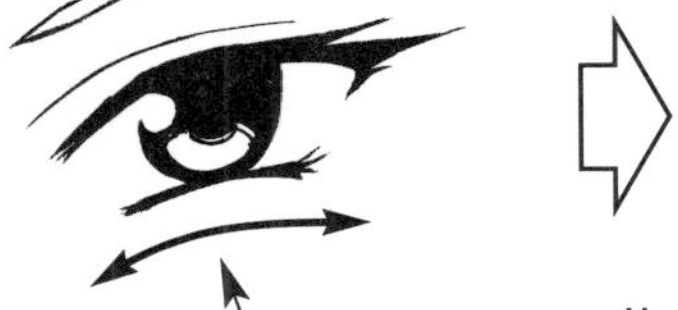

The lower eyelid takes an upward arcing curve.

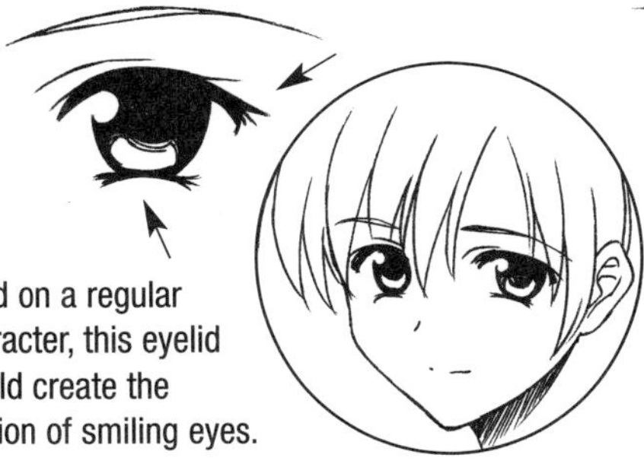

Used on a regular character, this eyelid would create the illusion of smiling eyes.

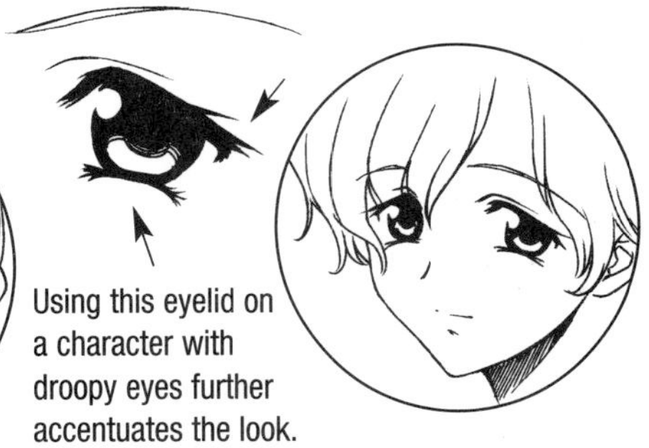

Using this eyelid on a character with droopy eyes further accentuates the look.

Changing the Head Angle to Produce Dramatization Effects

Showing her looking away from rather than directly at other characters when she is speaking helps create the mood that she is verbally assaulting or picking on that character.

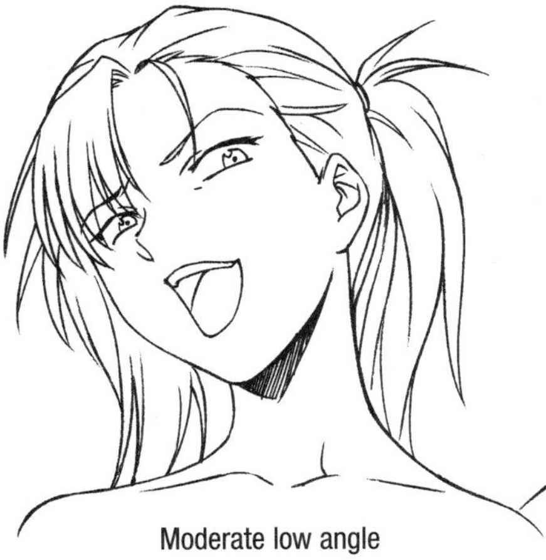

Moderate low angle

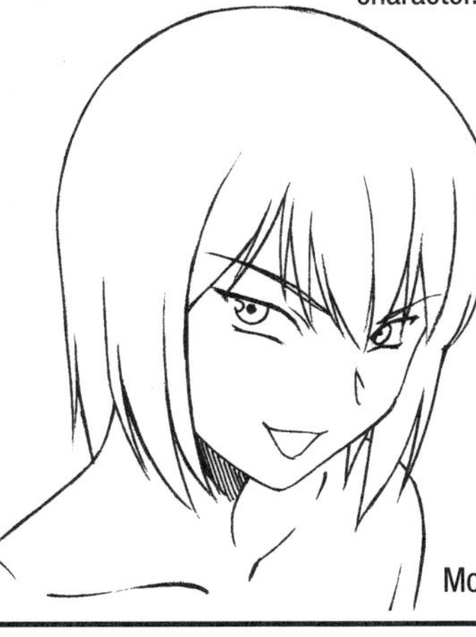

Moderate high angle

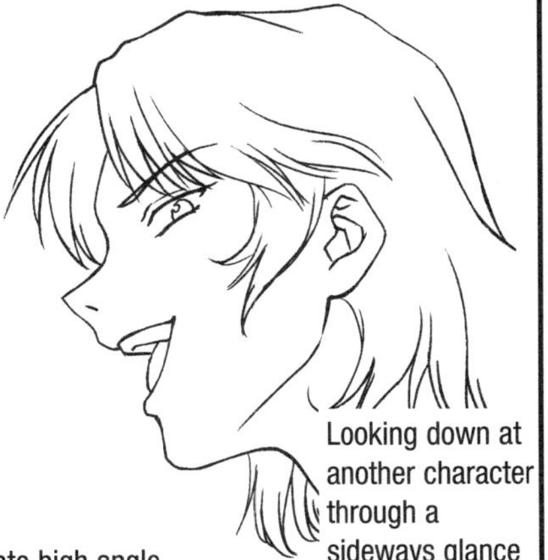

Looking down at another character through a sideways glance

Full Figure

Since mean or aggressive personalities are usually extroverted, draw the Bully's hair flipping outward.

Narrowness and angularity are visually associated with a cold-hearted atmosphere, so use angles in her collar and shoulders.

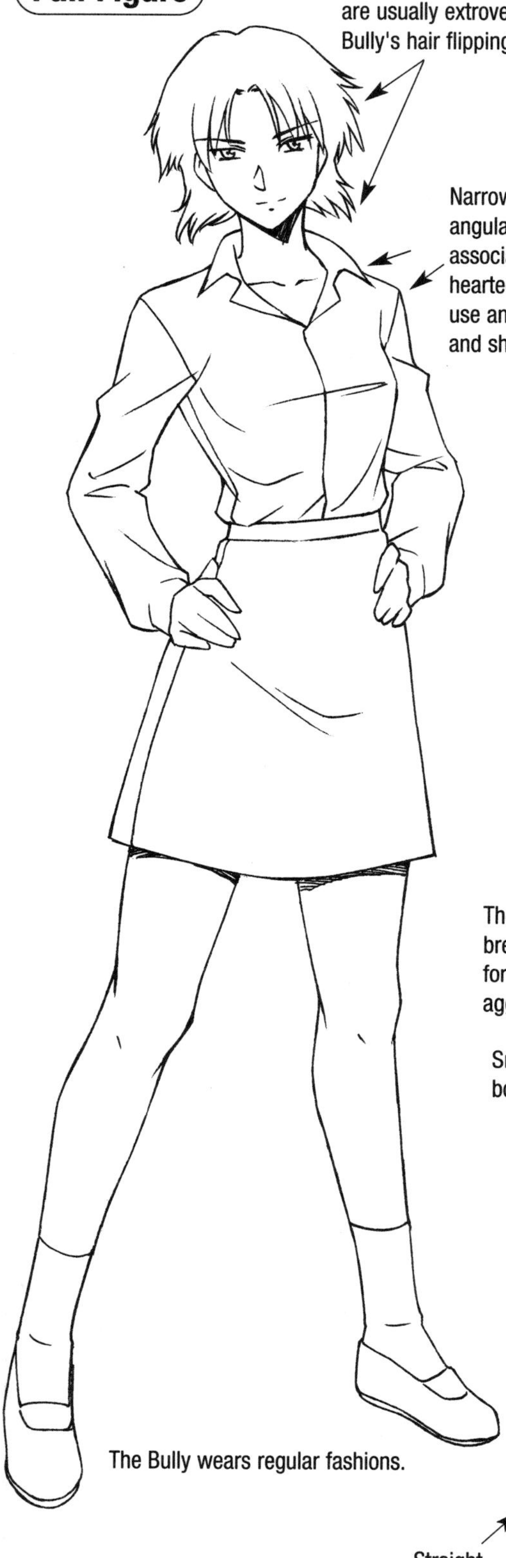

The Bully wears regular fashions.

• Boniness Is the Key

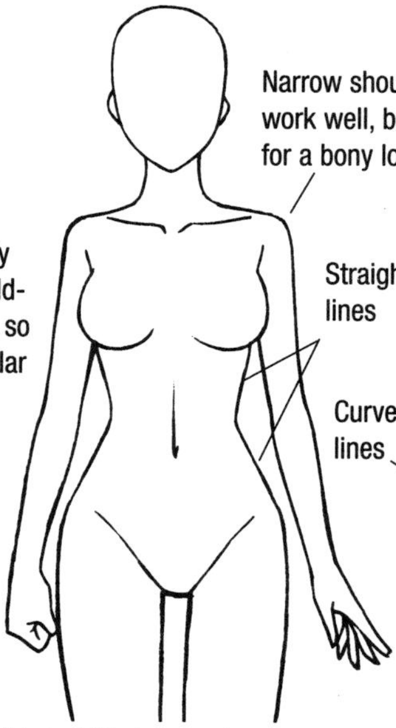

Narrow shoulders work well, but strive for a bony look.

Straight lines

Curved lines

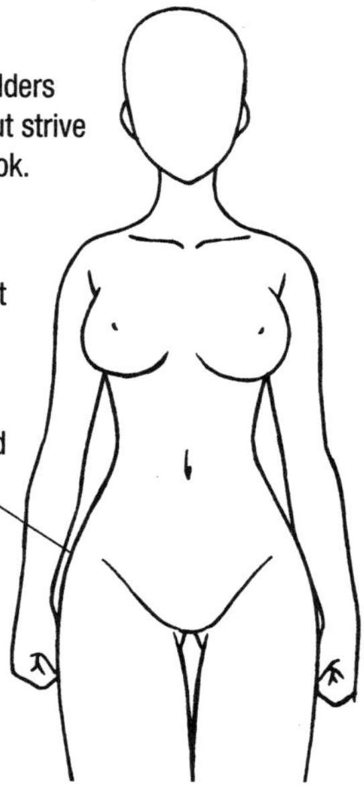

This build helps create a lean, cold-hearted image. Squared shoulders, flattish pelvis, and skinny arms and legs constitute key points.

This image shows a voluptuous, feminine build. The rounded shoulder, soft breasts, large, round hips, and generous thighs are distinguishing elements.

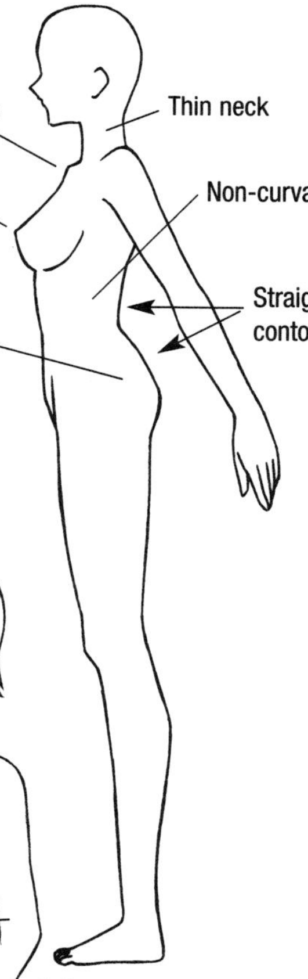

Collarbone

Thin neck

The ends of the breasts are thrust forward in an aggressive manner.

Non-curvaceous waist

Straight contours

Small, childlike or boyish posterior

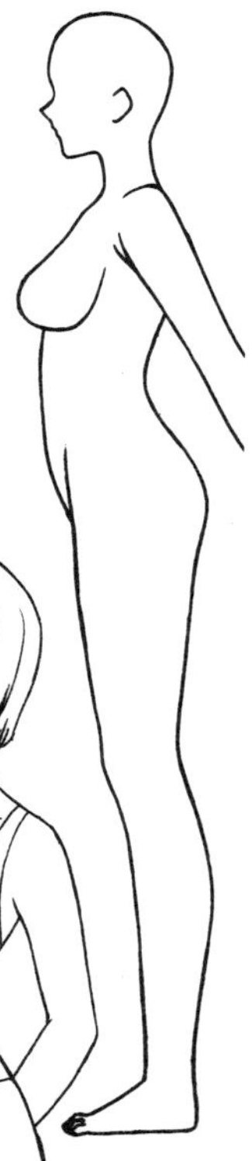

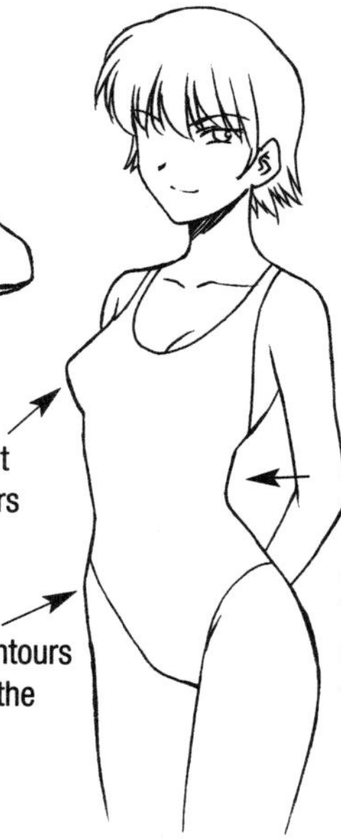

Straight contours

The pelvic bone contours become evident in the silhouette.

A flat, straight figure—the opposite of the typically soft feminine form

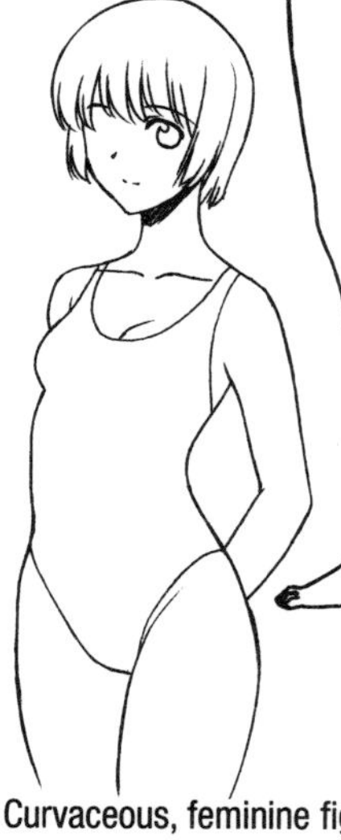

Curvaceous, feminine figure

Standard Fashions

Make an effort to dress her in clothing that will project a lean, mean, angular image. (Visualize a male character.)

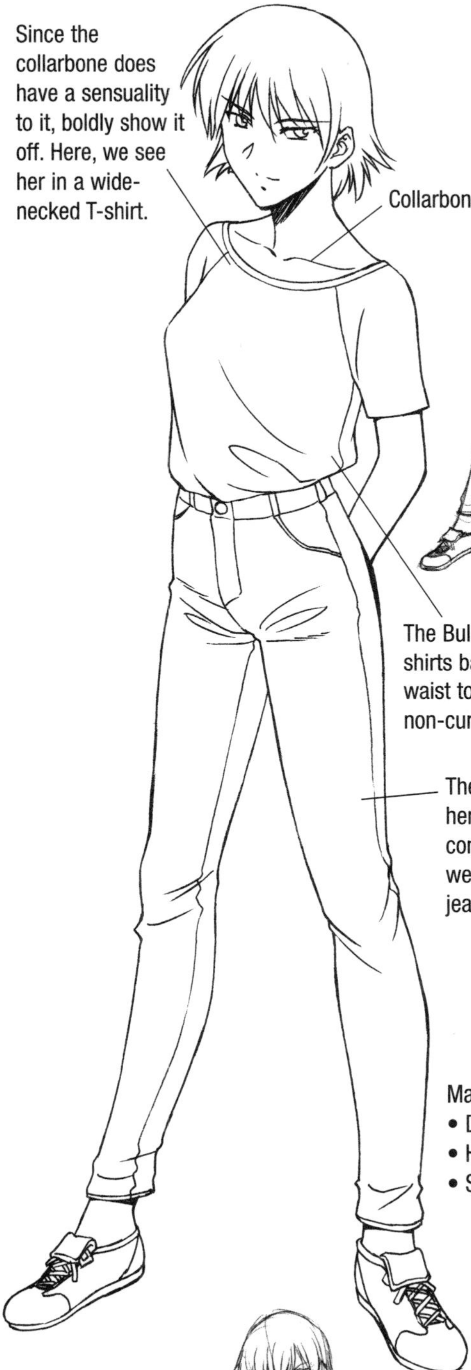

Since the collarbone does have a sensuality to it, boldly show it off. Here, we see her in a wide-necked T-shirt.

Collarbone

The Bully wears her shirts baggy at the waist to conceal her non-curvaceous waist.

The Bully is proud of her thin legs and consequently prefers wearing slim-cut jeans and the like.

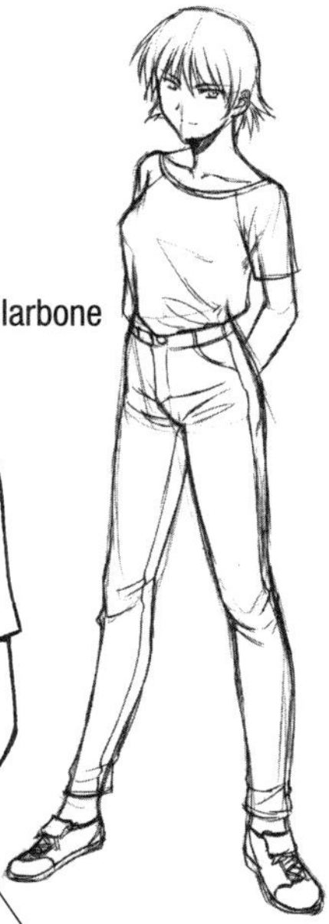

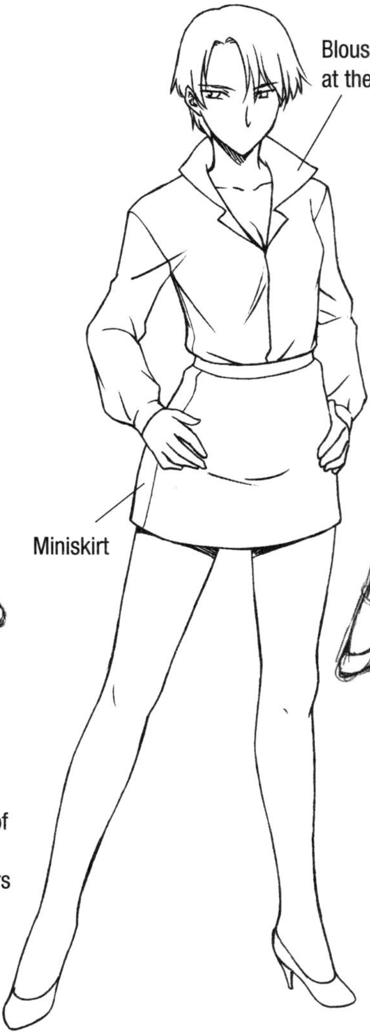

Blouse open at the neck

Miniskirt

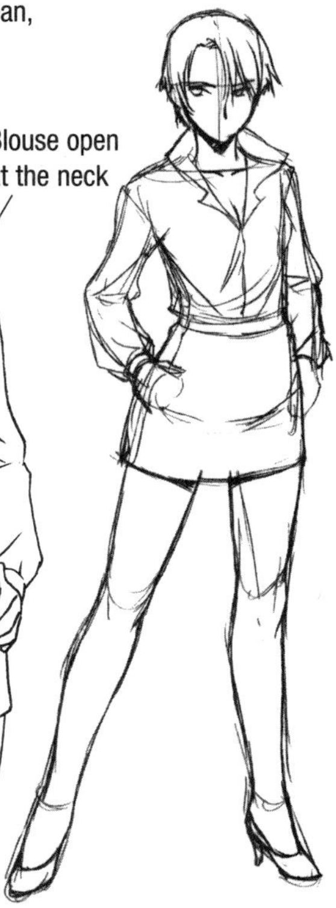

Main points in costume selection:

- Drawing attention to the chest
- Hiding the waist
- Showing confidence in the legs

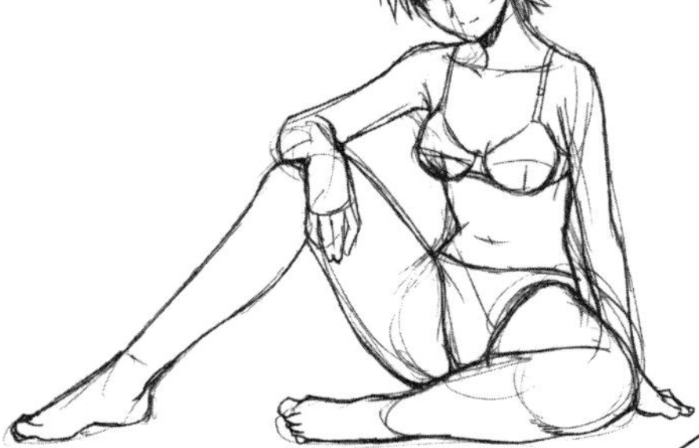

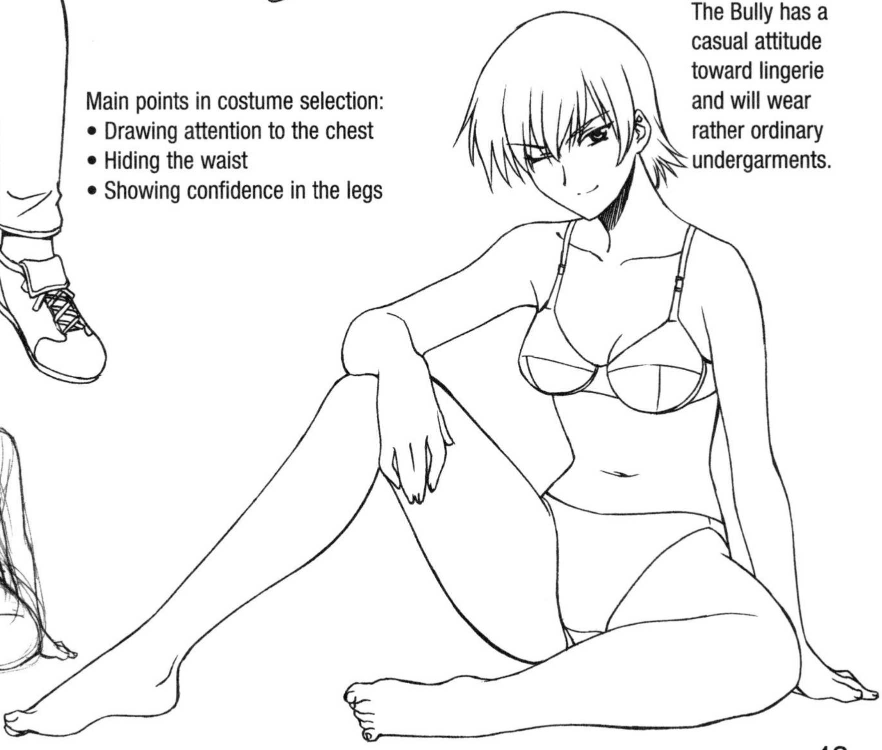

The Bully has a casual attitude toward lingerie and will wear rather ordinary undergarments.

09 The Older Girl

The foundation of this character lies in her mature face. Be sure to give her an oval face, defined nose bridge, and smallish eyes.

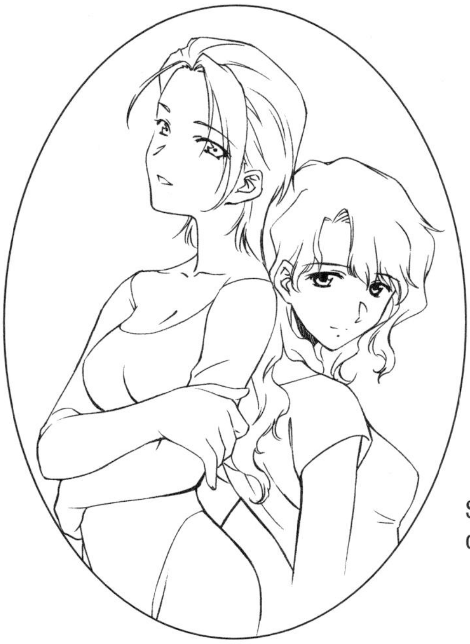

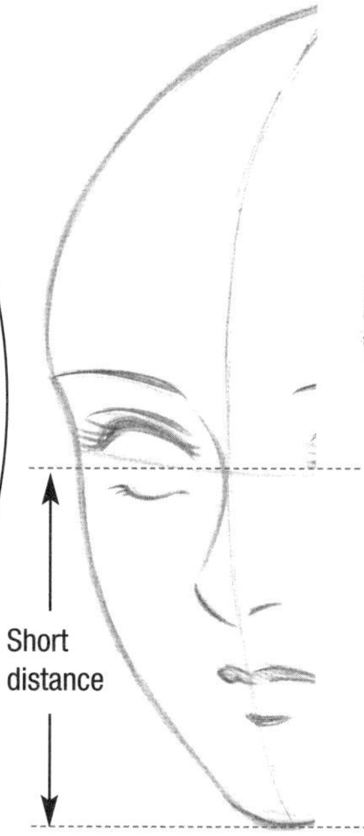

Ref. Fig. Childlike face
Note the large eyes.

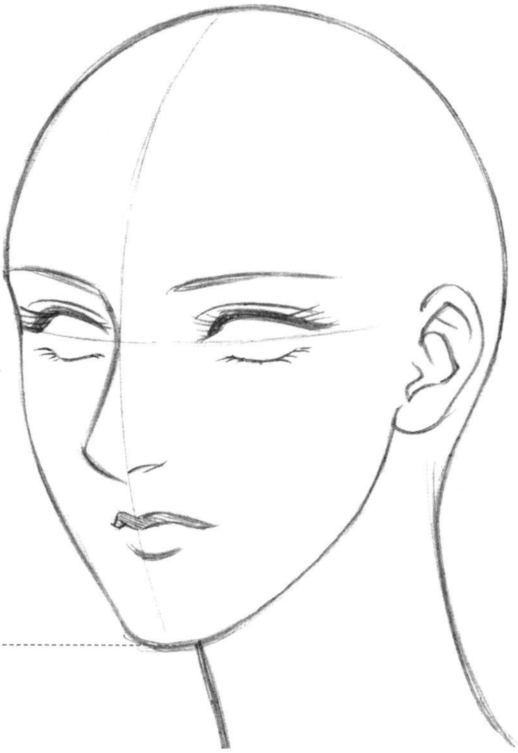

Basic Points

- There are two types of "the Older Girl": dynamic and calm.
- Dynamic type: Athletic
  —focus on spunky and active qualities when drawing.
- Calm type: Artsy
  —focus on creating a gentle, graceful atmosphere.

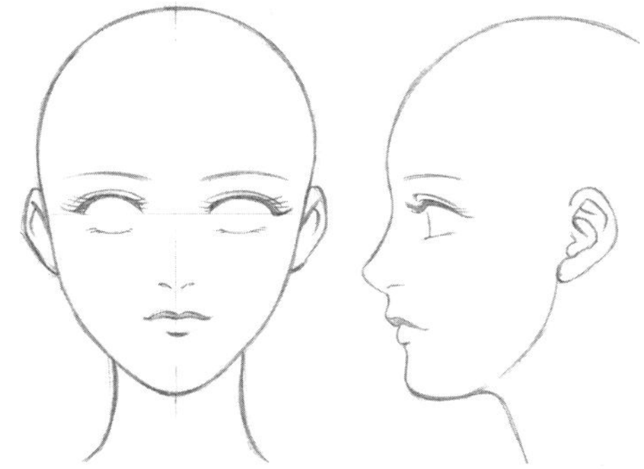

The neck is shorter on a young girl character.

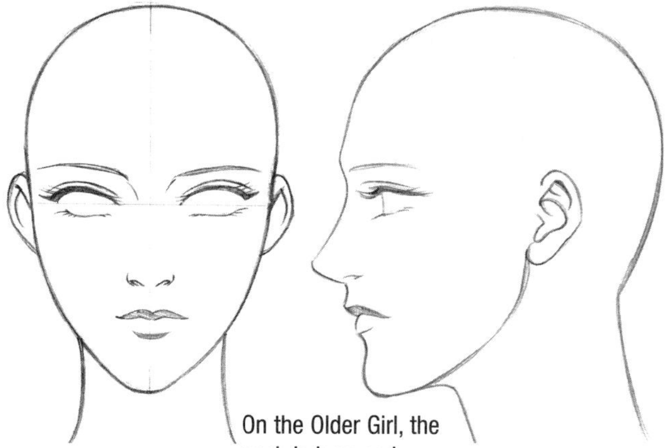

On the Older Girl, the neck is long and somewhat thicker.

Athletic vs. Artsy Older Girl

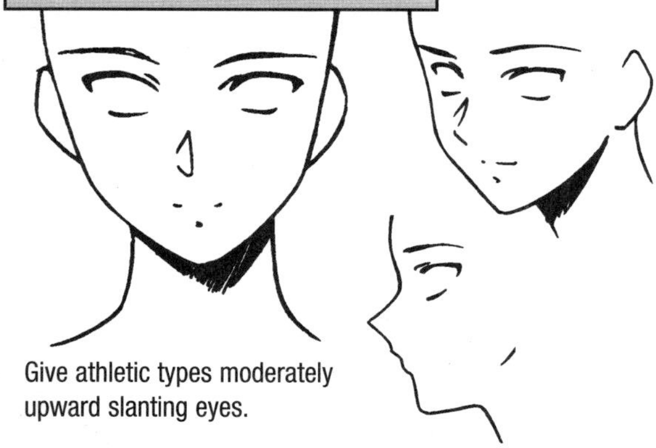

Give athletic types moderately upward slanting eyes.

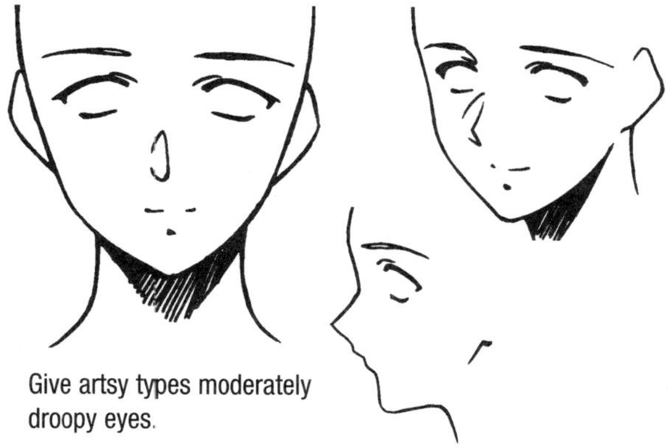

Give artsy types moderately droopy eyes.

Key Variation Points Transforming a Young Girl into a Woman

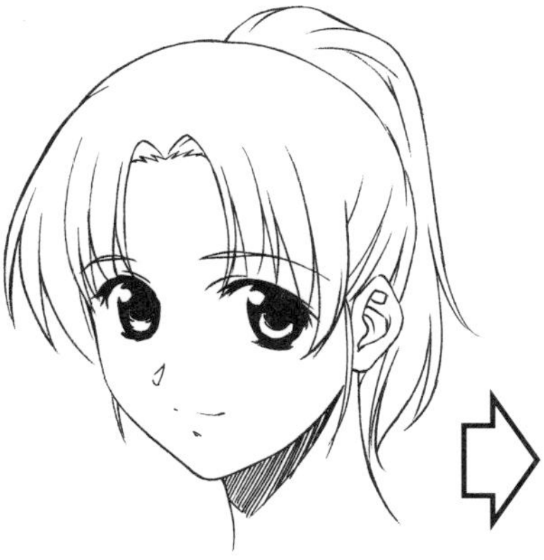

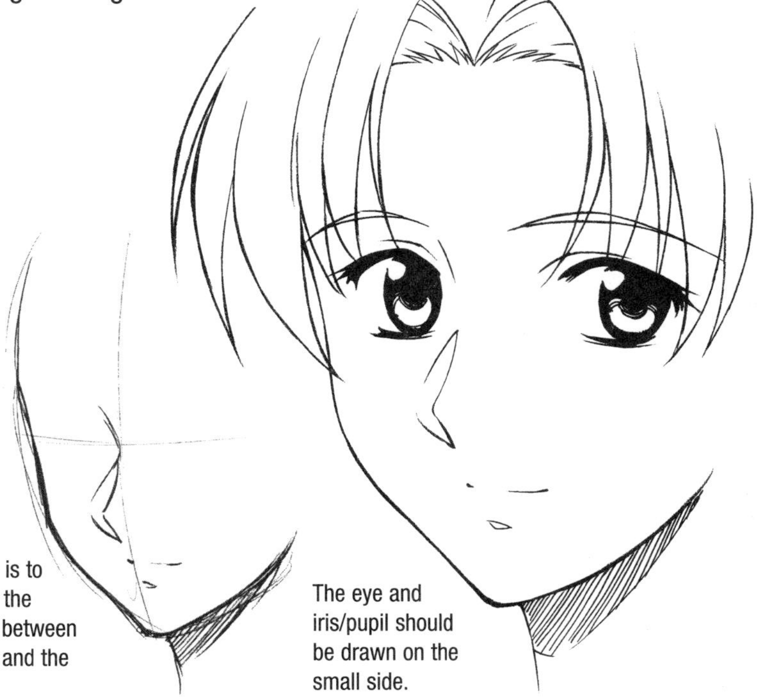

The eye and iris/pupil should be drawn on the small side.

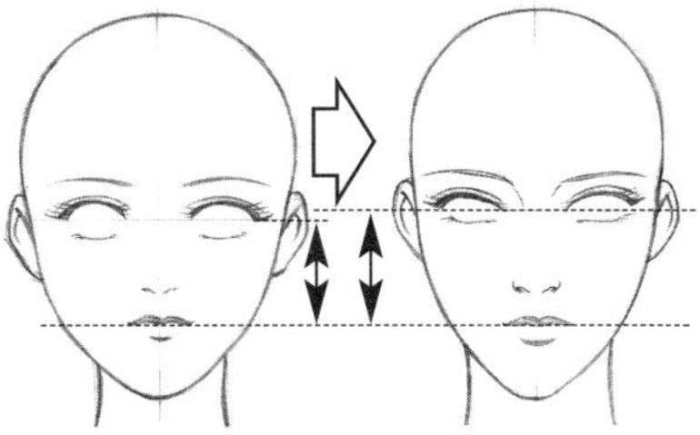

The trick is to lengthen the distance between the eyes and the mouth.

Young Girl **Woman**

Standard Face

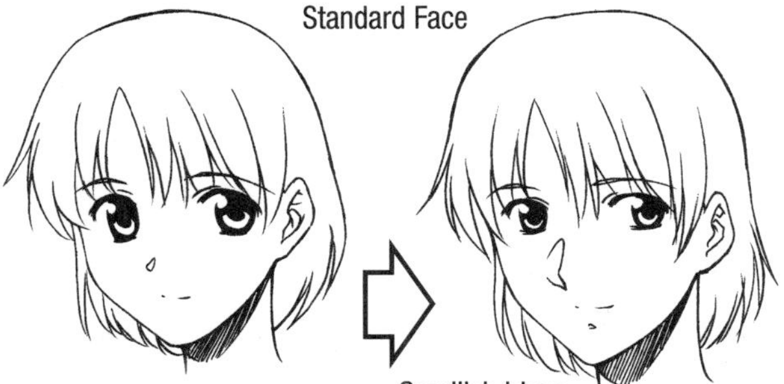

Smallish irises

Upward slanting eyes (Spunky, dynamic characters)

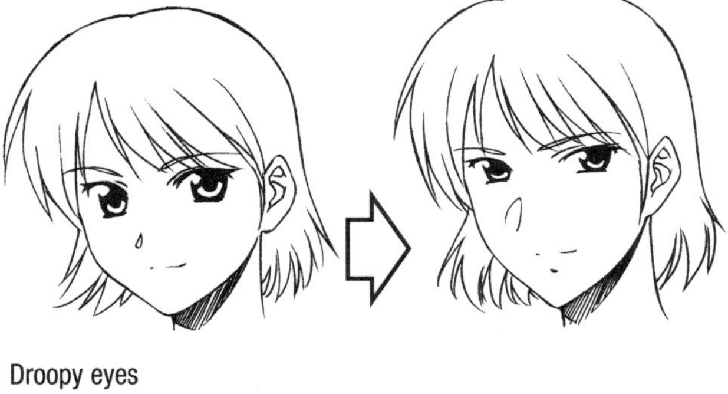

Droopy eyes (Quiet, gentle characters)

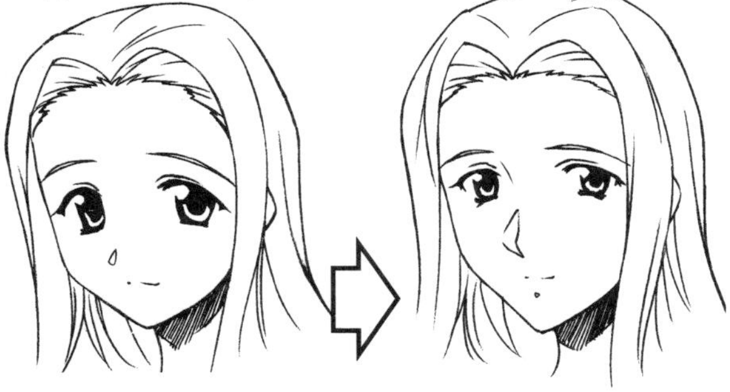

Suggesting lipstick

Accentuating the lips can facilitate creating an adult atmosphere.

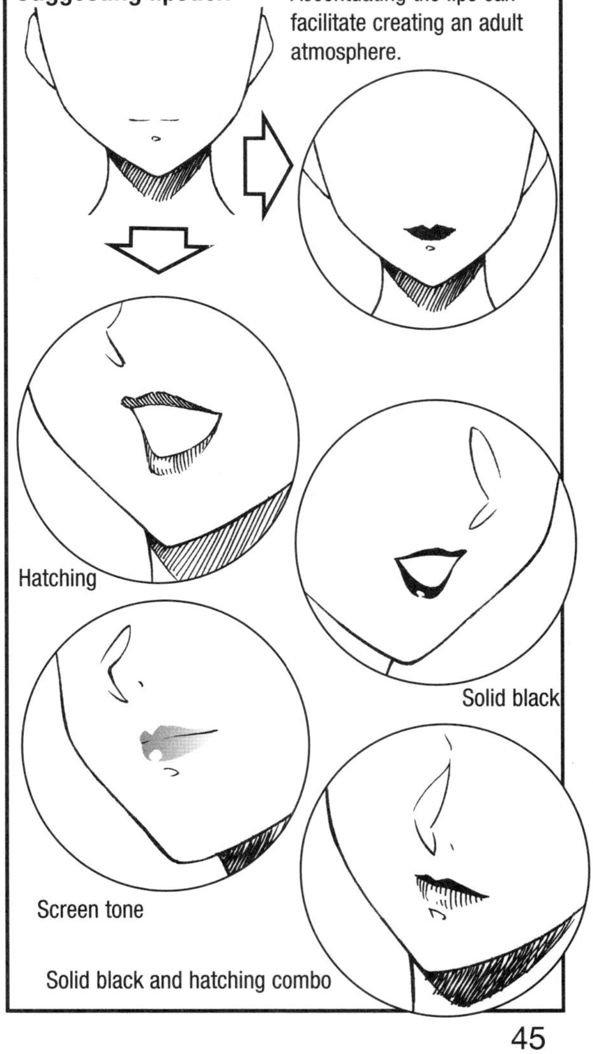

Full Figure

The Older Girl should always have broad shoulders, regardless of her personality type.

Contrast the two personality types: The athletic older girl is active and sports miniskirts and short hair. The artsy older girl is non-athletic and wears both her hair and skirts long.

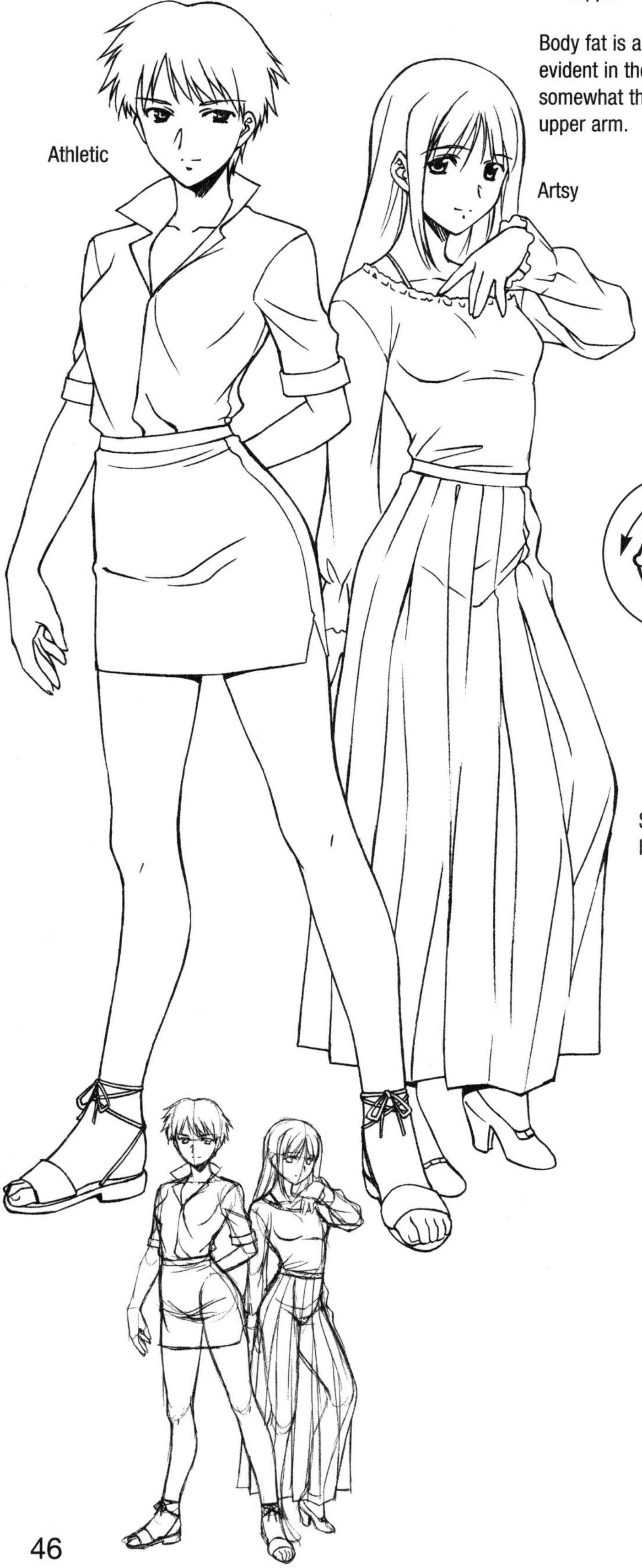

• Mature Figure: Large Chest and Hips

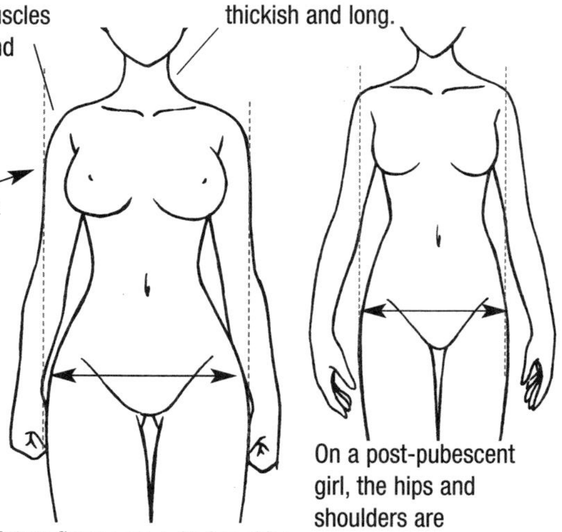

Mature figures are suited to older girl characters. The hips should be wider than the shoulders.

On a post-pubescent girl, the hips and shoulders are approximately the same width. The upper arm and thighs are slim.

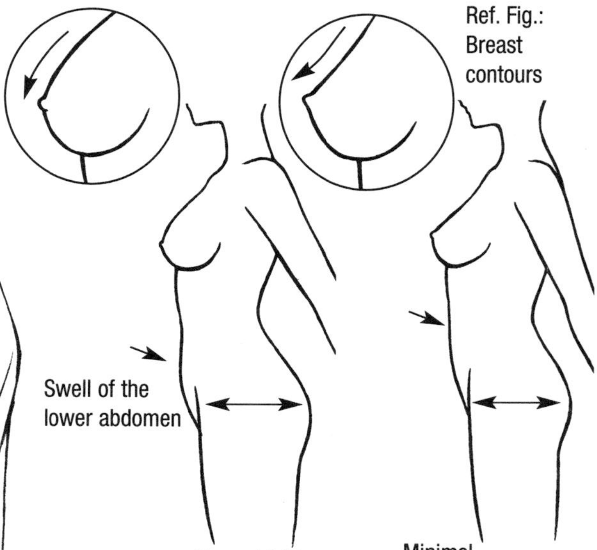

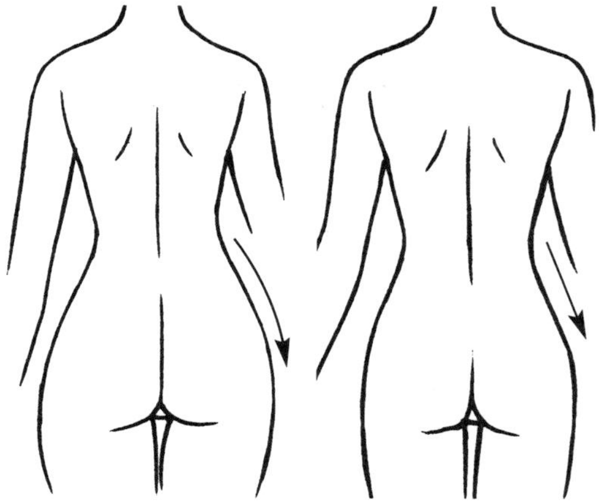

Standard Fashions

Dress the Older Girl in simple fashions and items that show off her figure.

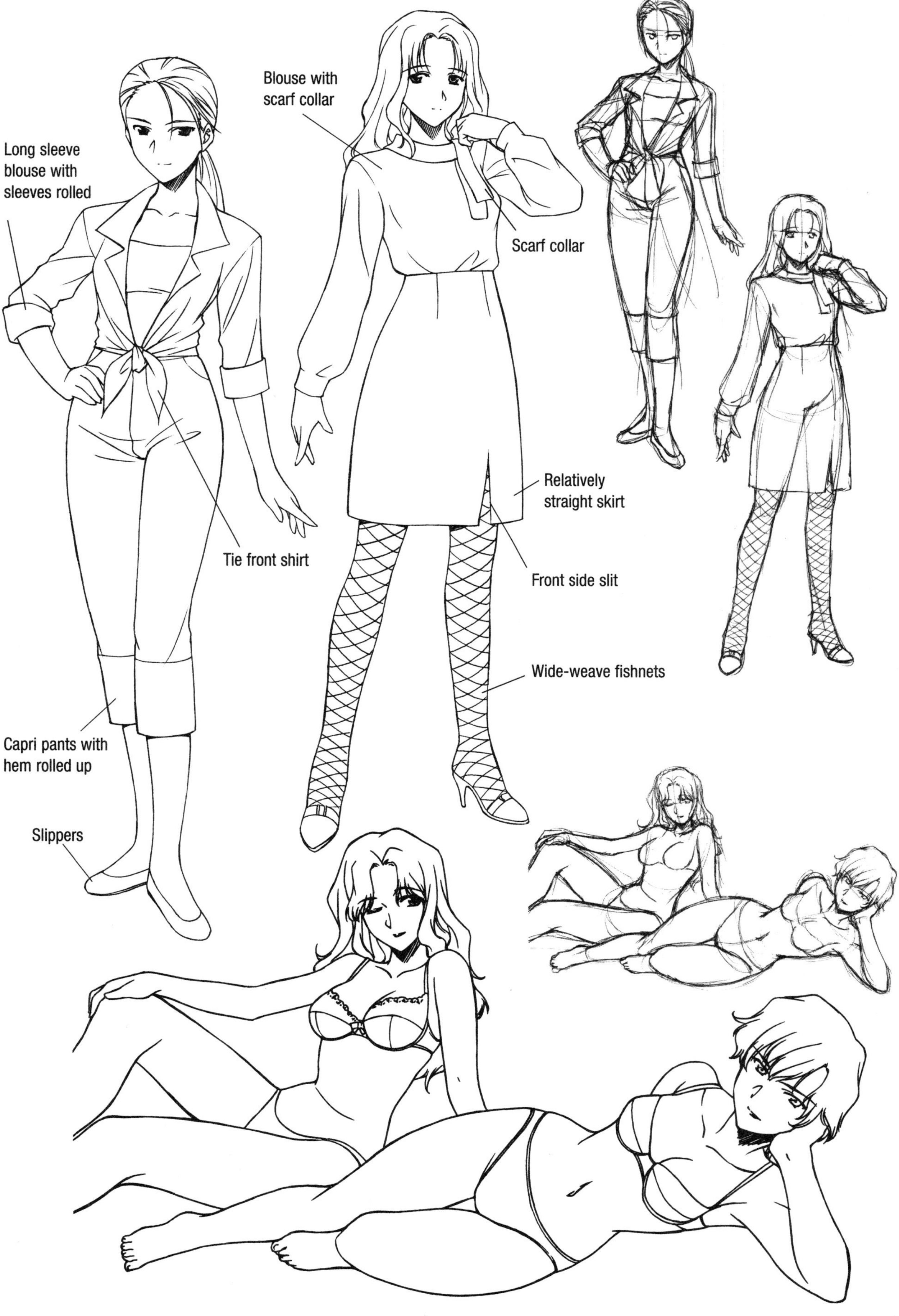

10 The Kid

Key features are a large head, a round face, large eyes, and round irises.

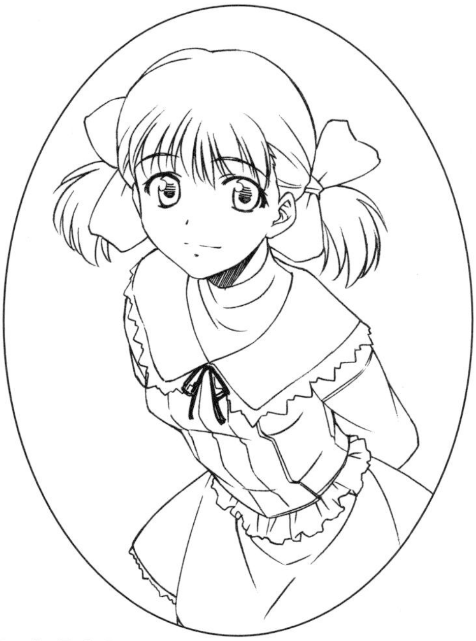

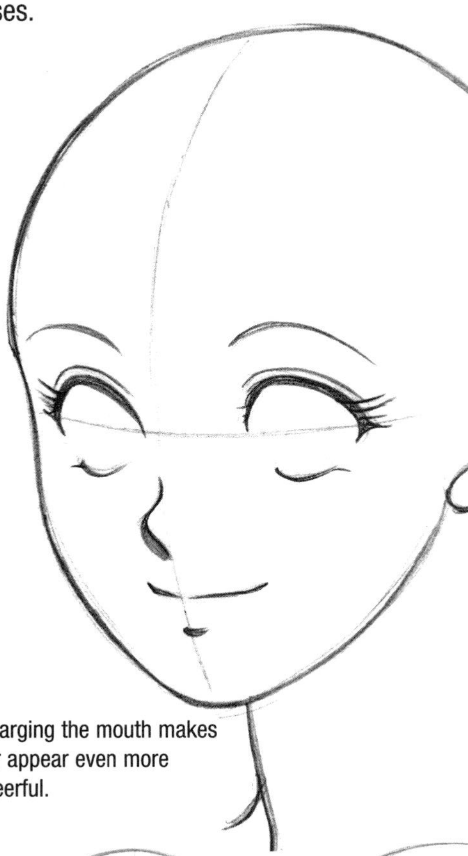

Basic Points

- "The kid" is not an actual child, but rather simply childlike in height, fashion, and outer appearance.
- Draw the head largish.
- Use large bows and lace as accessories or clothing accents.
- Basic character traits are innocent, naive, and spunky.

Enlarging the mouth makes her appear even more cheerful.

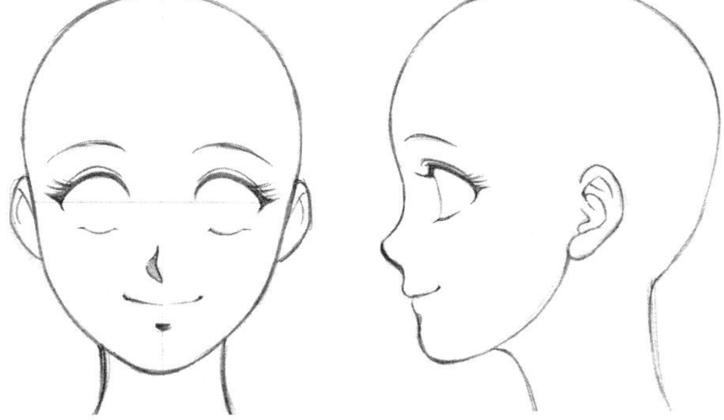

Large Head and Costume Effects

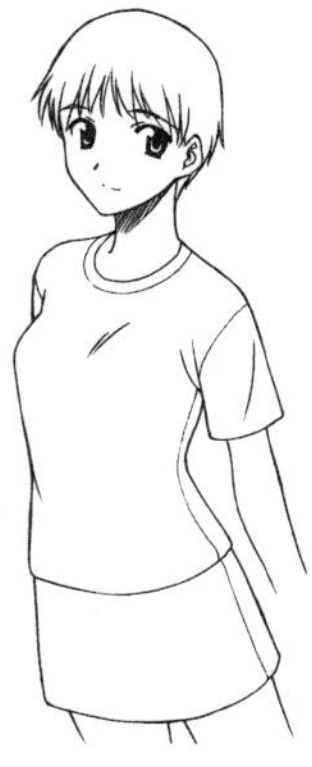

Typical character

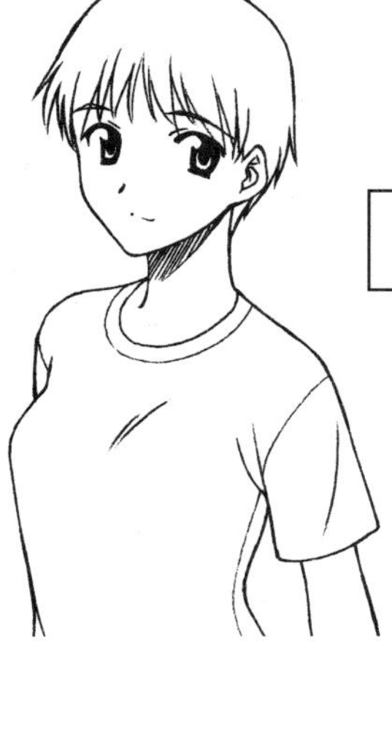

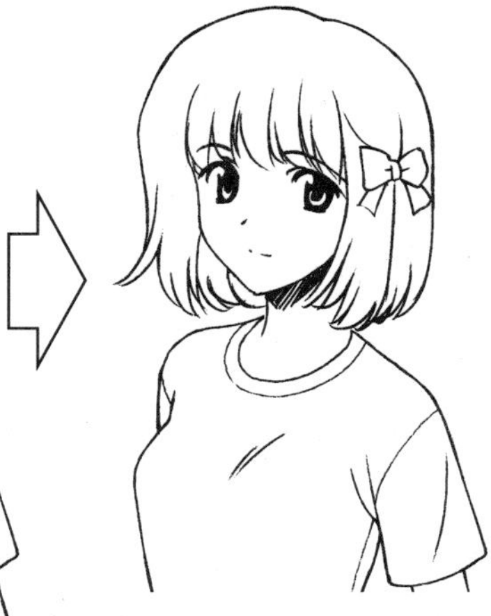

Adding a large wig and bow results in a childish-looking character.

Good

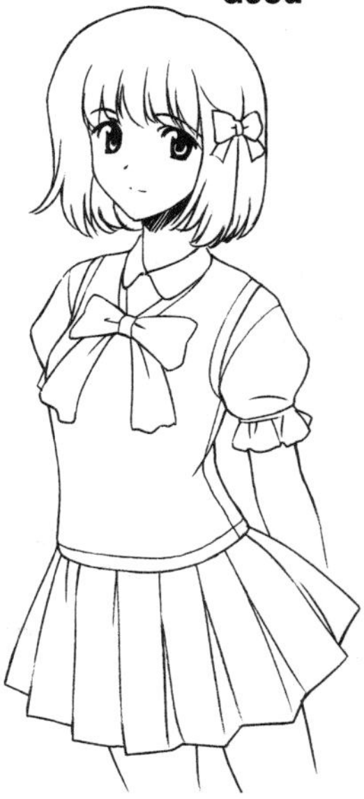

Not good

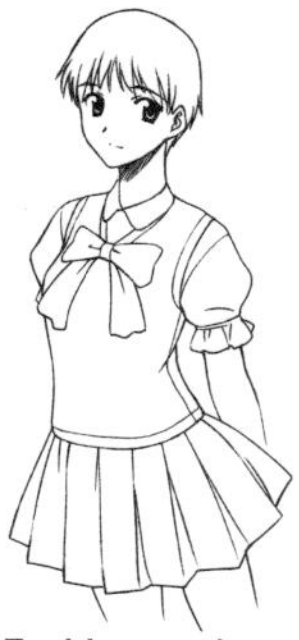

Fashions not suited for typical characters look terrific on the kid.

Popular Youthful Hairstyles

Pigtails

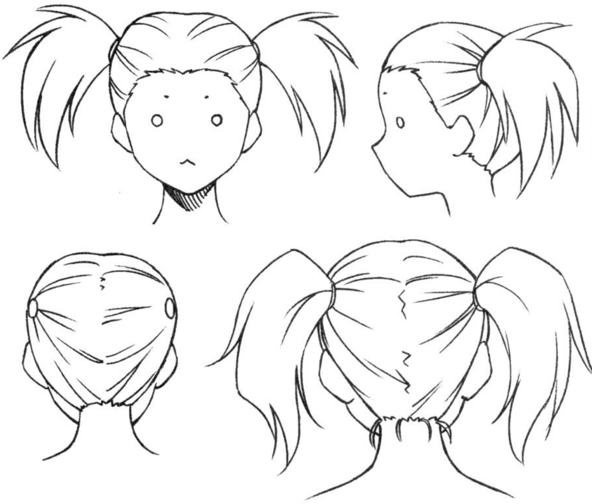

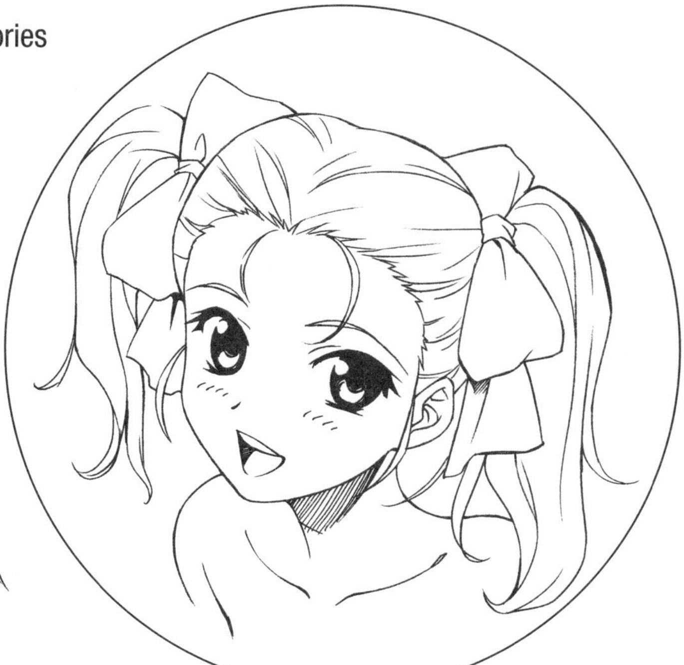

Side ponytail

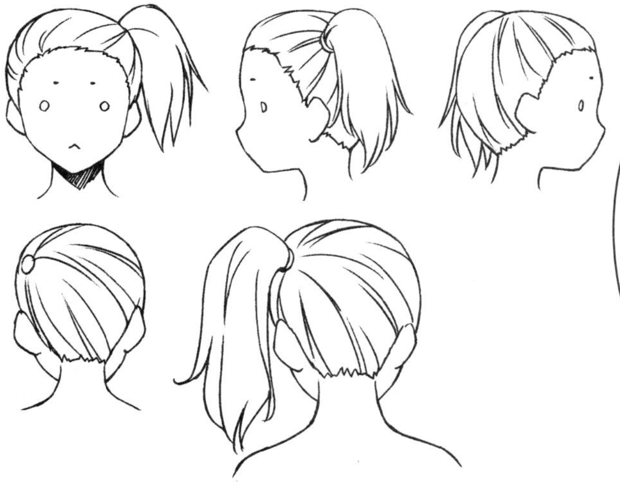

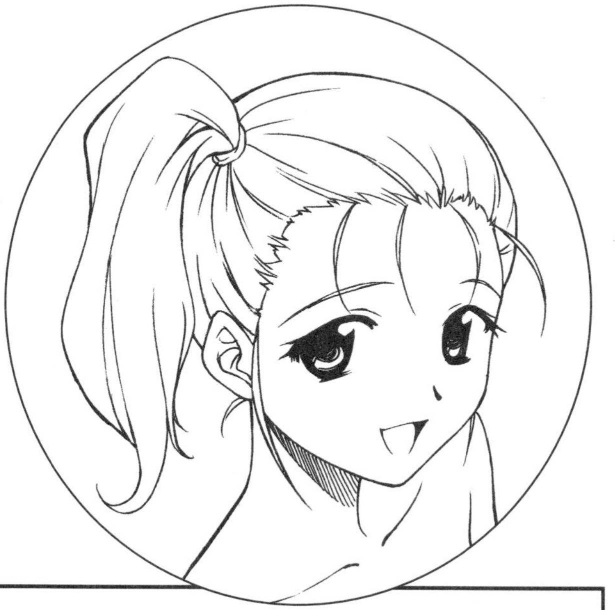

Secret Ingredient: Bows (Assorted Ties)

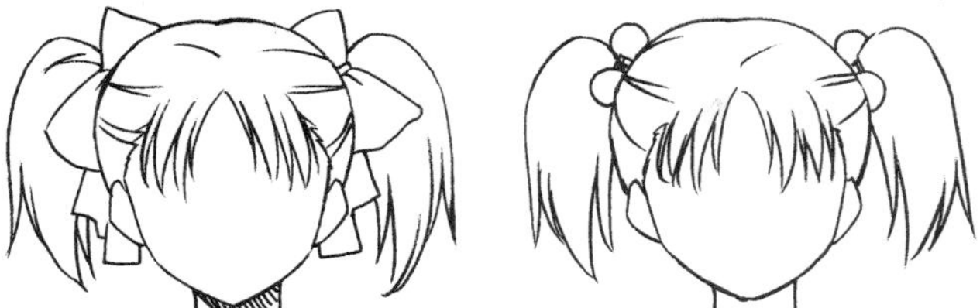

The accessory should be of a conspicuous size.

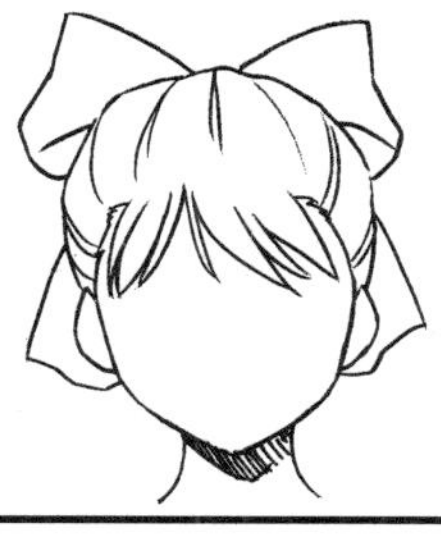

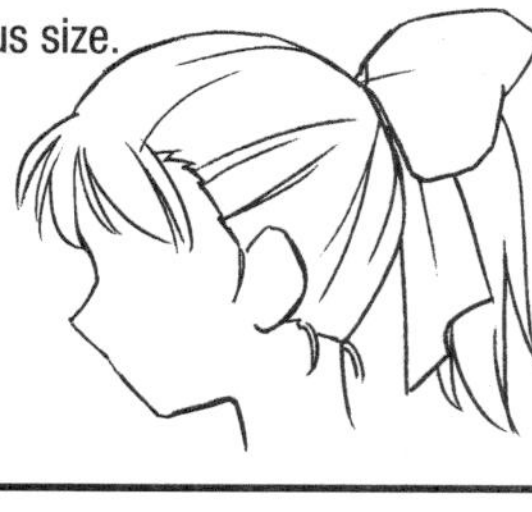

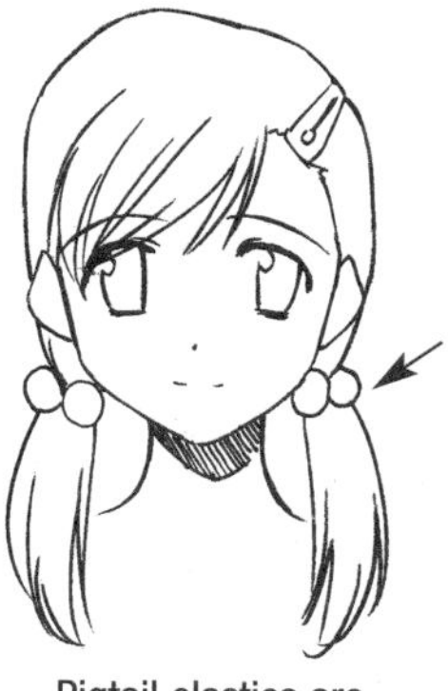

Pigtail elastics are also effective.

Not good

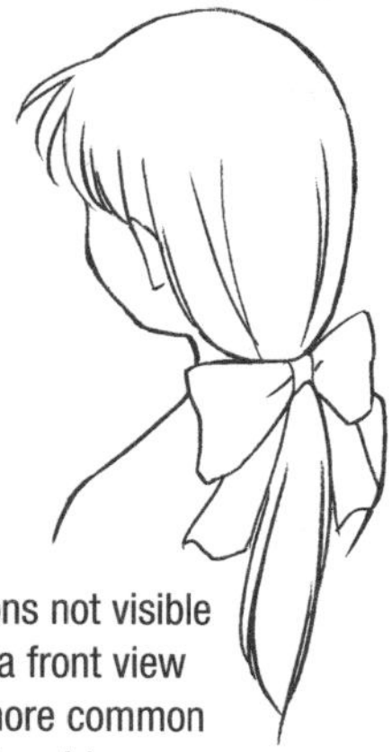

Ribbons not visible from a front view are more common to older girl characters.

Full Figure

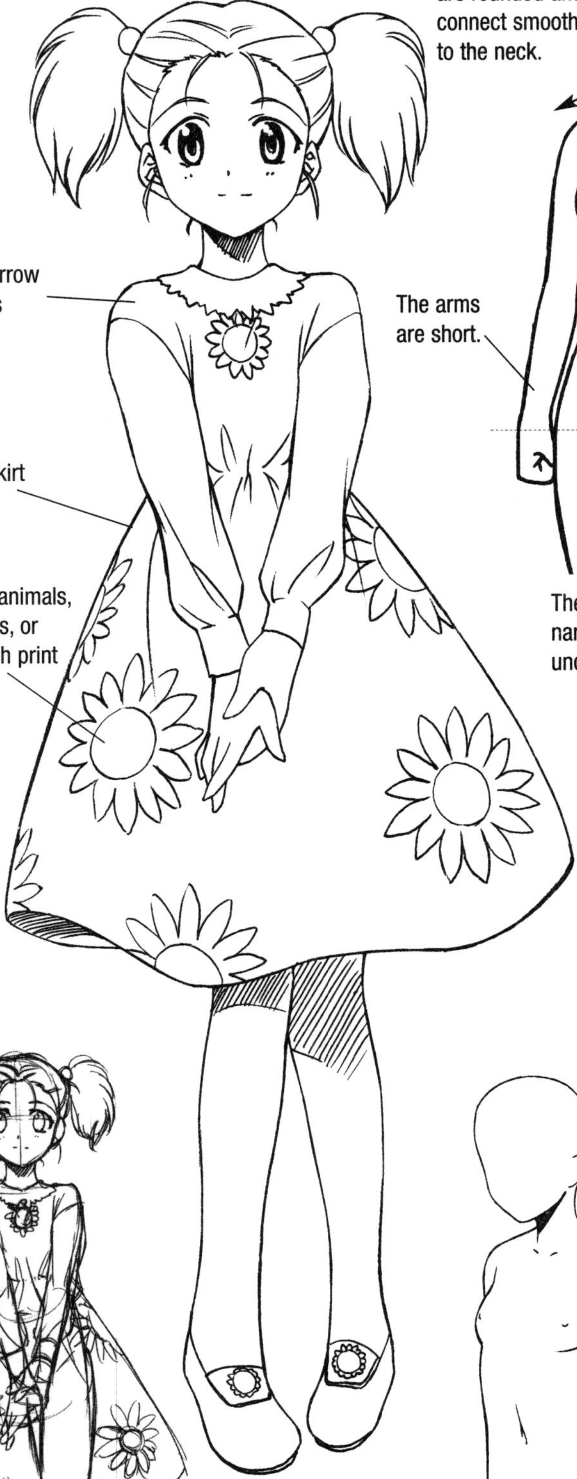

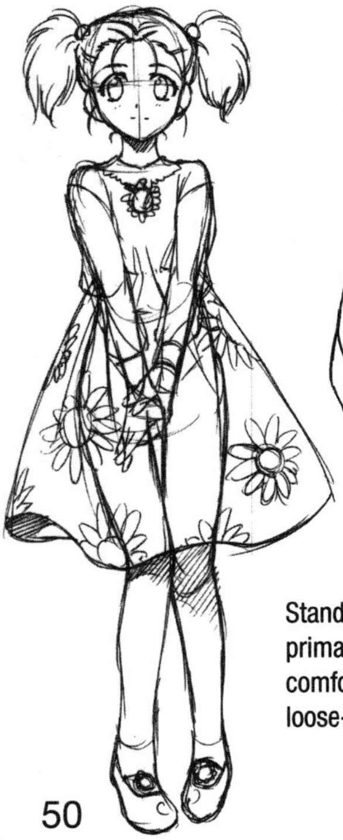

Standard fashions for the kid primarily consist of comfortable clothing. Select loose-fitting, baggy items.

• Small Chest and Preadolescent Figure

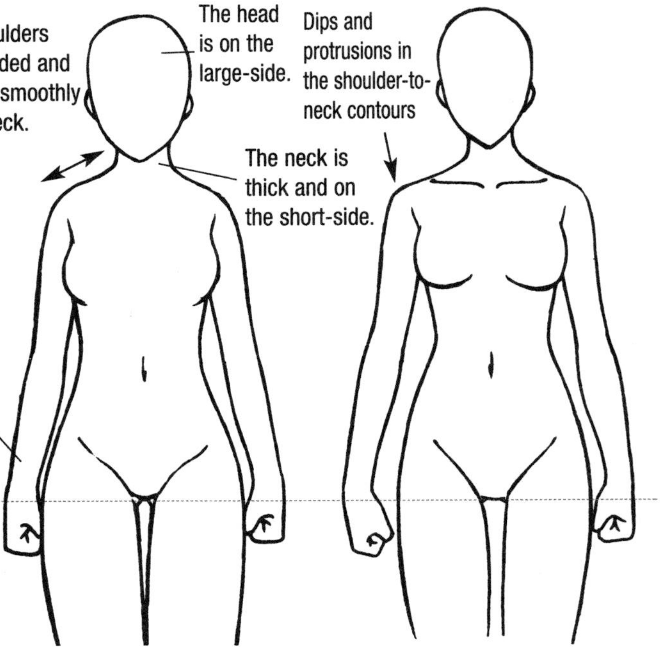

The kid's build features narrow shoulders and an understated chest.

Typical, mature figure

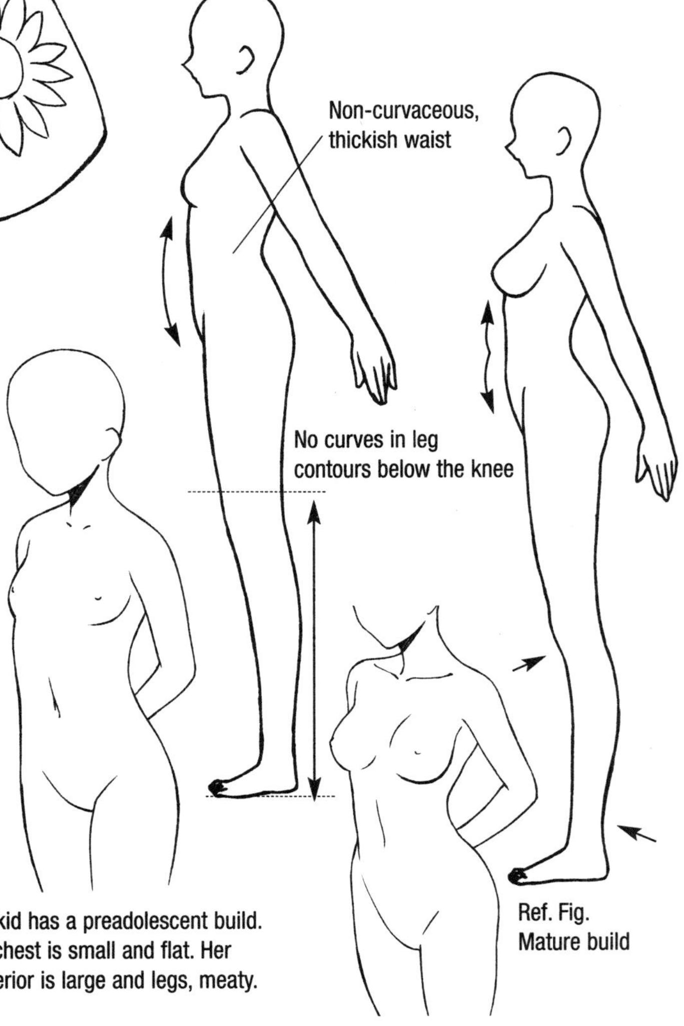

The kid has a preadolescent build. Her chest is small and flat. Her posterior is large and legs, meaty.

Ref. Fig. Mature build

Standard Fashions

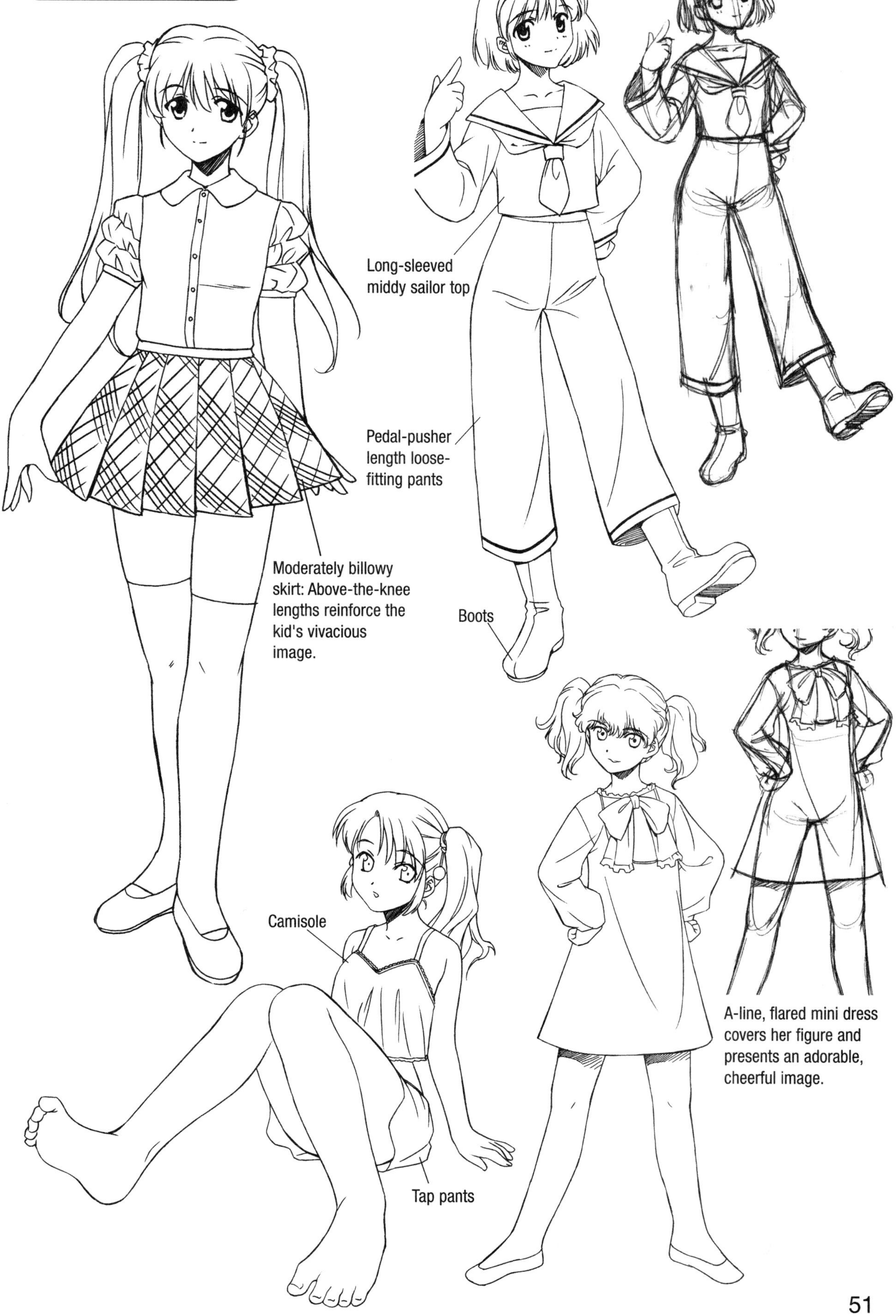

11 The Princess

The Princess's distinguishing features are large, droopy eyes and a slightly dim-witted look. Draw her in extravagant or expertly coiffed hairstyles.

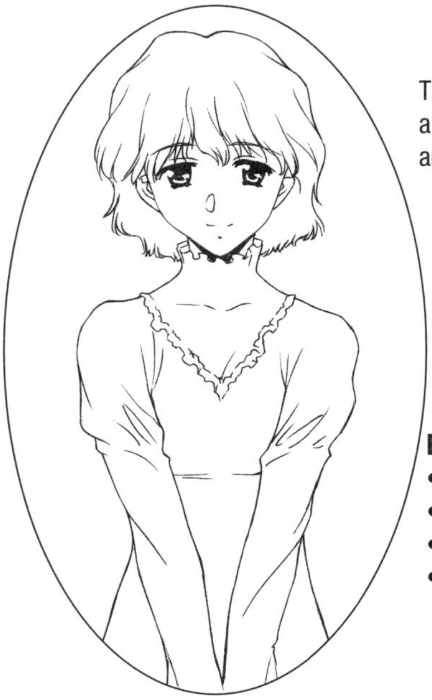

Thick eyebrows evoke a sense of strong will and inner fortitude.

Large eyes with eyelid folds somehow suggest an unexceptional sense of kindness and dim-wittedness.

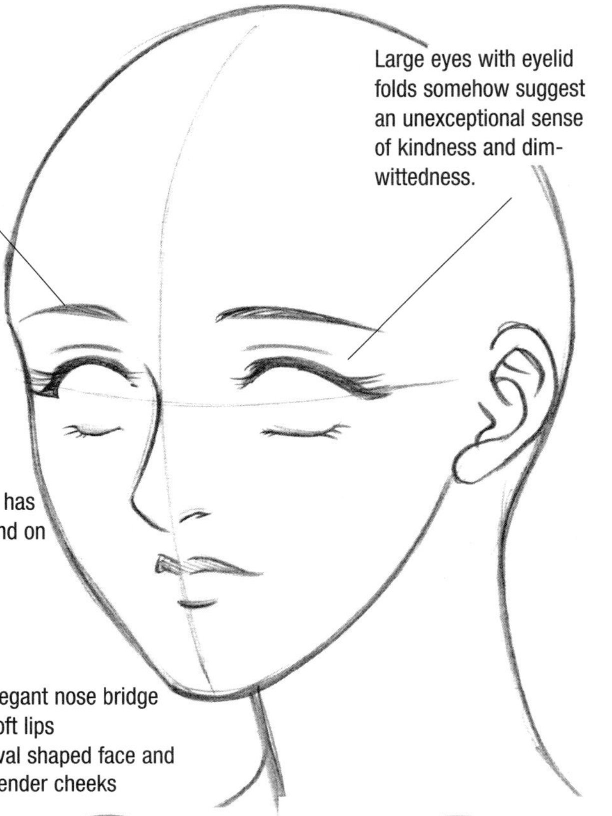

Basic Points
- Naïve
- Not too bright
- Wealthy
- Lots of free time (I.e. has plenty of time to spend on fussy hairstyles and elaborate clothing.

- Elegant nose bridge
- Soft lips
- Oval shaped face and slender cheeks

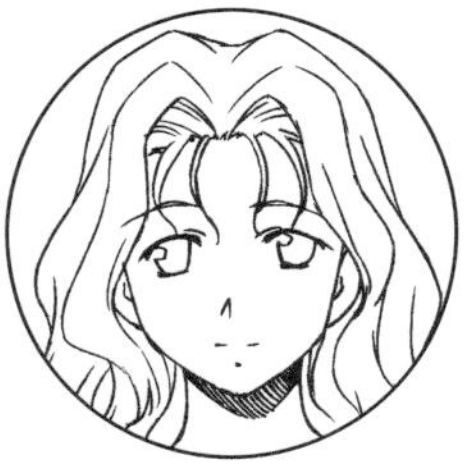

Sweet-tempered Princess
- Large irises: Suggest innocence
- Eyelid fold and droopy eyes: Indicate a gentle disposition.
- Small mouth: Suggests a reserved, mild personality.
- Round face: Suggests a mild, sweet disposition.

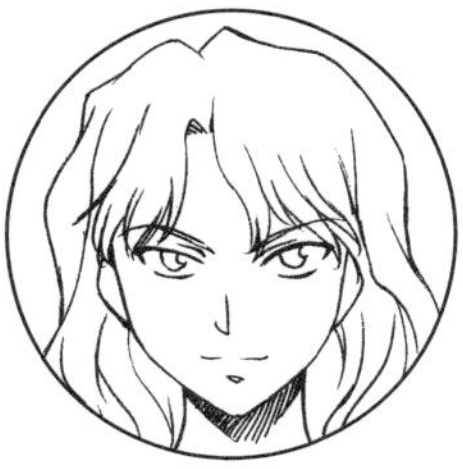

Scary Princess
- Thin, angular chin
- Small irises, upward slanting eyes, large mouth
- Mean-spirited, selfish air
- Short, thin eyebrows also project an intimidating, cold-hearted image.

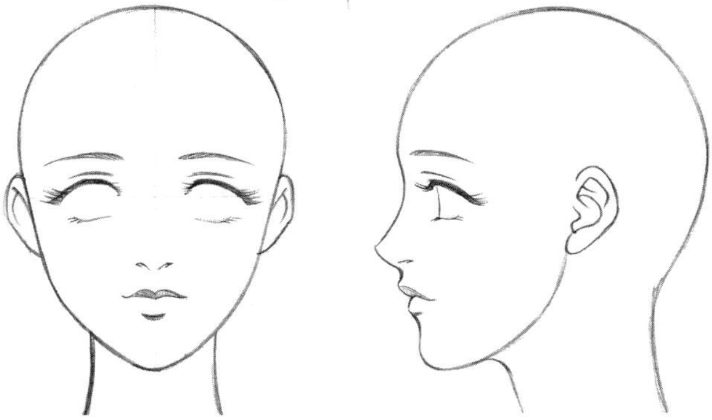

Two Diametric Princess Types

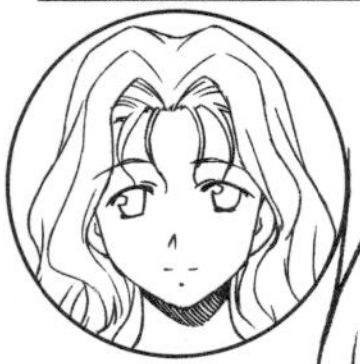

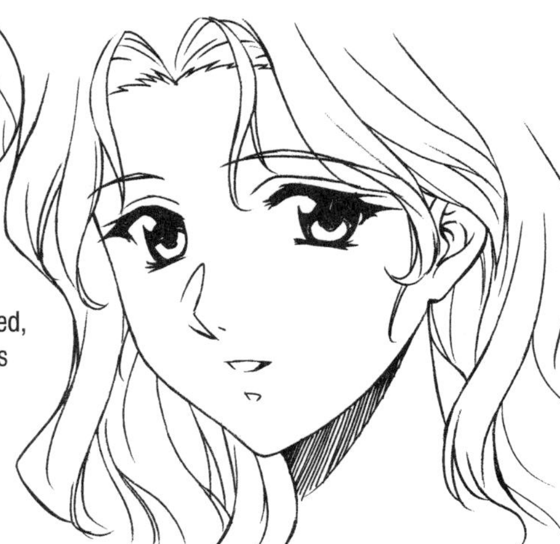

The gently raised, refined princess

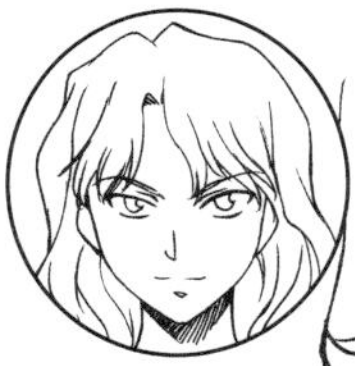

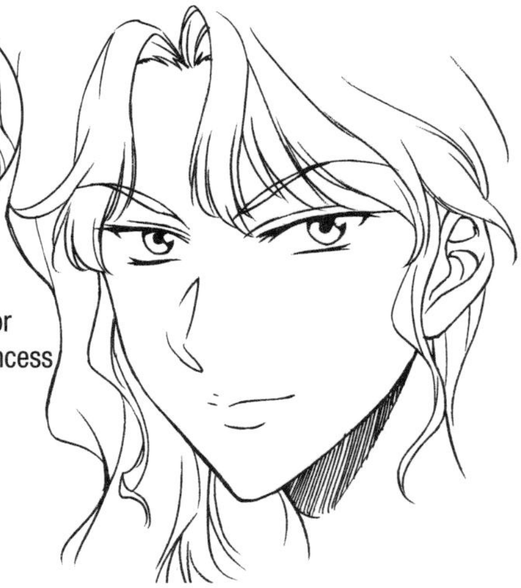

The tomboy or villainous princess

Key Variation Points Use hairstyles to suggest a character with Western or Japanese values

Western-Style Princess

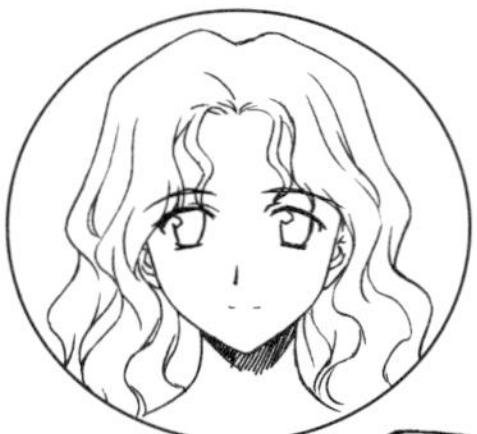

Select sumptuous hairstyles featuring waves or ringlets.

Wavy hair with center part

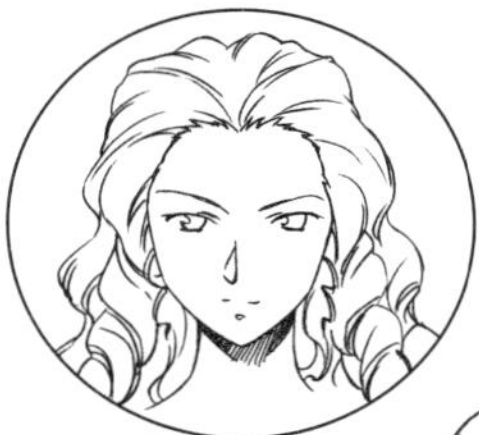

Swept back with ringlets

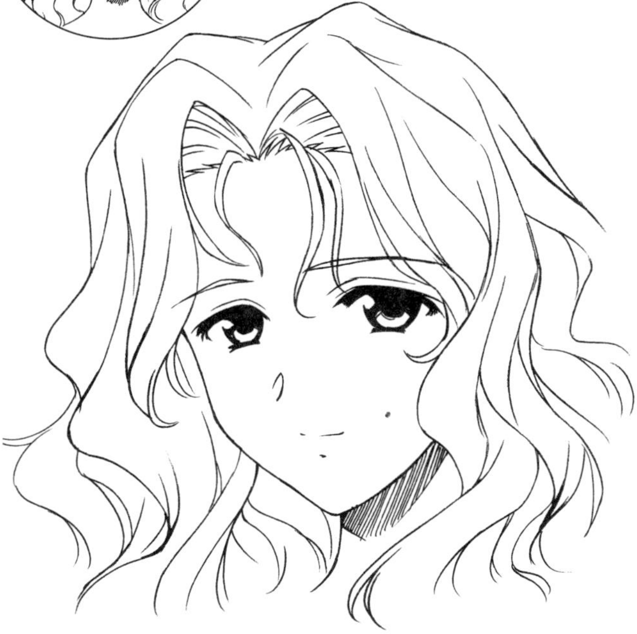

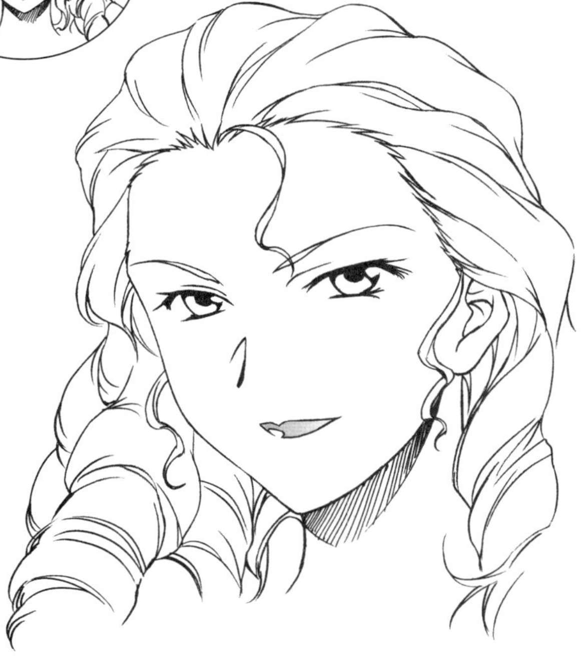

Japanese-Style Princess

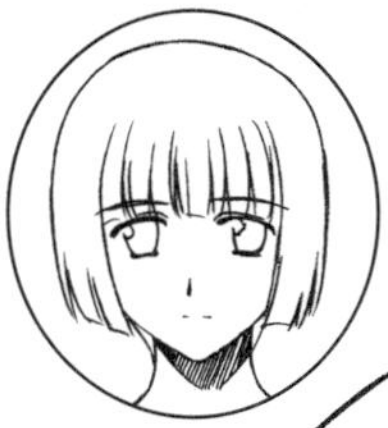

Emphasize straight, black hair.

Short hair concealing the forehead

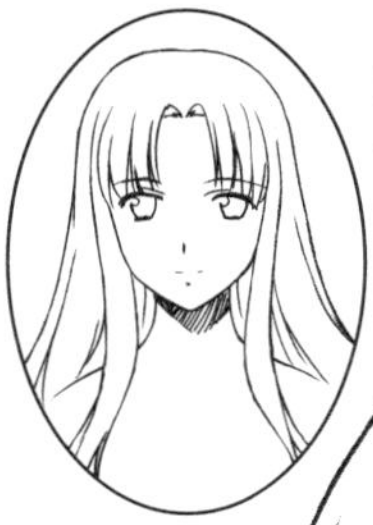

Long hair with center part

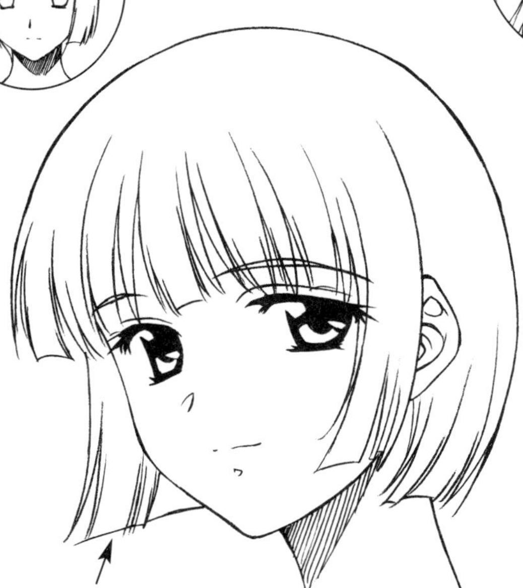

Evenly trimmed ends

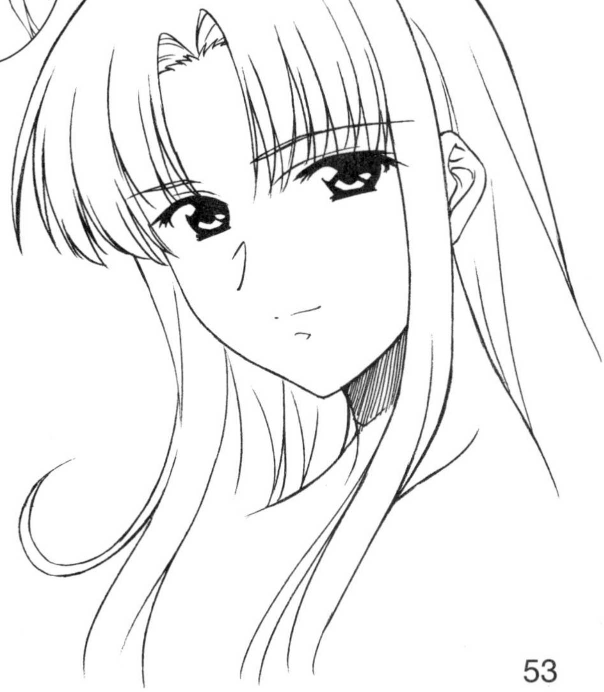

Full Figure

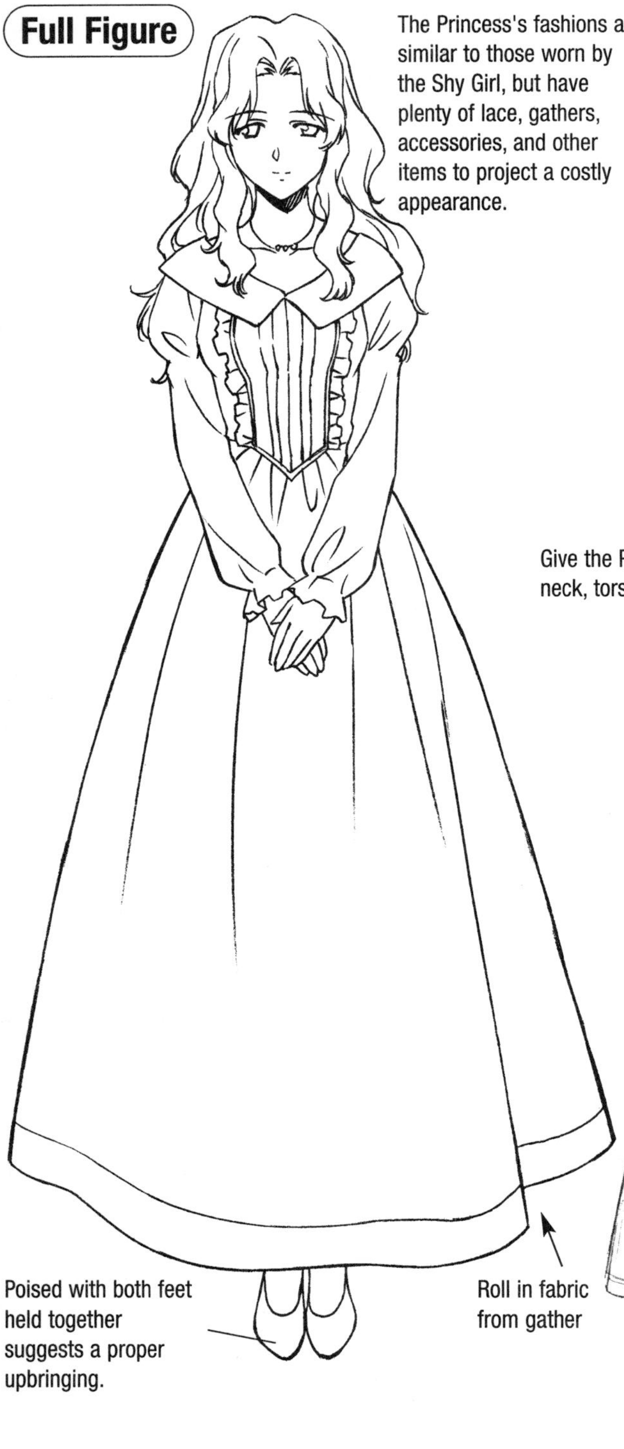

The Princess's fashions are similar to those worn by the Shy Girl, but have plenty of lace, gathers, accessories, and other items to project a costly appearance.

Poised with both feet held together suggests a proper upbringing.

Roll in fabric from gather

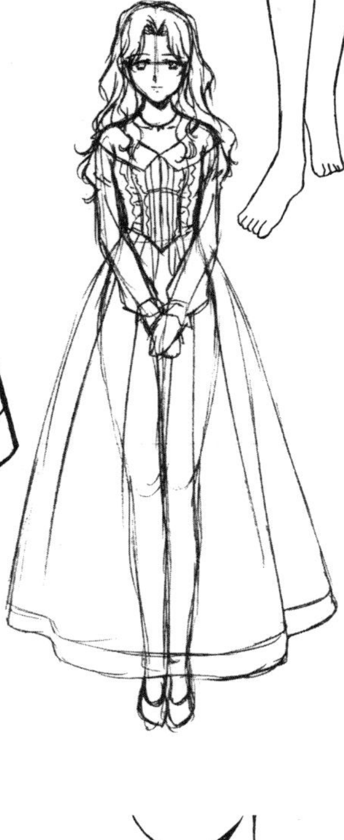

• Slim Torso, Arms, and Legs

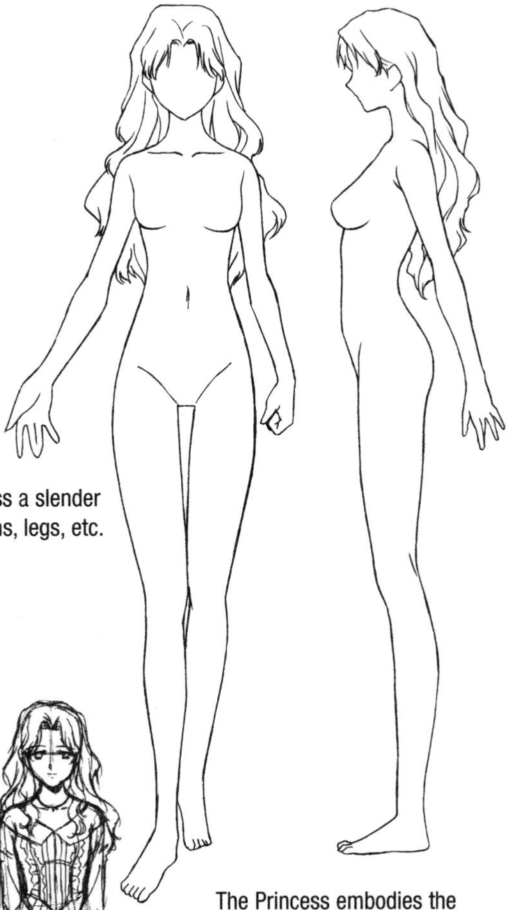

Give the Princess a slender neck, torso, arms, legs, etc.

The Princess embodies the image of a delicate, gently raised girl. Consequently, you should conceive of her build overall as slender.

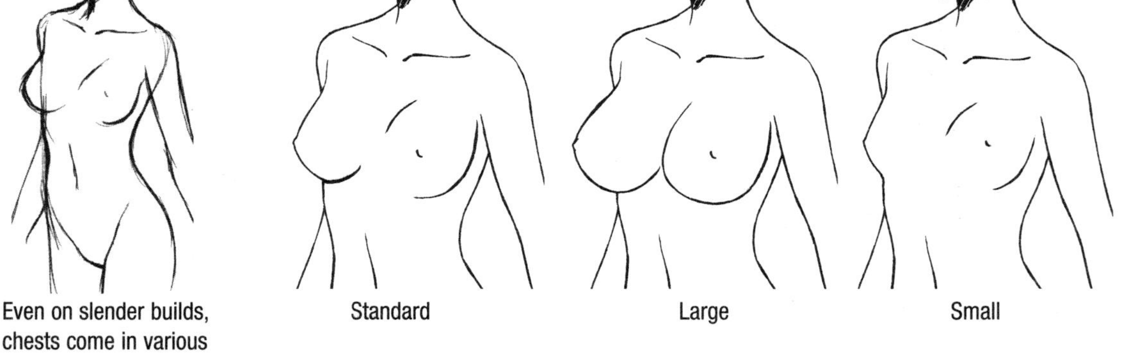

Even on slender builds, chests come in various shapes and sizes.

Standard

Large

Small

Standard Fashions

Take care to give the Princess a simple, elegant wardrobe.

For a casual look, a plain blouse and slacks, a straight skirt, and the like (reminiscent of the Straight-laced Girl) seem appropriate.

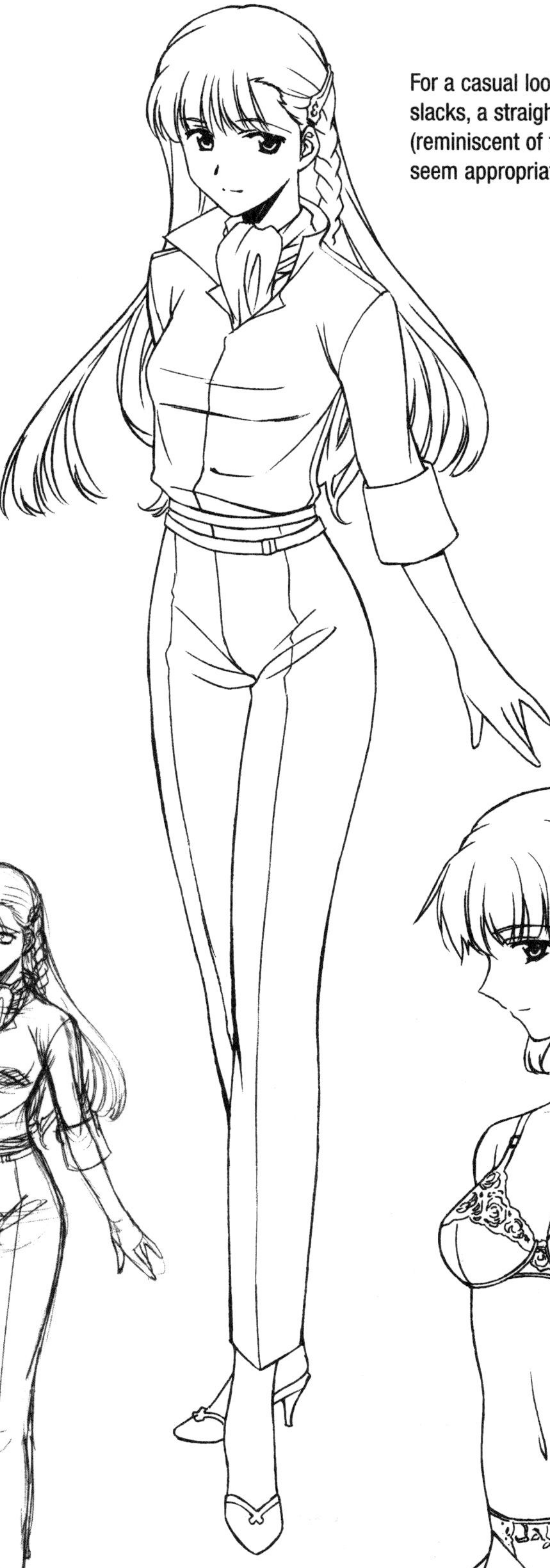

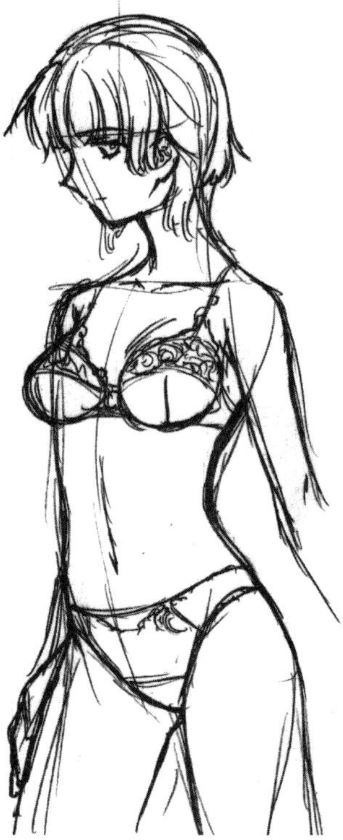

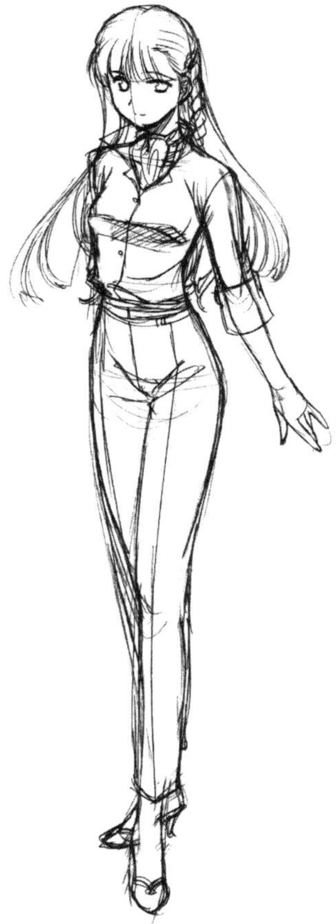

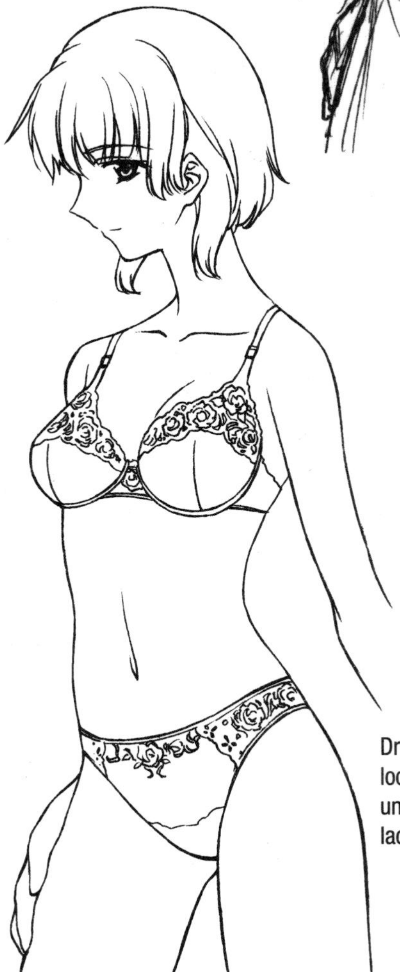

Dress her in expensive-looking, ornate undergarments full lace, etc.

12 The Bad Girl

Key features are her strong-willed, upward slanting eyes (intimidating almond-shaped eyes) and a large mouth.

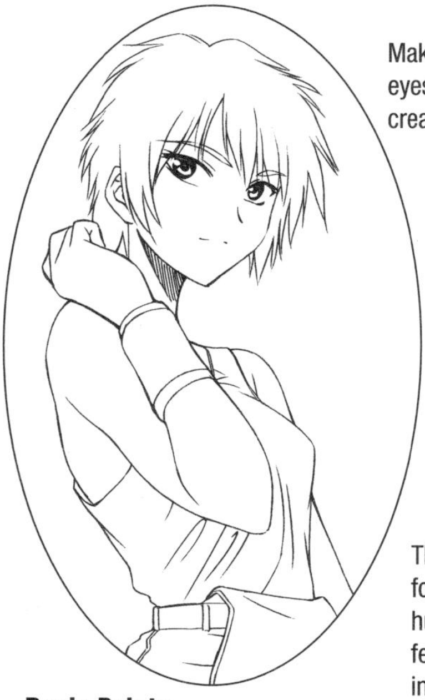

Making the corners of her eyes dark and upward sloping creates a daunting look.

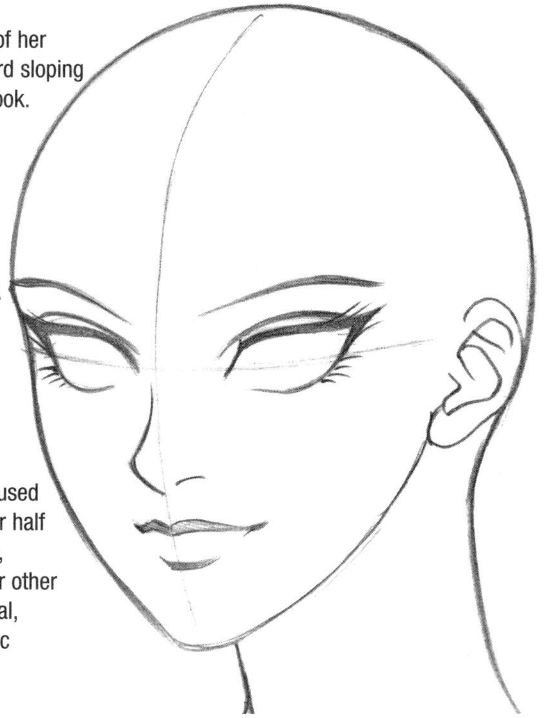

This type is often used for preternatural or half human characters, female warriors, or other inhuman or atypical, somehow eccentric character types.

Basic Points

- Spunky and individualistic
- Wild
- While she does not play the villain, narrowing her eyes would result in a stereotypical baddie.

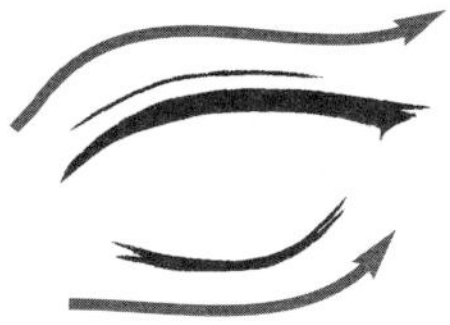

Stern, almond-shaped eyes

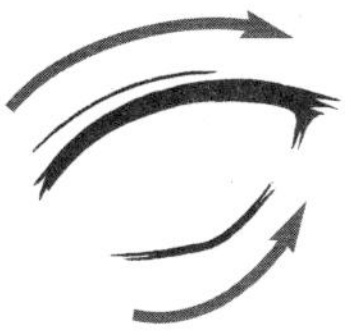

Typical eyes

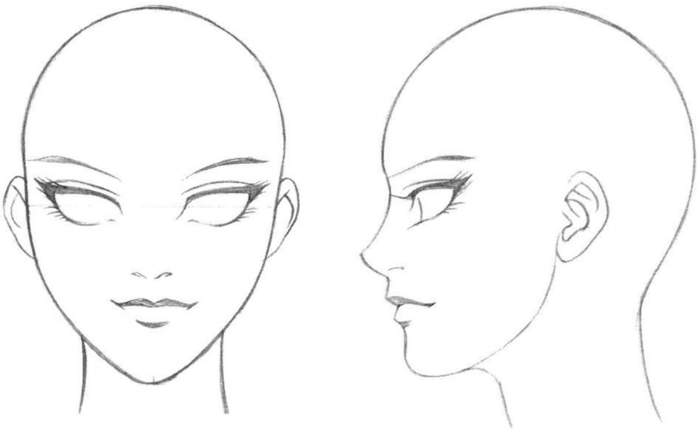

Impressions Resulting from Iris Size

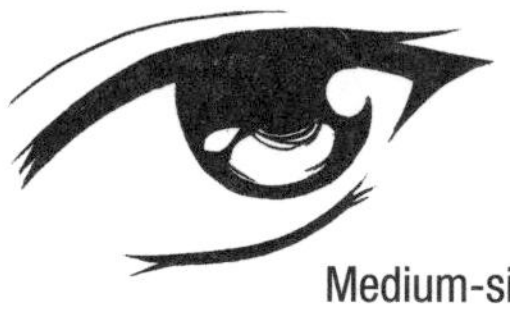

Medium-sized iris

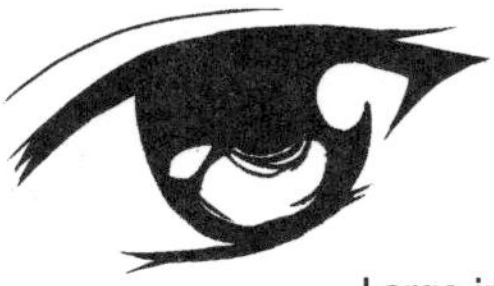

Large iris

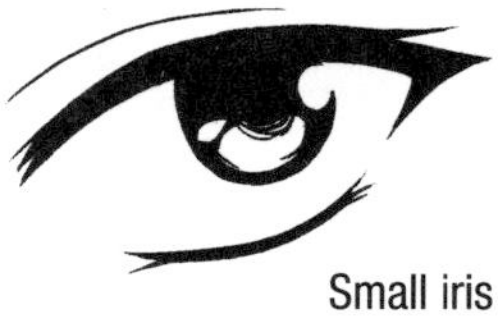

Small iris

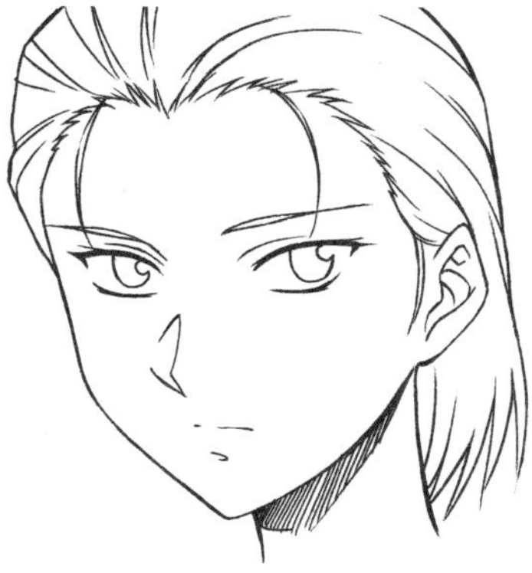

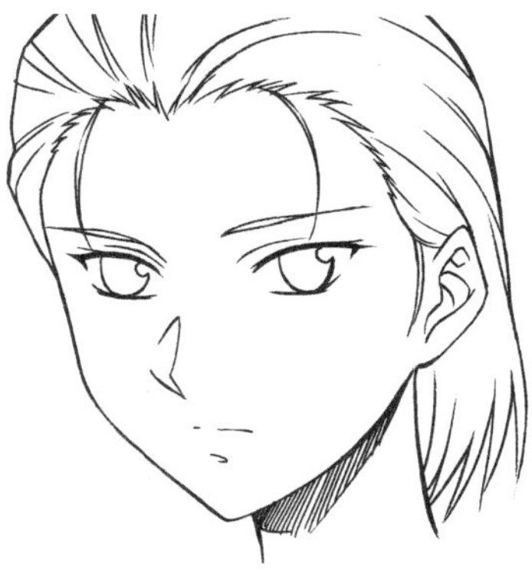

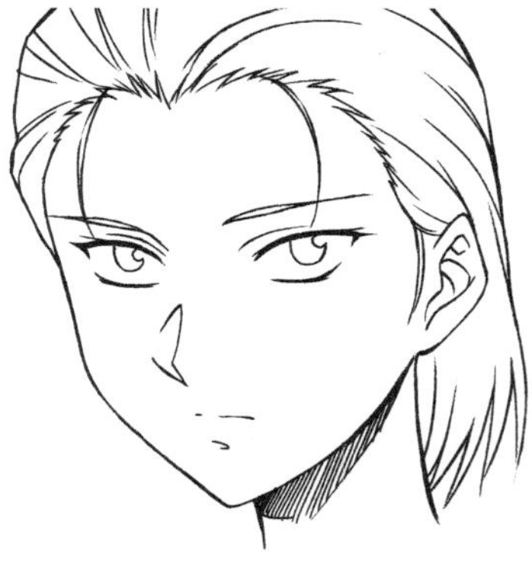

Standard Hairstyles for Quickly Reinforcing an "Individualistic" Look

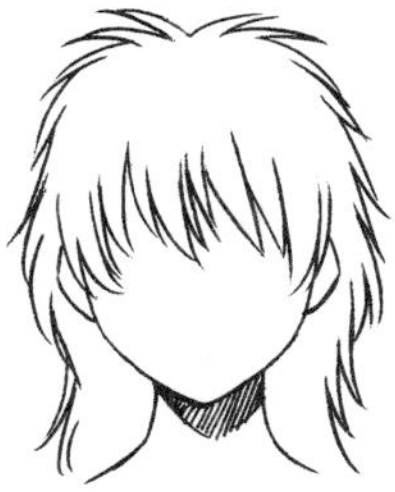

Long Bangs
- Hang over the eyes.
- Hide the eyes.

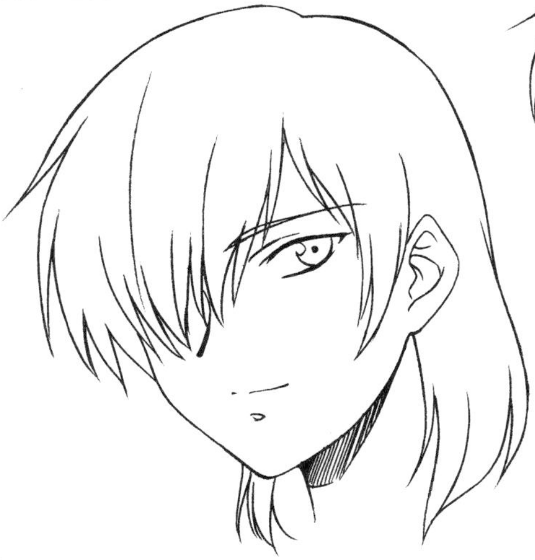

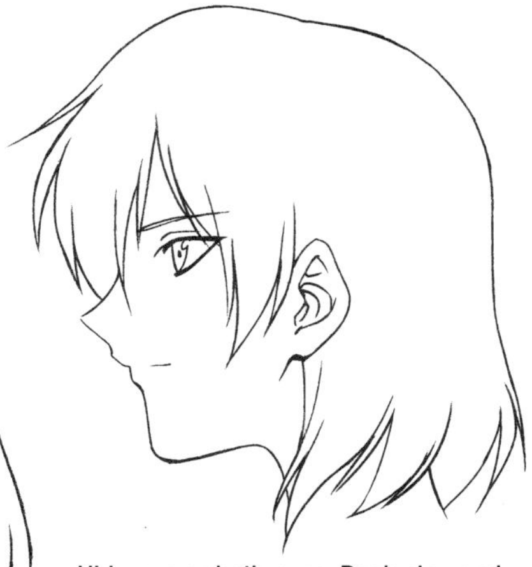

Hide one or both eyes. Designing and portraying hairstyles planned around the eyes are easy and strongly convey a sense of individuality.

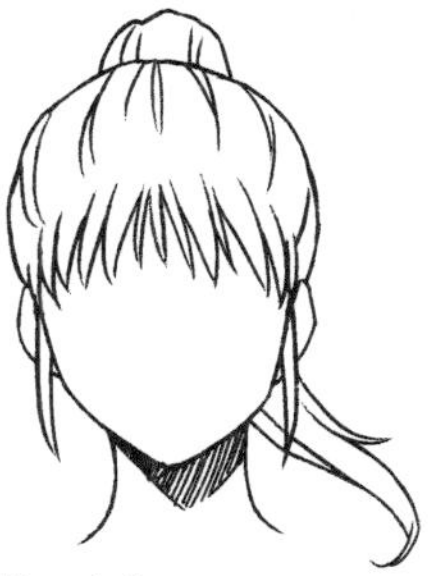

Ponytail
- Note the side tendrils.

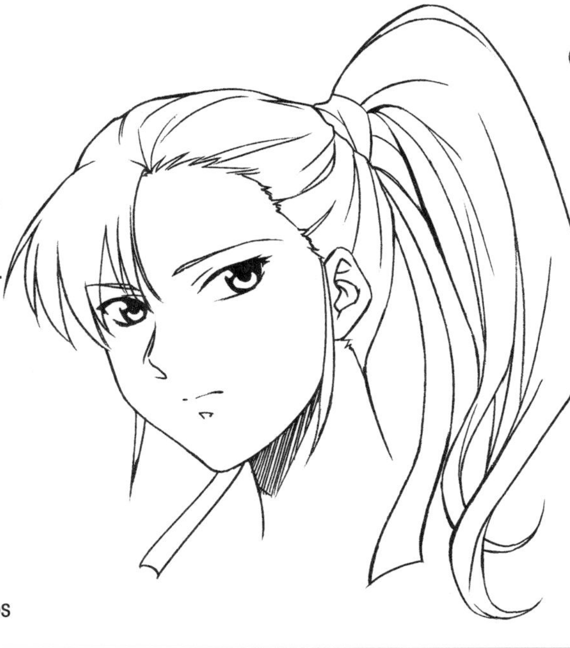

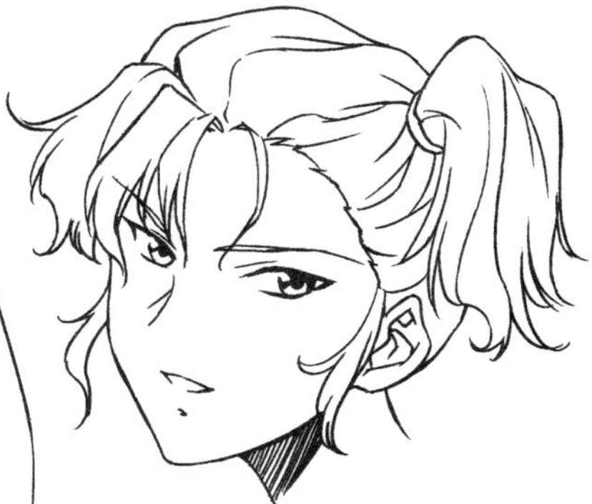

Adjusting the condition of the hair, the way it's tied, where it's tied, and its length allow for a variety of looks.

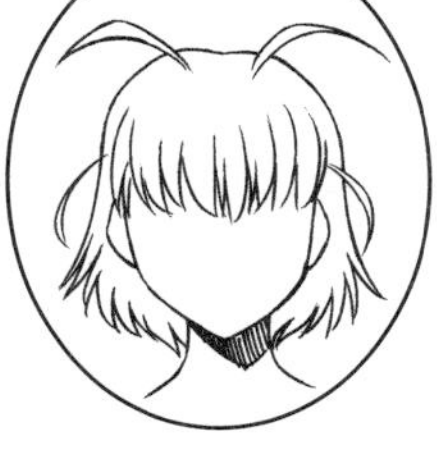

Antenna-style hair wisps

Items to Bring out Her Bad Girl Nature

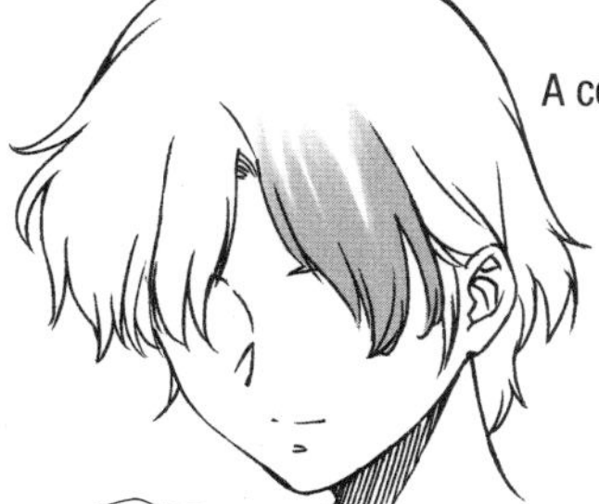

A colored lock of hair

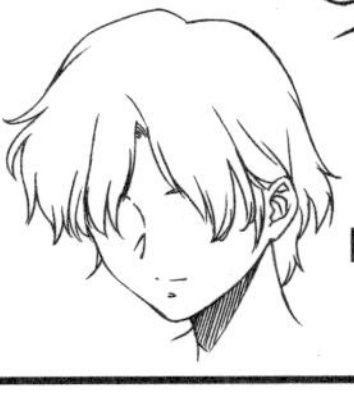

Natural color

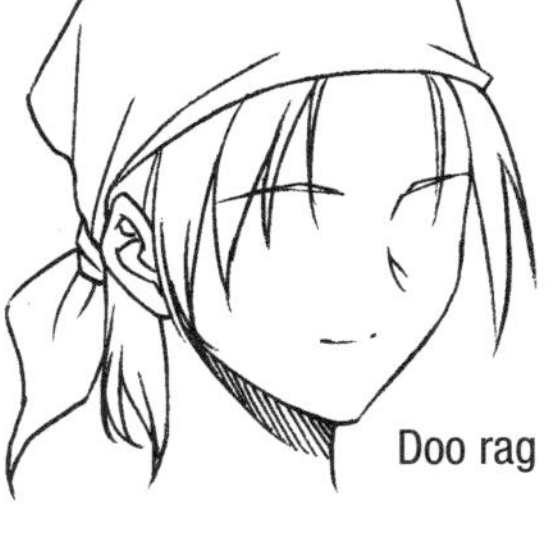

Doo rag

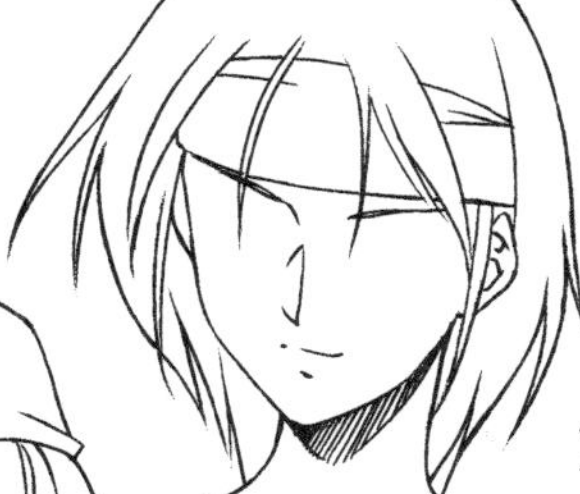

Wide headband or bandana

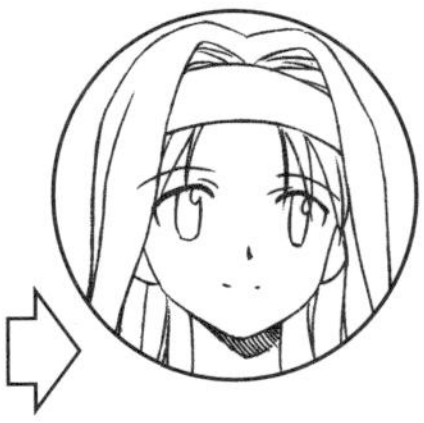

Big or droopy eyes generate an adorable, stylish look.

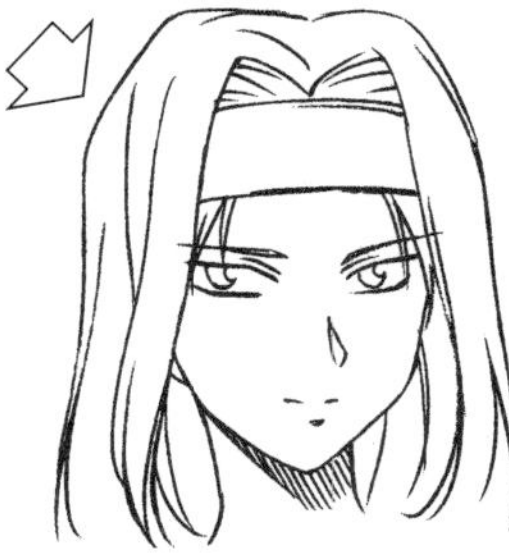

Stern eyes reinforce the notion of a distinctive personality.

Full Figure

Use hard rock or punk fashions for reference.

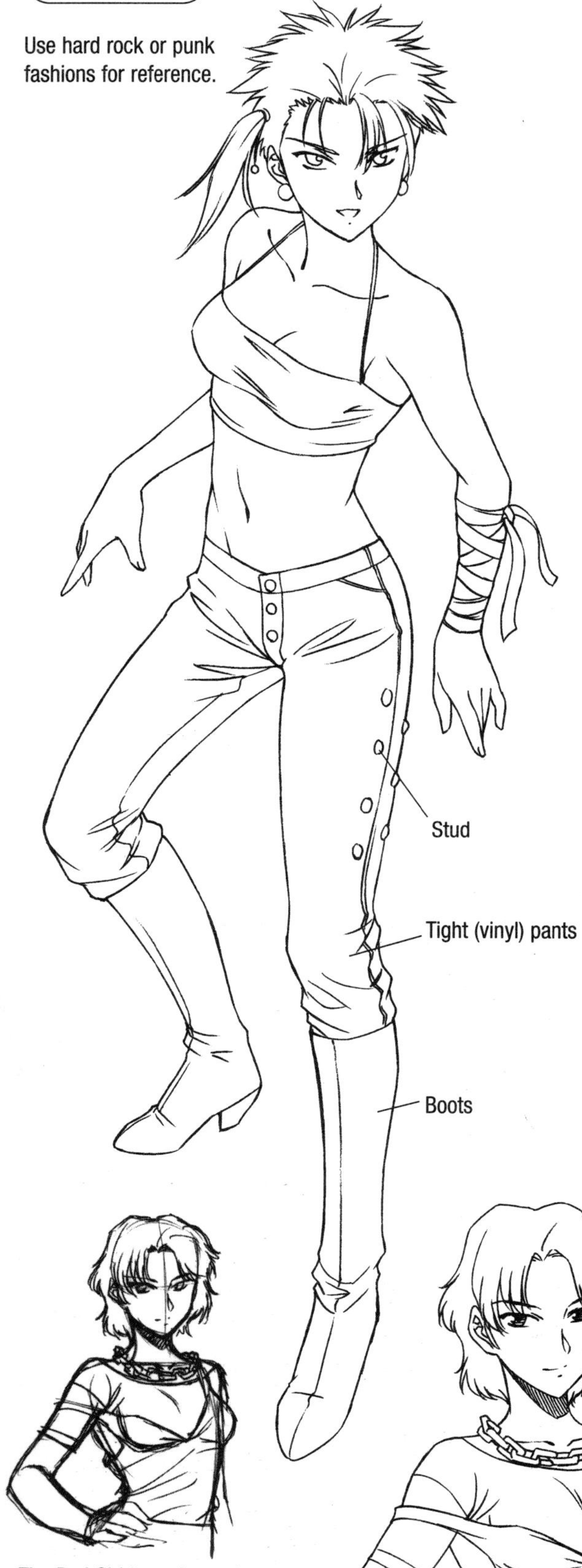

The Bad Girl turns layered clothing, tops with unattached or slipping straps, items with holes, chains, studs, etc. into fashion statements.

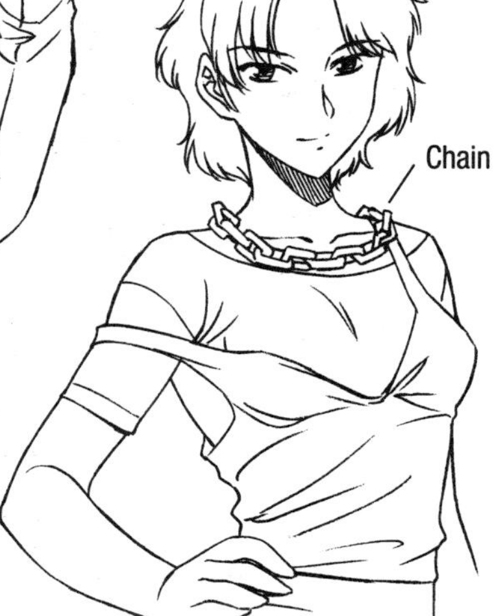

• Emphasizing Musculature and Skeletal Structure

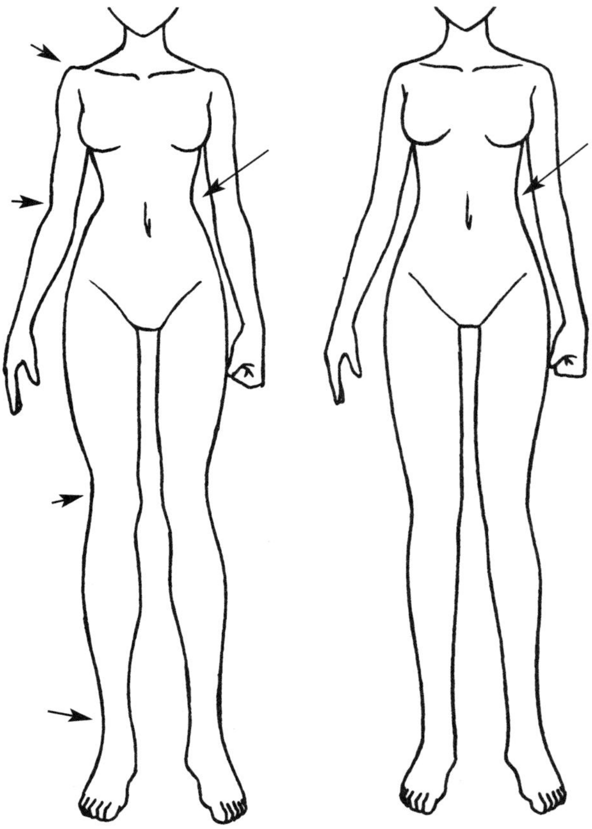

For the Bad Girl's build, accentuate contour line dips and bulges at the joints: the shoulders, the elbows, the knees, the ankles, the waist, etc. This will create the look of defined muscles.

On a typical build, the arms' and legs' display gracefully curved lines.

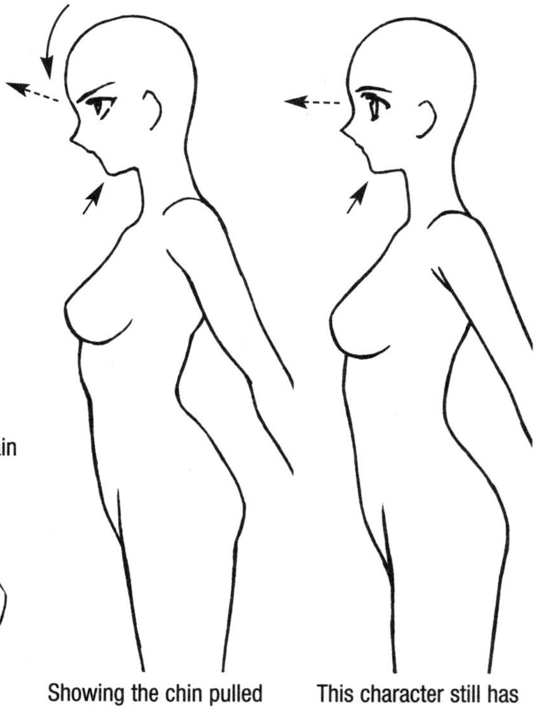

Showing the chin pulled in, glancing up under lowered brows creates a combative mood.

This character still has her chin pulled in even when looking directly at another character.

Standard Fashions

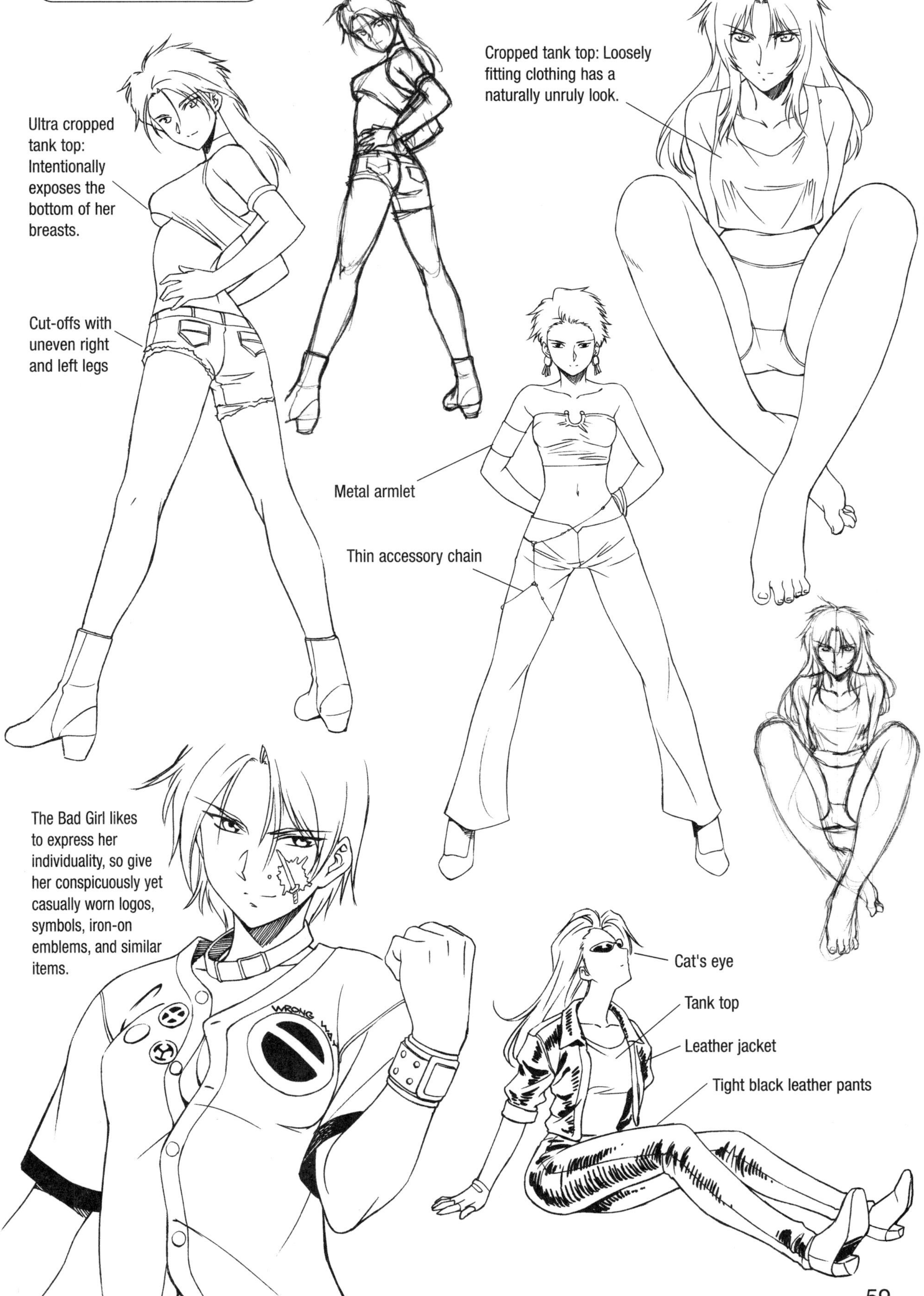

Height Distinctions

Height distinction is an important aspect of distinguishing characters. The protagonist should be used as the standard in establishing which characters are taller and shorter.

Three Categories: Average (the Standard), Tall, and Short

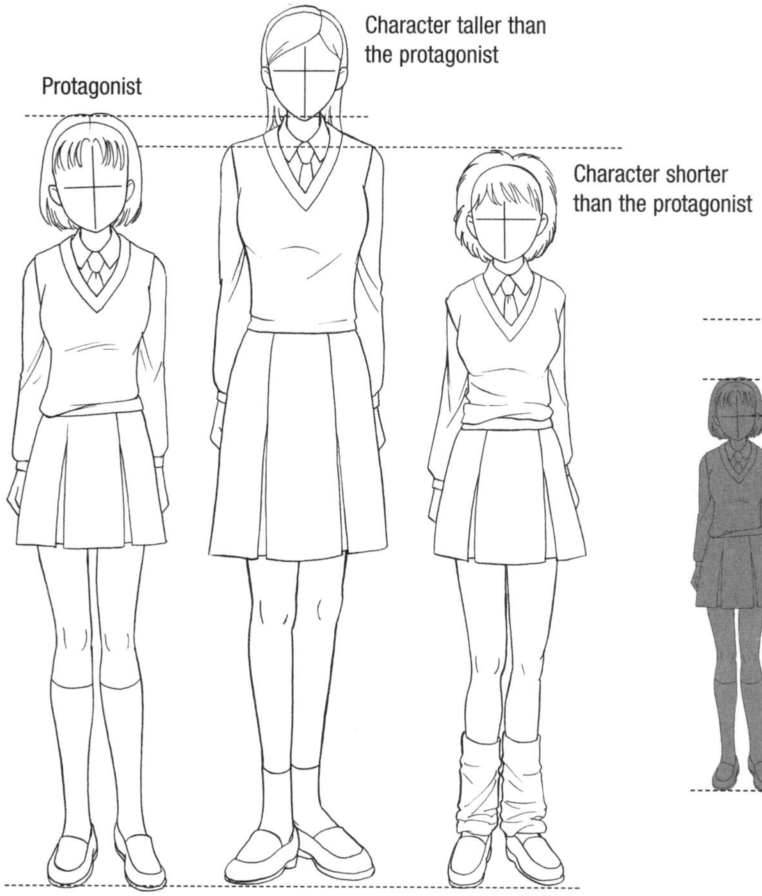

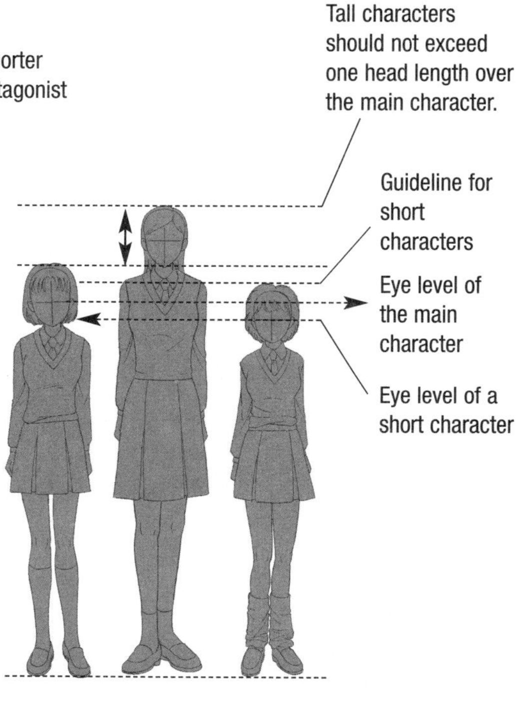

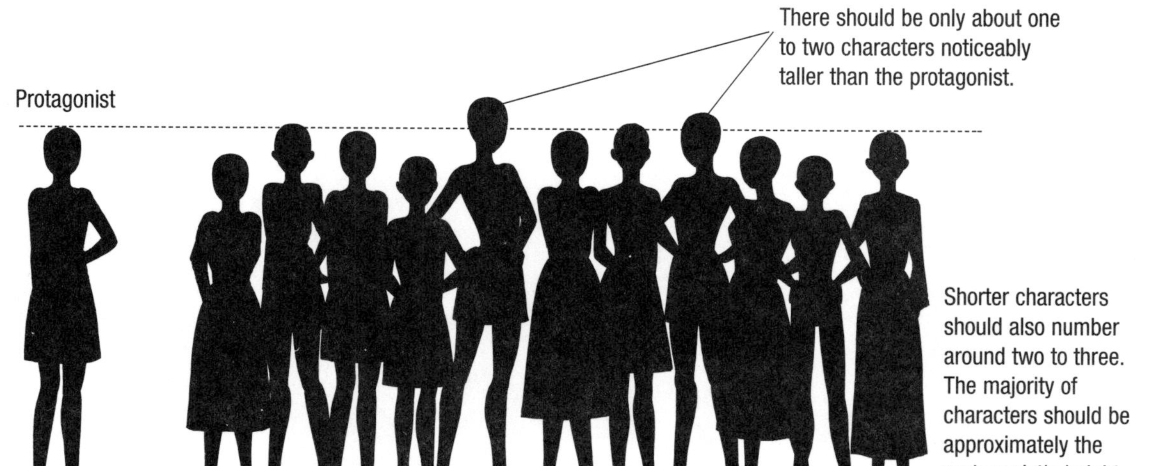

Hair Effects Exploit hair volume and style to create perceptual differences in height, even when the characters' heights are actually the same.

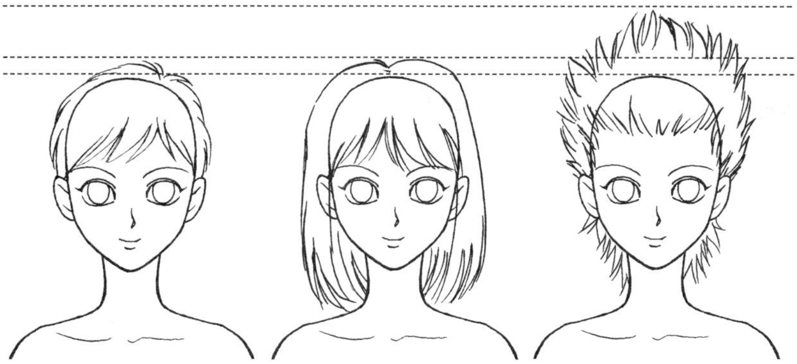

Heel Height Heel height changes how actual height is perceived.

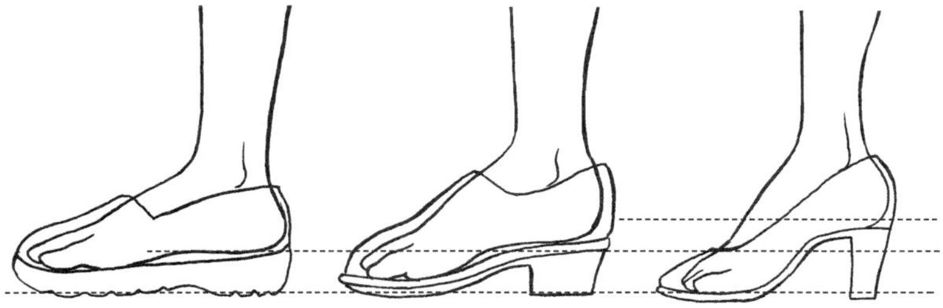

Thickly soled sneaker

Leather shoes with a medium heel

High-heeled shoe (Boots, pumps, etc.)

• Changes According to Heel Height

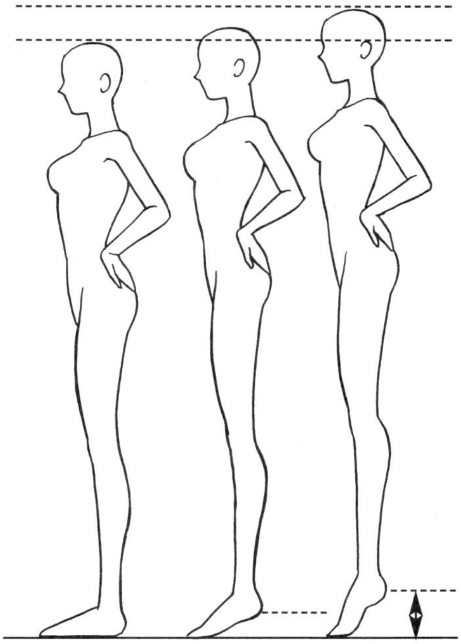

The character's height increases by the heel's height.

Key Points in Modifying Appearances

Have each character pose differently by adjusting their hands and feet. This will give you a more natural look.

• Adjusting the Face's Direction

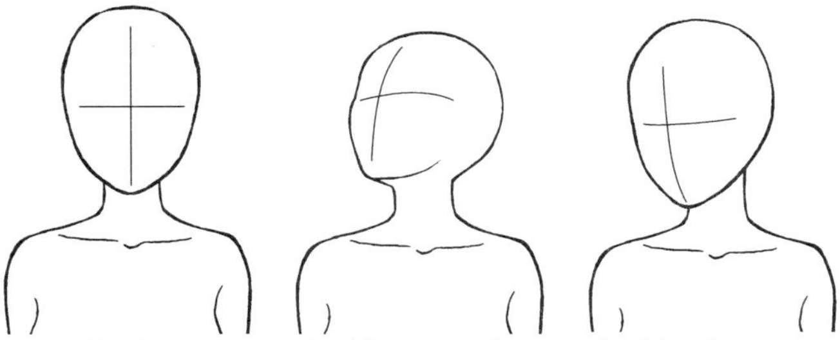

Front

Looking up, gazing absent-mindedly

Looking down, hunching forward

• Adjusting the Torso's Direction

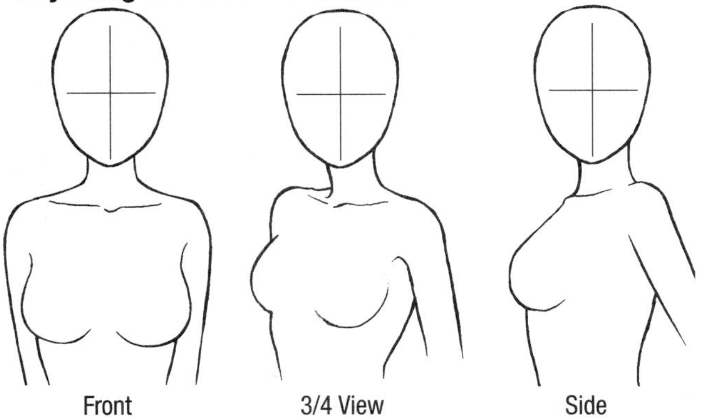

Front

3/4 View

Side

• Positioning of Hands

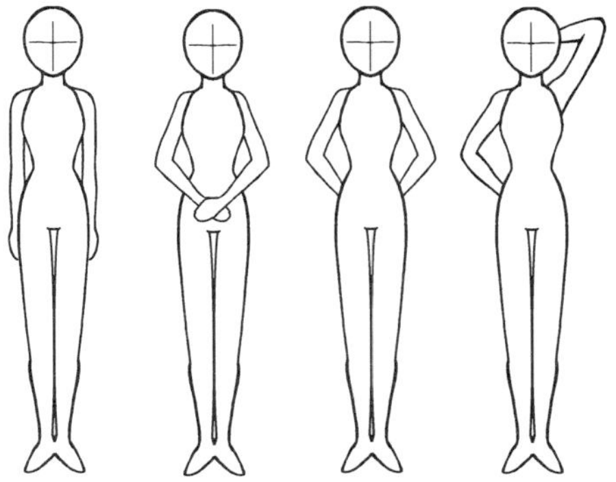

Bolt upright

Hands clasped in front

Hands clasped in back

Intentional pose

• Positioning of Feet

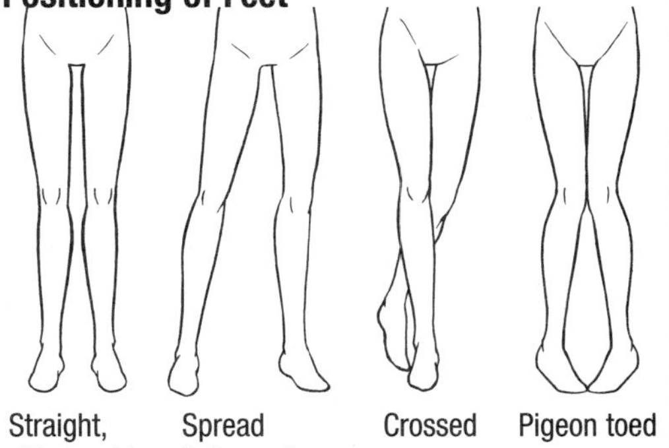

Straight, side by side

Spread "at ease"

Crossed

Pigeon toed

Height Portrayal Samples

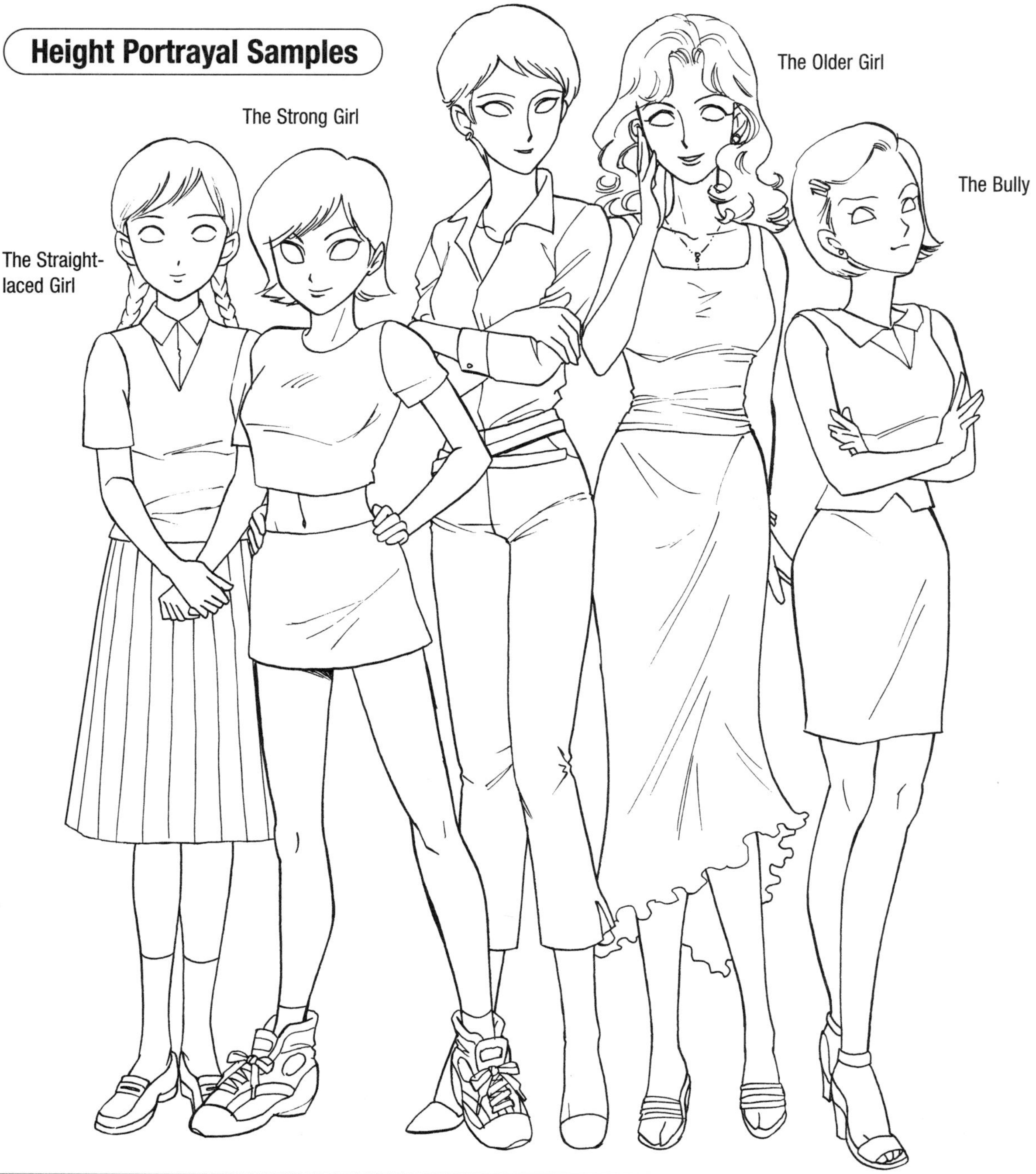

Effects in Distinguishing Height

E.g. All characters of equal height:

E.g. All characters of different height

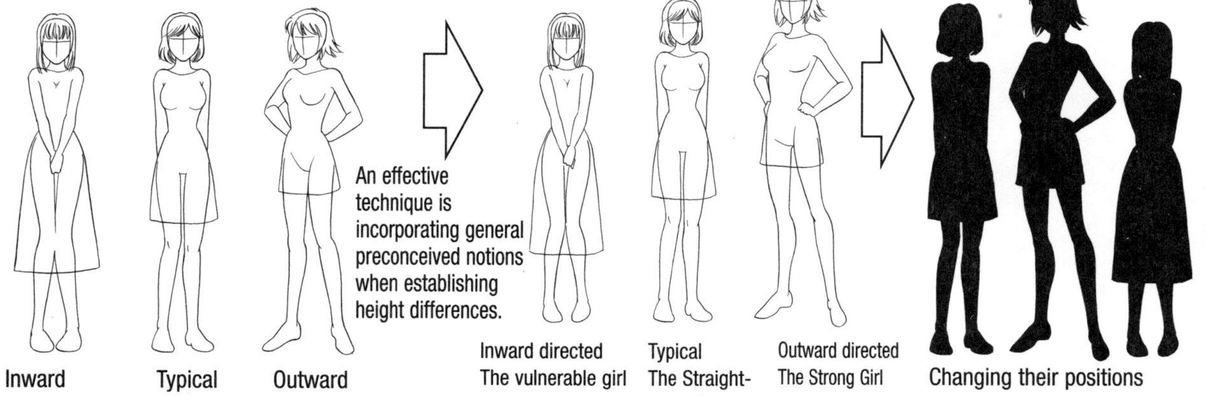

An effective technique is incorporating general preconceived notions when establishing height differences.

Changing their positions affects the visual composition.

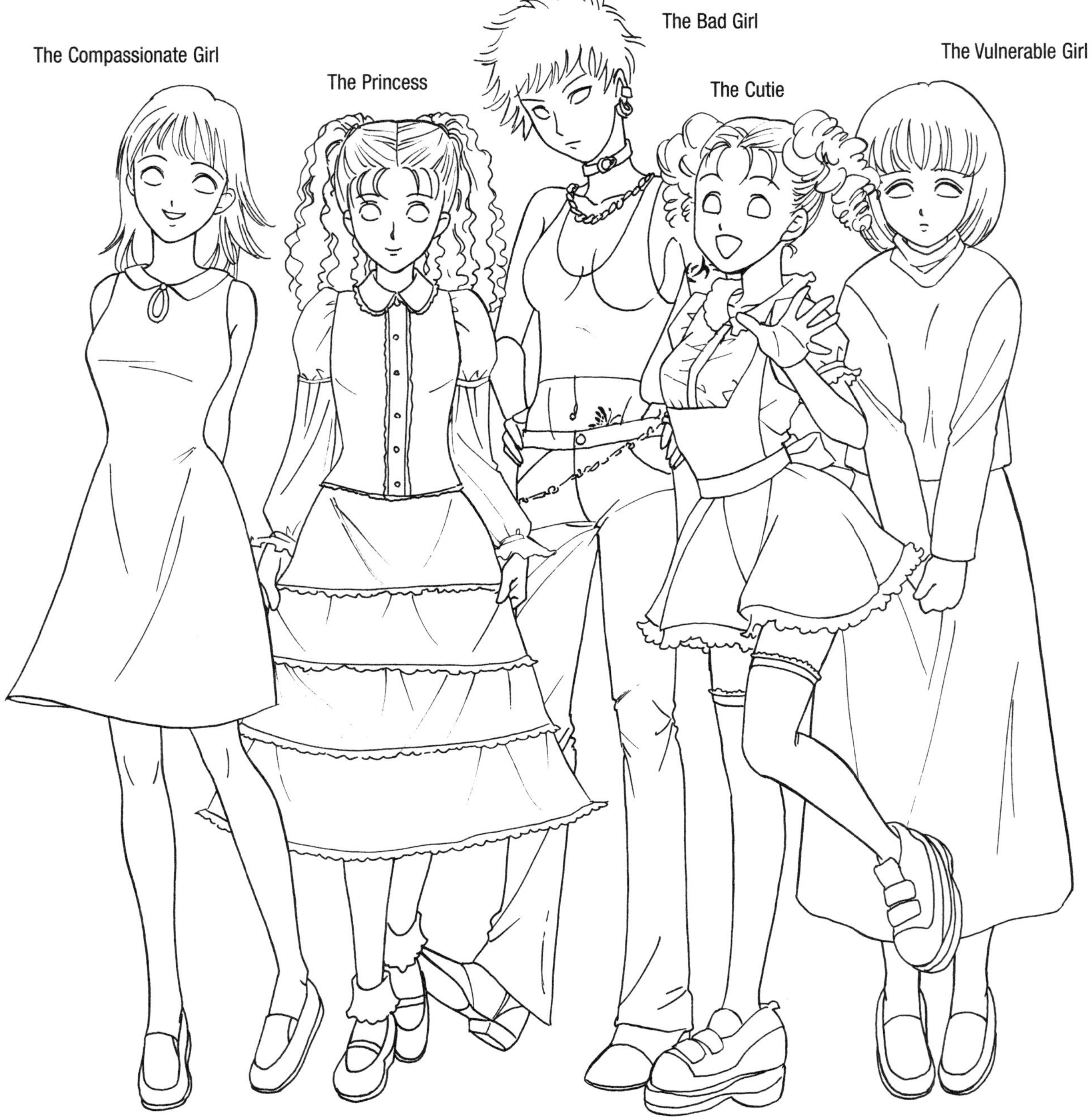

Undermining Preconceived Notions

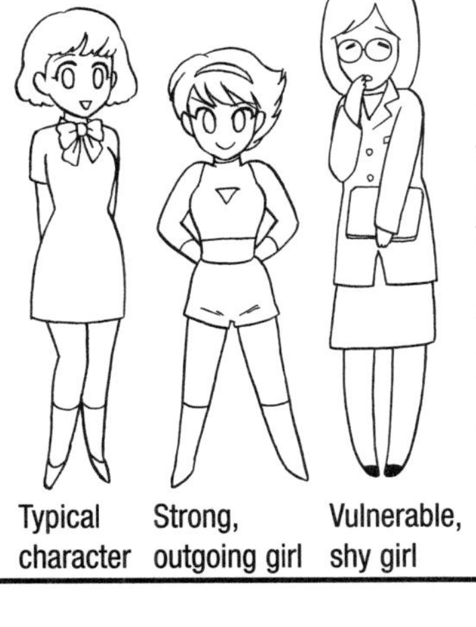

Normally, artists draw vulnerable, shy types as the smallest in stature and strong types the tallest. Here, I have intentionally made the character with the smallest image—the shy character—the tallest. This is one *manga* portrayal technique.

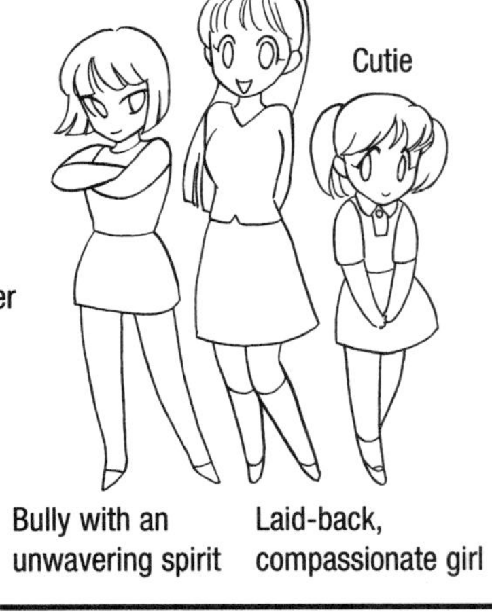

Selecting Costumes That Match the Character

Costume designing typically divides into two categories: concealing and revealing. Let's take a look using generally inactive (introverted) versus dynamic (extroverted) character types as our bases.

Concealing Fashions

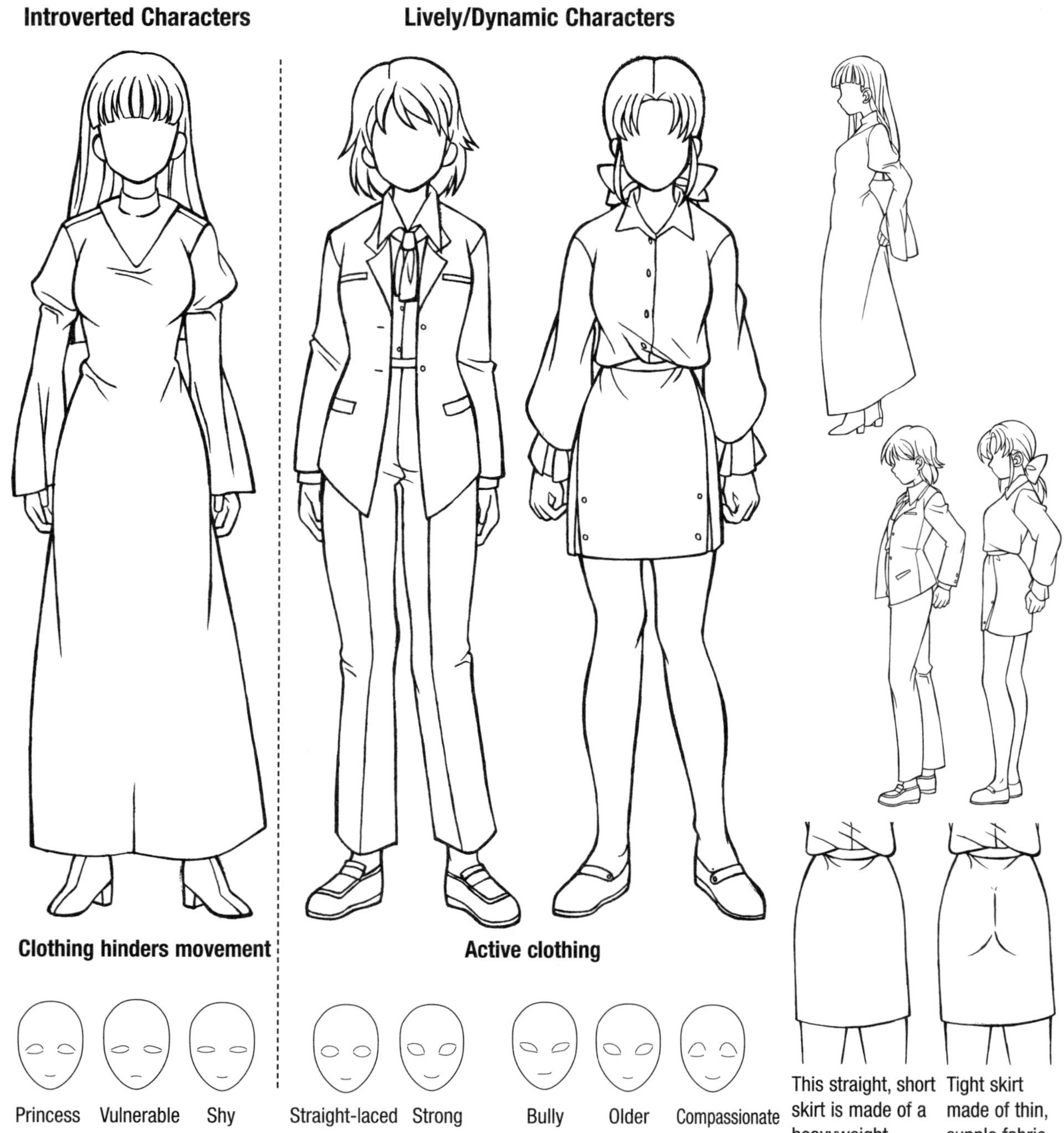

This straight, short skirt is made of a heavyweight fabric, so the shape of the posterior does not show.

Tight skirt made of thin, supple fabric

Body Conscious and Revealing Outfits

These fashions are favored for dynamic, lively (extroverted) characters.

Revealing

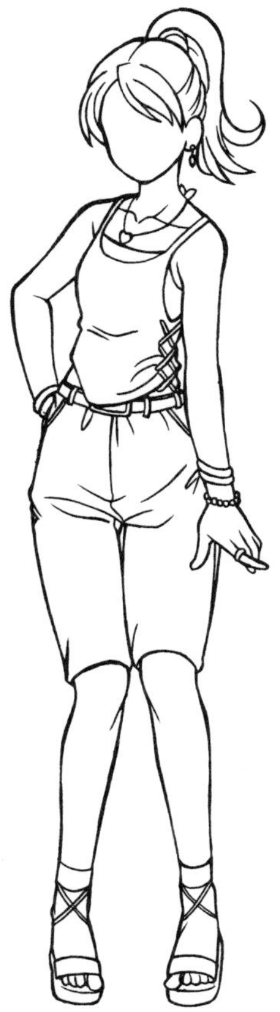

Body Conscious

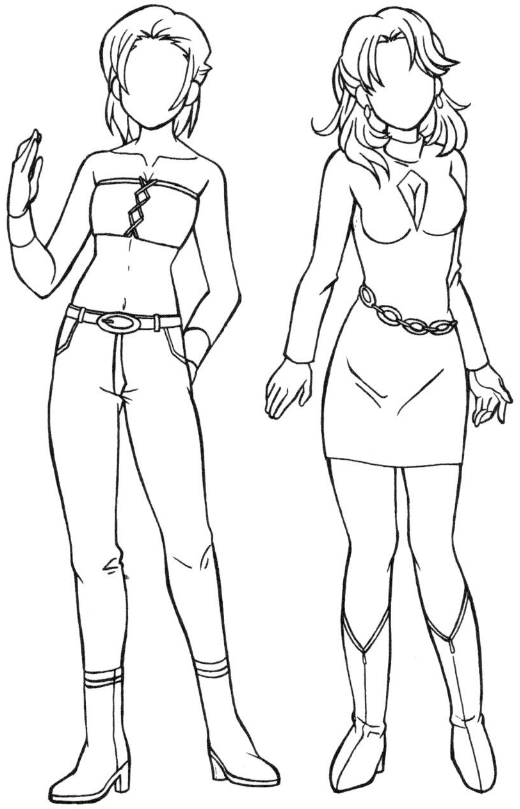

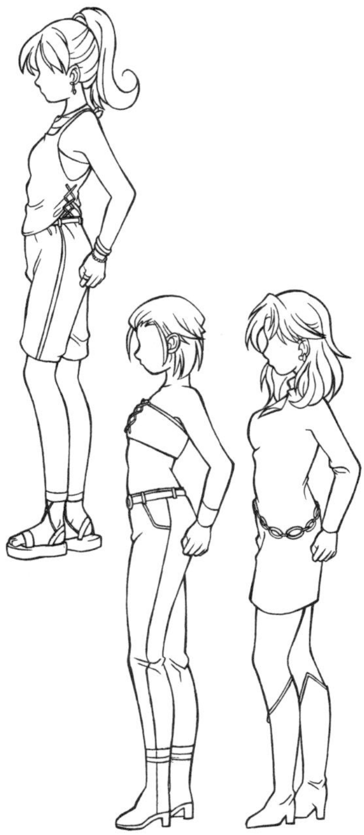

Intermediate Fashions

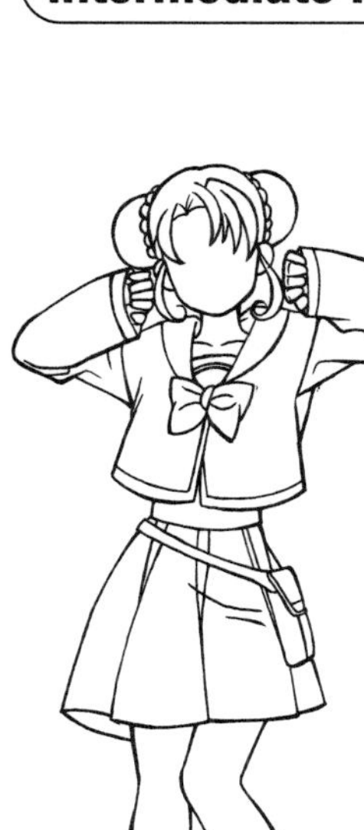

The cutie

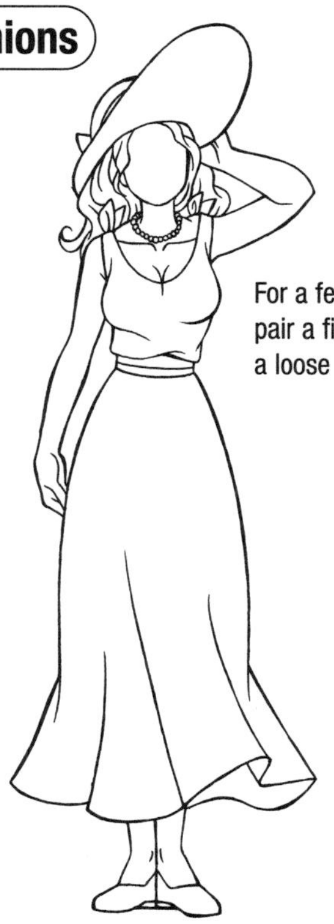

For a feminine look, pair a fitted top with a loose skirt.

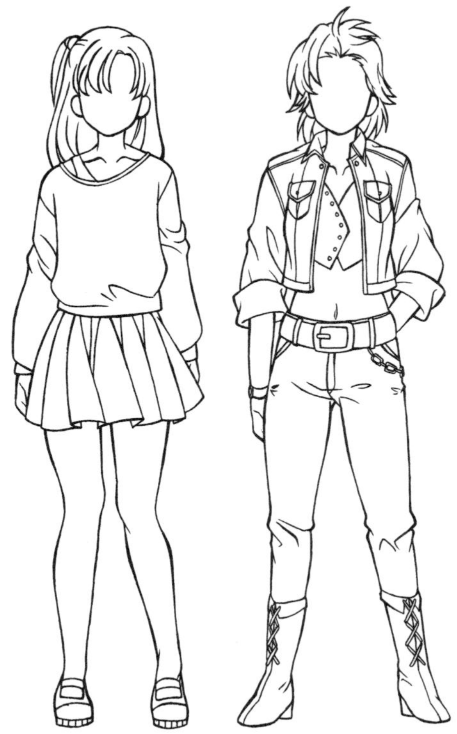

For a sloppy or tough look, pair a loose-fitting top with tight-fitting pants or a miniskirt.

Uniform Portrayal

Uniforms with Blazers

The most common uniforms in Japan consist of blazers and sailor suits. Each comes in four variations derived from the original standard.

Six Modifiable Details

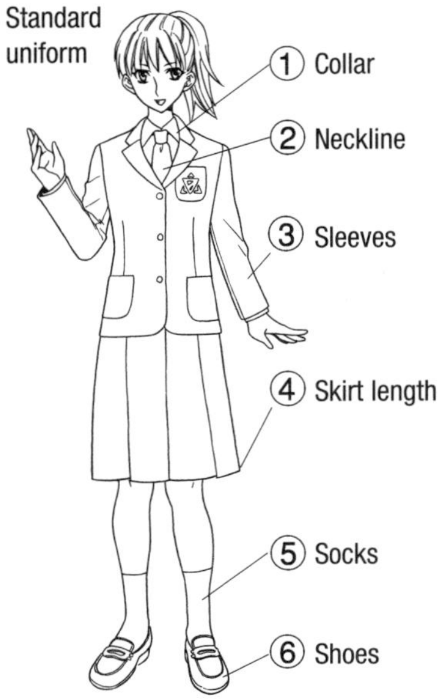

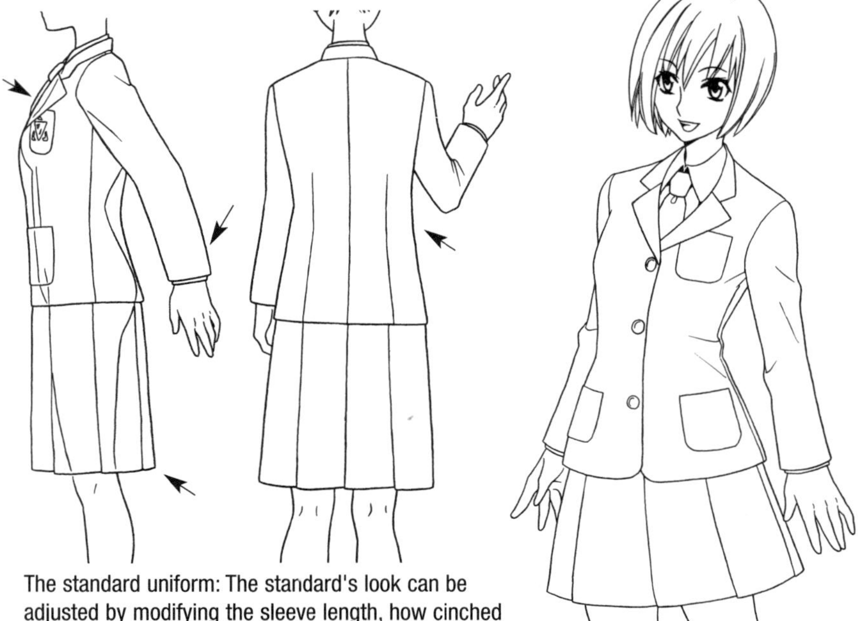

The standard uniform: The standard's look can be adjusted by modifying the sleeve length, how cinched the uniform is at the waist, seams, and other details according to personal taste.

Four Common Variations

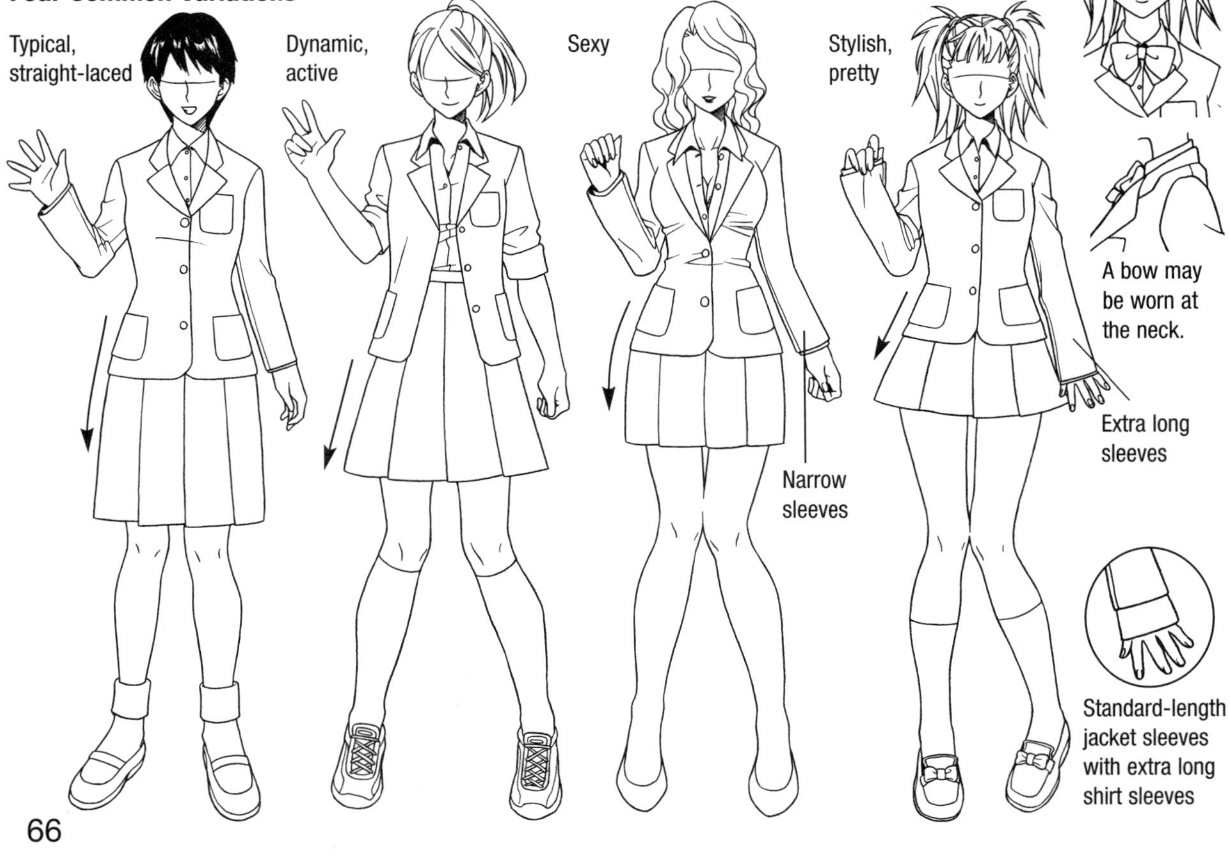

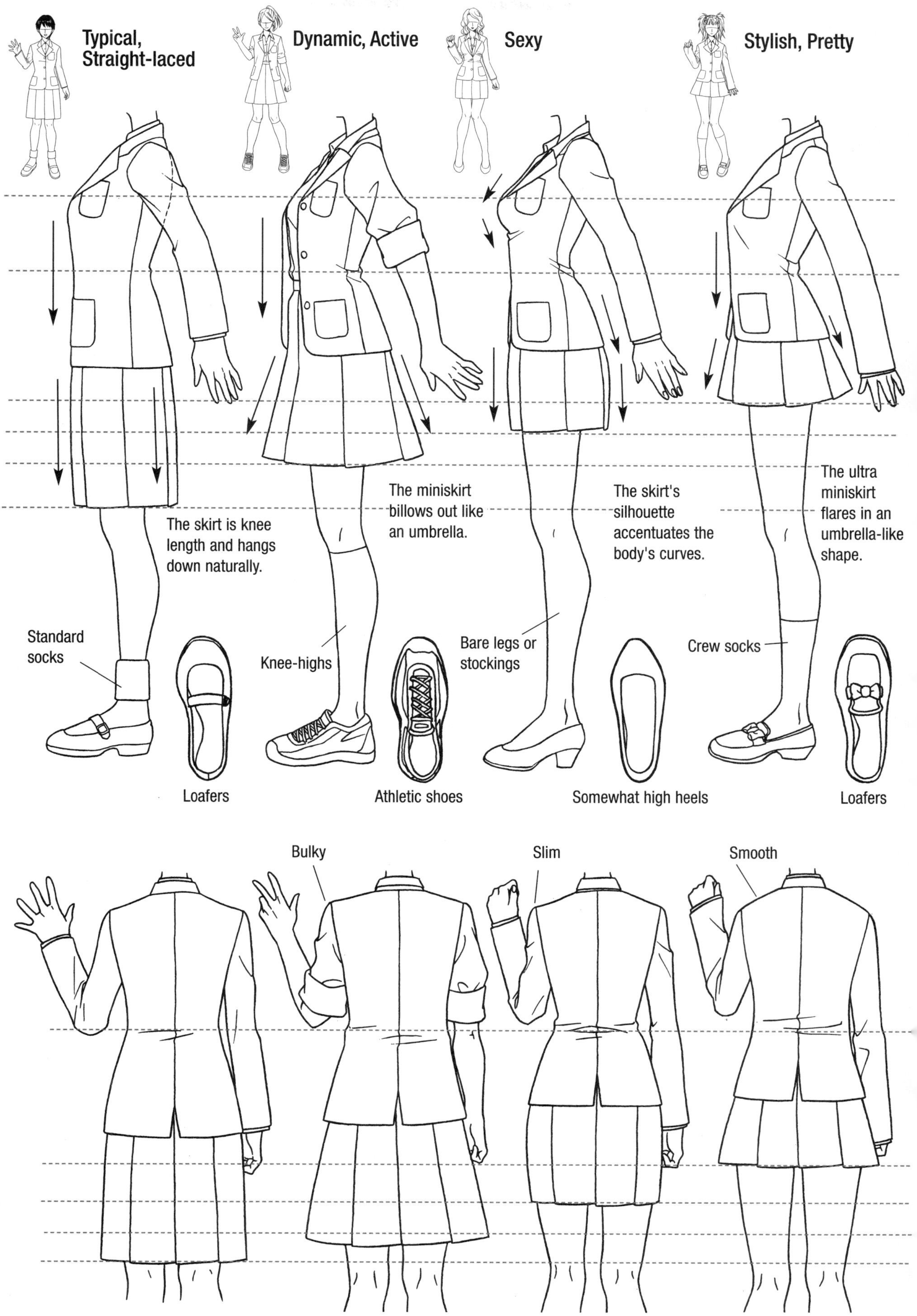
Typical, Straight-laced
Dynamic, Active
Sexy
Stylish, Pretty
The skirt is knee length and hangs down naturally.
The miniskirt billows out like an umbrella.
The skirt's silhouette accentuates the body's curves.
The ultra miniskirt flares in an umbrella-like shape.
Standard socks
Knee-highs
Bare legs or stockings
Crew socks
Loafers
Athletic shoes
Somewhat high heels
Loafers
Bulky
Slim
Smooth

Glancing over the Shoulder

Typical, Straight-laced

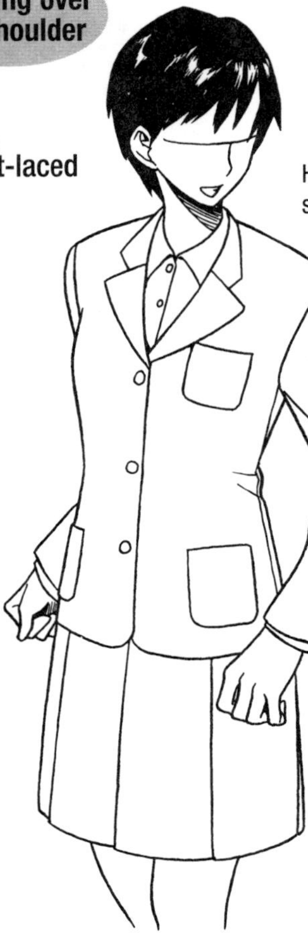

Dynamic, Active

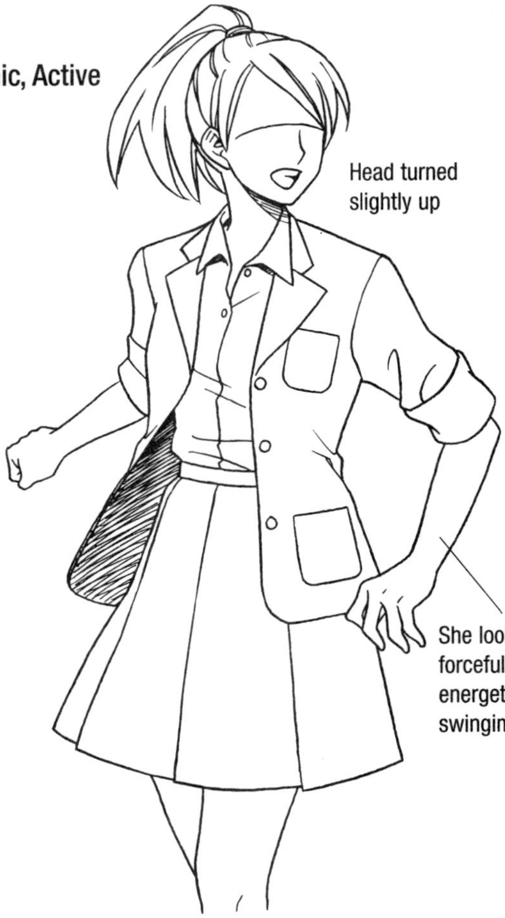

Sexy

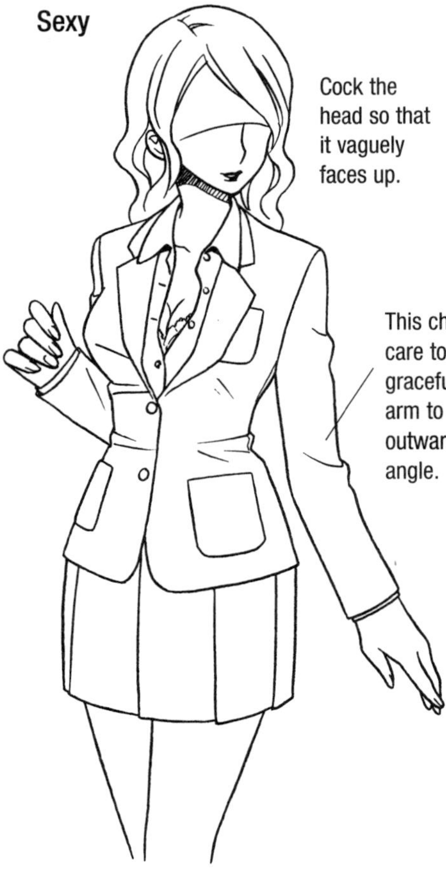

Stylish, Pretty

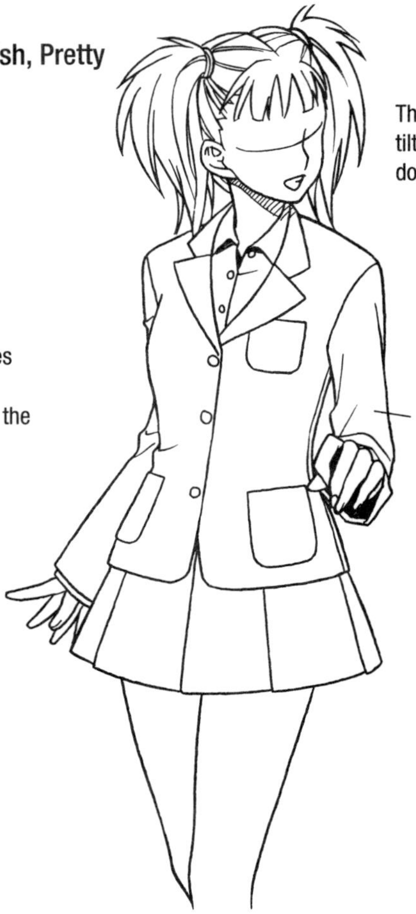

Sitting

Each character should have her own style of cocking her head, or placing or hands and feet.

Typical, Straight-laced

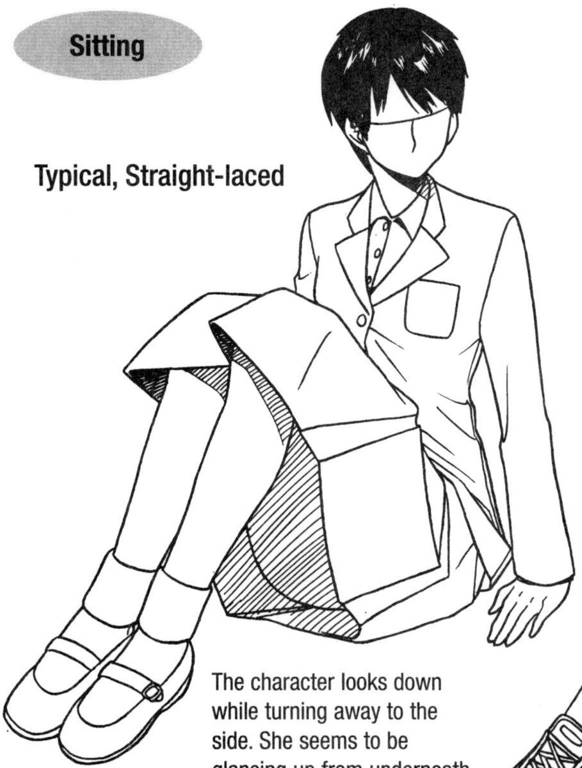

The character looks down while turning away to the side. She seems to be glancing up from underneath her brows, creating a tense or anxious mood.

Dynamic, Active

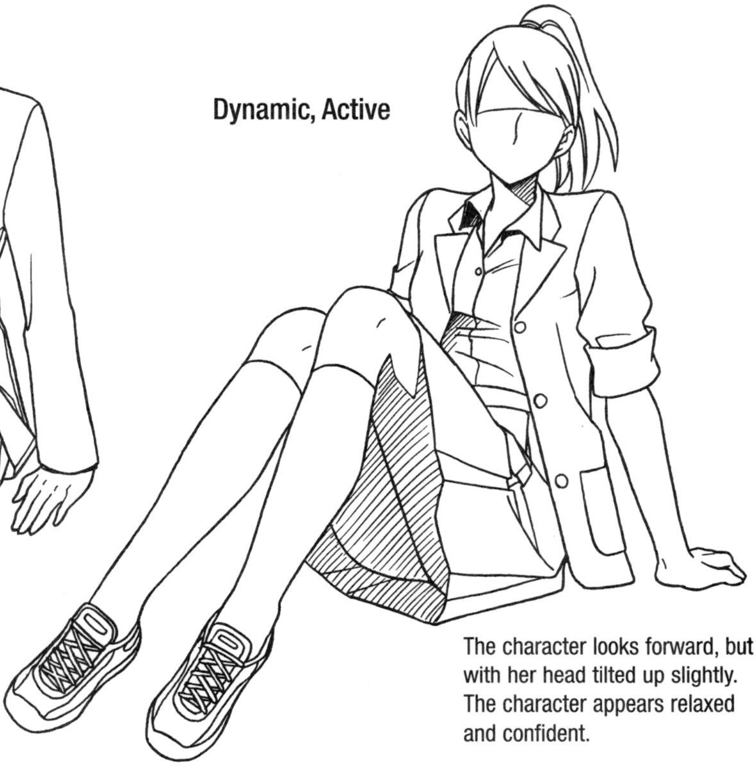

The character looks forward, but with her head tilted up slightly. The character appears relaxed and confident.

Sexy

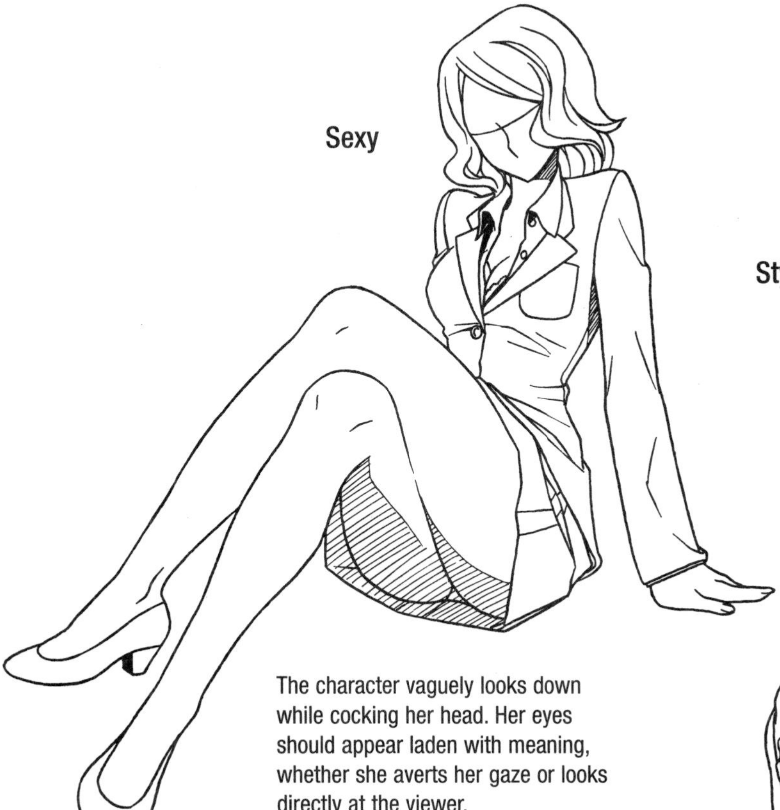

The character vaguely looks down while cocking her head. Her eyes should appear laden with meaning, whether she averts her gaze or looks directly at the viewer.

Stylish, Pretty

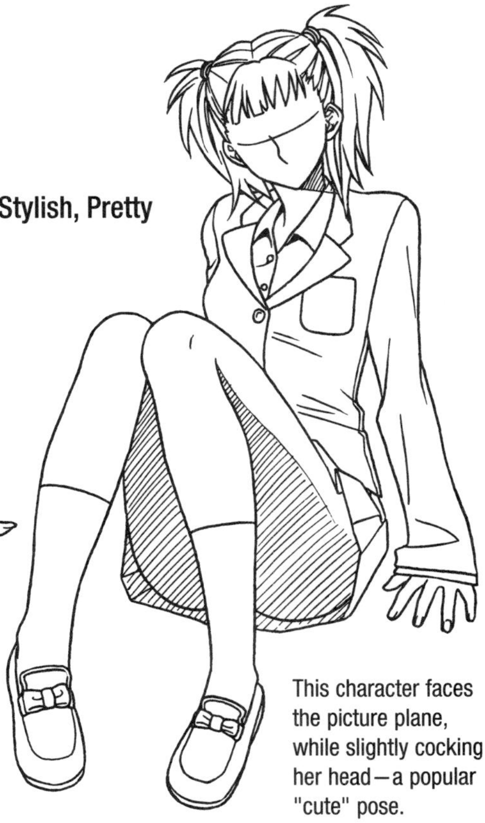

This character faces the picture plane, while slightly cocking her head—a popular "cute" pose.

Sailor Suits

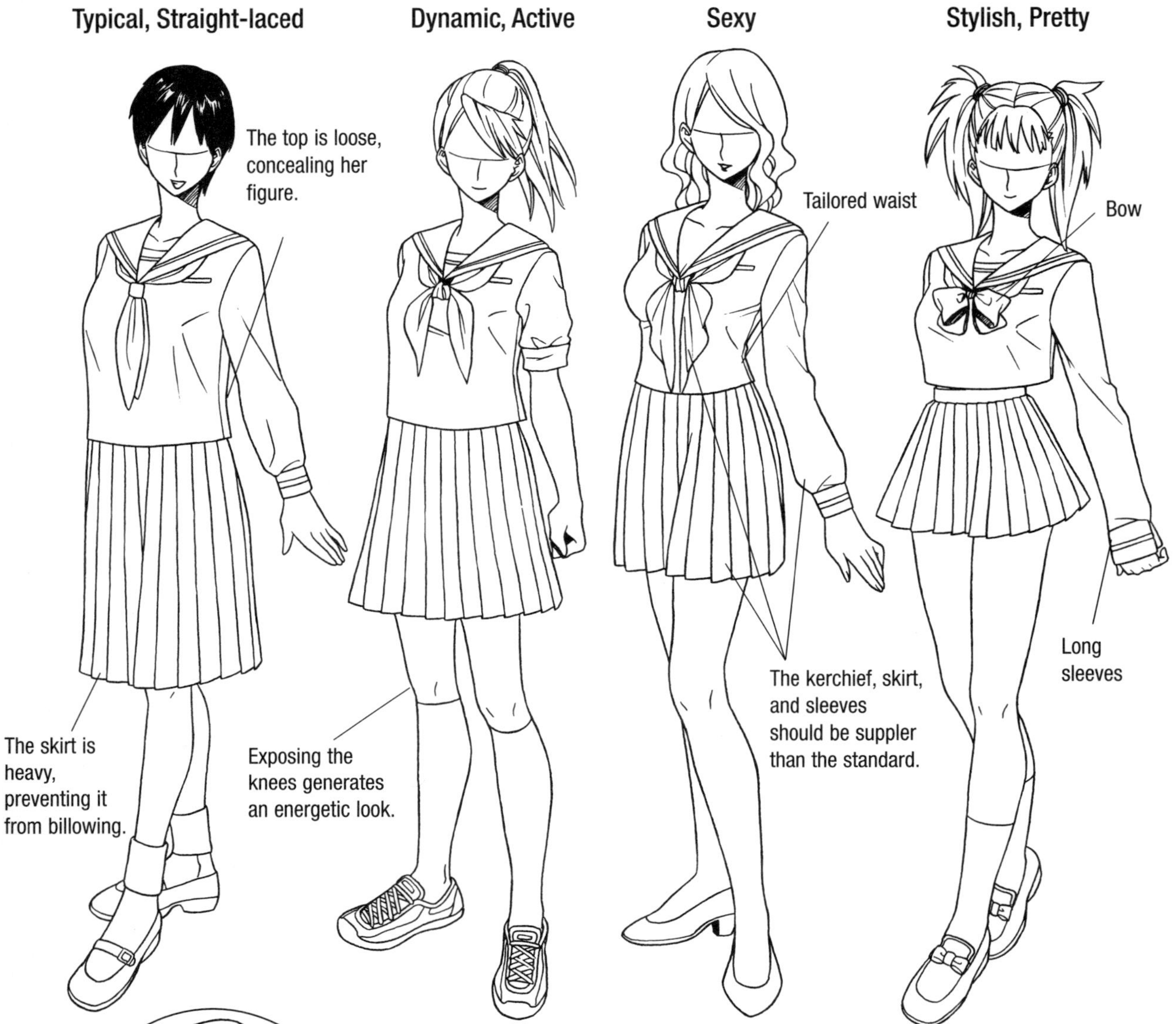

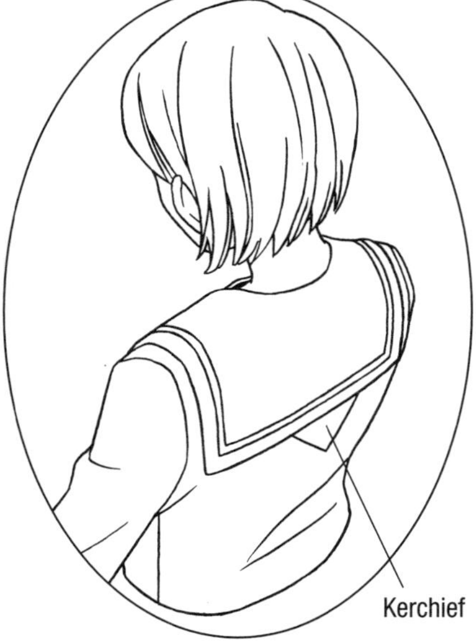

Back view of standard sailor collar: All variations share the same collar.

Kerchief The kerchiefs may either be slipped through a ring or tied. With kerchiefs coming in a range of suppleness, stylistic variations are plentiful.

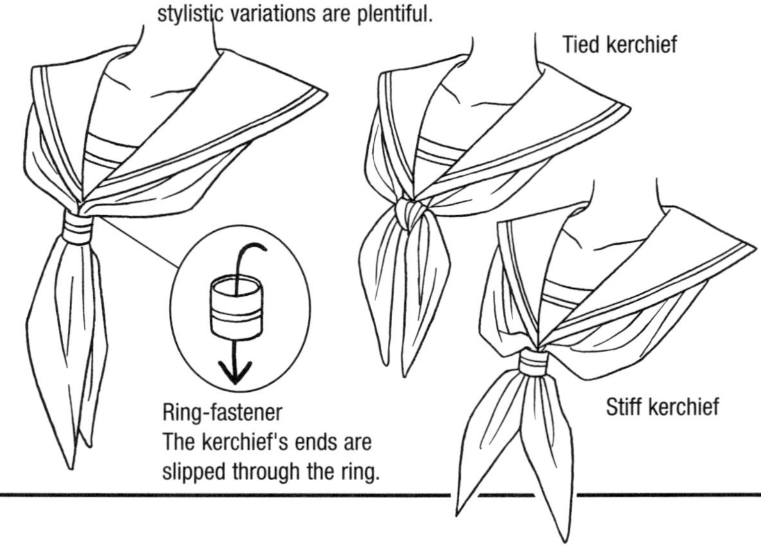

Running

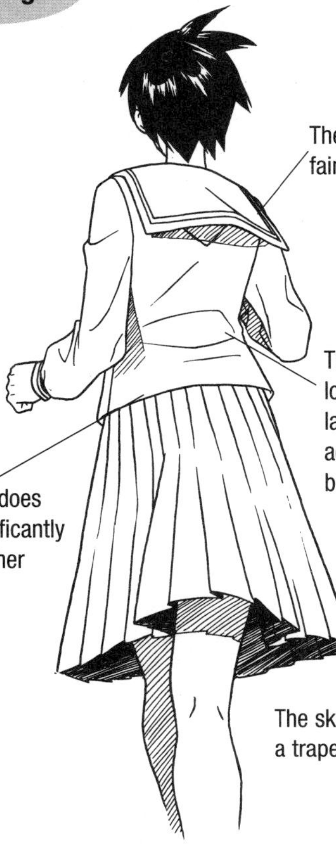
The sailor collar faintly flutters.
The blouse has a loose fit, allowing large creases to form according to the body's movements.
The blouse does not lift significantly away from her torso.
The skirt billows in a trapezoidal shape.

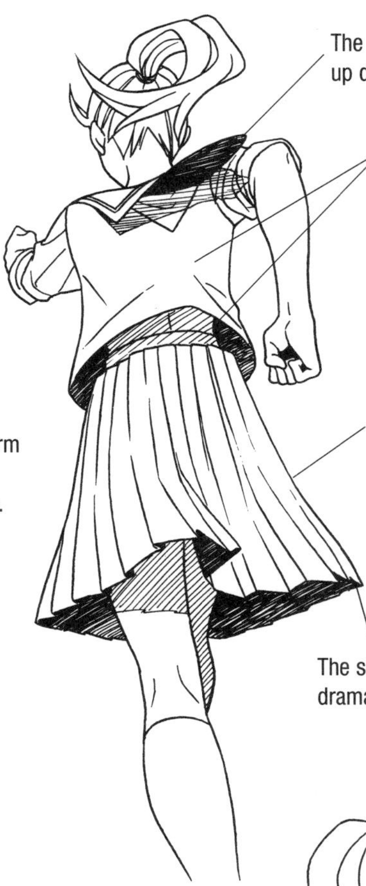
The sailor collar flips up dramatically.
This blouse has an exceedingly loose fit, allowing the fabric to lift away from the torso. Shallow creases form according to the fabric's movement.
The skirt begins to flare about halfway down its length.
The skirt billows dramatically.

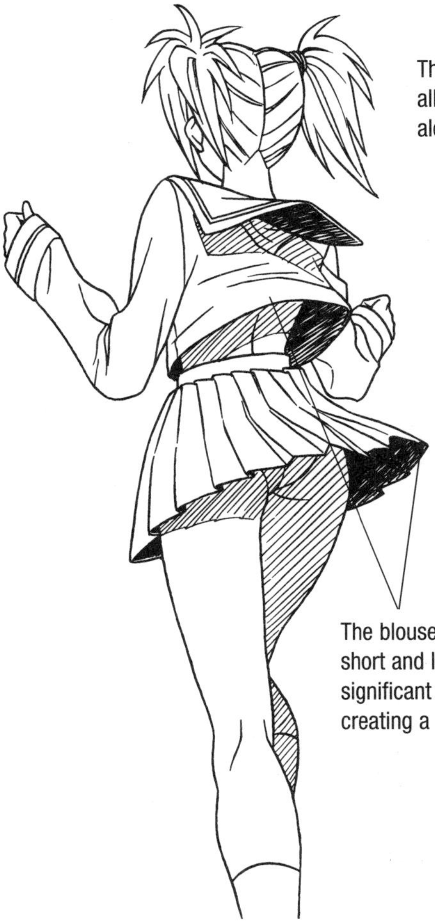
The blouse and skirt are short and light, giving them significant lift, and thus creating a charming image.

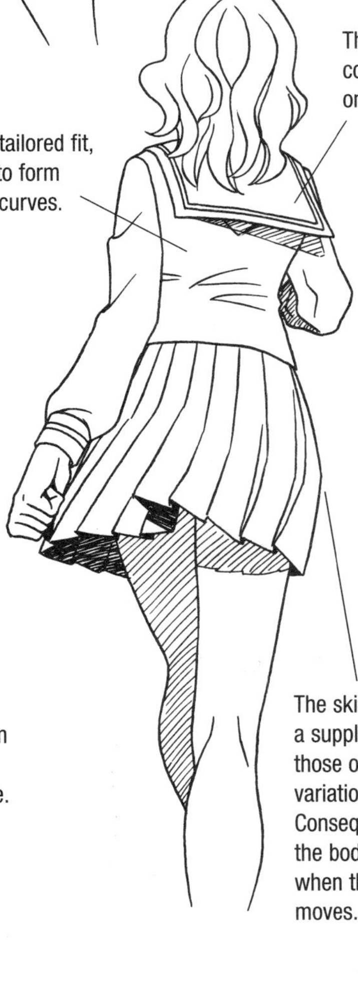
The sailor collar flutters only slightly.
The blouse has a tailored fit, allowing creases to form along the waist's curves.
The skirt is made of a suppler fabric than those of the other variations. Consequently, it hugs the body's contours when the character moves.

Tricks to Designing Uniforms for the Twelve Character Types

In addition to blazer-style uniforms and sailor suits, uniforms can come with jackets or sweaters, or in dress form. Match different collars, sleeves, skirts, shoes, and other separates to modify your designs.

Key Design Points

• Collars

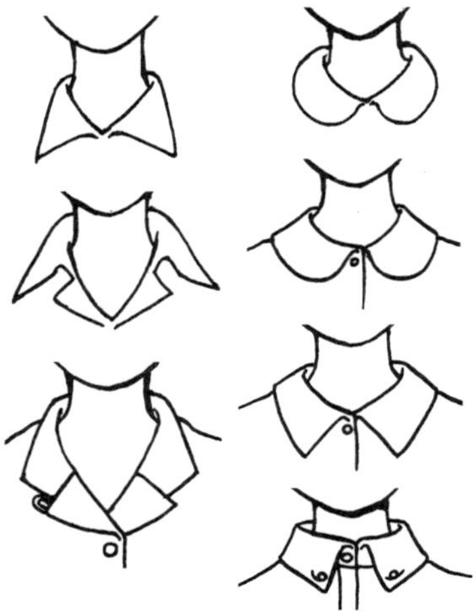

• Neckties

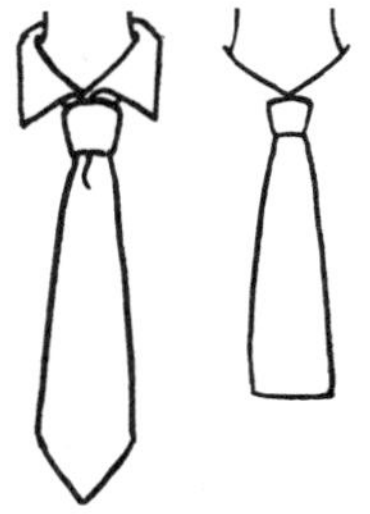

Adjust the length and width.

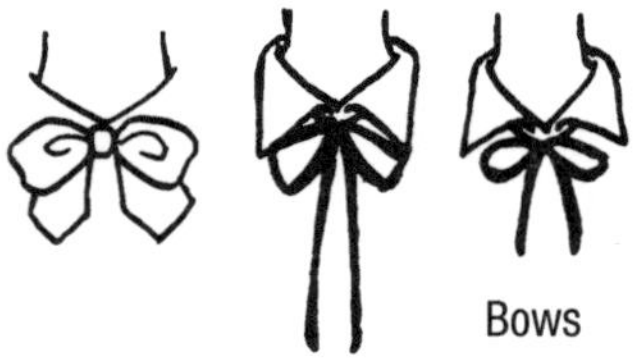

Bows

• Popular Sock Styles

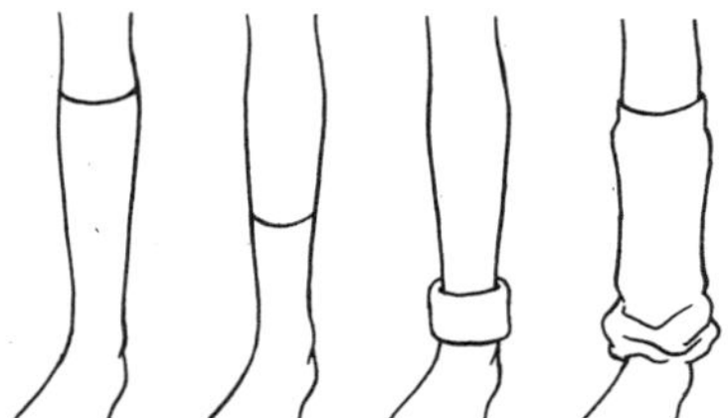

Blazer-Style Uniforms

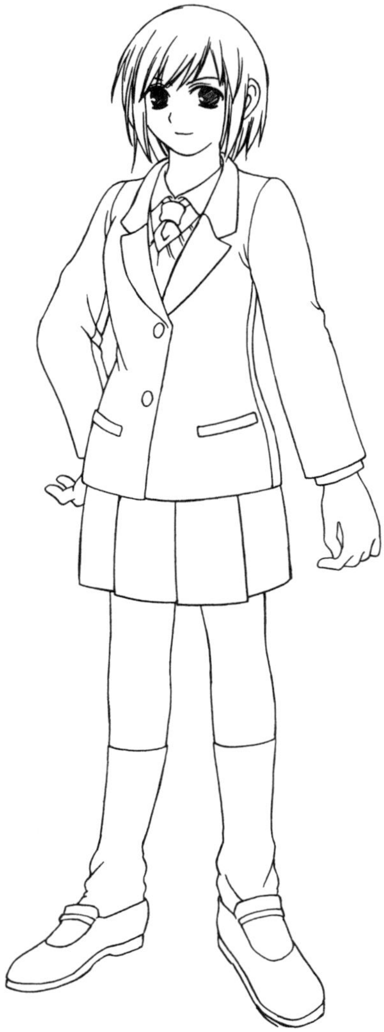

• Popular Shoe Styles

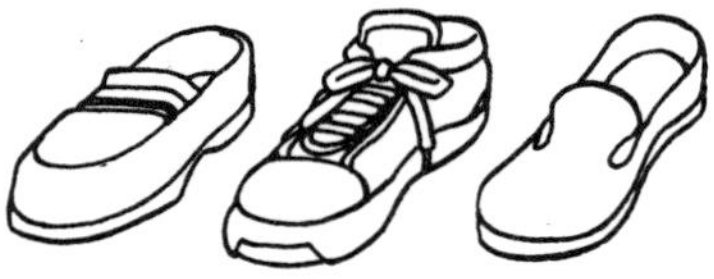

• Two Main Vest Types

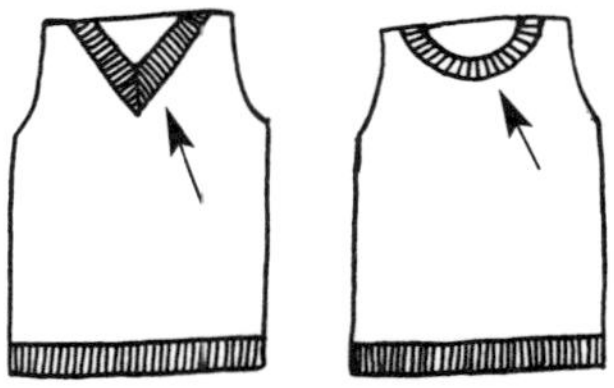

Adjust the deepness of the neckline to expand design possibilities.

• Jackets

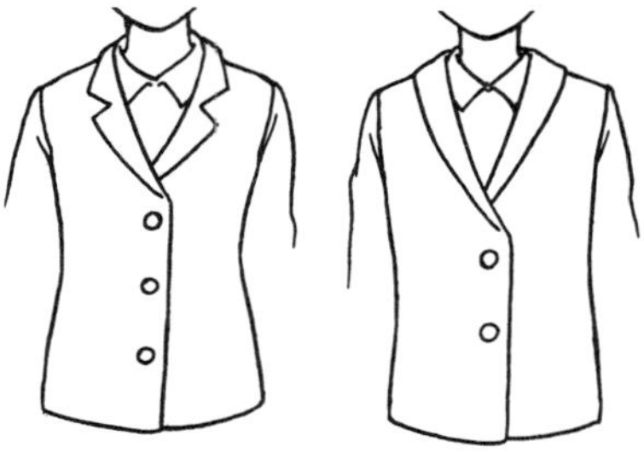

The collar generally comes in two forms: two-button and three-button.

• Common Skirt Styles

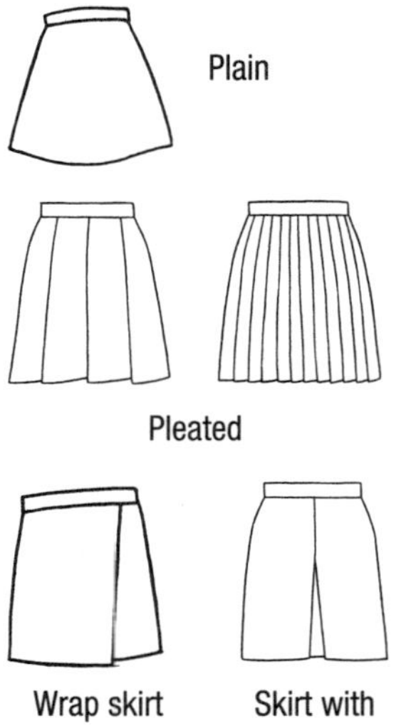

Essential Items: Pockets and School Insignia

Adjusting the school insignia or pocket's shape creates the look of a different school's uniform even without modifying the blazer design.

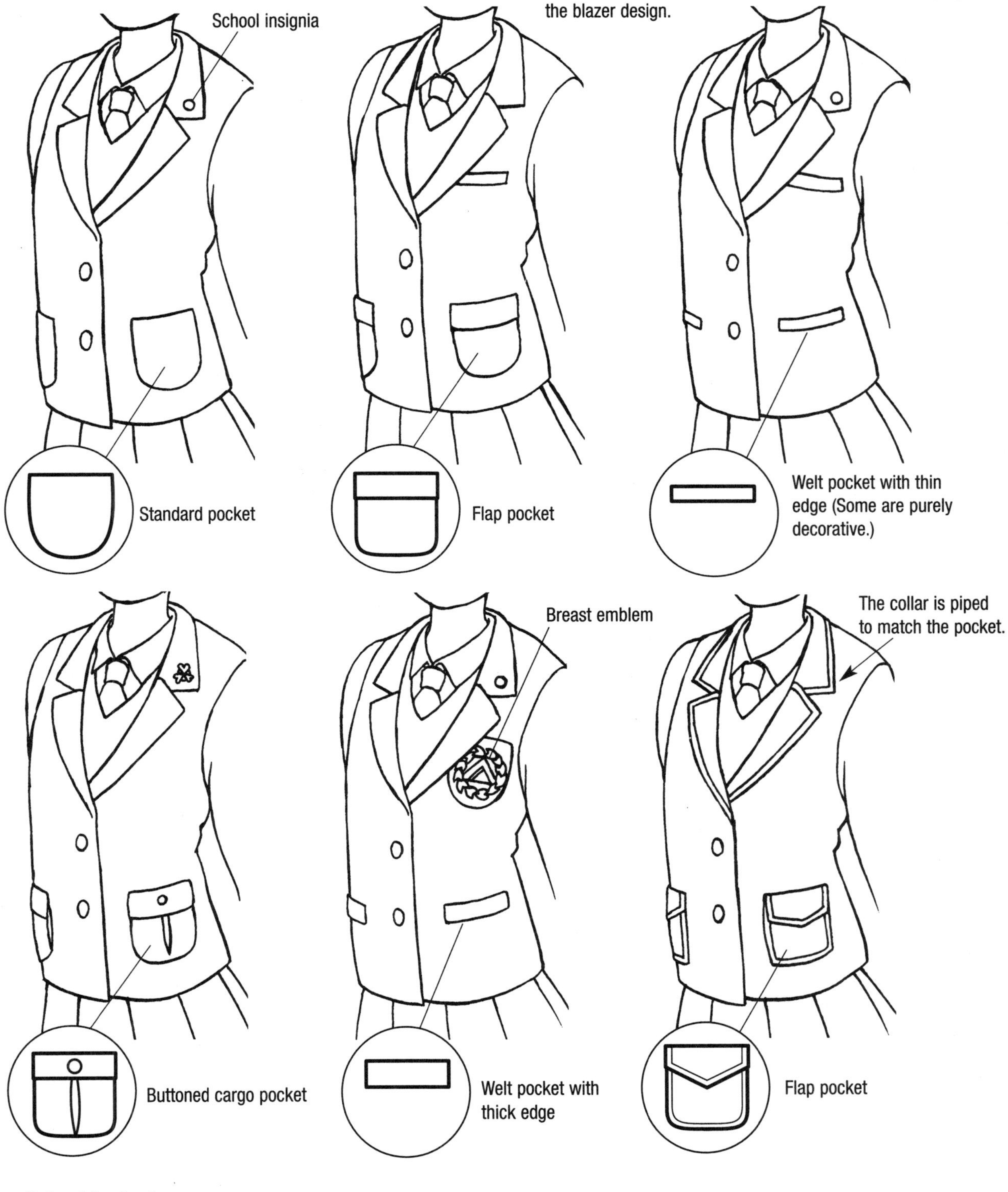

School Insignia

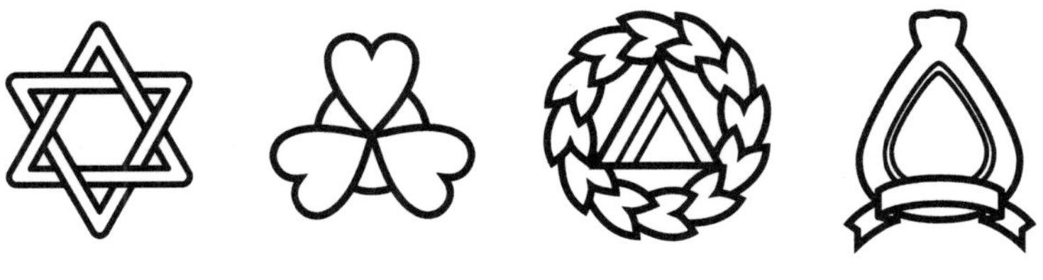

For easy insignia designing, take a simple shape and then repeat it.

Blazer-Style Uniforms

Design uniforms so that they can be distinguished from a distance at a single glance. Take care to make the collar, skirt, socks, shoes, and sleeves different for each uniform.

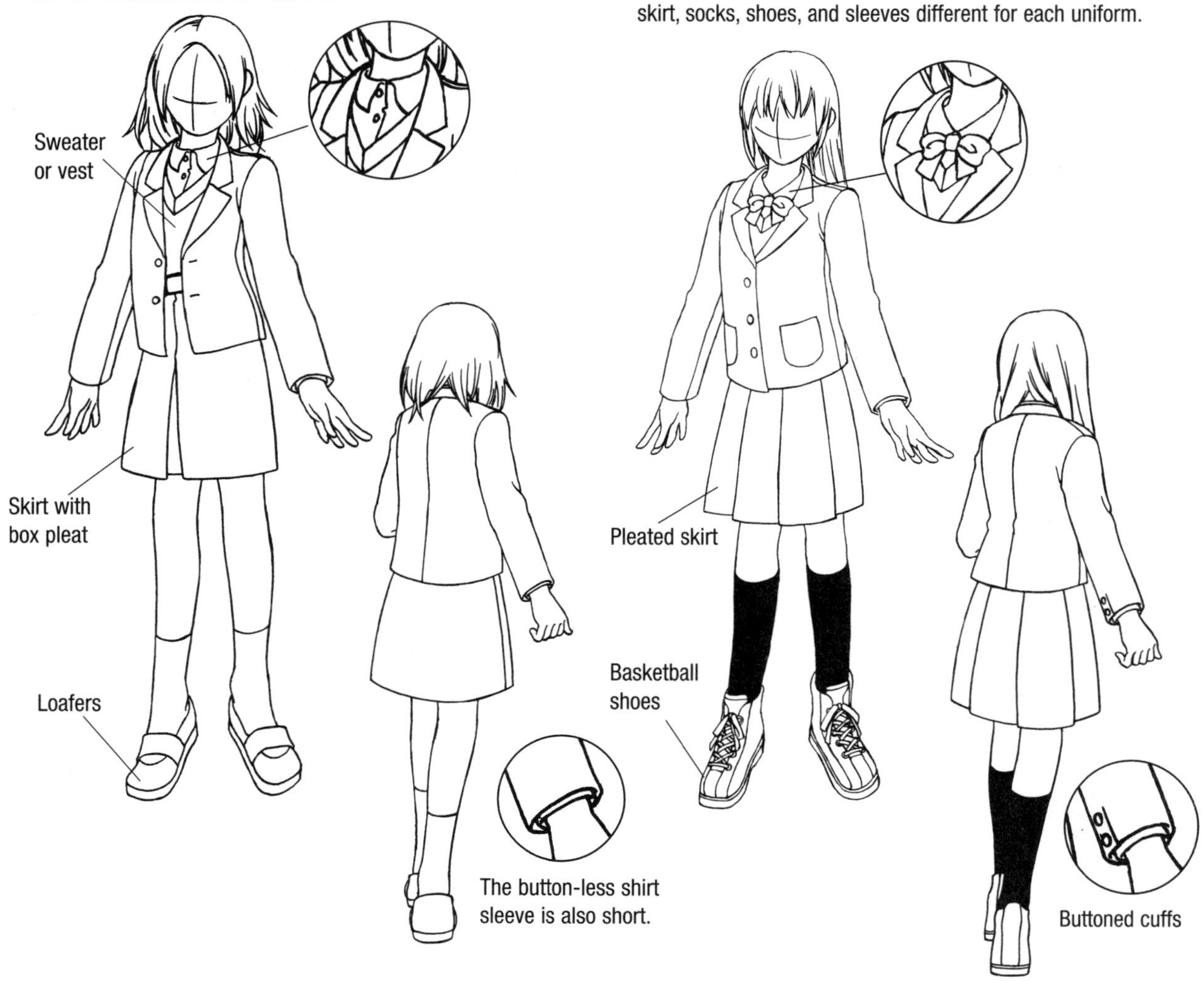

Point for Consideration: The Jacket Collar

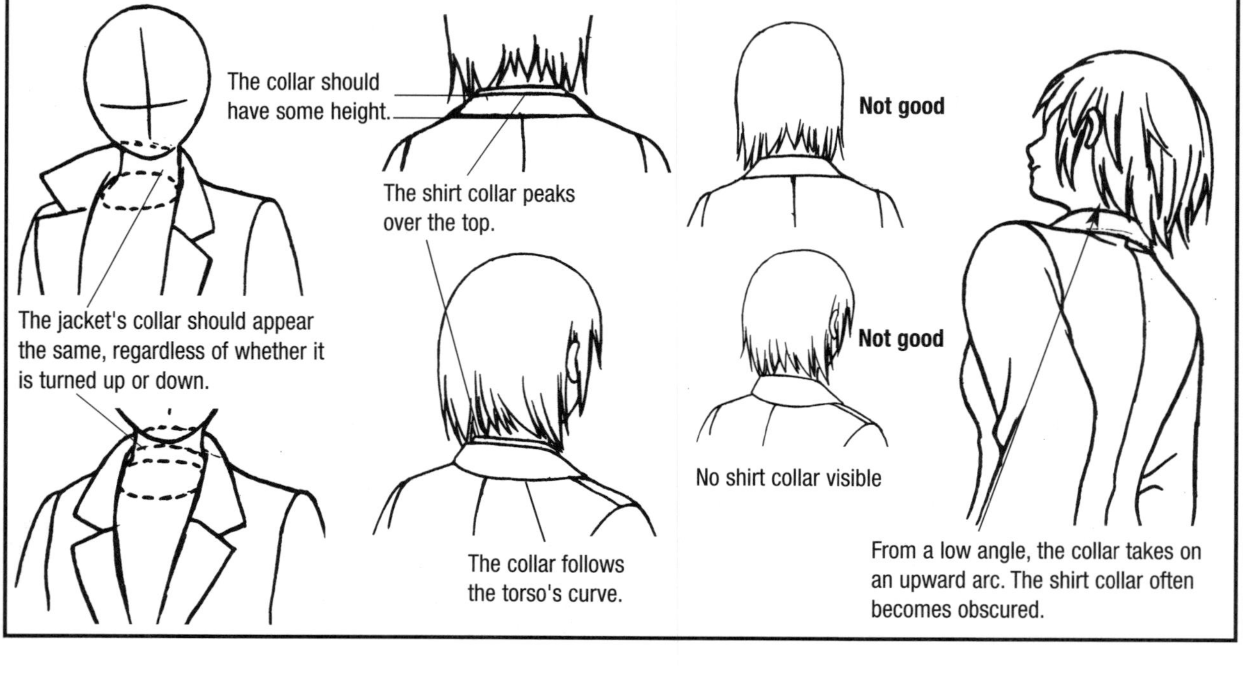

Jacket-Style Uniform

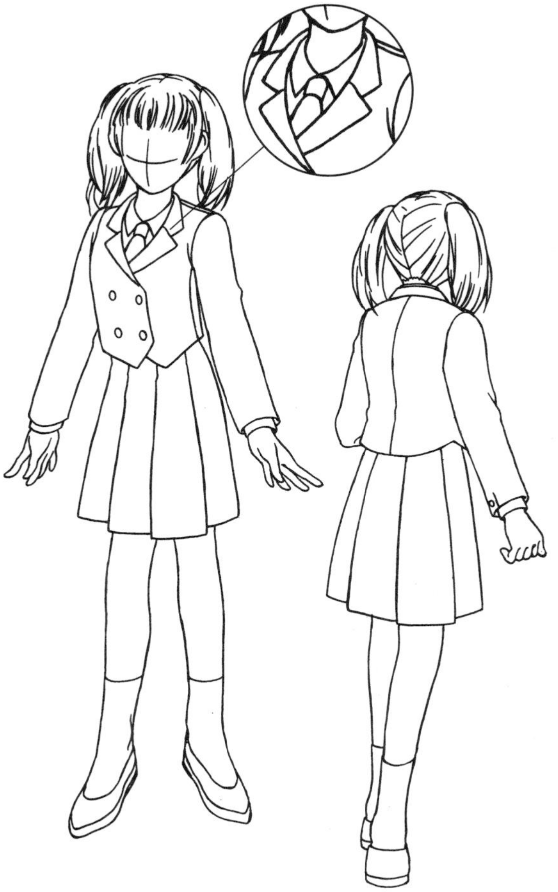

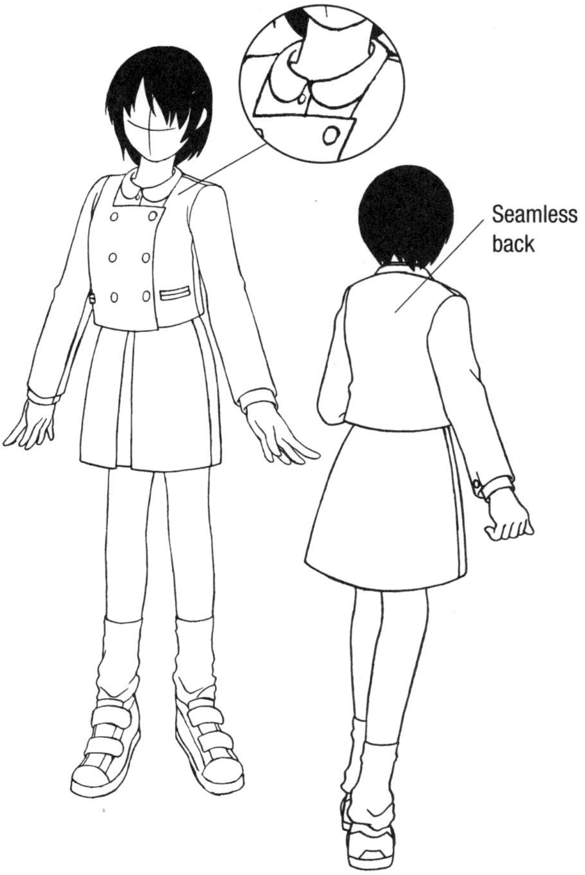

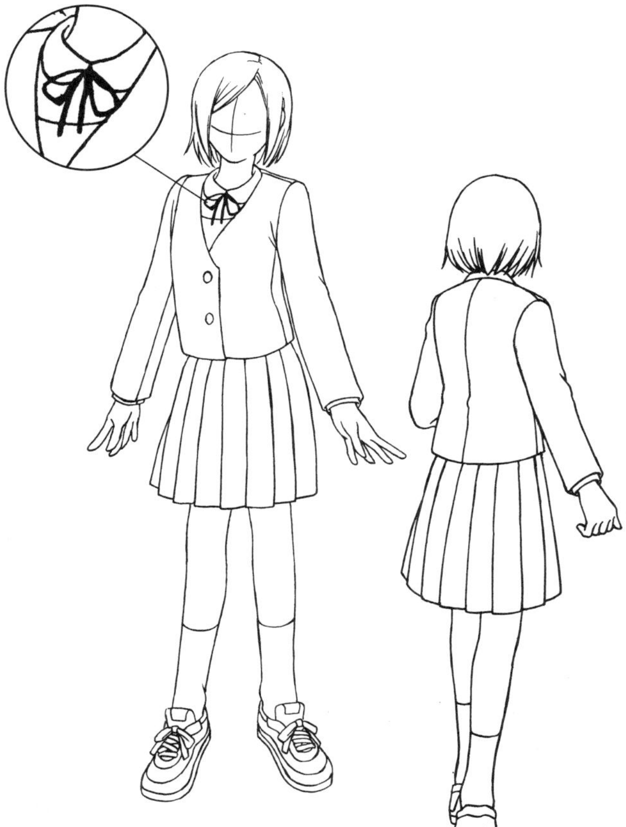

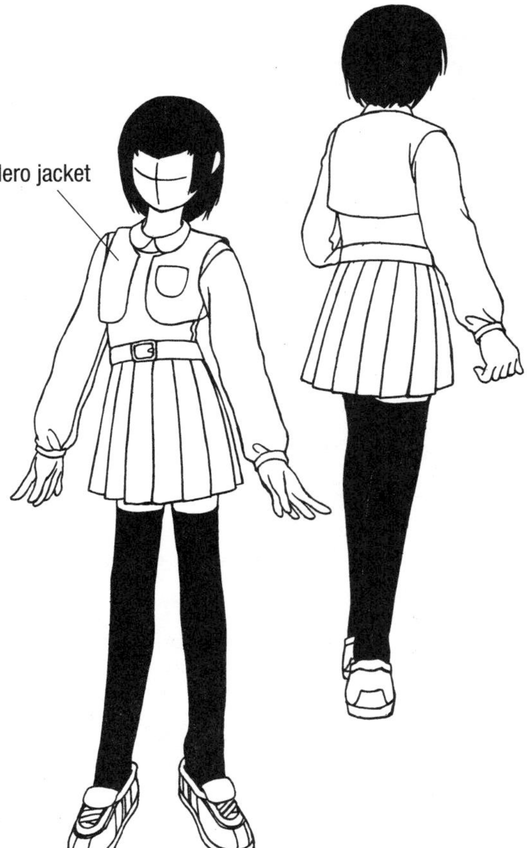

Sailor Suits

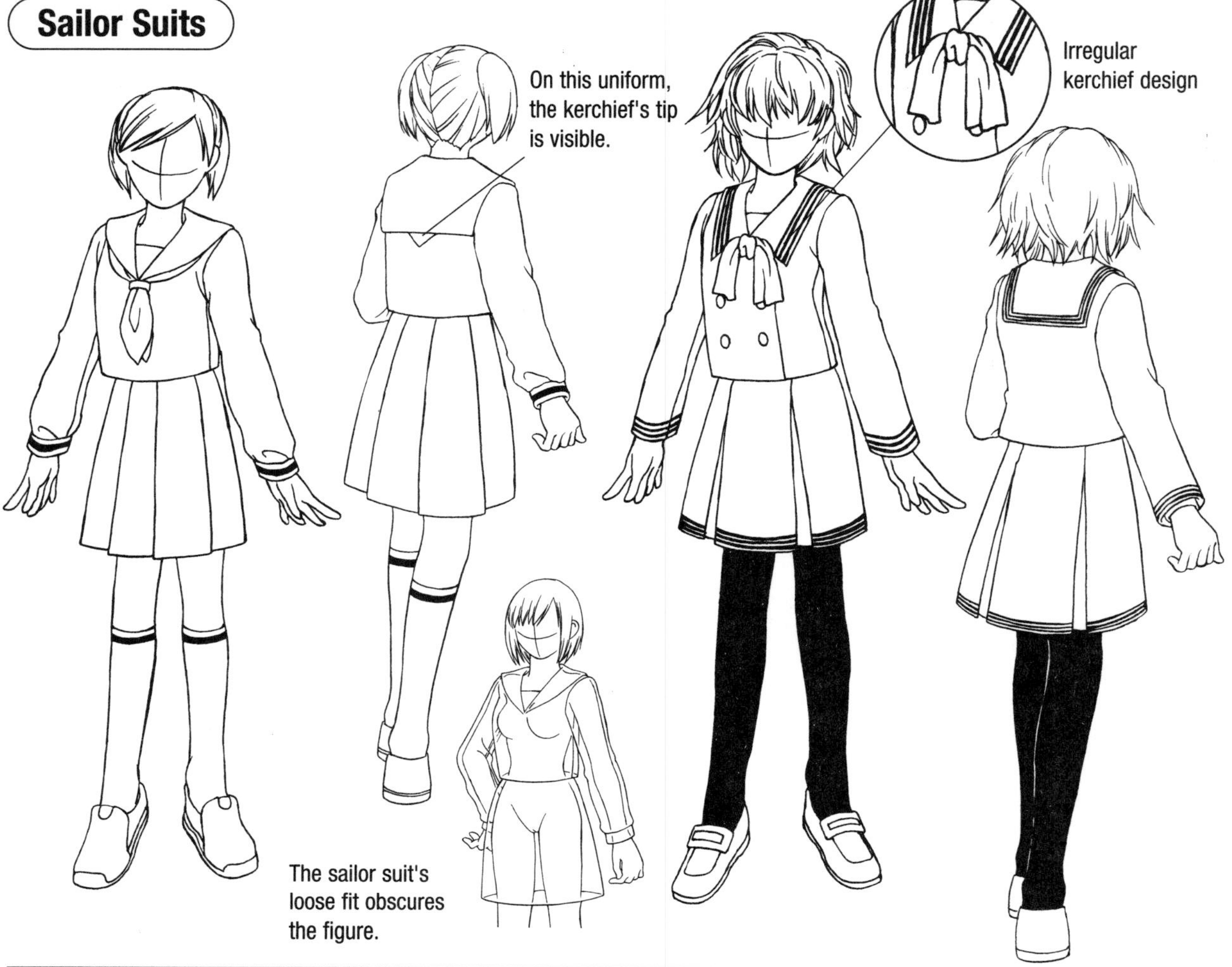

Collars and Kerchiefs

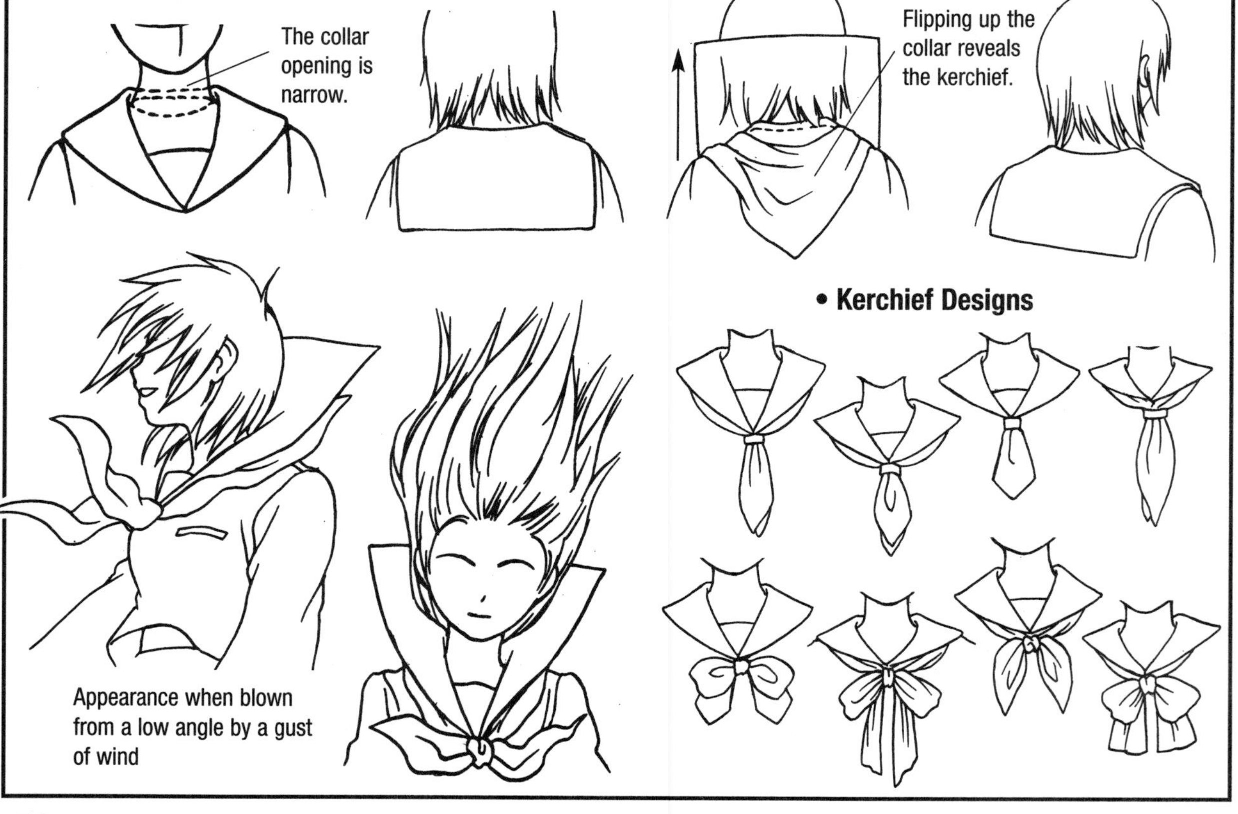

Dress-Style Uniforms

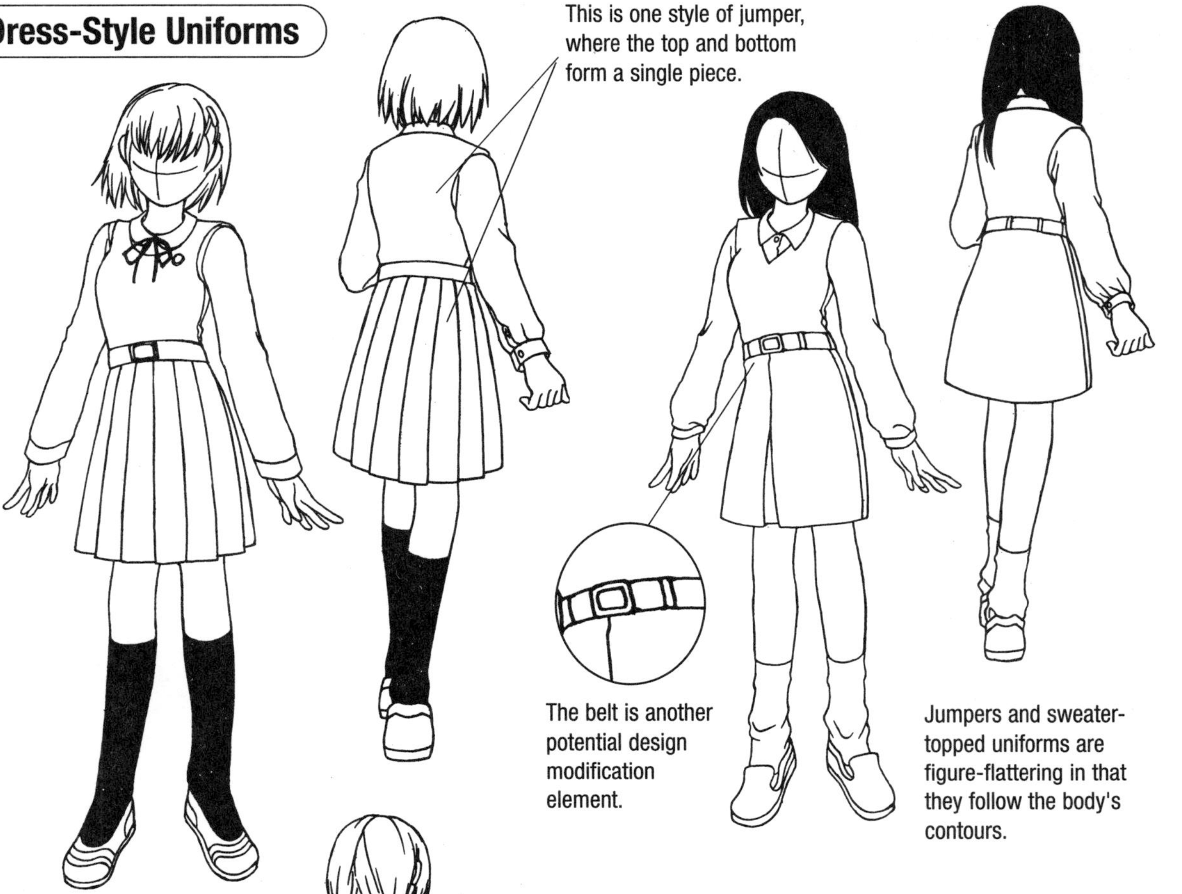

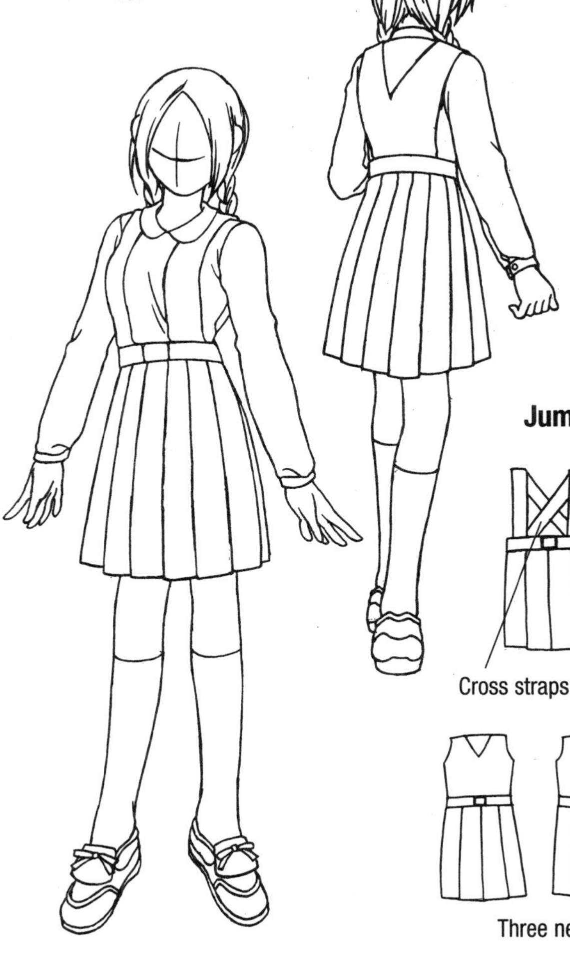

Uniforms with Sweaters

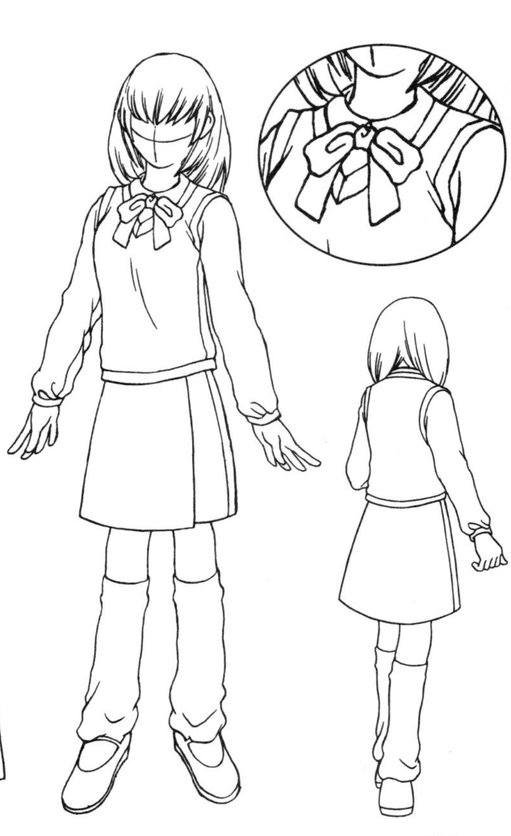

Jumper Designs

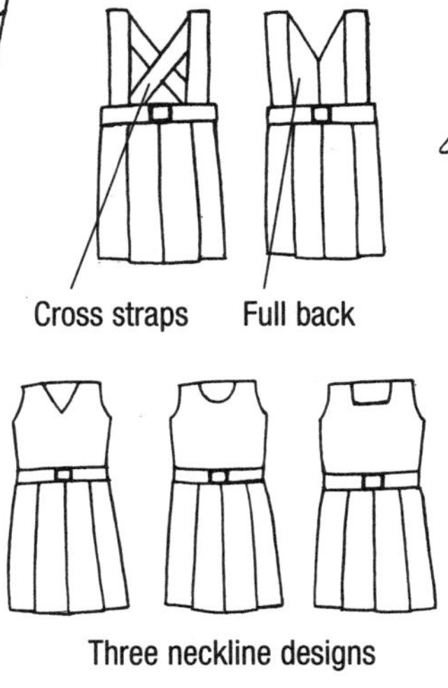

Techniques in Character Image Design

Hairstyle is a critical element in establishing a character's image. There are innumerous hair designs, but the artist must give consideration to whether the ears and the forehead should be exposed.

Percentage of ear exposed: 0% (Ear hidden)
Percentage of forehead exposed: 0% (Bangs conceal forehead)

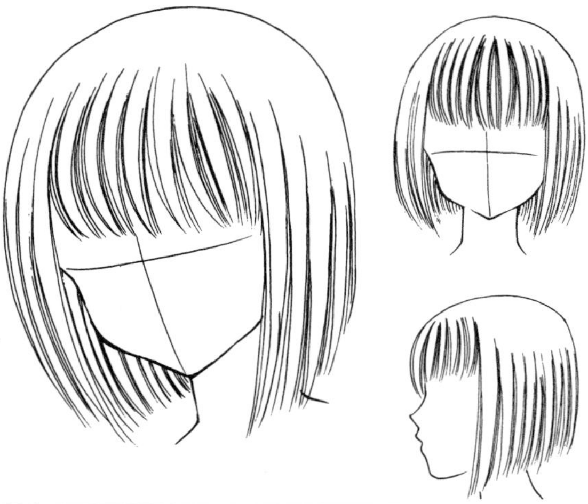

Percentage of ear exposed: 100% (Ear visible)
Percentage of forehead exposed: 100% (Forehead visible)

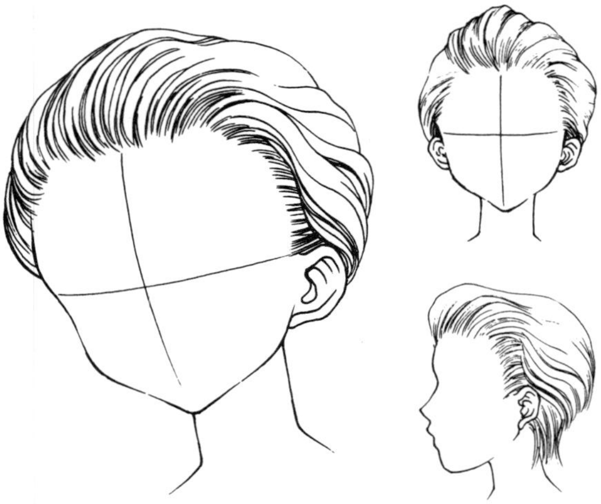

Percentage of ear exposed: 100% (Ear visible)
Percentage of forehead exposed: 0% (Bangs conceal forehead)

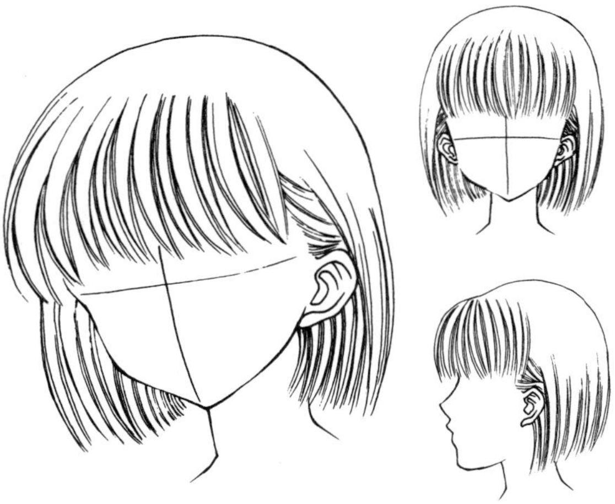

Percentage of ear exposed: 0% (Ear hidden)
Percentage of forehead exposed: 100% (Forehead visible)

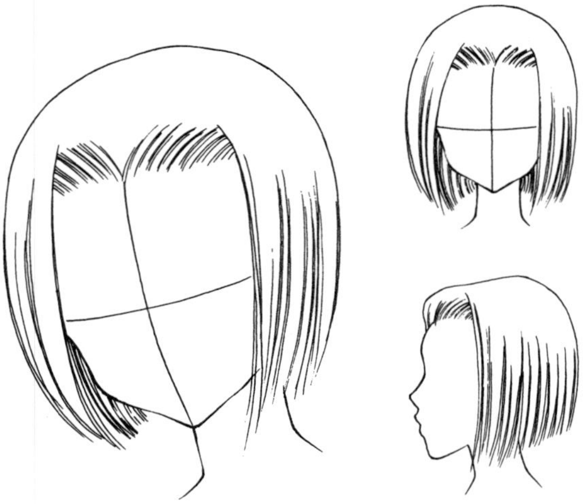

Popular Hairstyles That Leave Half the Forehead Visible (50% Exposed)

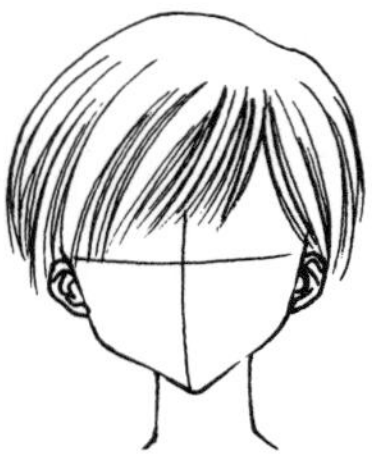

Side part

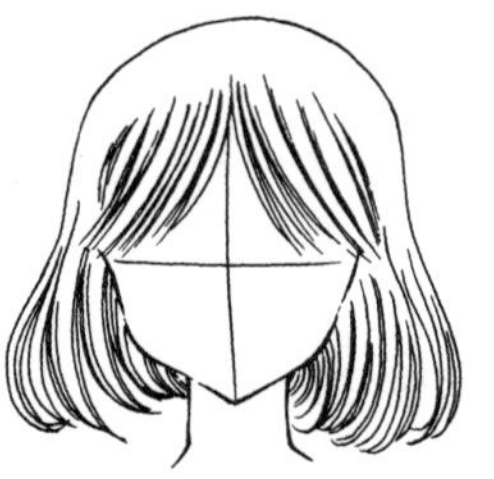

Center part

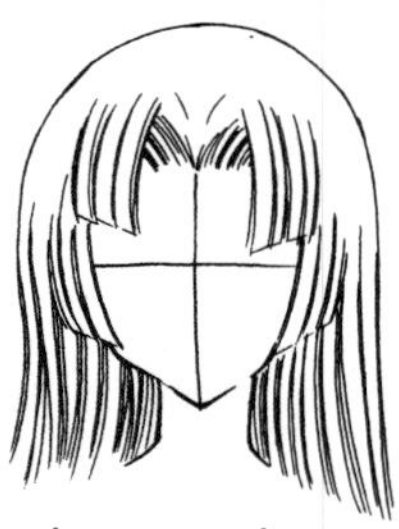

Japanese princess-style hair

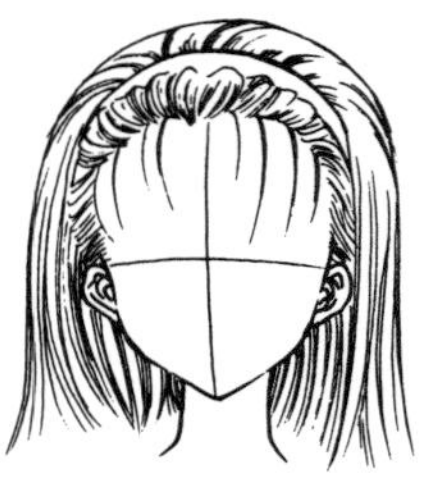

Wispy bangs

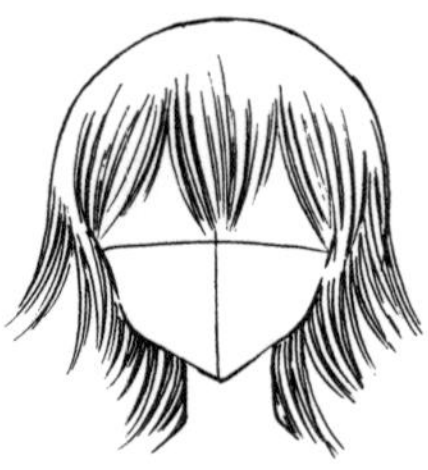

Wedge-shaped bangs

	Percentage of Forehead Exposed: 0% (Forehead Hidden)	Percentage of Forehead Exposed: 50% (Half of Forehead Visible)	Percentage of Forehead Exposed: 100% (Forehead Visible)
Percentage of Ear Exposed: 0% (Ear Hidden)	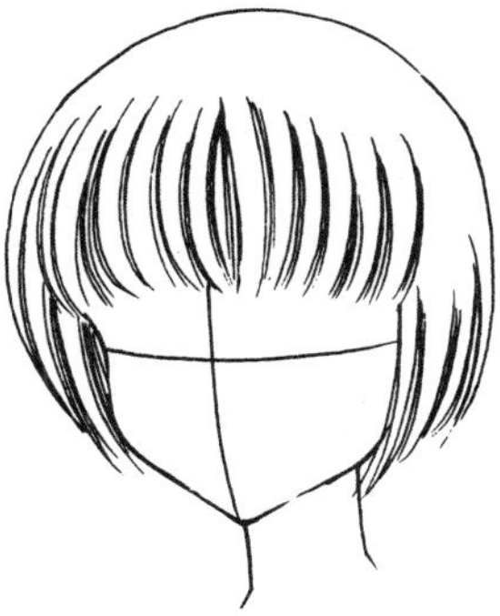	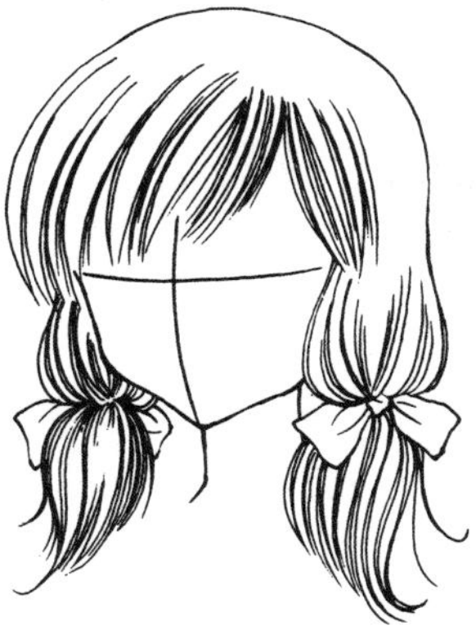	The hair is often shown tied in the back. 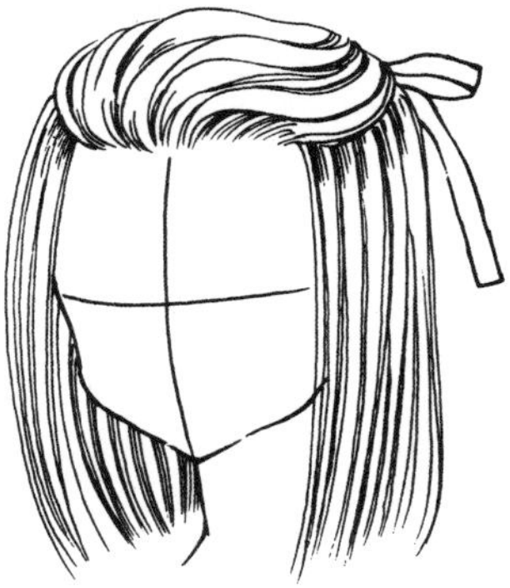
Percentage of Ear Exposed: 50% (Half of Ear Visible)	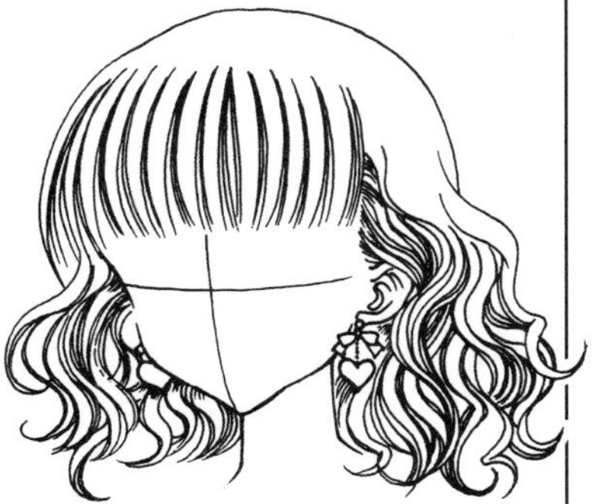 This style is great for showing off earrings. Artists often draw wavy hair or show the hair flipping outward.	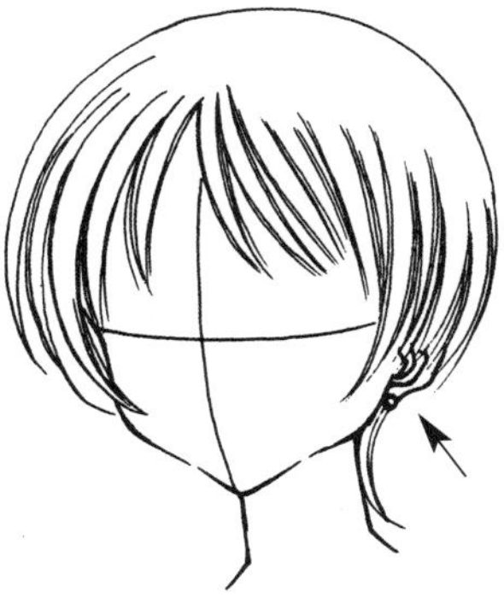	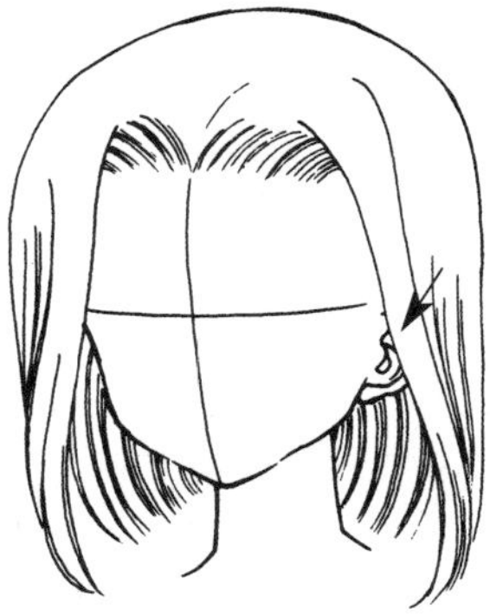
Percentage of Ear Exposed: 100% (Ear Visible)	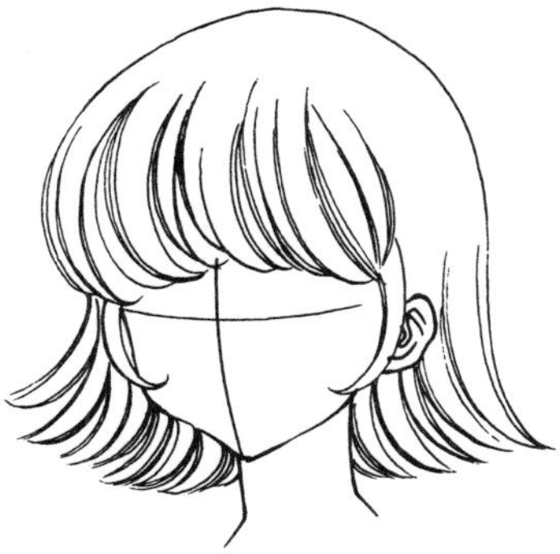 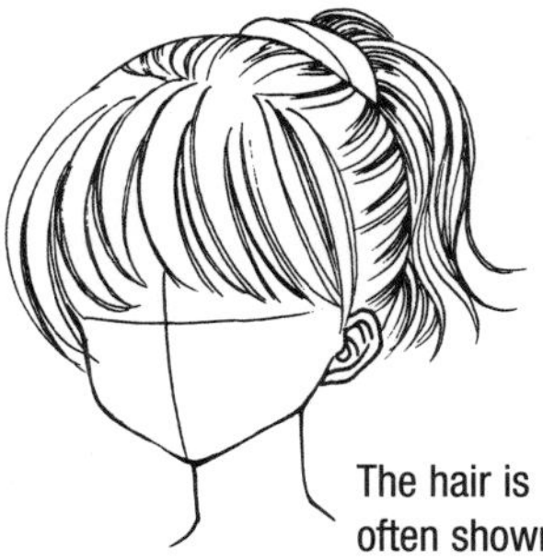 The hair is often shown tied back in a ponytail, etc.	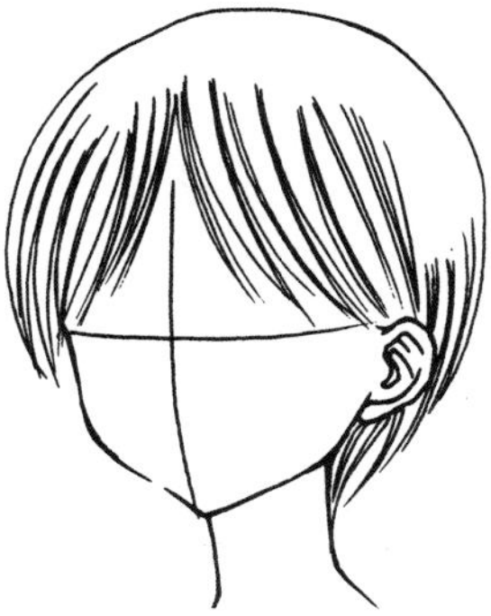 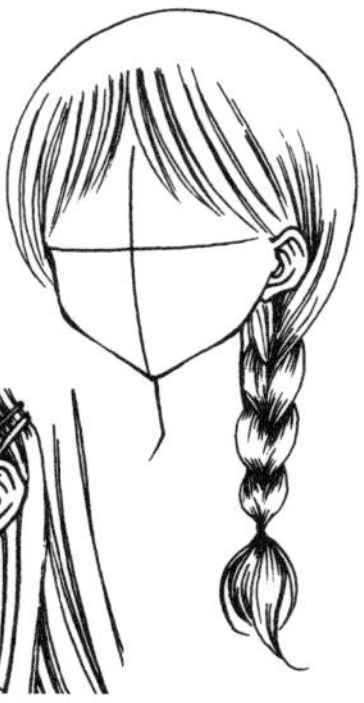 Long hairstyles 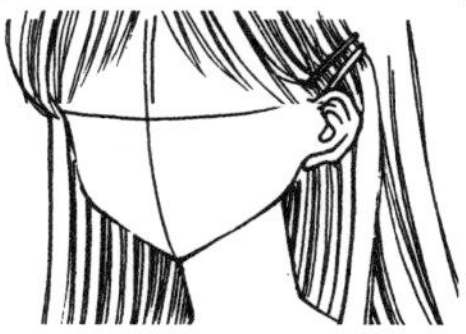	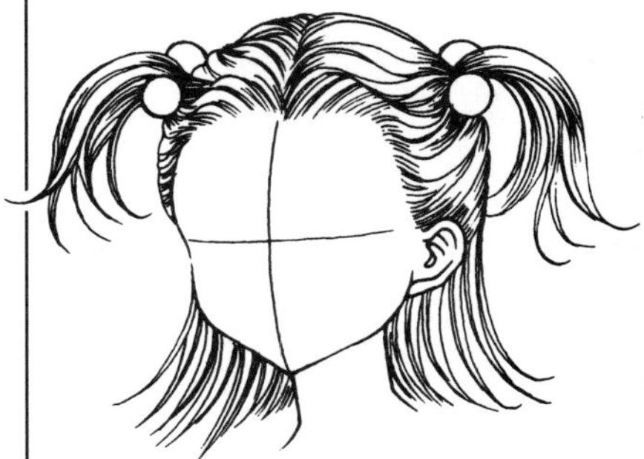 The hair is often pinned back. 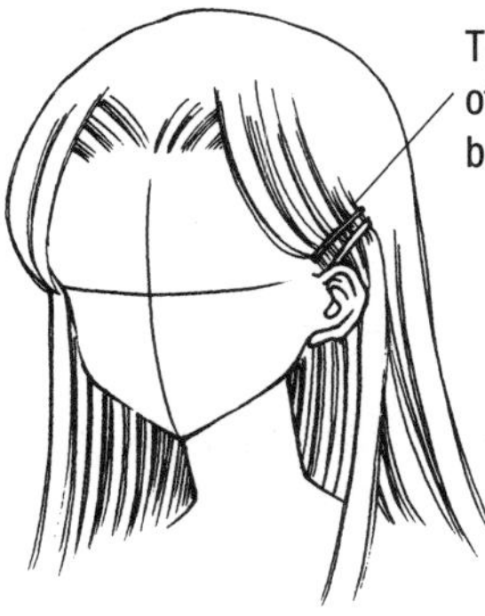

List of Distinguishing Eye Features

The eyes' shape is a key ingredient for distinguishing a character. Try playing around with the eyes' length, height, and upper and lower lids.

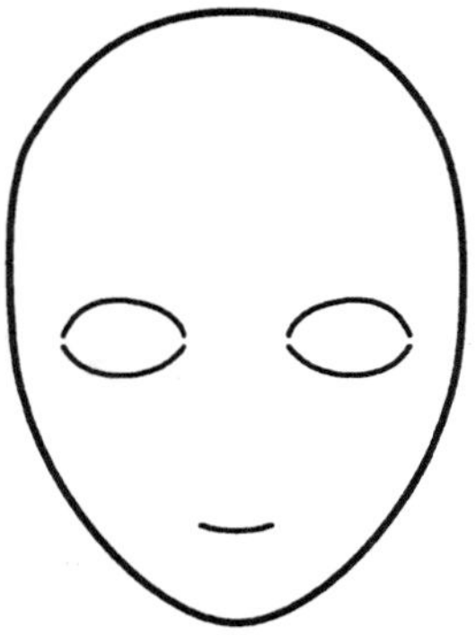

Standard Eye:
The Straight-laced Girl

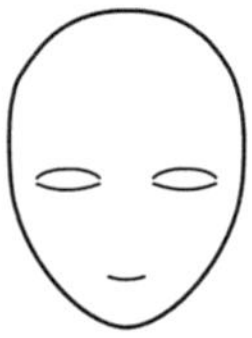

Narrow standard:
- The Shy Girl
- The Older Girl

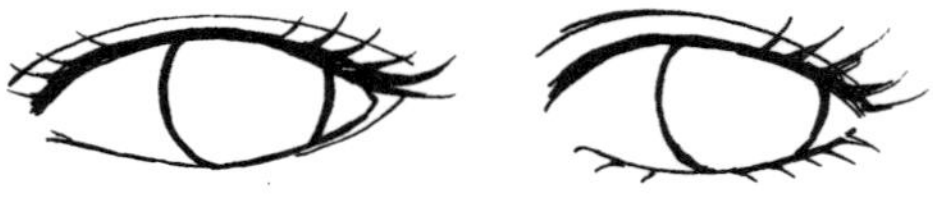

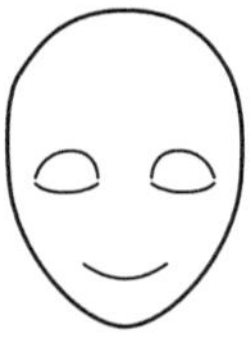

Average:
- The Cutie
- The Imp
- The Kid

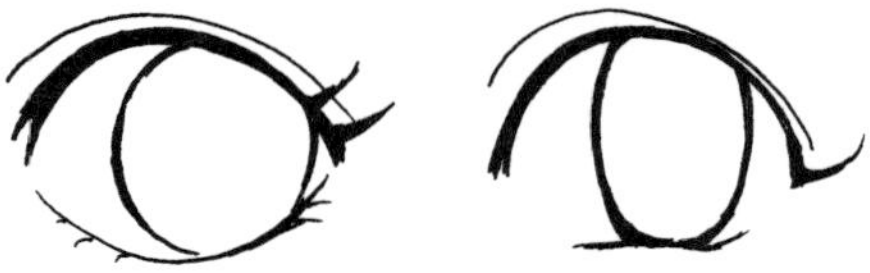

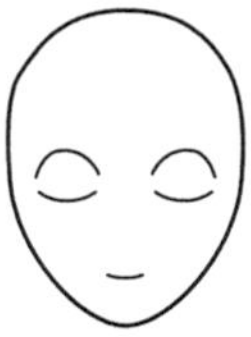

Large standard:
- The Cutie
- The Kid

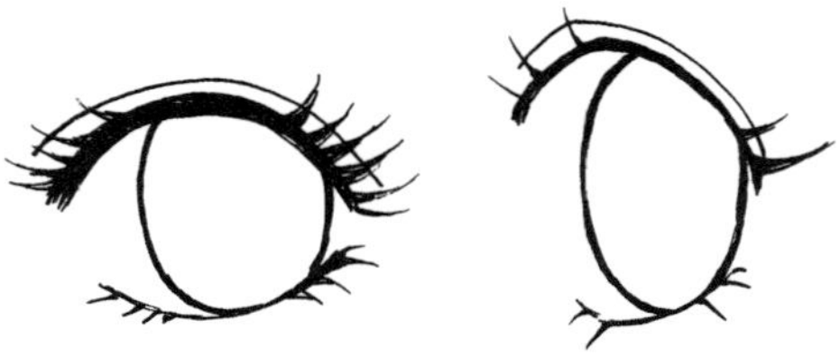

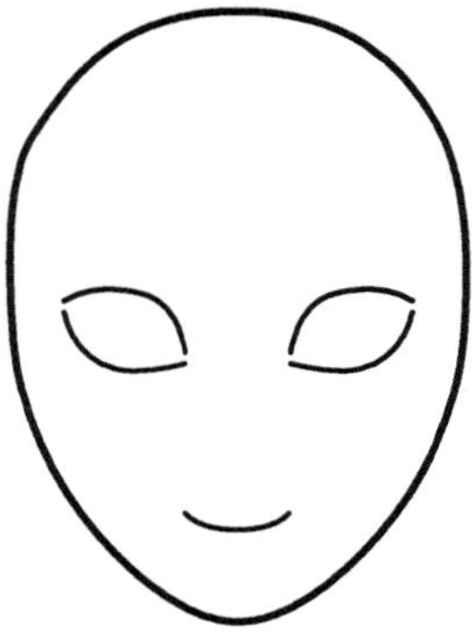

Upward Slanting Eyes:
The Strong Girl

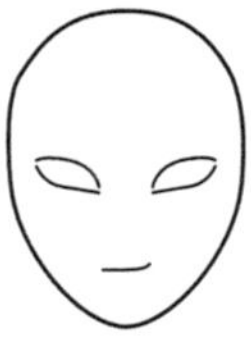

Narrow upward slanting:
- The Bully

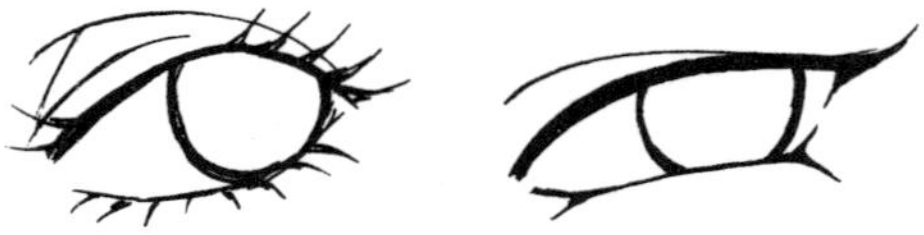

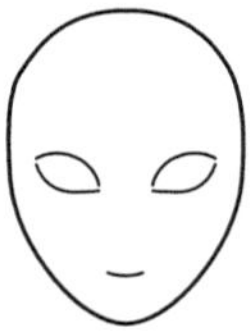

Average upward slanting:
- The Older Girl

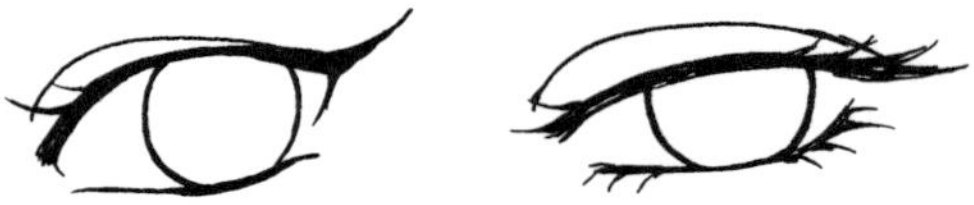

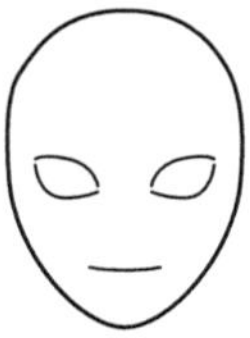

Large upward slanting:
- The Bad Girl

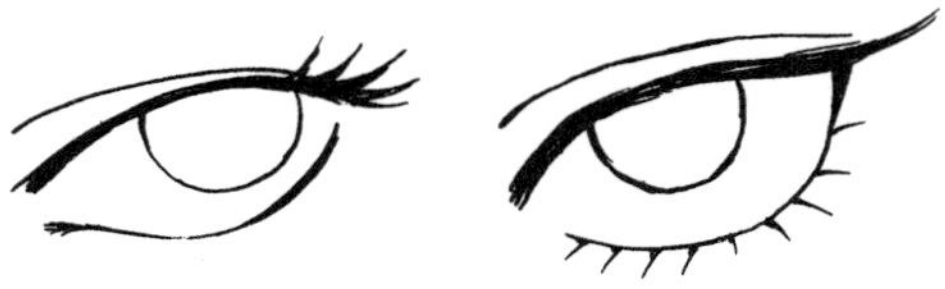

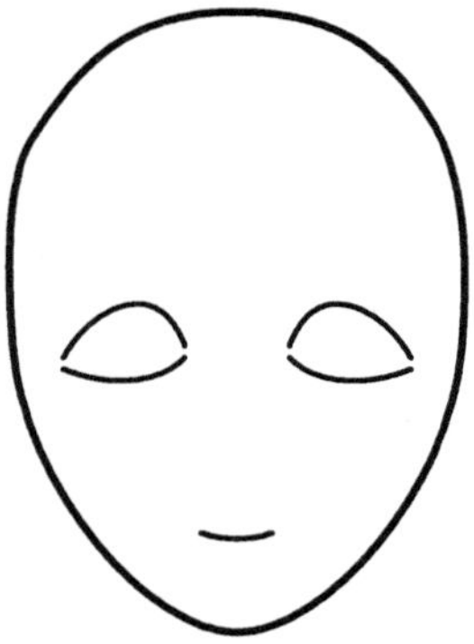

Downward Slanting Eyes:
The Vulnerable Girl

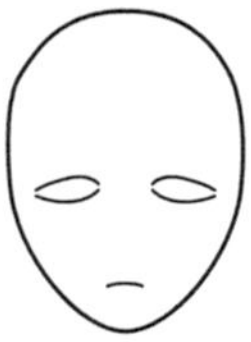

Narrow downward slanting:
- The Vulnerable Girl

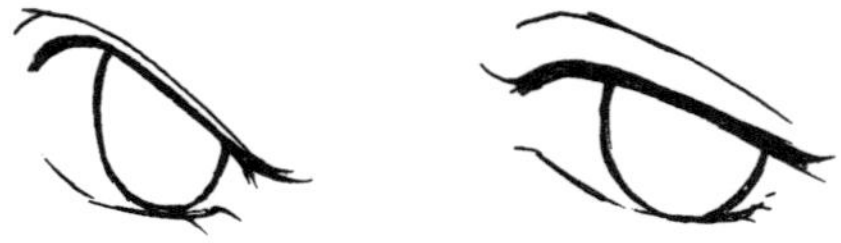

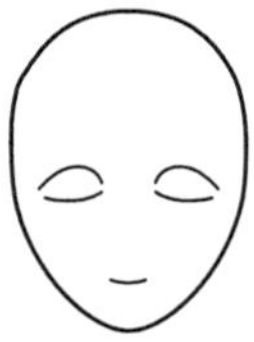

Average downward slanting:
- The Shy Girl
- The Older Girl

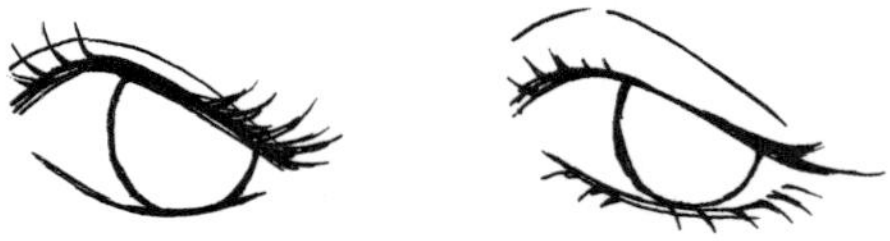

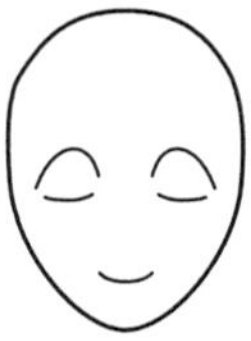

Large downward slanting:
- The Cutie
- The Kid

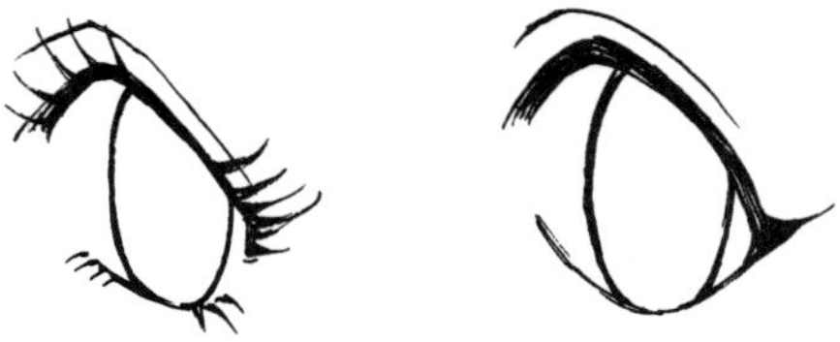

Chapter 2

Making the Figure Move

Create Vibrant Characters by Successfully Portraying the Way They Walk, Sit, and Gesture

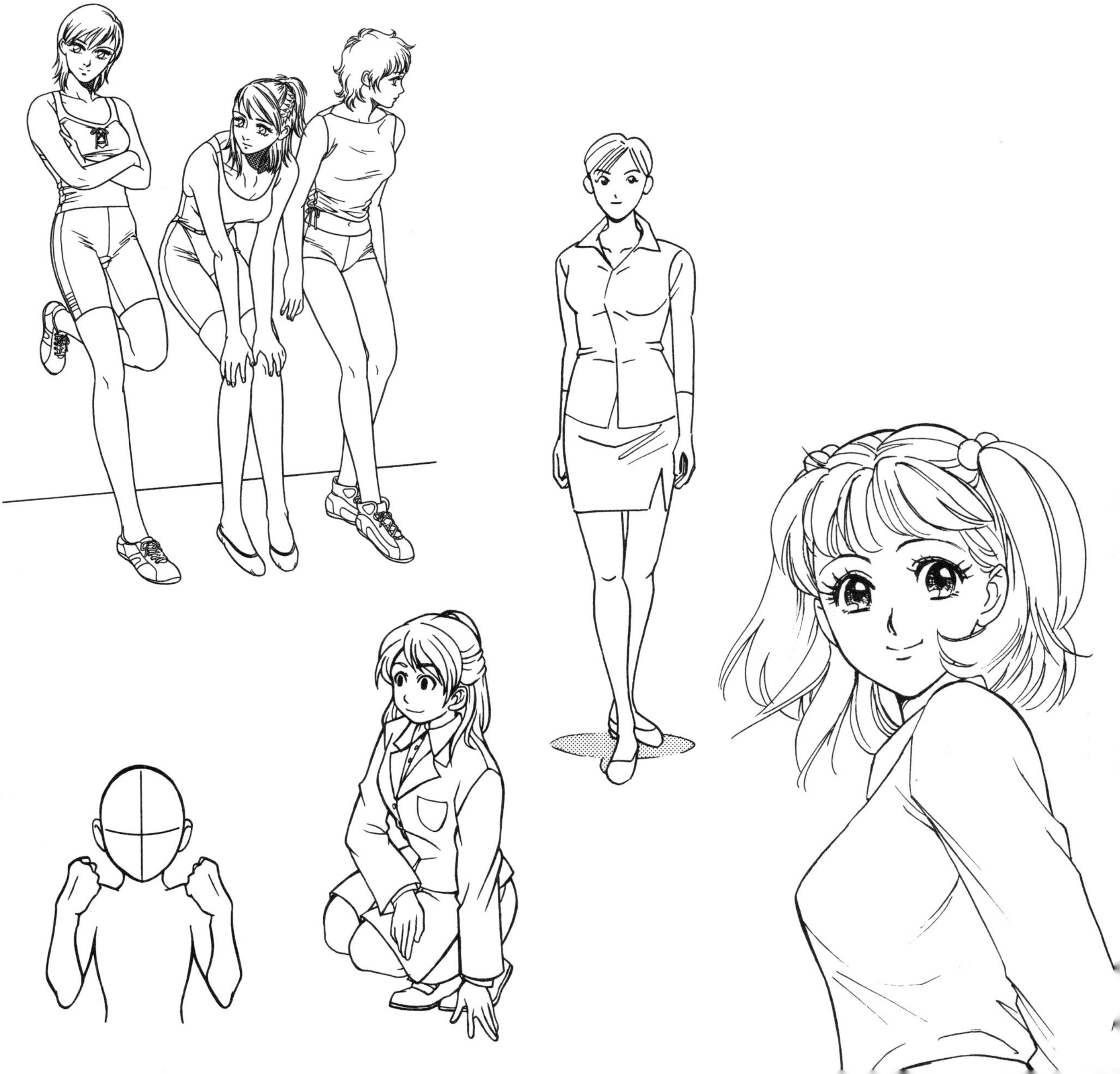

The Fundamentals of Character Movements

The human body is a three-dimensional object covered with curved surfaces. Generally speaking, rendering a standing pose from a slightly high angle makes for a pretty impressive composition. Start by drawing a sketch using curved lines to capture the pose.

Front View

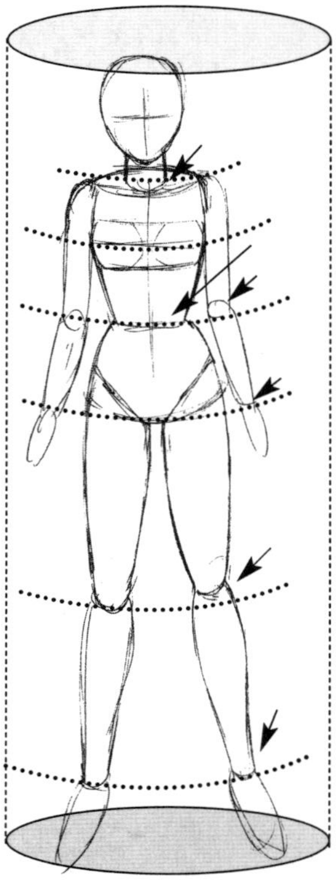

Rendering the rough layout sketch in curved lines makes it easier to generate a sense of flesh and solidity that is attractive.

The neck, waist, and lowered arm and leg joints all take downward curves.

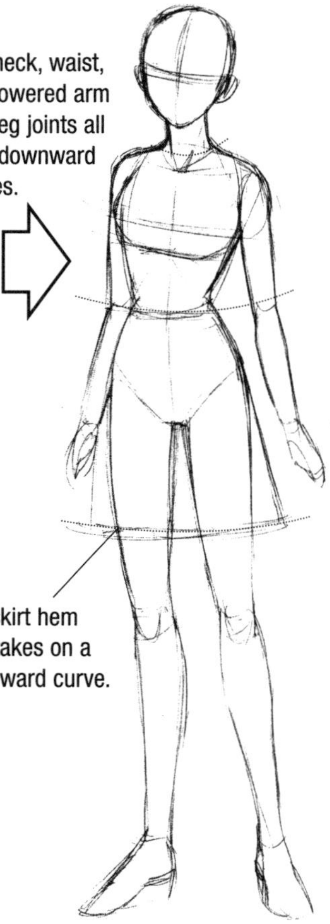

The skirt hem also takes on a downward curve.

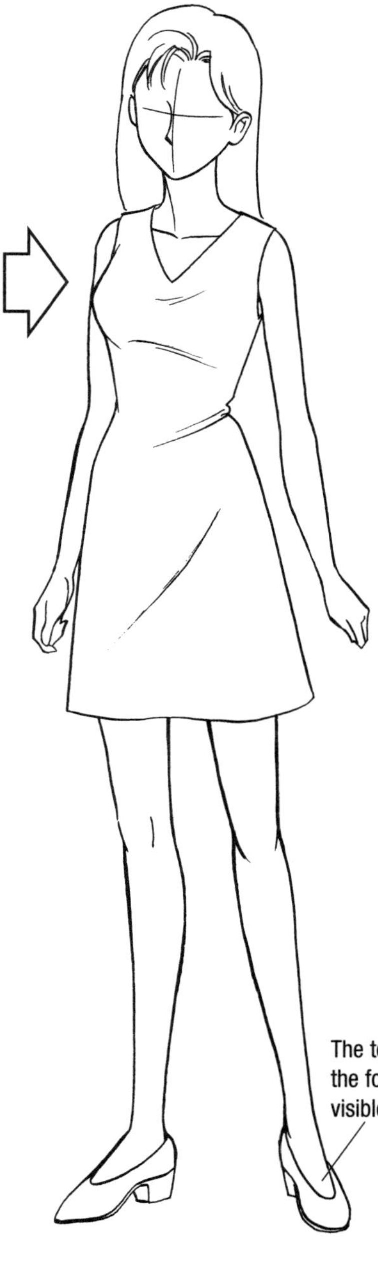

The top of the foot is visible.

Shoes Rendered from Straight-on When Composing from a Low Angle

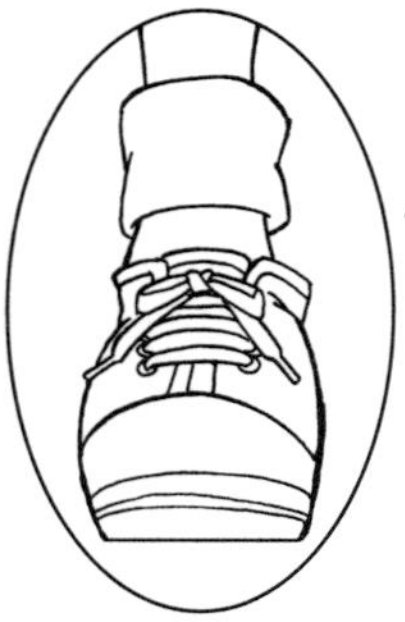

The front of the shoe is only visible when the figure is drawn in upward arcing curves (i.e. from a low angle).

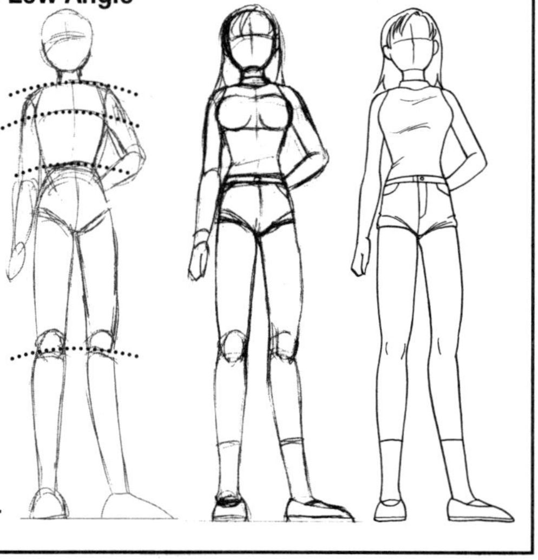

3/4 View

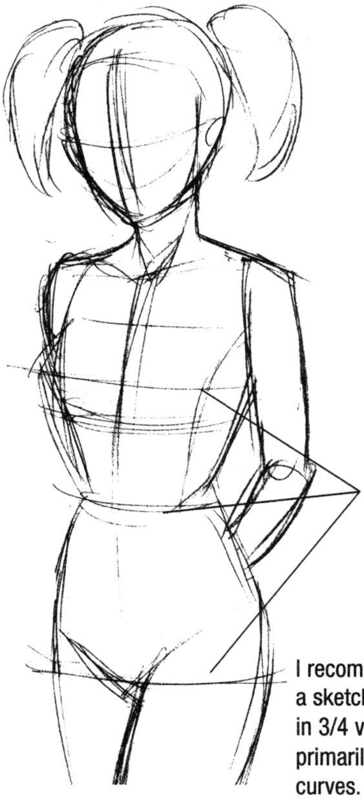

Downward curves

I recommend rendering a sketch of a character in 3/4 view using primarily downward curves.

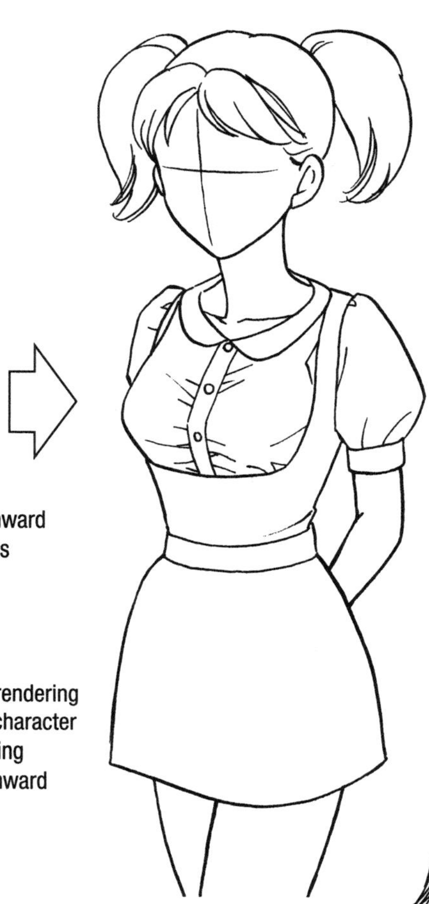

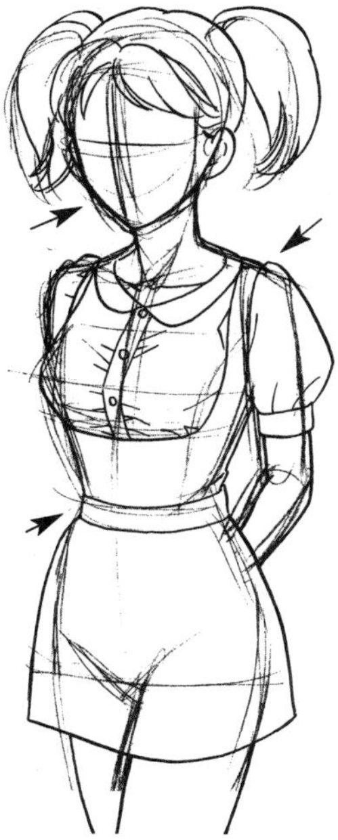

Be sure to capture the head, shoulders, and waist's positions accurately in the layout sketch stage.

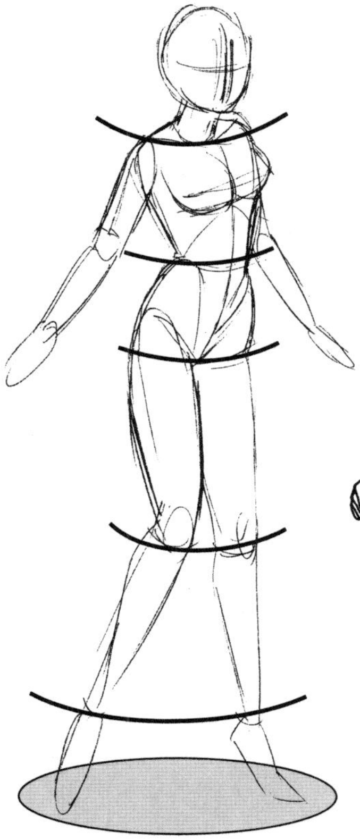

Layout curves are intended to serve as guidelines for the figure's curved surfaces and obtaining a sense of volume. Consequently, approximations will suffice.

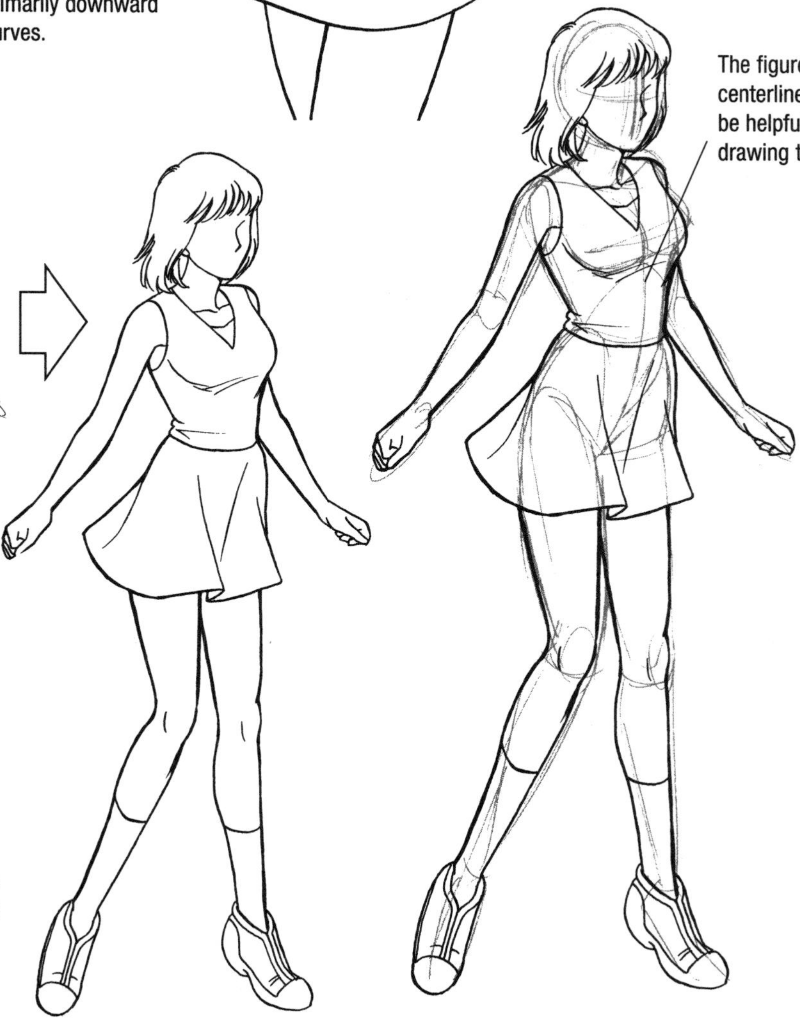

The figure's centerline (axis) will be helpful when drawing the clothing.

Moderate Low Angles

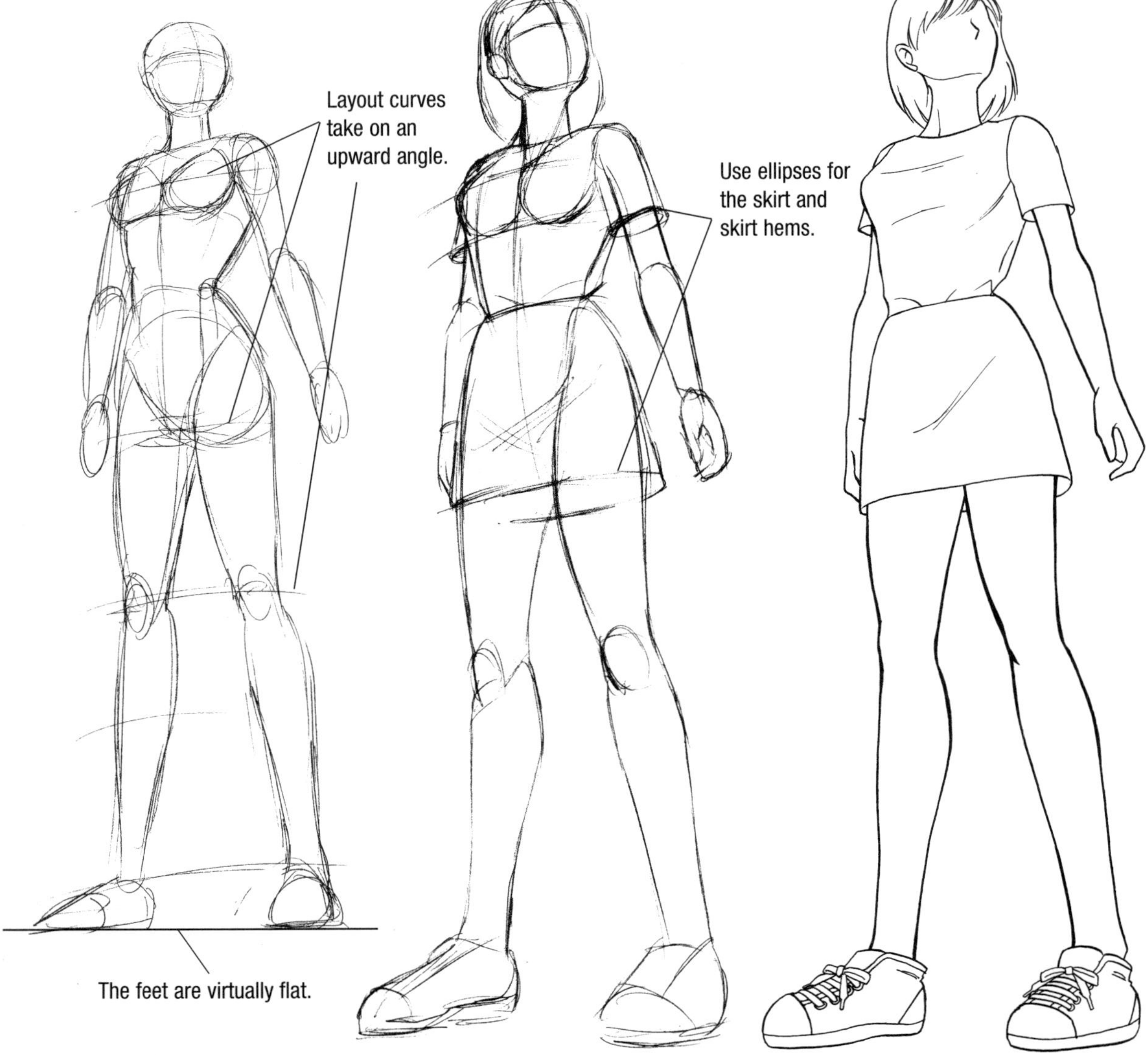

Low angles work well with graceful, poised characters or confident poses.

• Contrasting Low vs. Standard Angles

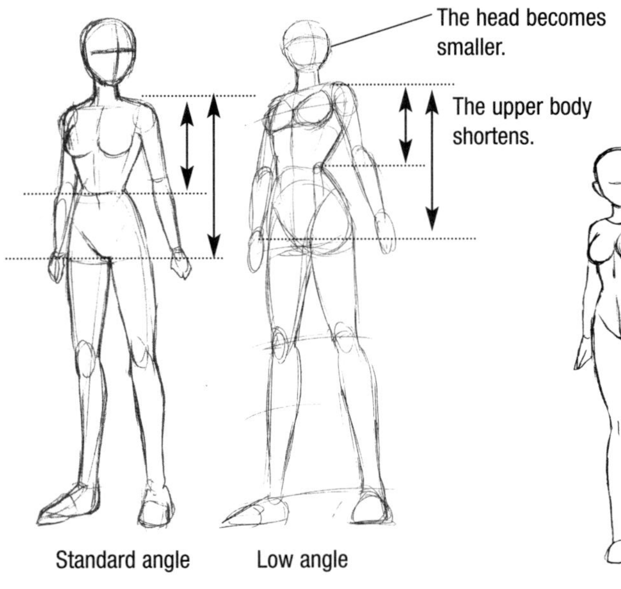

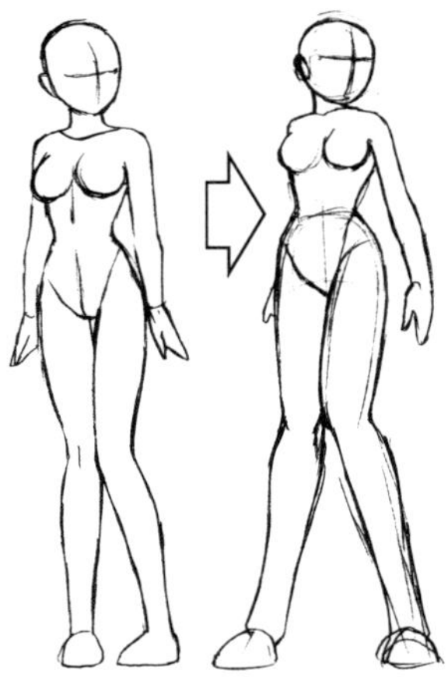

Low angle compositions are not commonly used with "cute" or typically feminine poses, such as where the figure is bending forward or its toes are pointed in.

Moderate High Angles

• Confident Poses

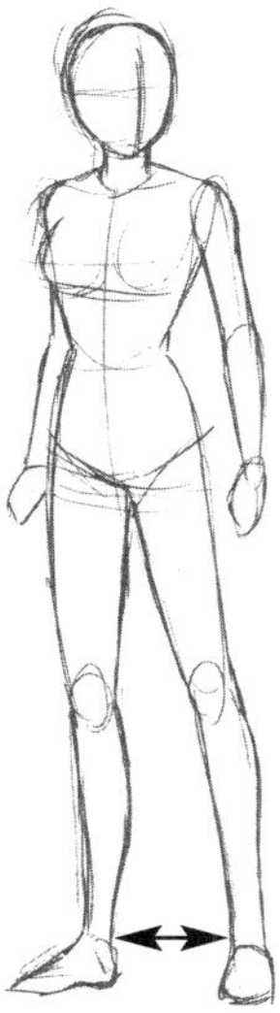

The legs are spread widely. The arms are pulled back somewhat.

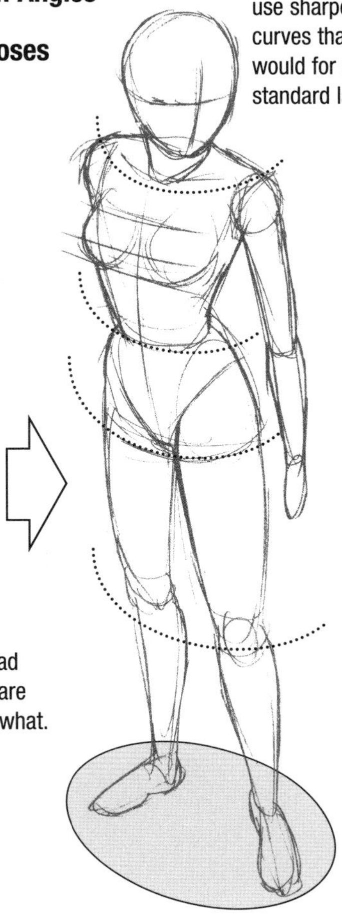

The trick here is to use sharper curves than you would for a standard layout.

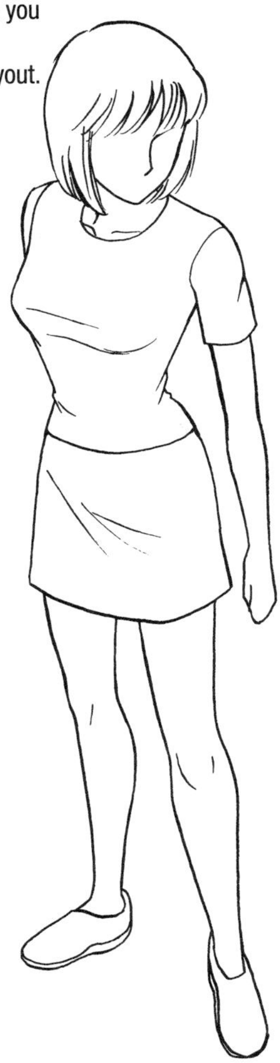

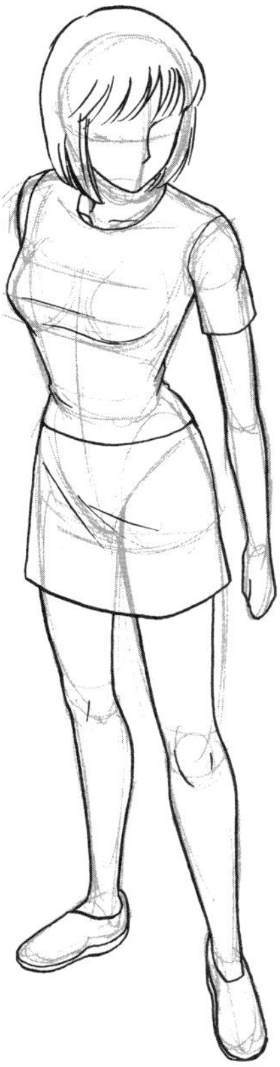

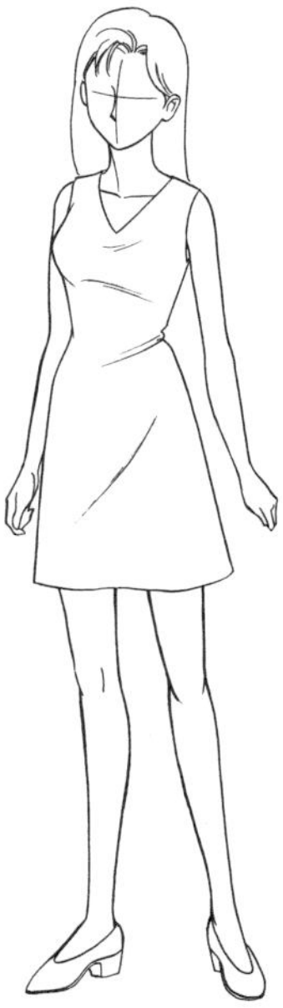

In contrast with a moderate high angle composition, greater proportions of the top of the head and chest are visible. The skirt hem comprises an ellipse.

• Feminine Poses

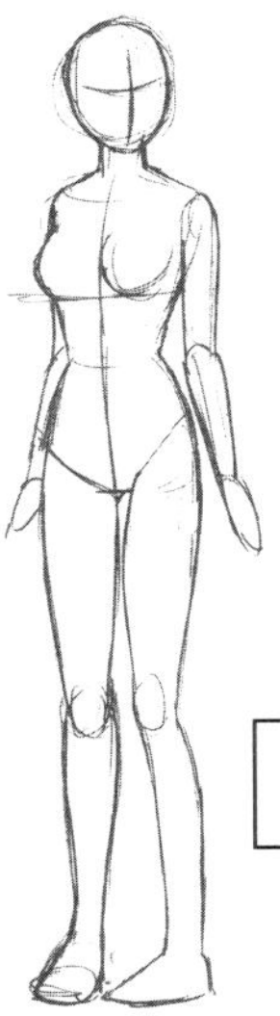

The toes point in, and the arms are pulled to the side, forming angles.

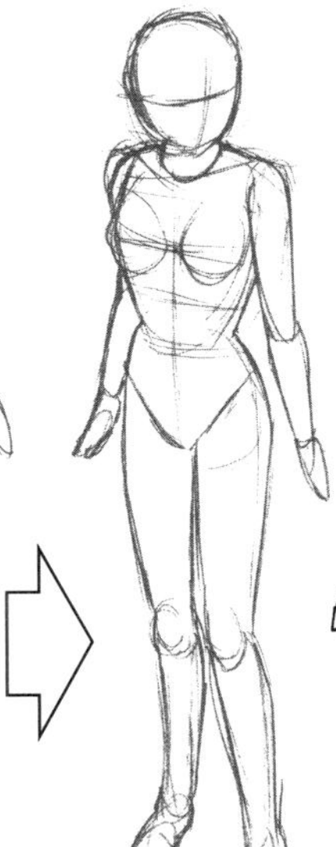

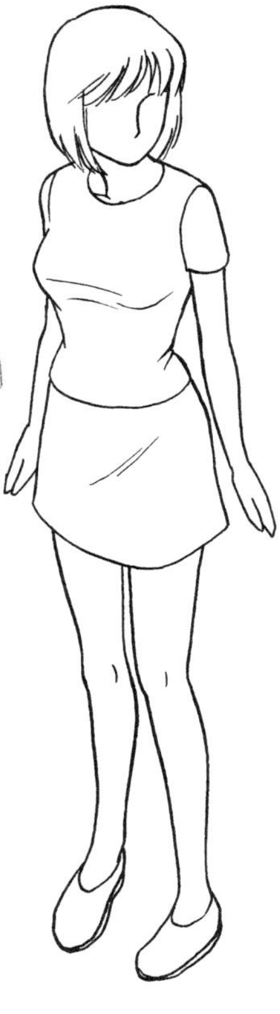

Application in "Walking" Scenes

The same upper body drawn in a standing pose may be used for a walking figure.

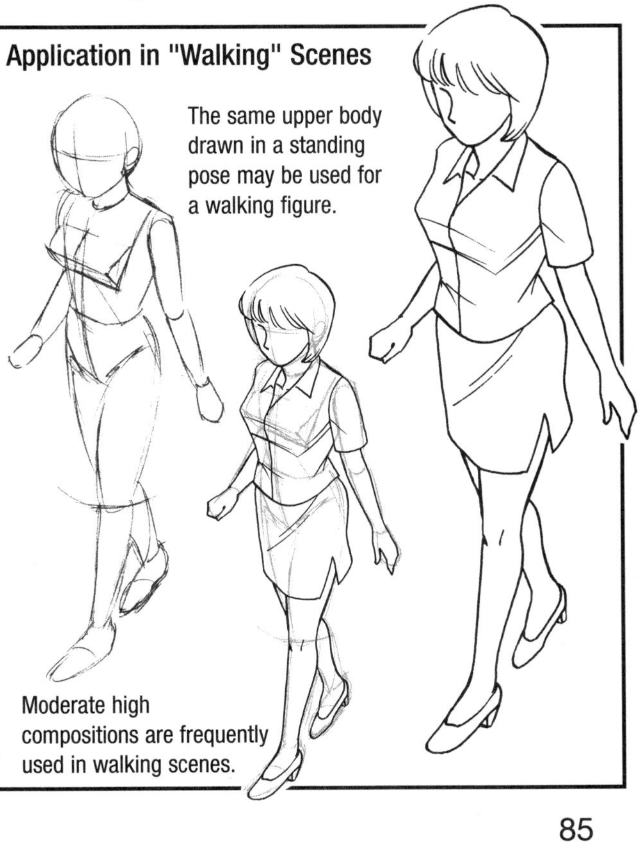

Moderate high compositions are frequently used in walking scenes.

Side View

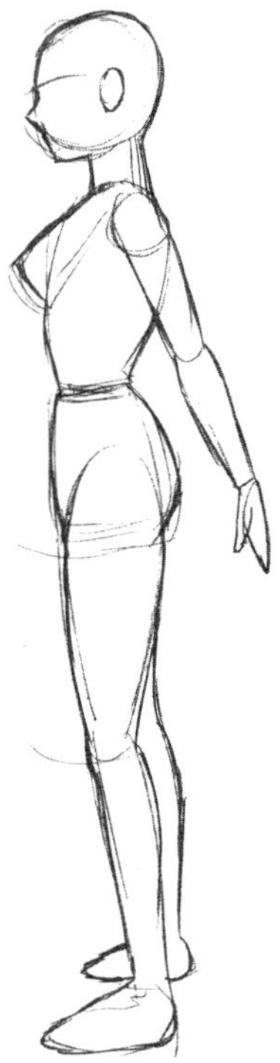

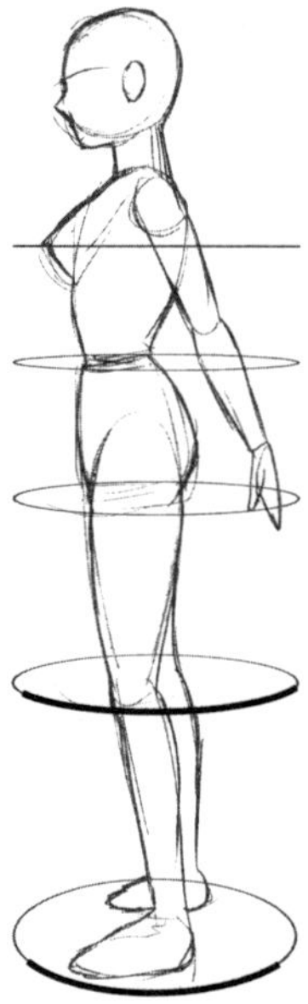

In full figure side views, layout curves become sharper as they approach the feet.

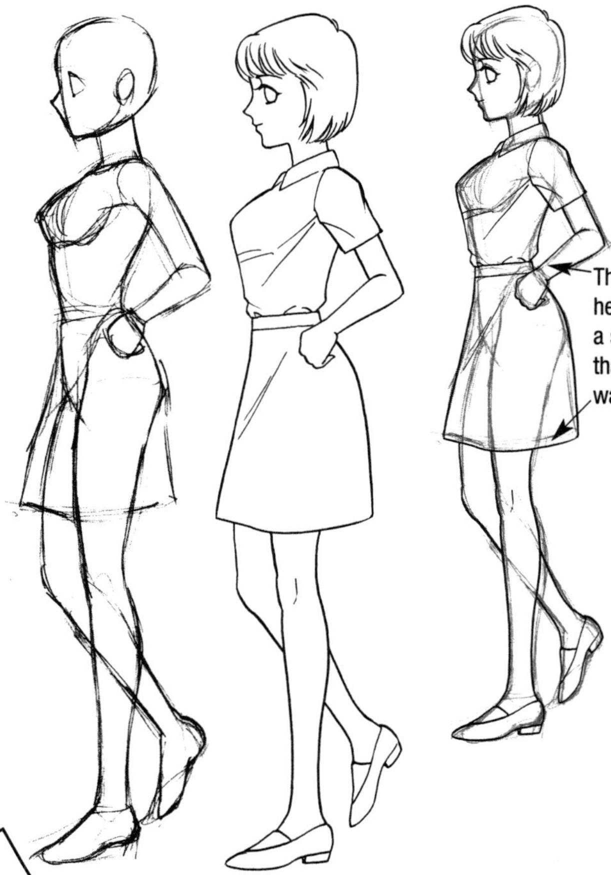

The skirt's hemline takes on a sharper curve than that at the waist.

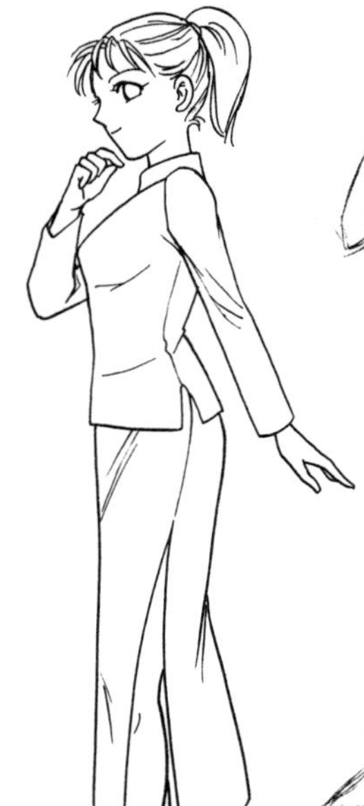

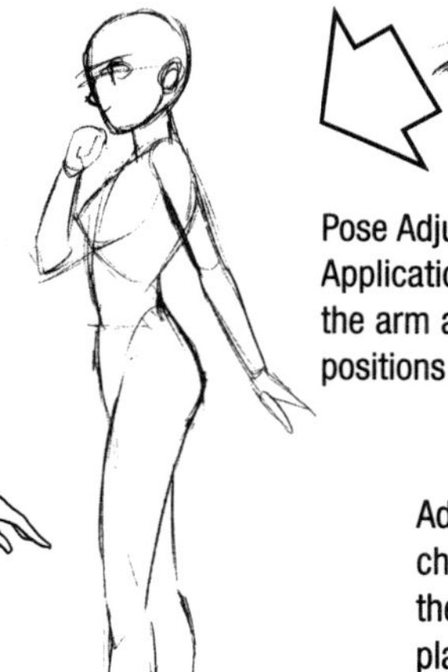

Pose Adjustment Application: I modified the arm and leg positions on this figure.

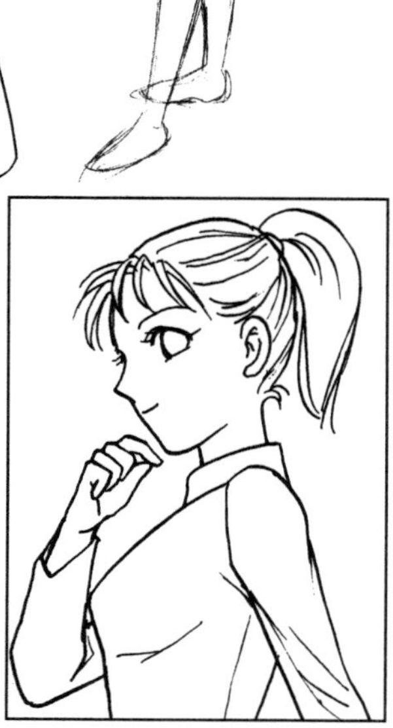

Side views are commonly used for bust shots.

Adjusted Side View: Drawing the character's body in side view but the face looking toward the picture plane creates a striking image.

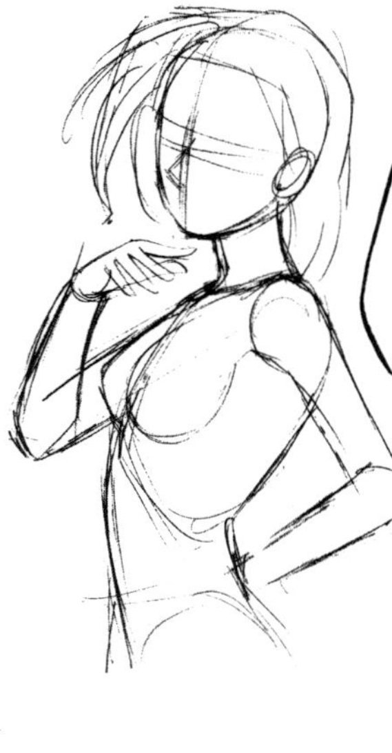

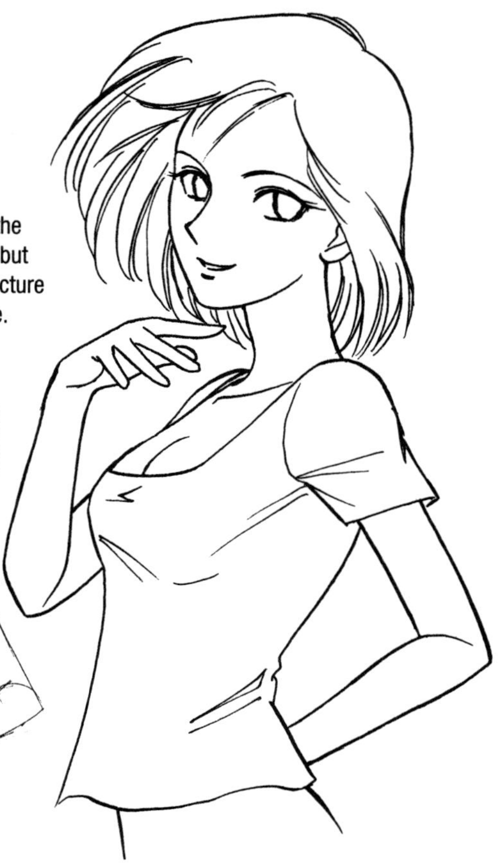

Low Angle Compositions

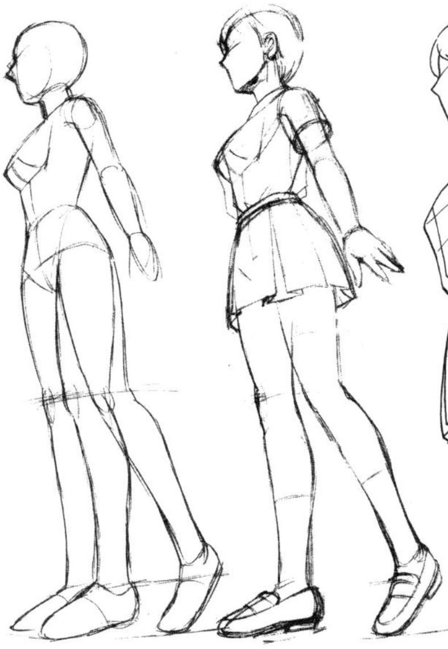

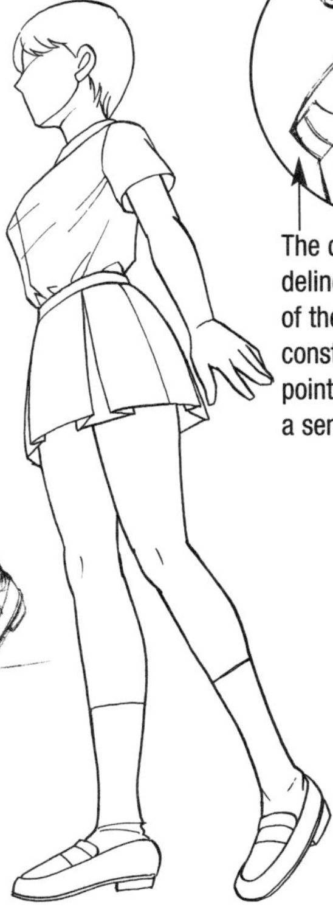

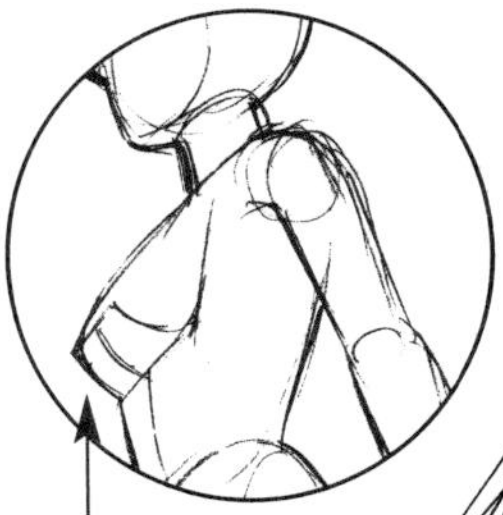

The clearly delineated underside of the breasts constitutes a key point in producing a sense of volume.

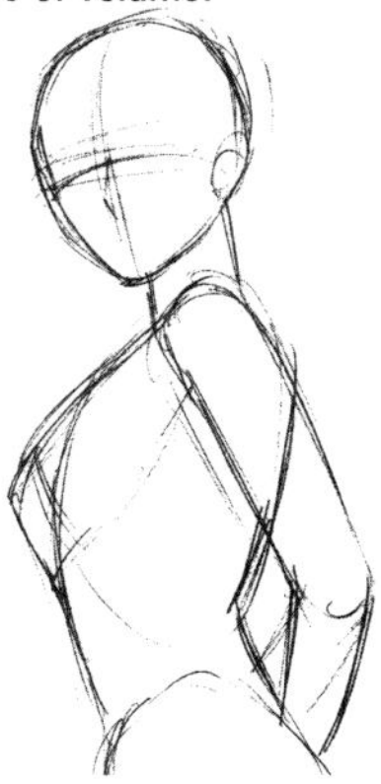

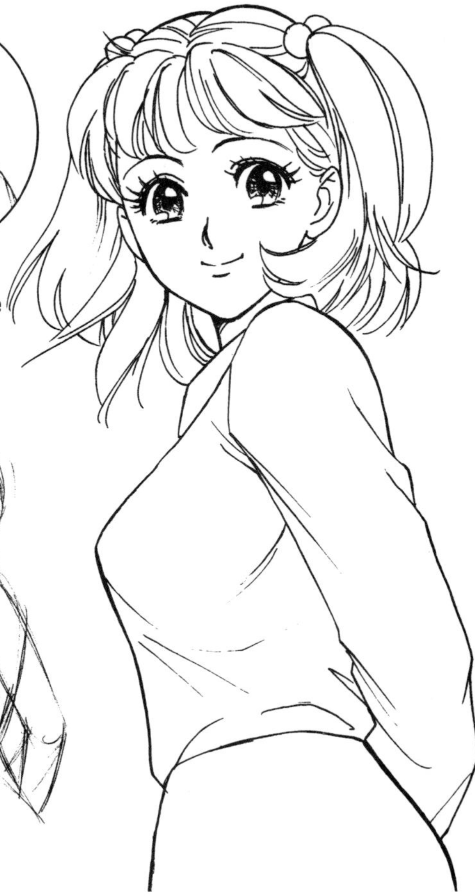

Side views of the full figure are not often composed from a low angle. However, when used in a bust shot, it creates an impressive image.

High Angle Compositions

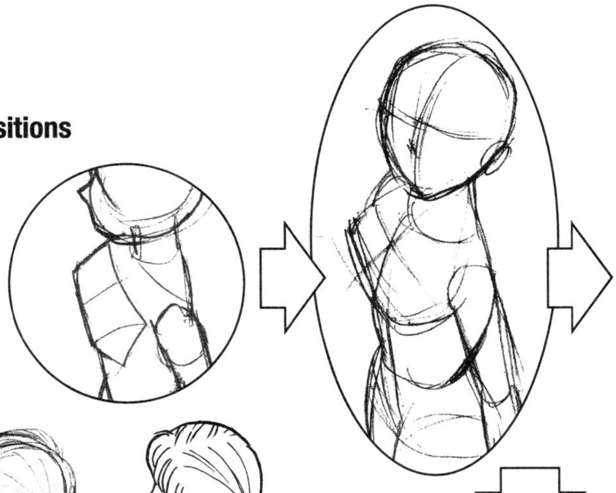

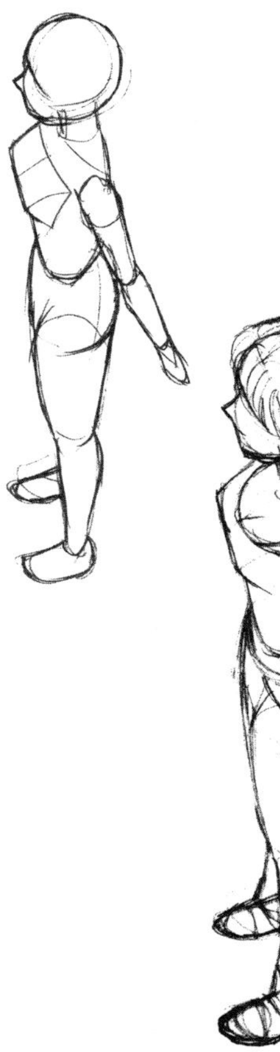

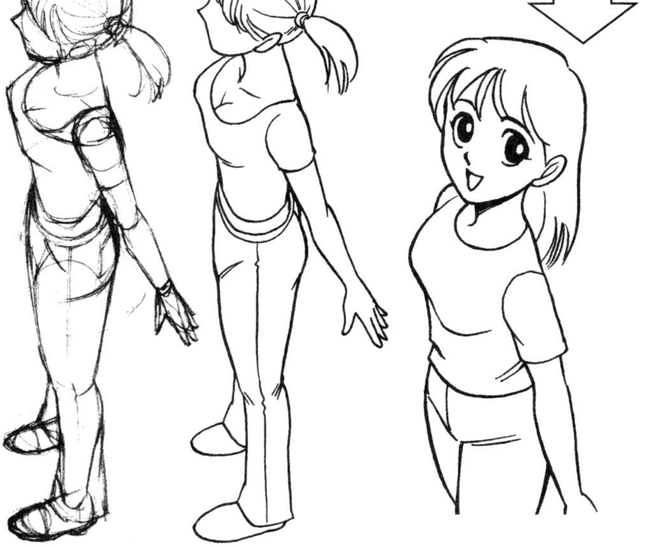

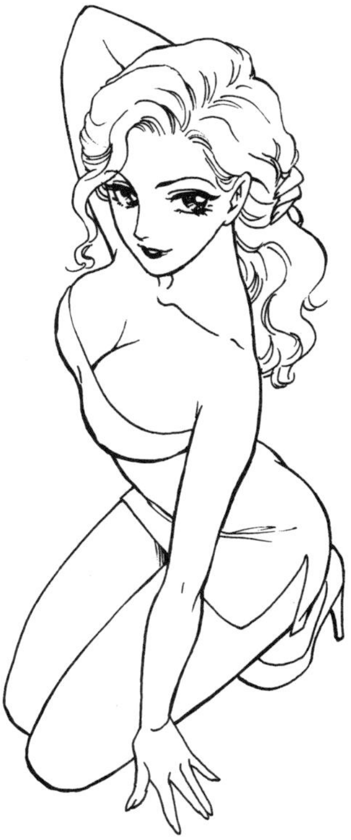

High angle compositions are great for emphasizing the figure, for book or magazine-style illustration compositions, and for *manga* title page illustrations.

Walking Scenes

Artists all need to become proficient at drawing walking scenes, given that they are repeatedly used, such as when a character makes his/her first appearance, for scenes changes, to suggest the passage of time, etc.

When Walking Scenes Appear in *Manga*

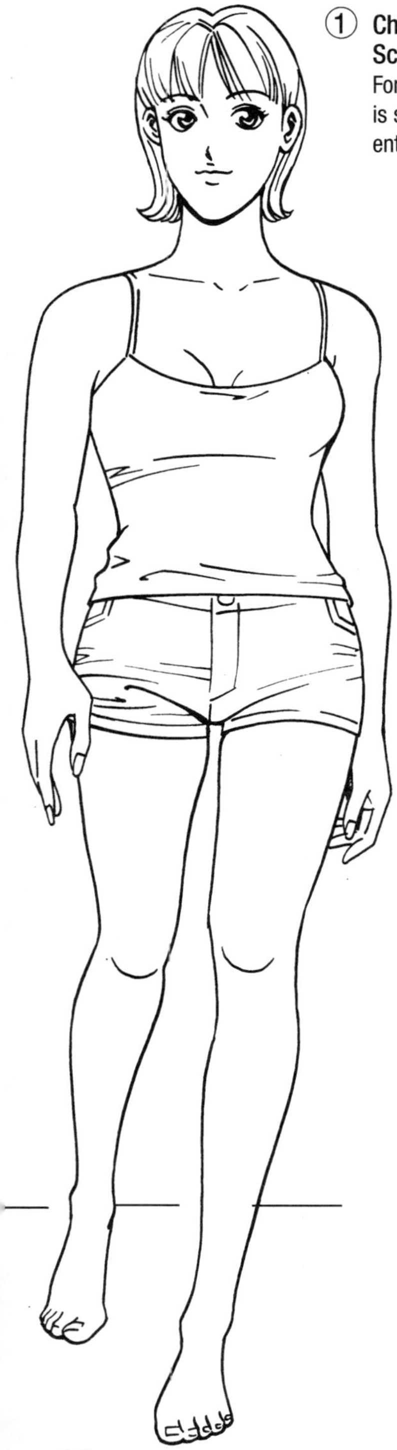

① **Character Introduction Scenes:**
For these, the full figure is shown starting to walk, entering a room, etc.

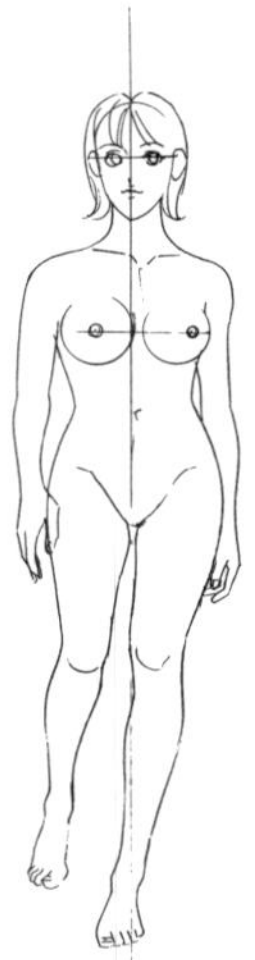

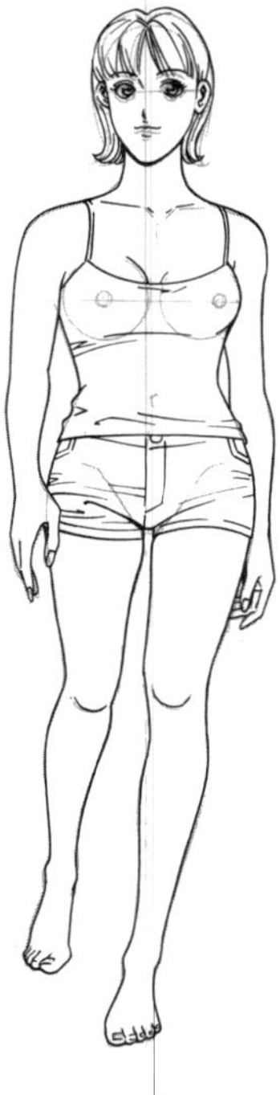

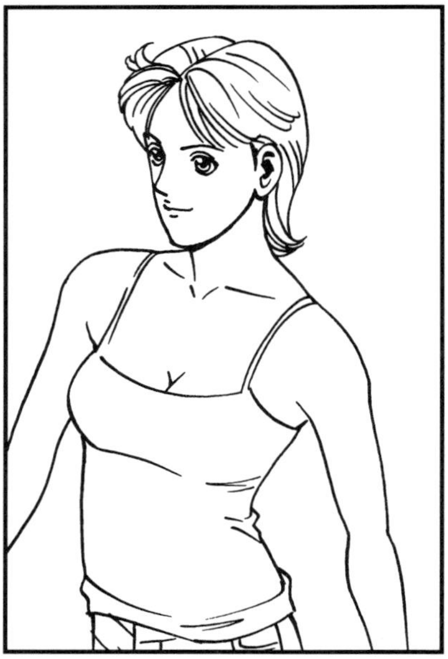

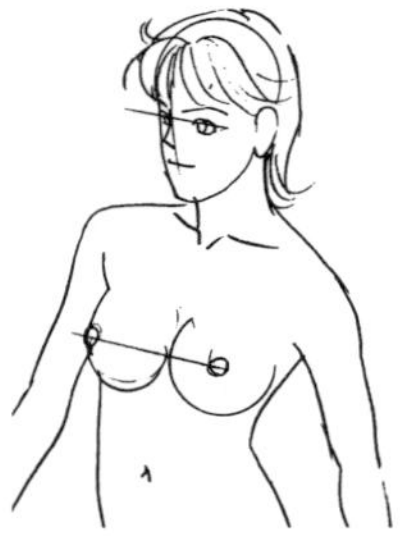

② **Scenes of the Character in Motion:**
These primarily tend to comprise shots of the upper body. Movement is represented as swinging arms or "wind" lines.

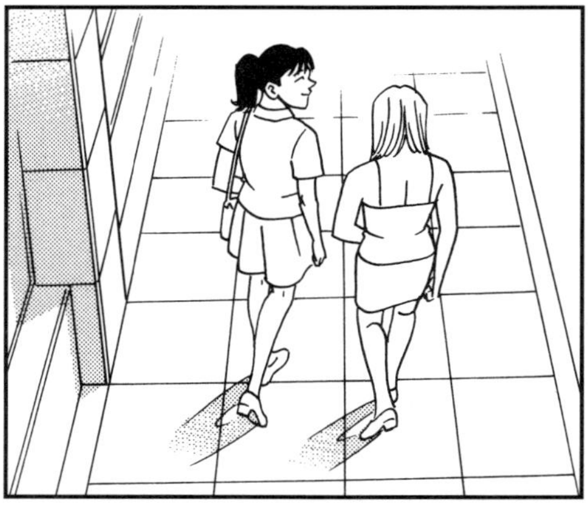

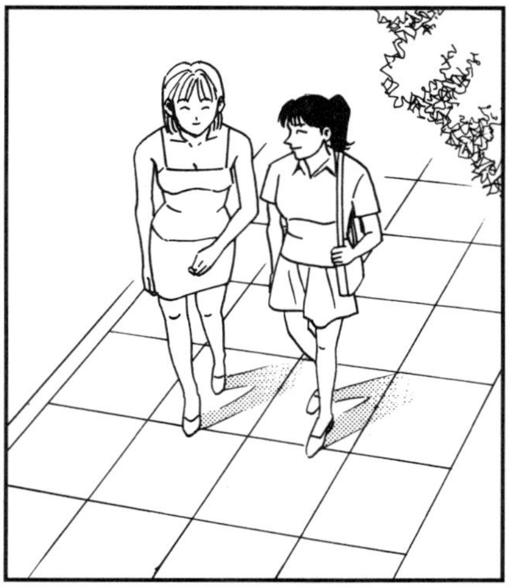

③ **Scene Changes and Establishment Scenes:**
These often comprise long shots of the full figure composed from a high angle.

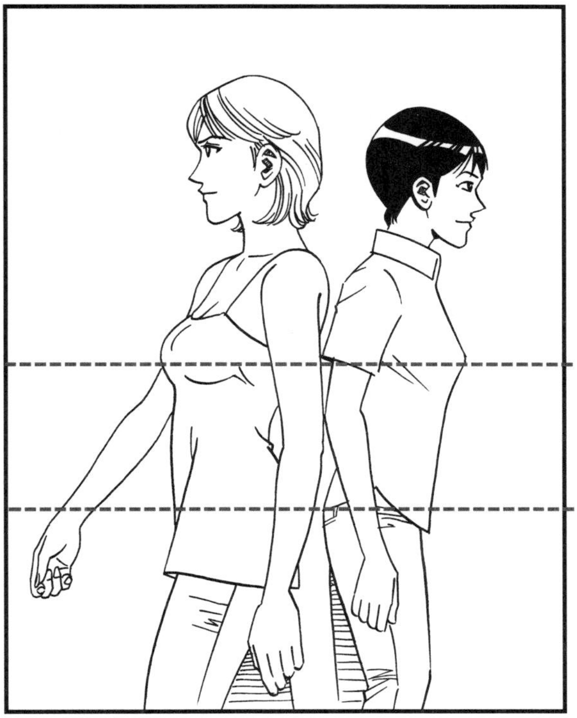

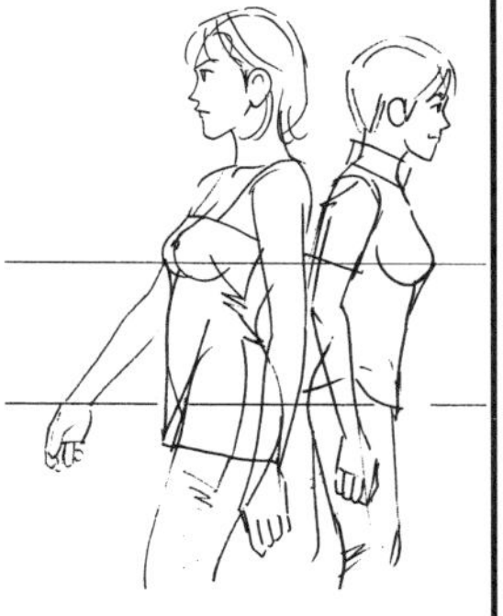

④ **Scenes of Characters Passing Each Other**

The figure is often shown from the shoulders or chest up. Images from the waist up are rare.

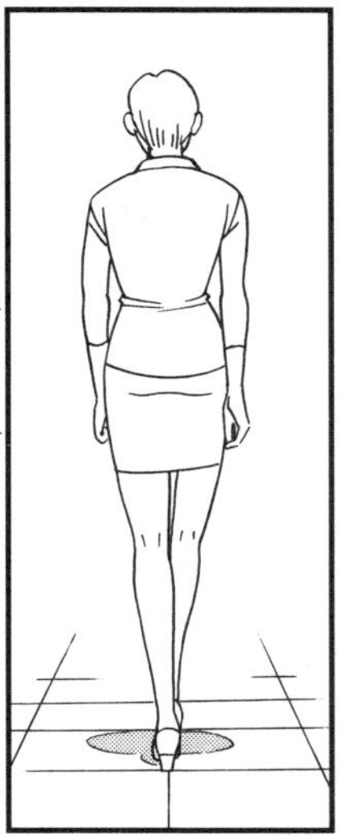

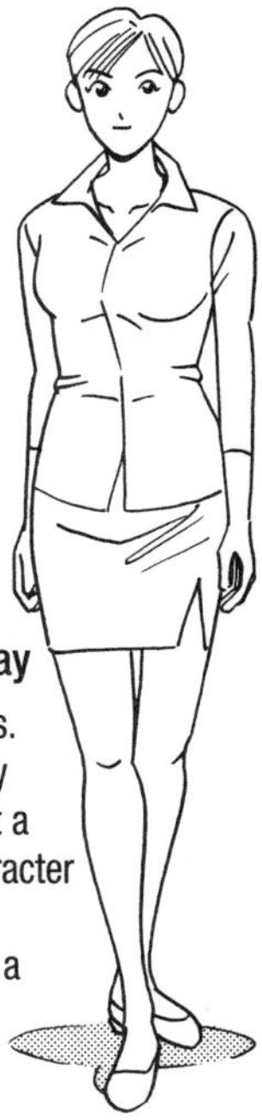

⑤ **Scenes of Walking Away**

These are basic full figure shots. When the character walks away dejectedly, artists usually select a back view, while when the character stands with poise and self-assurance, artists usually draw a front view.

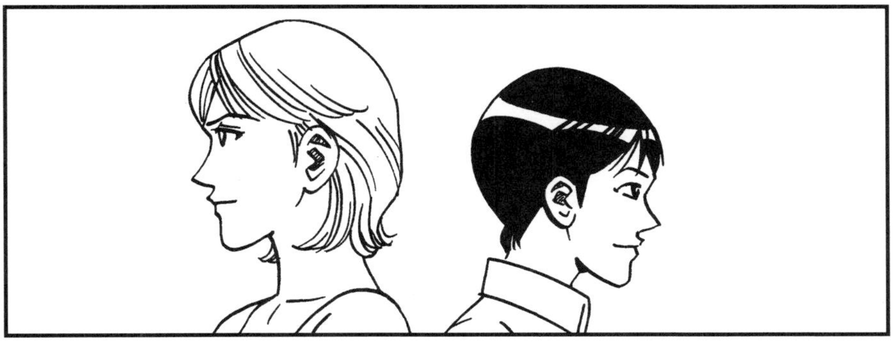

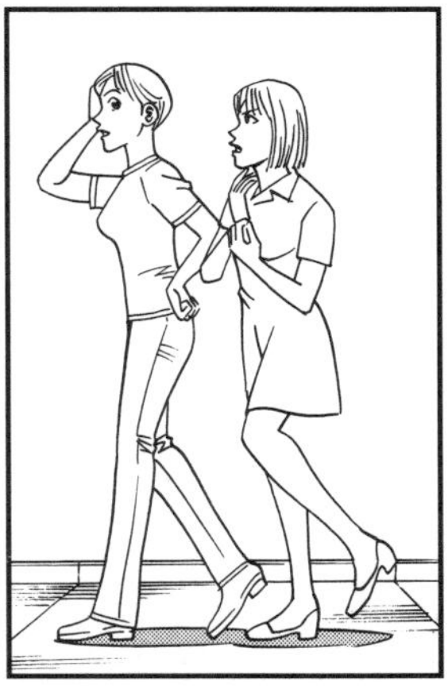

⑥ **Scenes of Talking, Discussing, or One Character Running after Another**

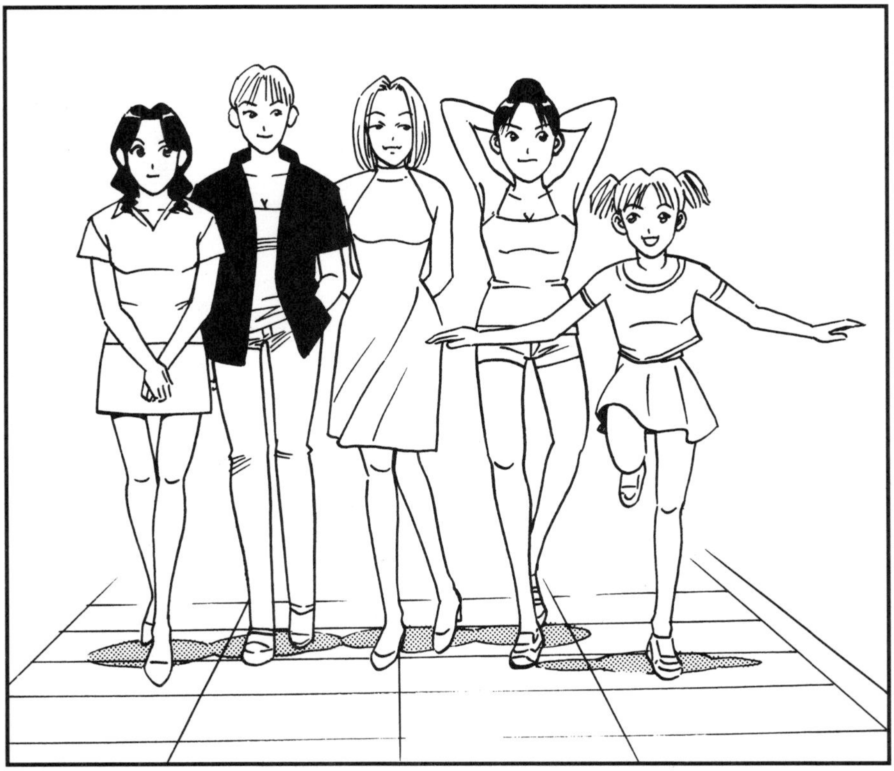

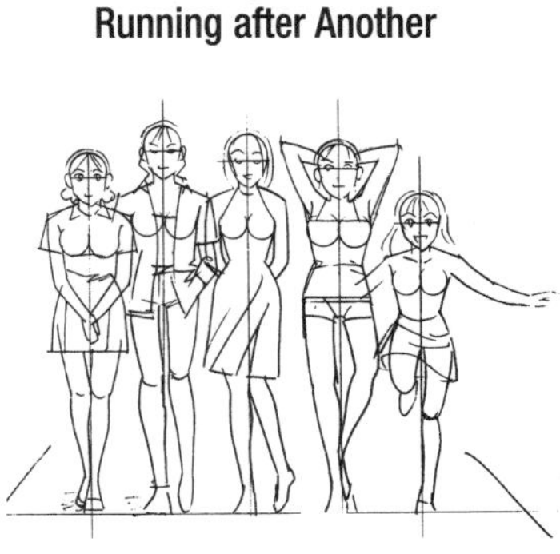

⑦ **Scenes of Characters Walking in a Group**

Showing characters walking side-by-side in a group offers a look common to movies and TV shows.

The Fundamentals of Walking

Walking normally

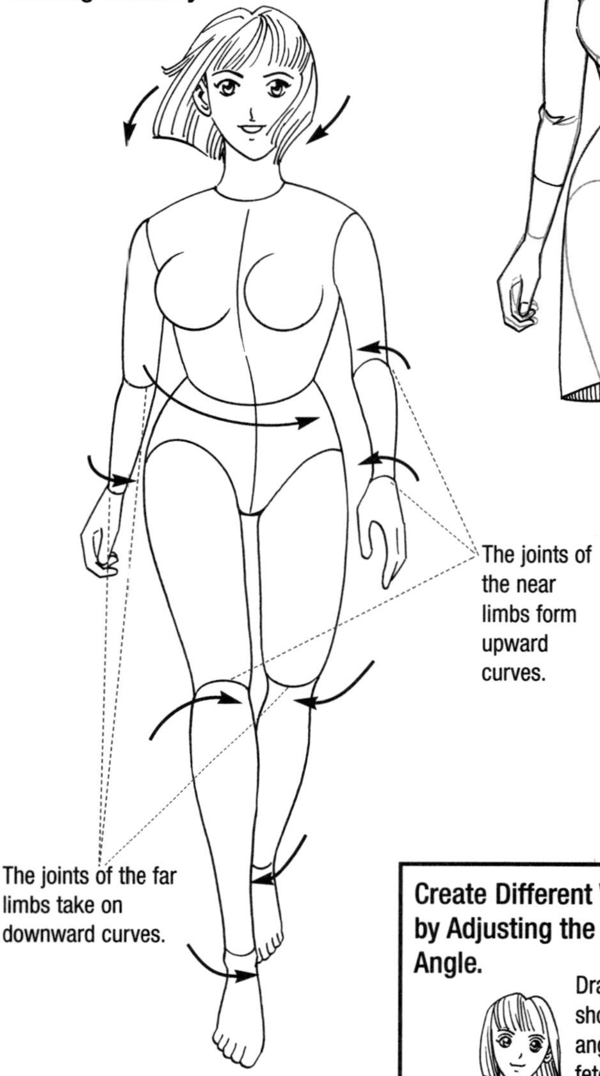

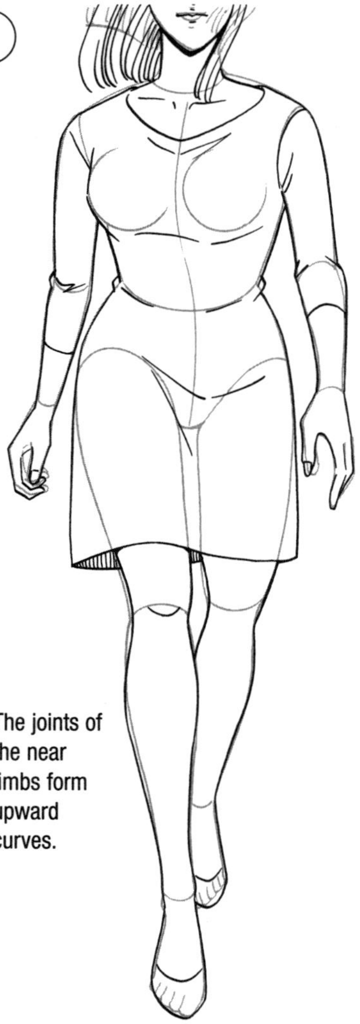

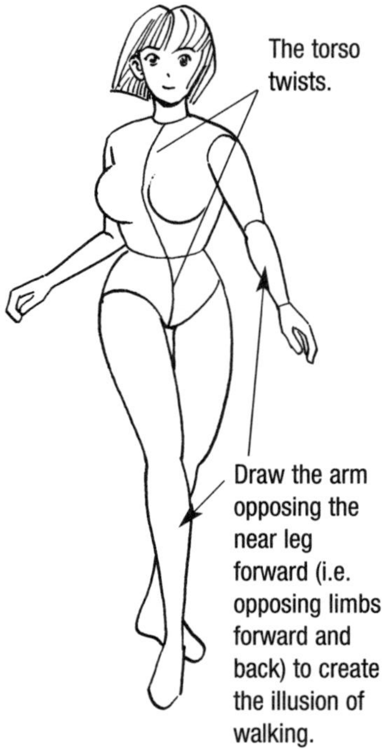

Create Different Walking Styles by Adjusting the Shoulders' Angle.

Adjusting the shoulders' angle, and the degree of motion in the neck and arms allow you to change the character's perceived mood.

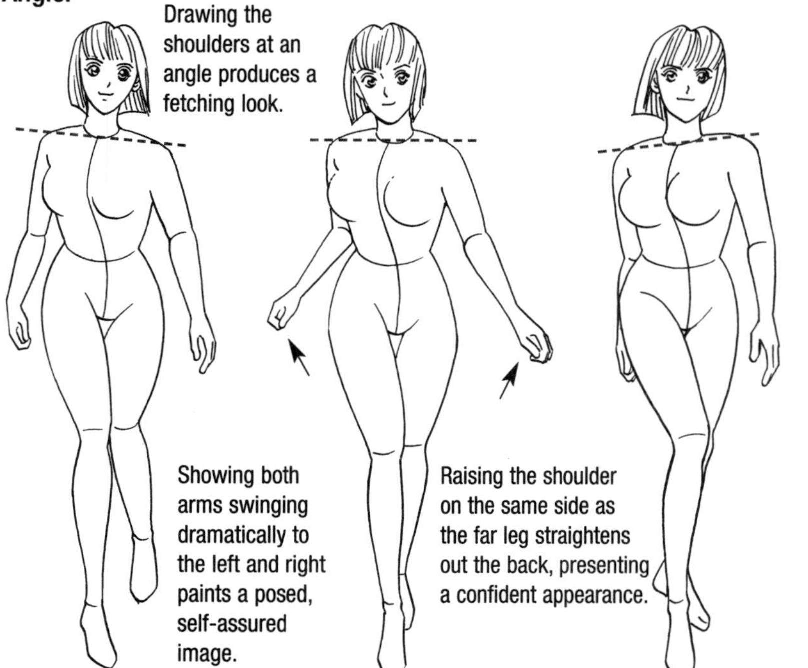

Differences in Pace

Breaking into a Trot

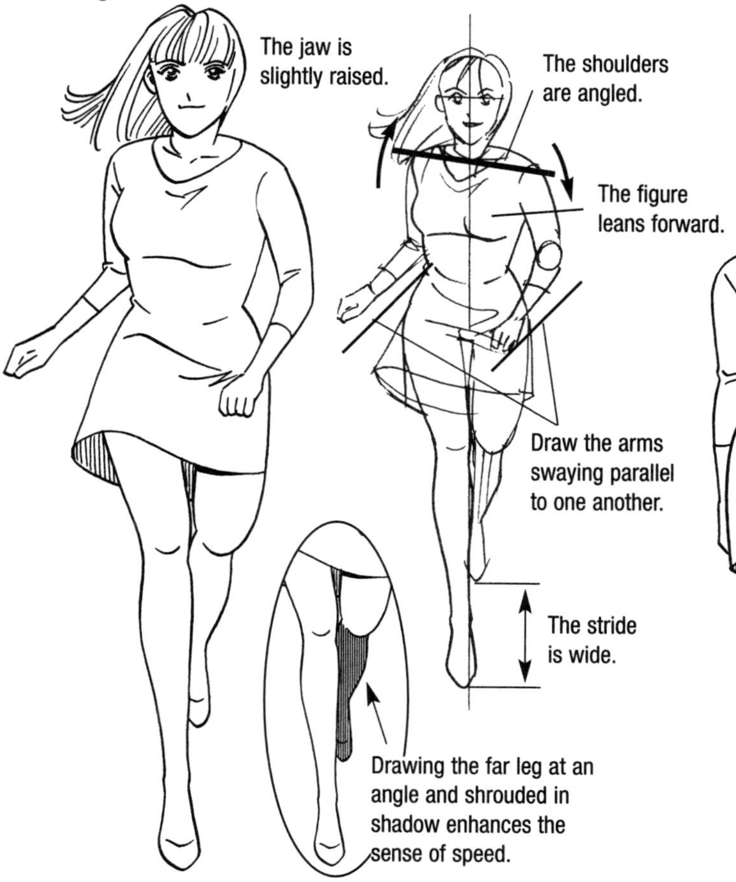

Plodding along

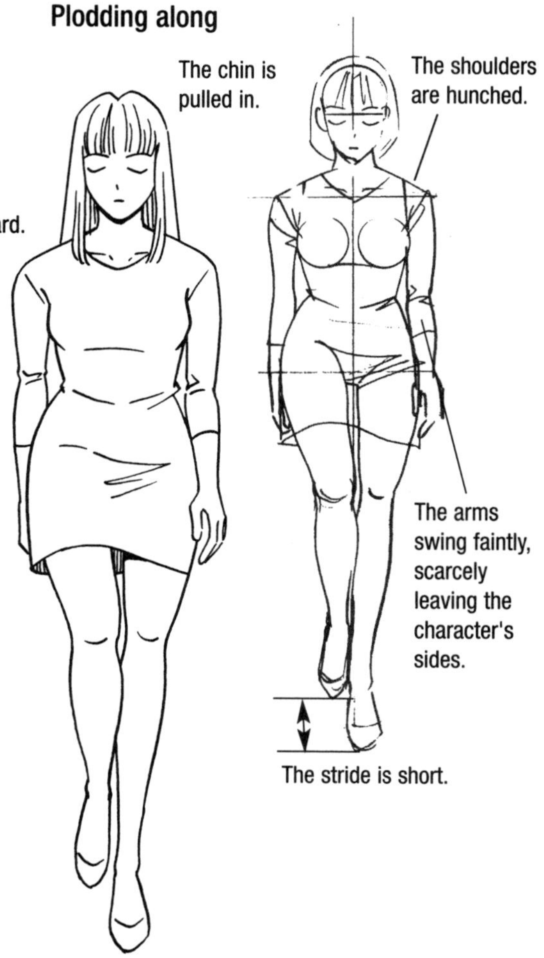

Walking Slowly

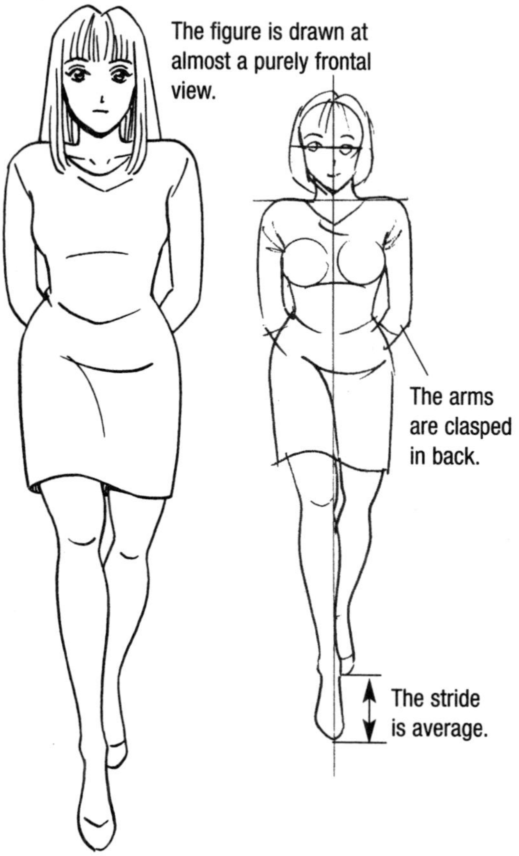

Hands Communicate the Emotional State

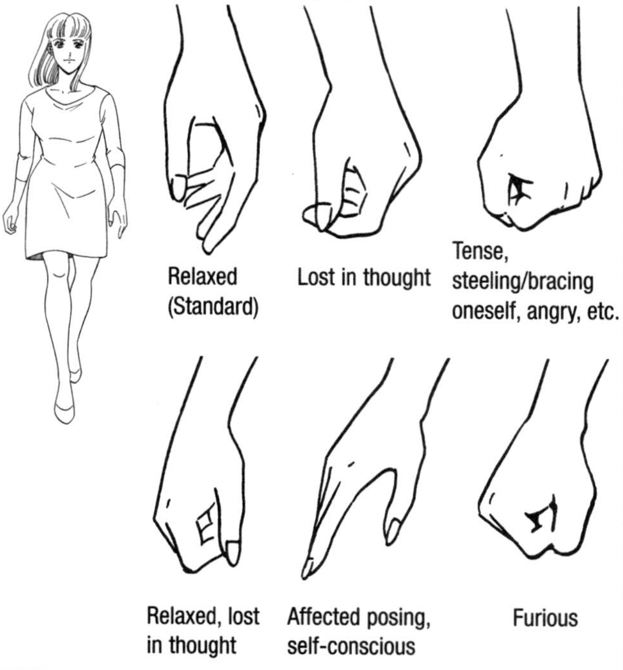

Using Bust Shots to Portray Walking

When using bust shots to portray walking, no torsion is visible in the torso, nor are the legs present. Consequently, care must be taken with the arms' angles to suggest that the arms are swinging while walking.

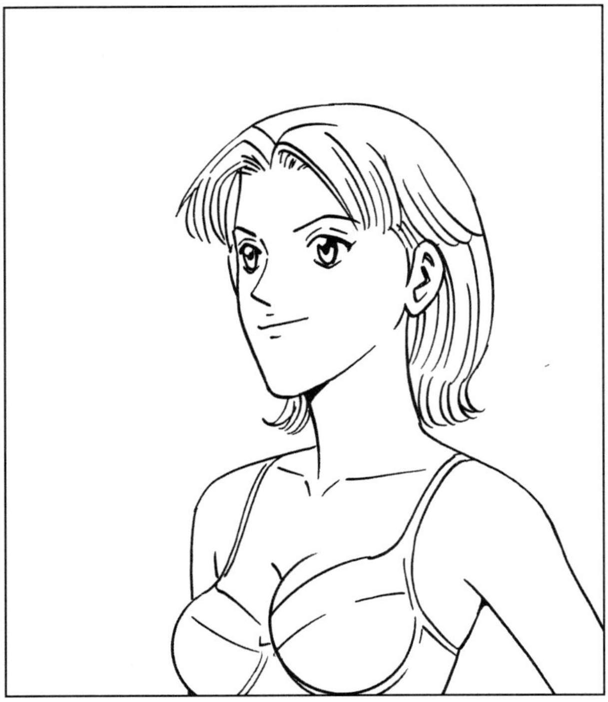

Leaving open space in front of, behind, and above the character suggests walking in an open area.

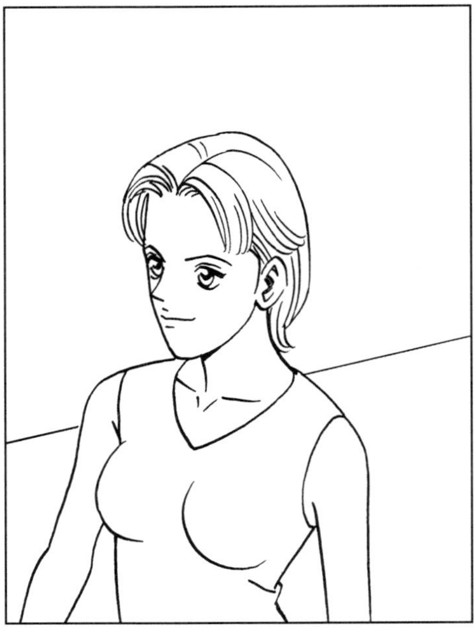

When composed from a moderately high angle, a single line suggests the ground—a common technique for creating the illusion of a corridor or road.

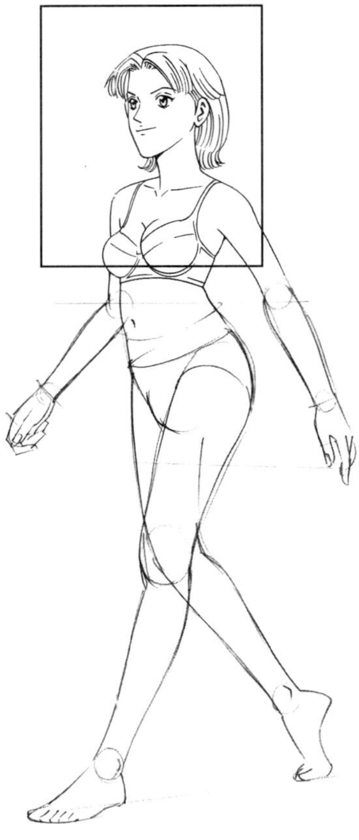

This figure includes those portions not appearing in the panel. The point of note is that even when artists are just producing a bust shot from a full figure, the full figure is still drawn walking.

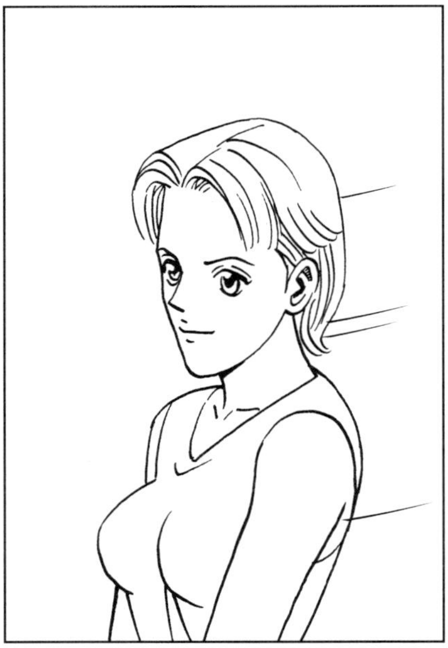

Special Effect Lines: Drawing short lines behind the figure suggests the character is moving.

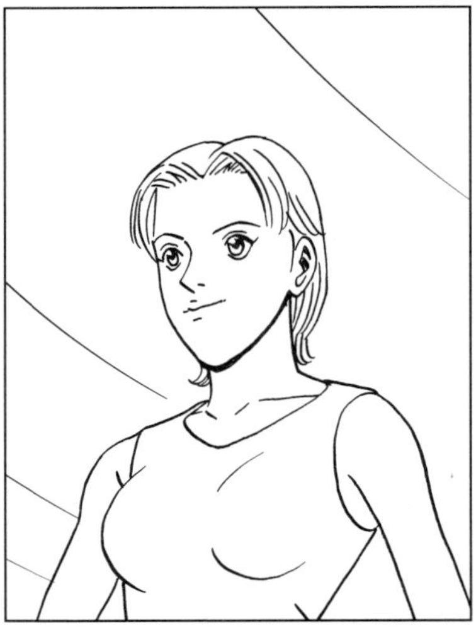

Here, subtly arcing lines in front of and above the character suggest a background shifting behind the character, creating the illusion of movement.

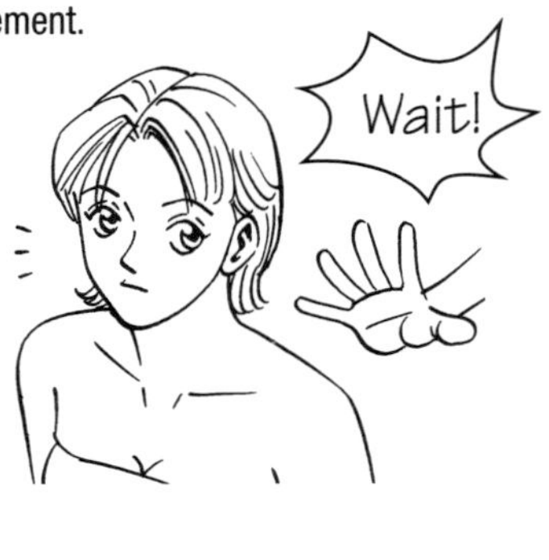

Dashes drawn around speech balloons and in front of the character's face suggest the instant a character stops moving.

Walking While Talking on a Cell Phone/Eating

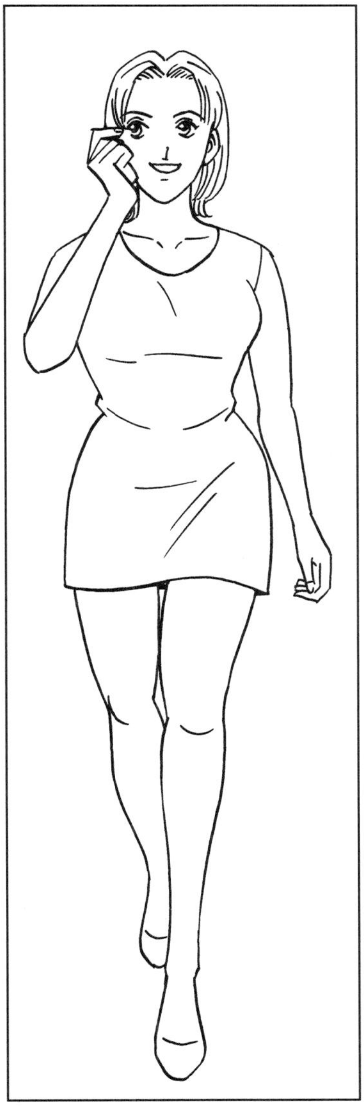

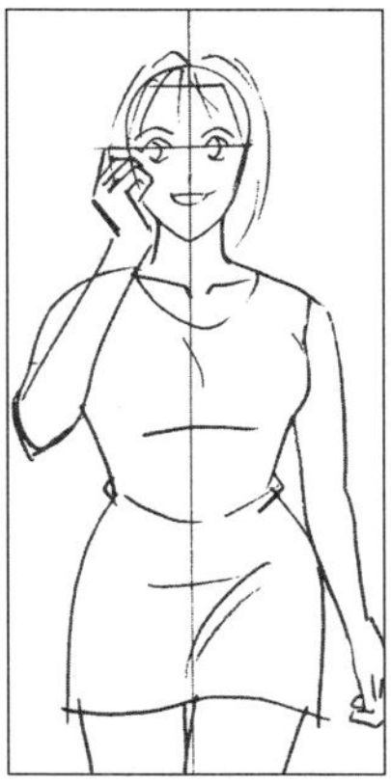

Since cell phones are obscured from view by the hand, the way the hand is held becomes crucial.

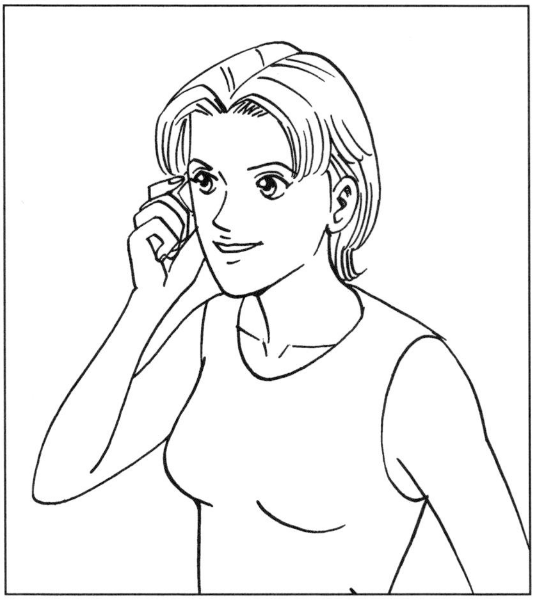

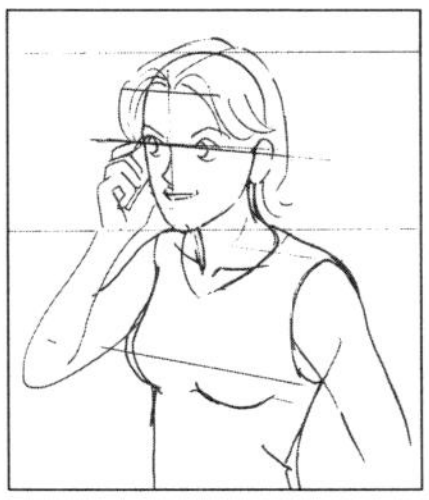

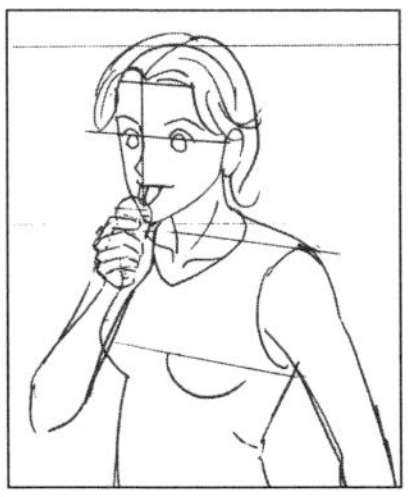

The face and torso are directed in the same angle. Note that the elbow changes position according to whether the hand is held by the ear or the mouth. The left arm is depicted swinging, thus suggesting motion.

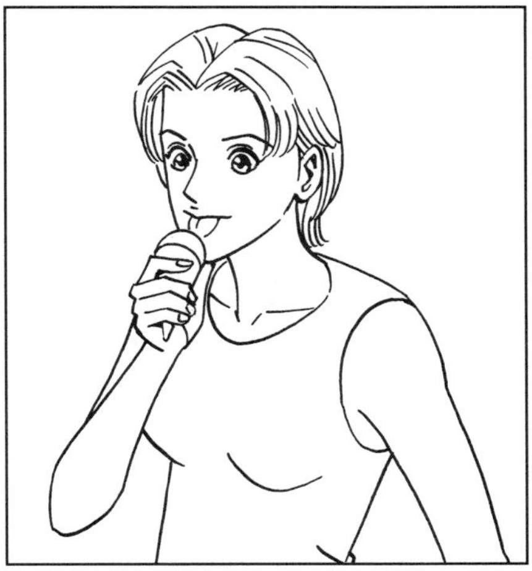

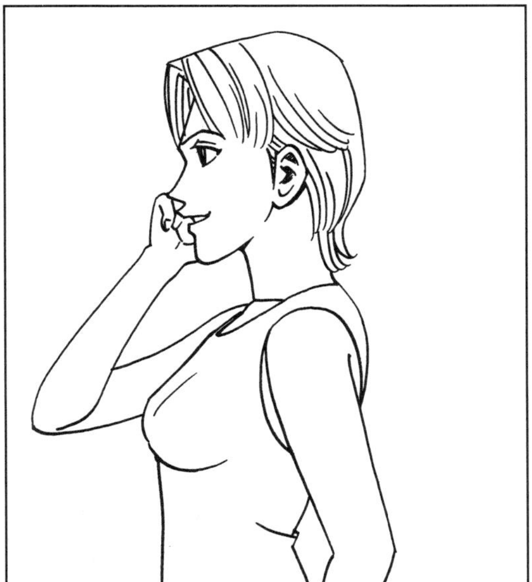

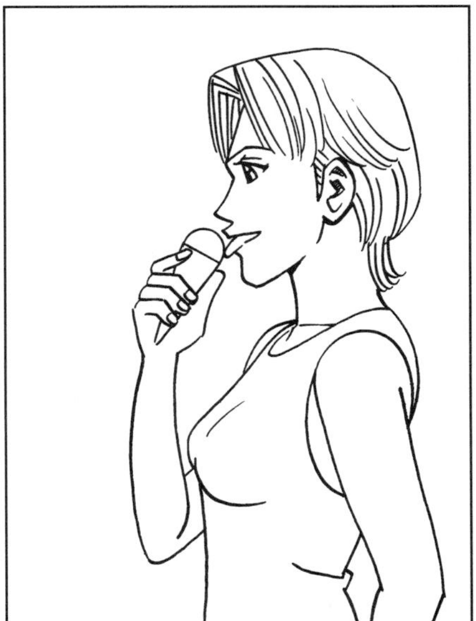

From a side view, open space should be left to the character's front and back. Take note that positioning the figure in the panel's center will create the impression that she is standing still.

Rear View/Leaving

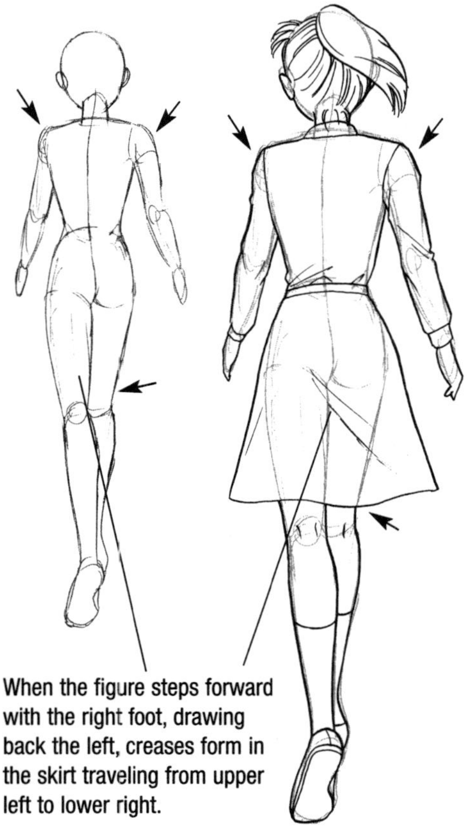

When the figure steps forward with the right foot, drawing back the left, creases form in the skirt traveling from upper left to lower right.

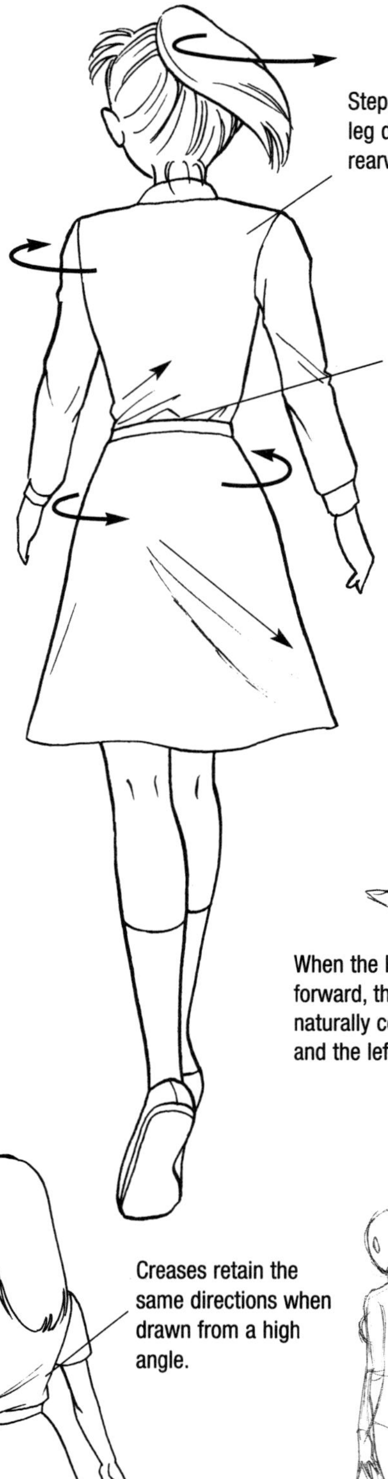

Stepping forward with the right leg draws the right shoulder rearward.

Stepping forward with the right leg, drawing back the left causes creases to form at the waist angling from upper left to lower right.

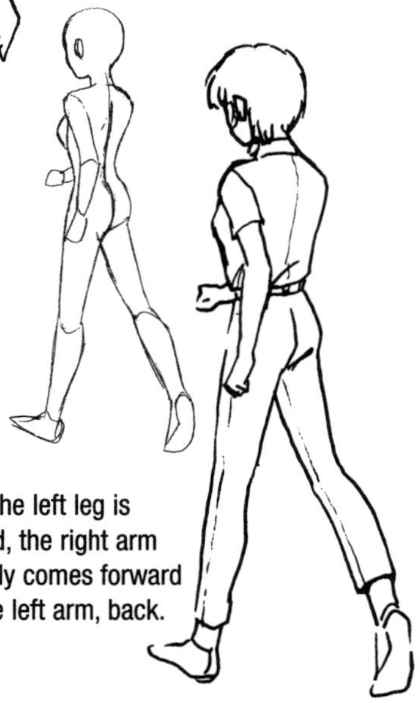

When the left leg is forward, the right arm naturally comes forward and the left arm, back.

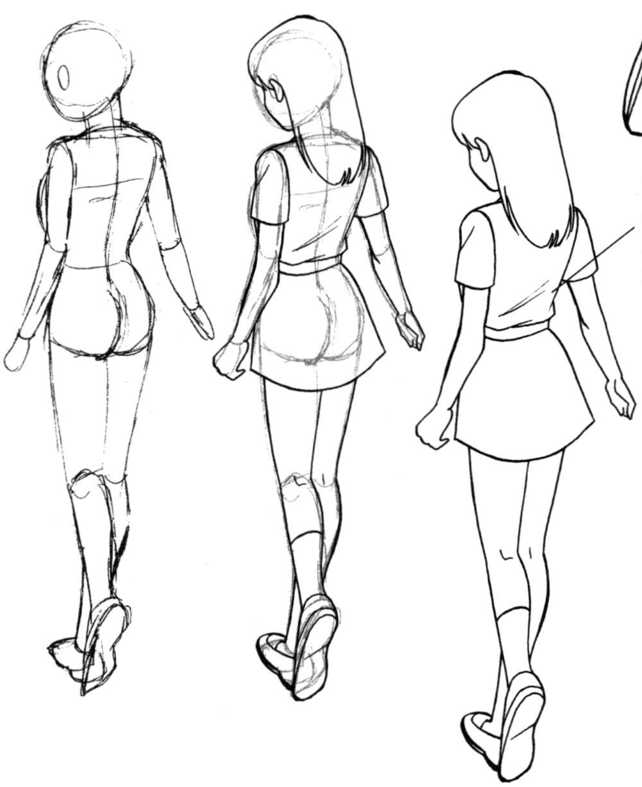

Creases retain the same directions when drawn from a high angle.

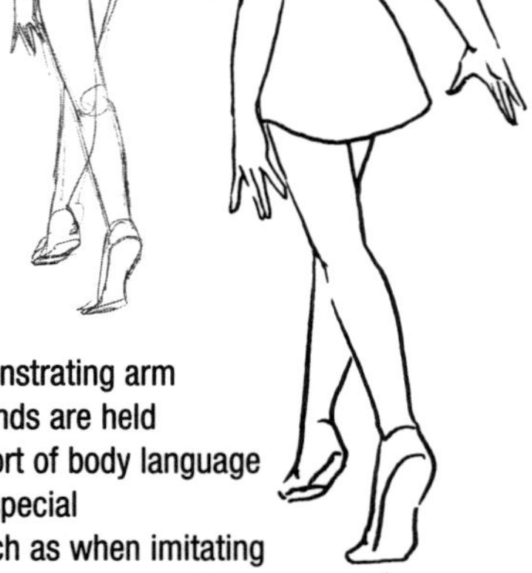

In this figure demonstrating arm positioning, the hands are held unnaturally. This sort of body language would be used in special circumstances, such as when imitating a modelesque-style walk or posing for some other purpose.

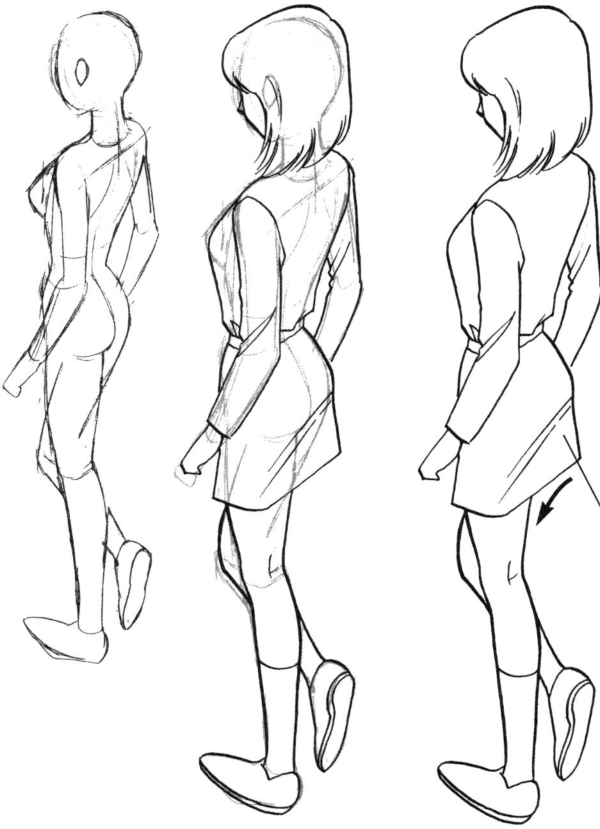

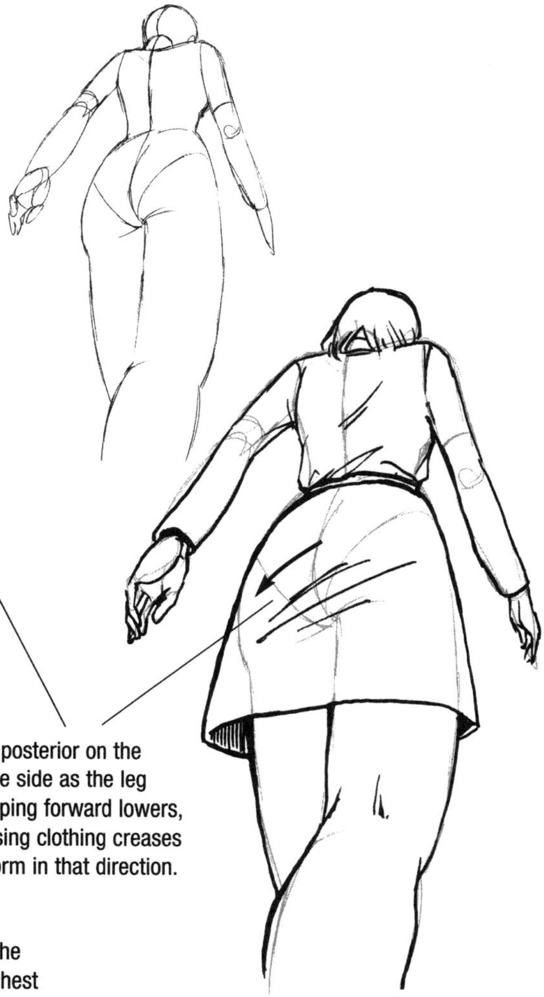

The posterior on the same side as the leg stepping forward lowers, causing clothing creases to form in that direction.

The back broadens as the shoulders roll forward and the head bent forward.

When the arms are brought around to the back, causing the chest to thrust out, the scapula become prominent.

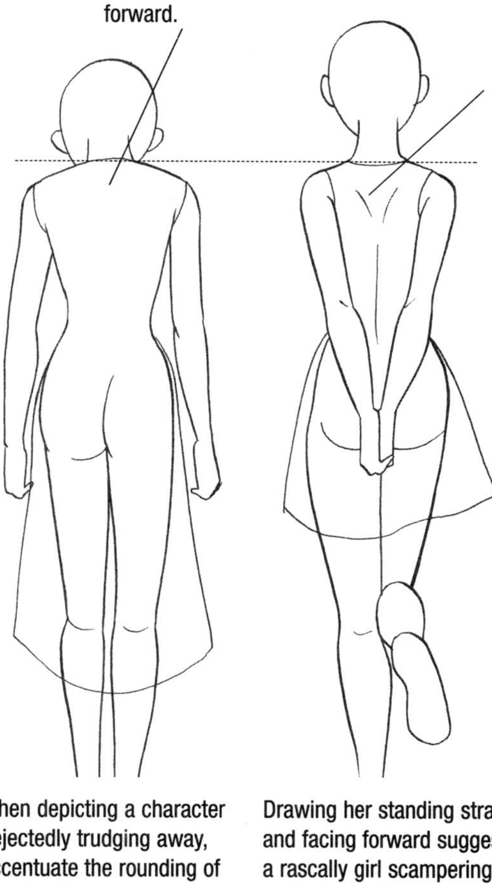

When depicting a character dejectedly trudging away, accentuate the rounding of the shoulders and show the figure hunched over.

Drawing her standing straight and facing forward suggests a rascally girl scampering off.

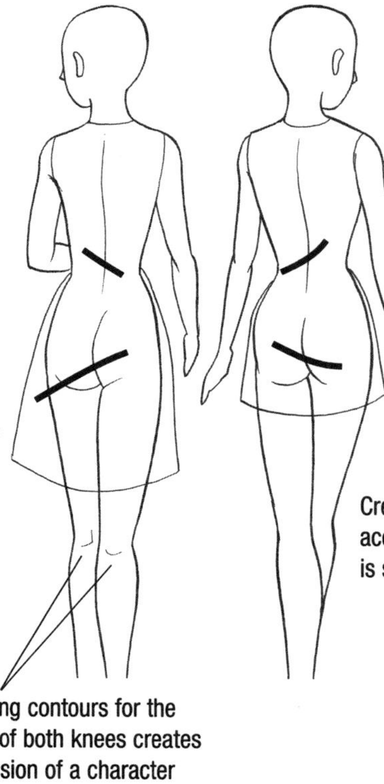

Crease angles vary according to which foot is stepping forward.

Including contours for the backs of both knees creates the illusion of a character walking while leaning slightly forward.

Scenes of Going to/Leaving School (Overhead Shots)

Walking scenes are often used for scene changes or explanatory scenes, and the prevalent composition seems to consist of an overhead angle. In scenes of going to or leaving school, characters often walk with their friends or classmates, allowing for the depiction of multiple figures.

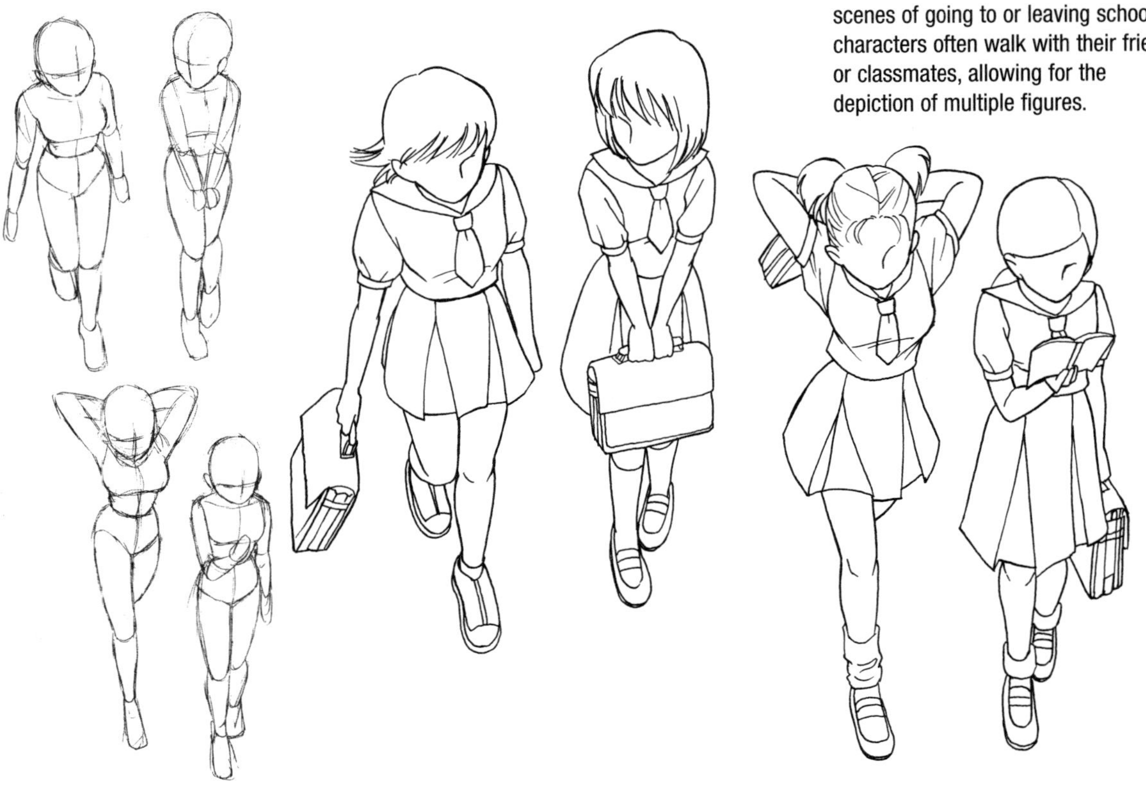

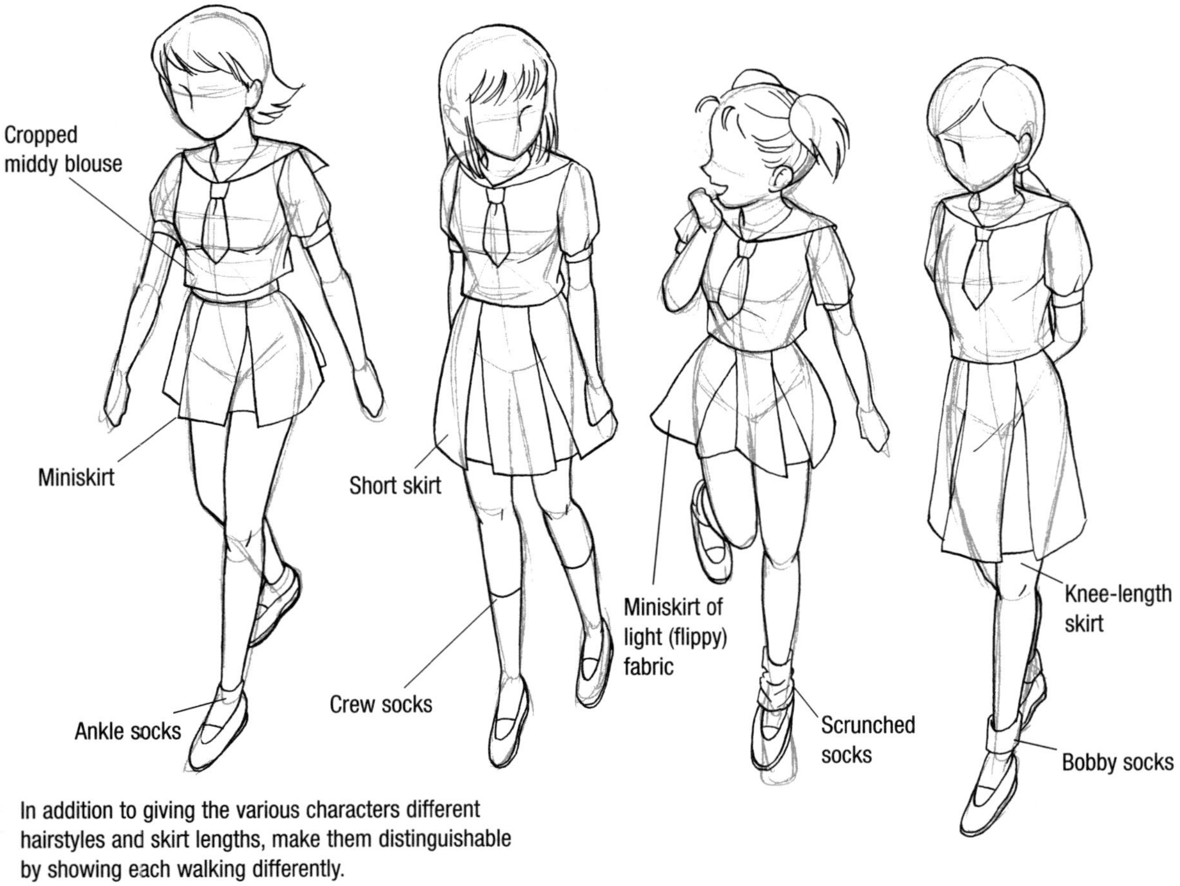

In addition to giving the various characters different hairstyles and skirt lengths, make them distinguishable by showing each walking differently.

Using Ingenuity When Lining up Characters

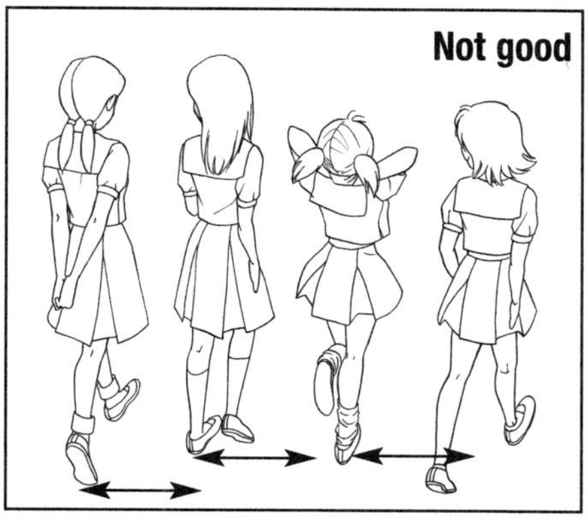

Here, the characters are spaced evenly, walking as a group side-by-side. While this is acceptable as a single mise-en-scéne, it does appear artificial and staged.

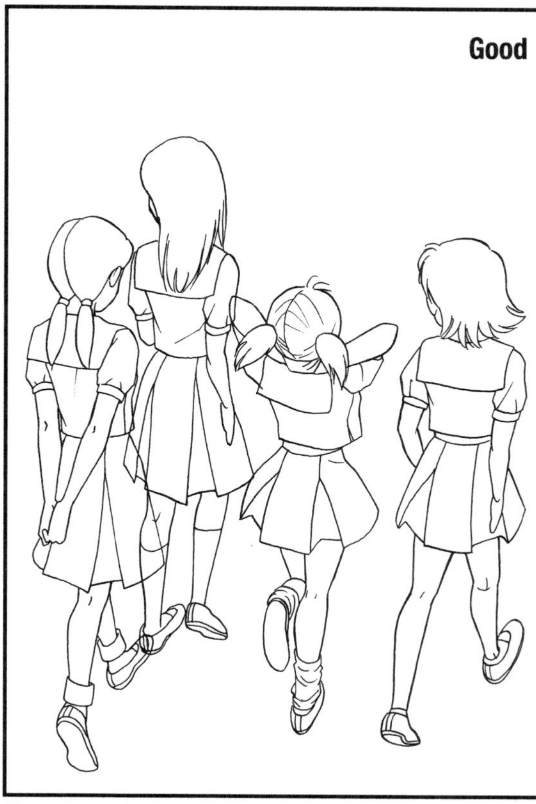

Show some characters walking in the front of the group and others lagging behind. Individuality in the line-up projects a more natural feel.

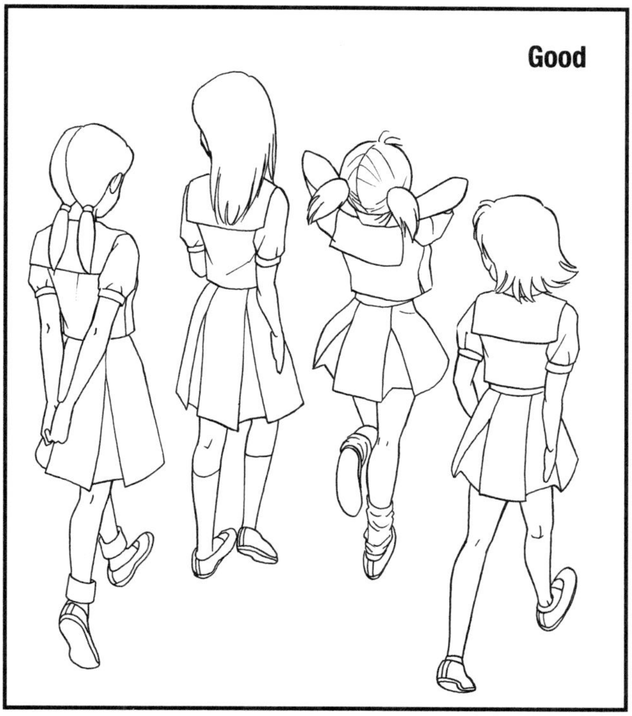

If you do opt to space the characters evenly, your group will appear more natural if some characters walk ahead while others fall back.

A character walking in front of the others in the group will need to be foreshortened. Make her one size smaller than the rest.

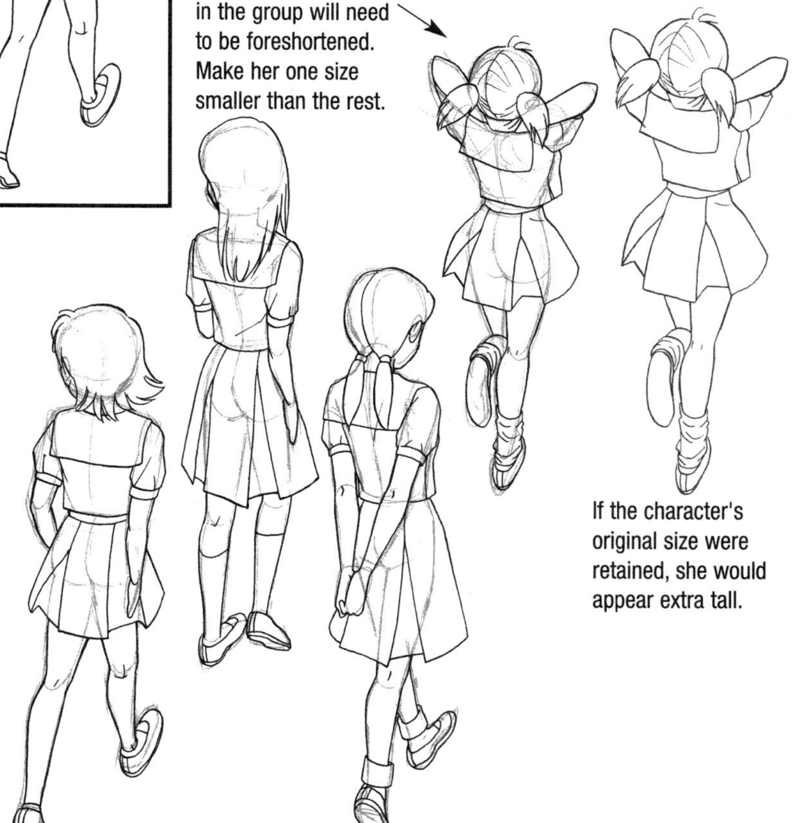

If the character's original size were retained, she would appear extra tall.

Style of Walking as Indication of Emotional State

Strive to indicate the characters' emotional states through her posture or body language (swinging or positioning of the arms and the direction of the head) even without having drawn the face.

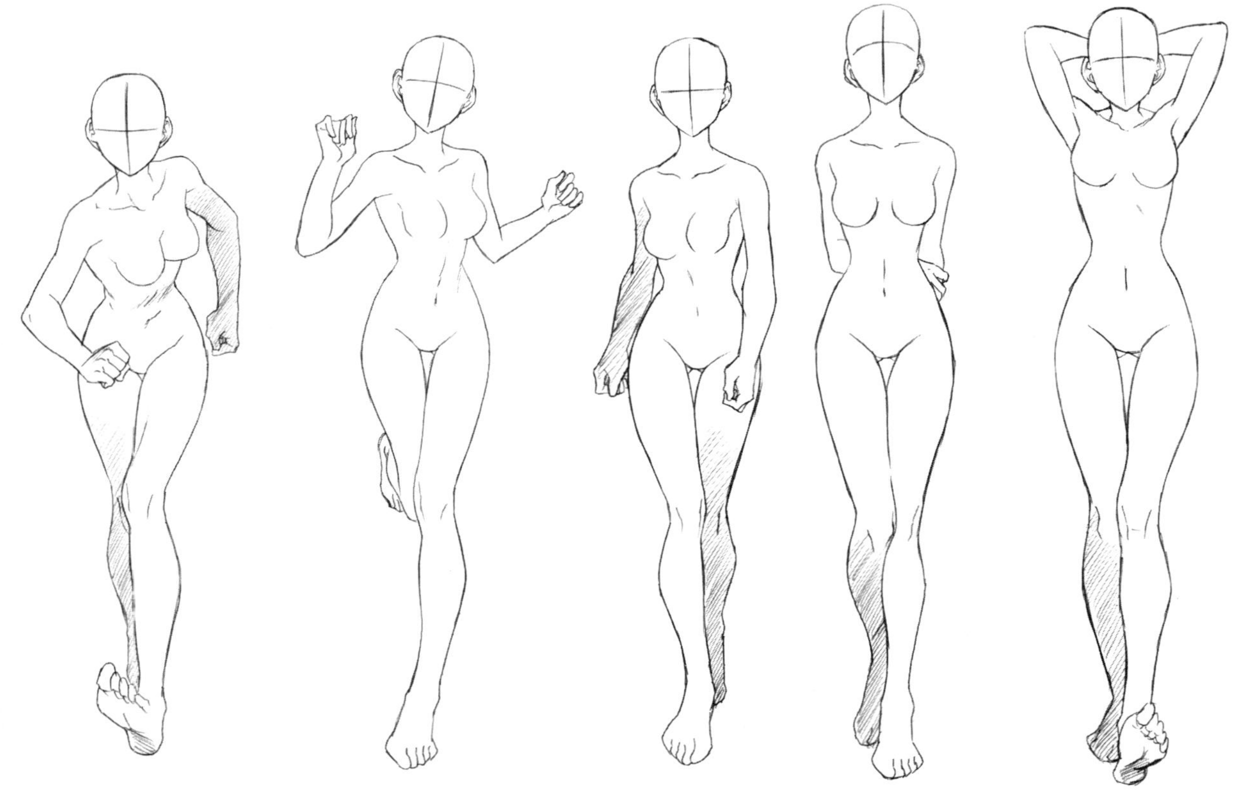

Large Stride (Confidence, Anger)

Excited, Gleeful

Serious

Lost in Thought

Bored

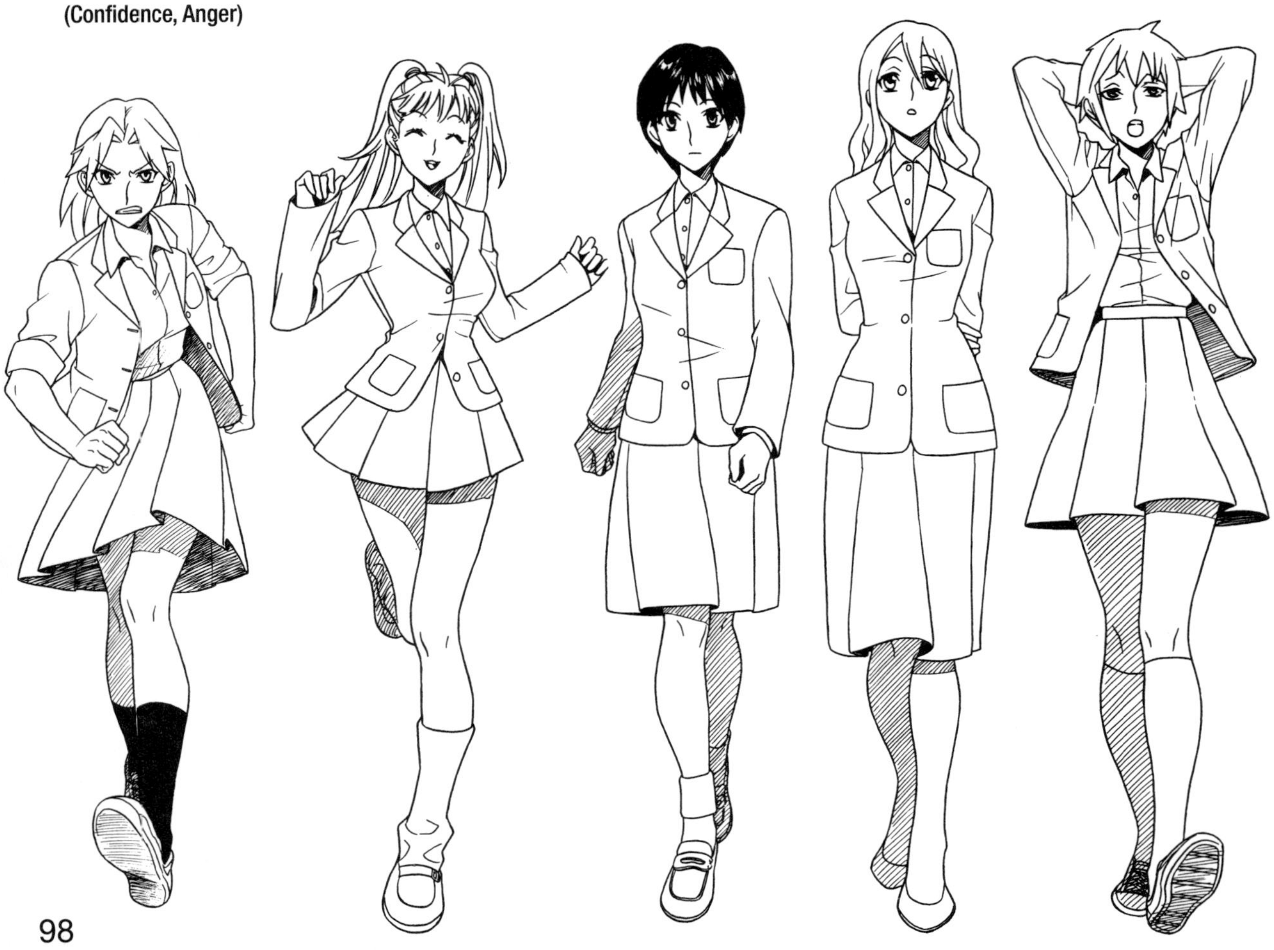

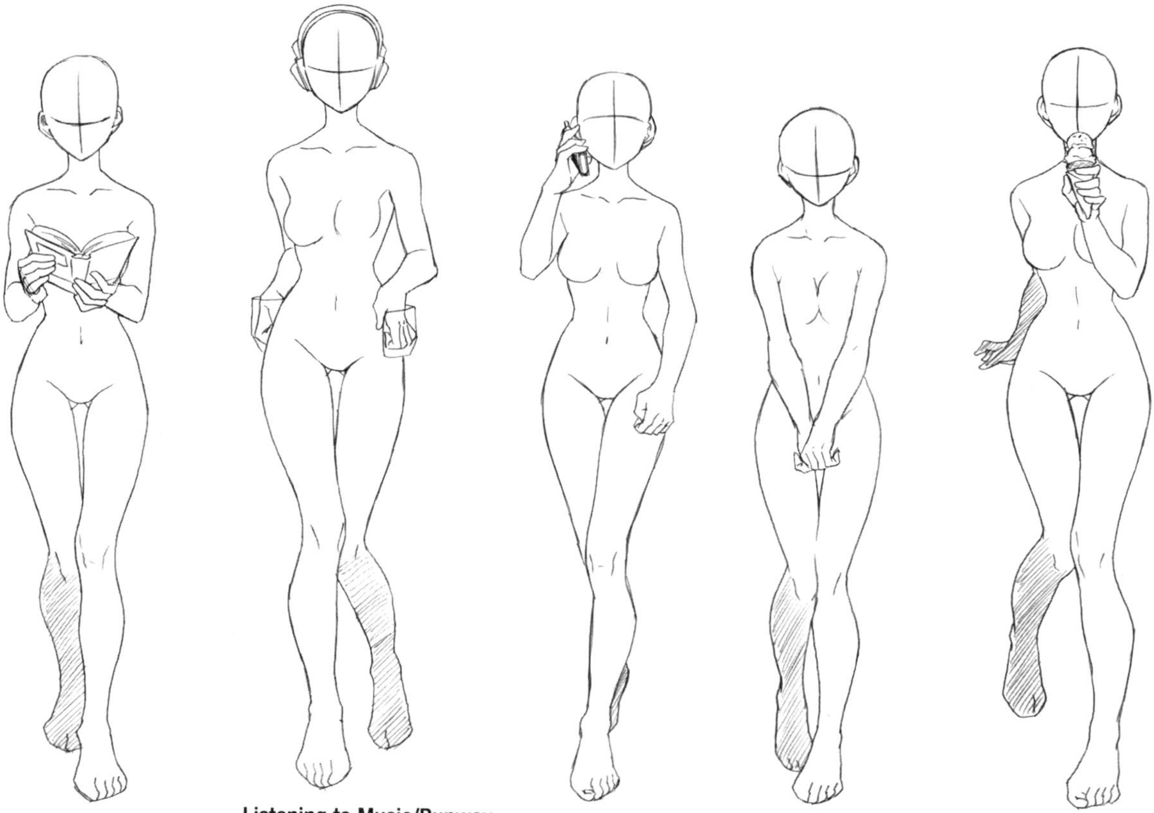

Reading

Listening to Music/Runway Model-Style

Talking on the Cell Phone

Plodding Along, Dejected

Eating, Hurrying

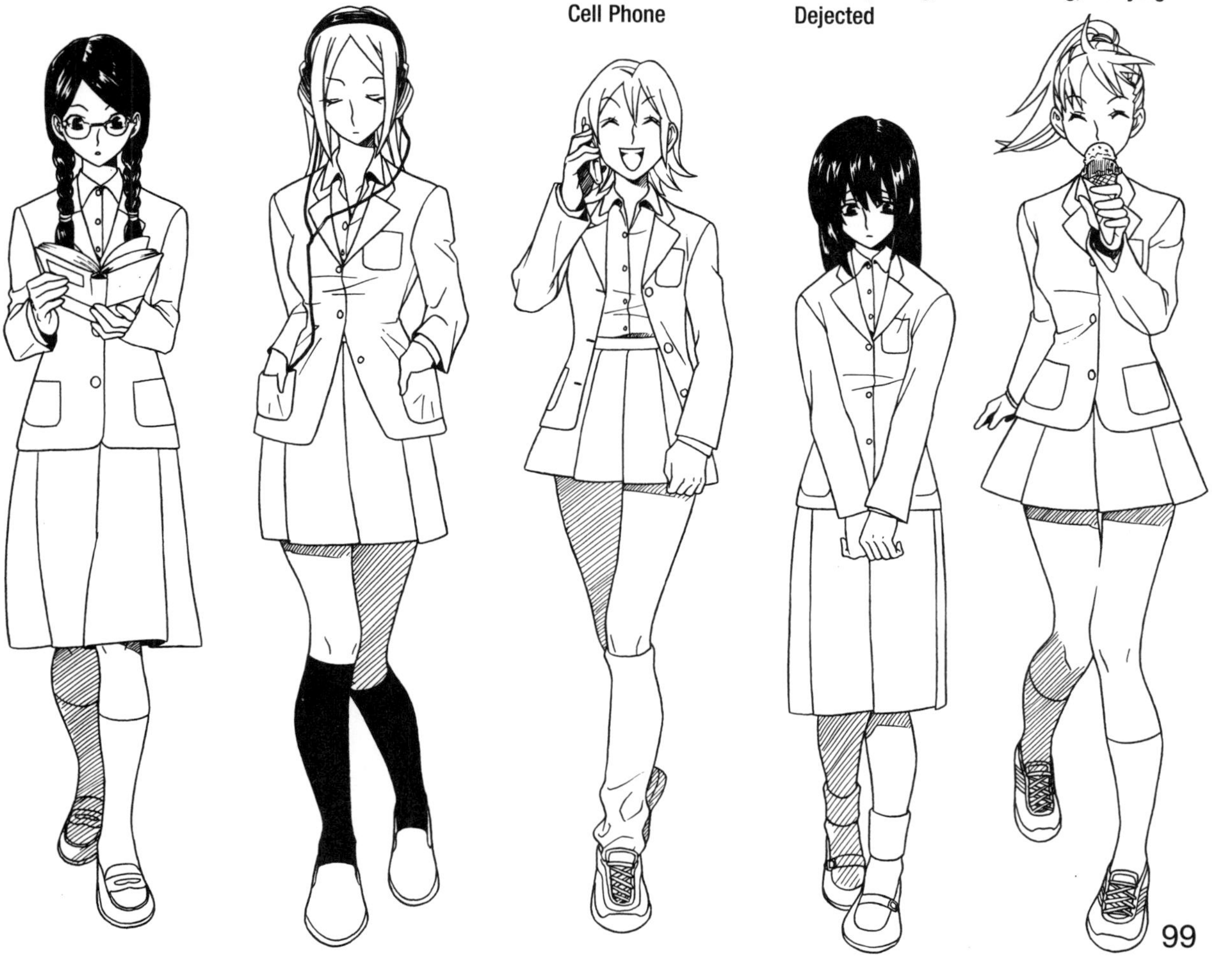

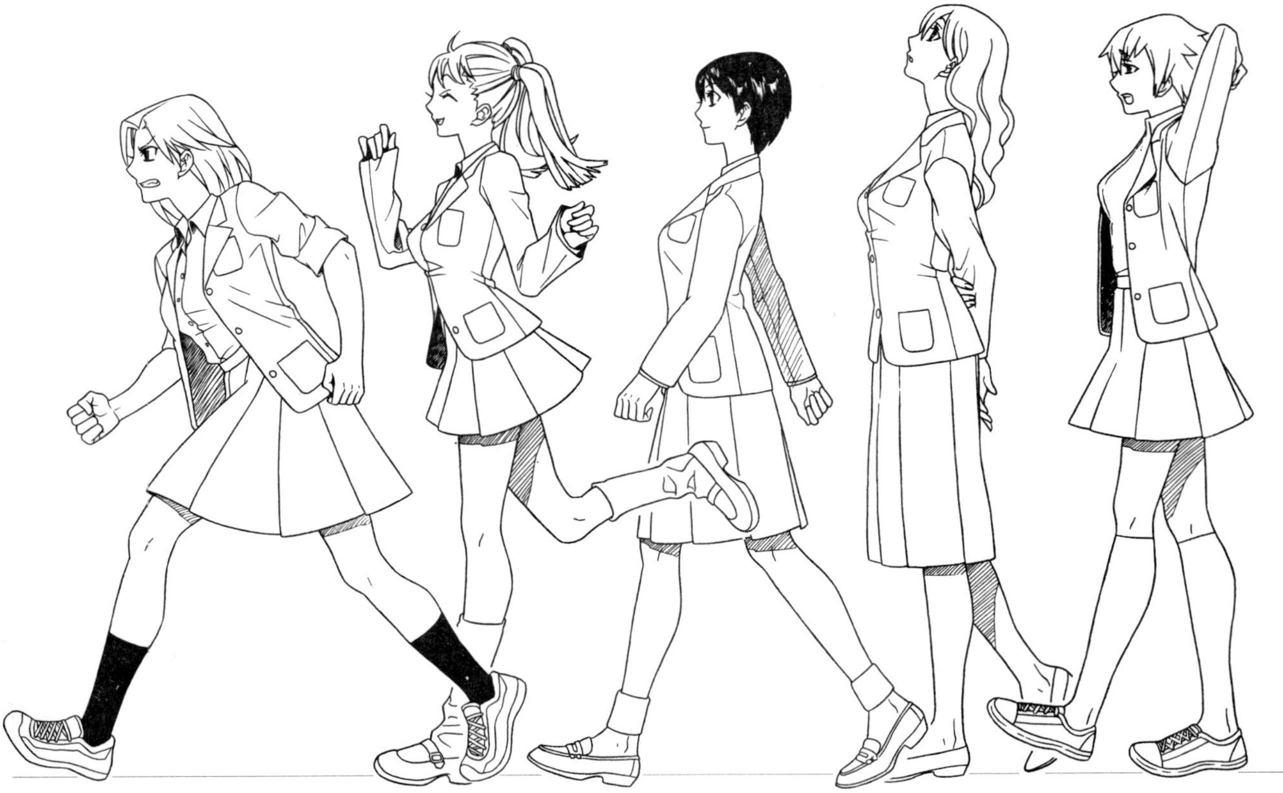

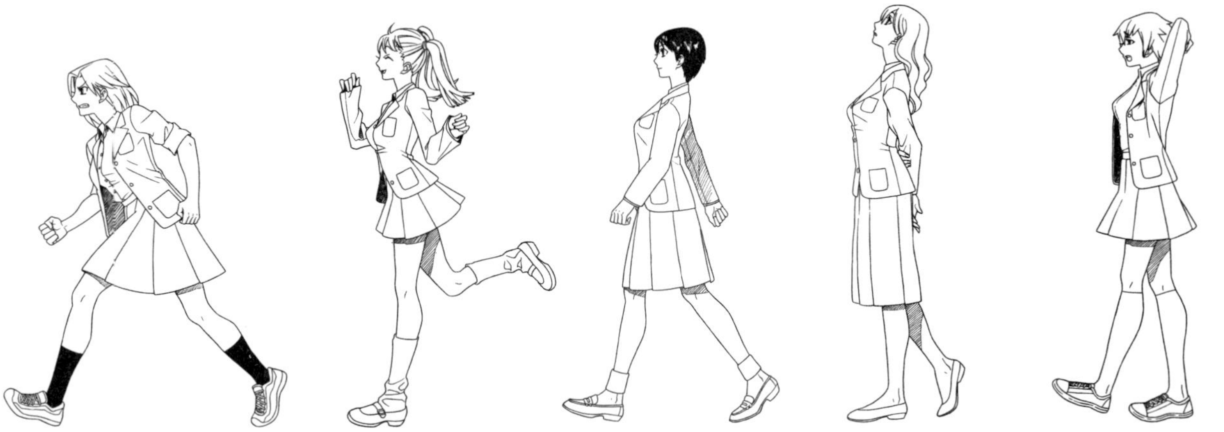

Large Stride (Confidence, Anger) | Excited, Gleeful | Serious | Lost in Thought | Bored

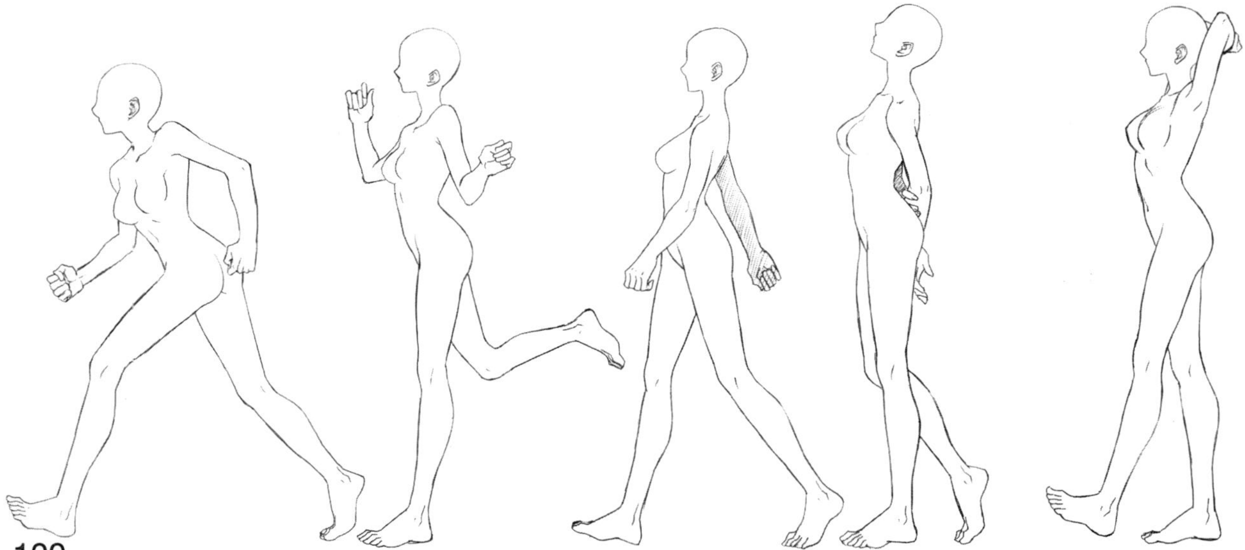

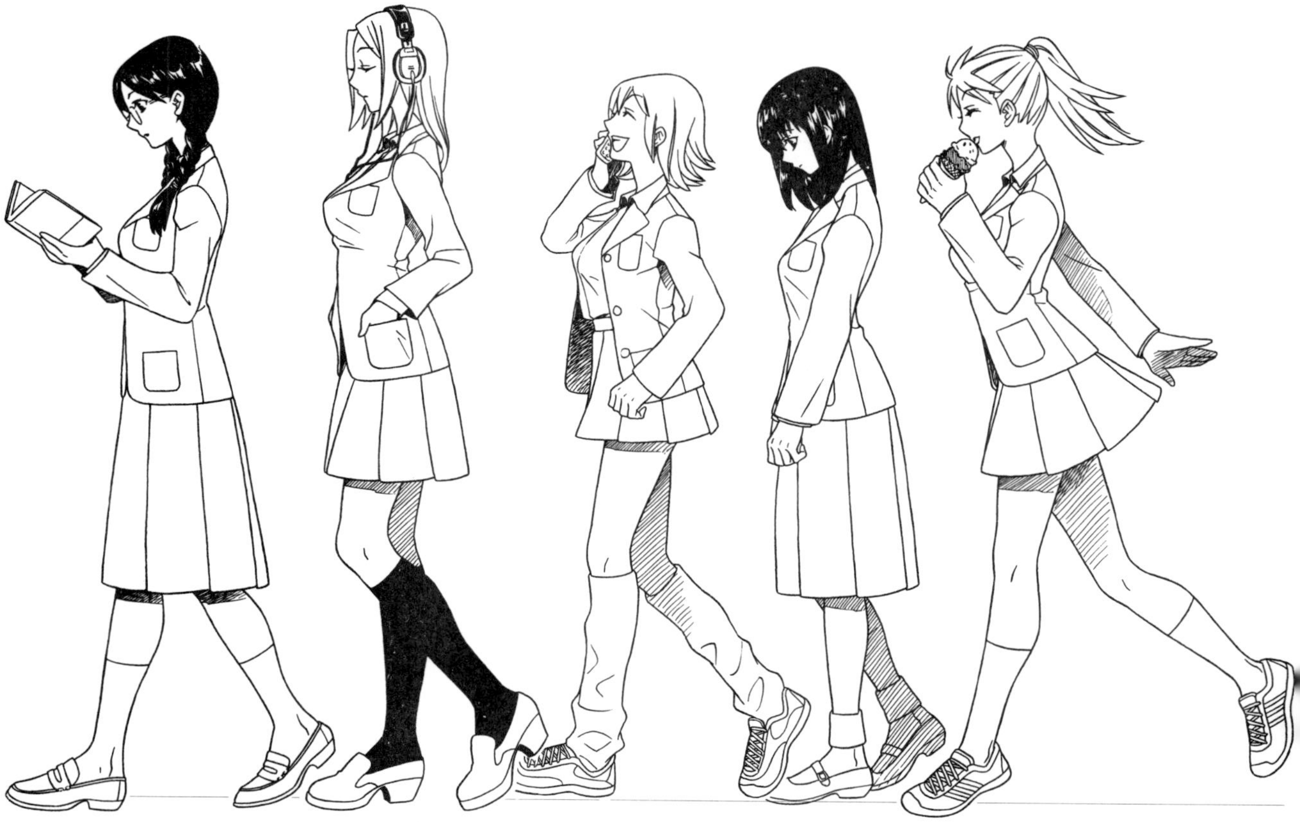

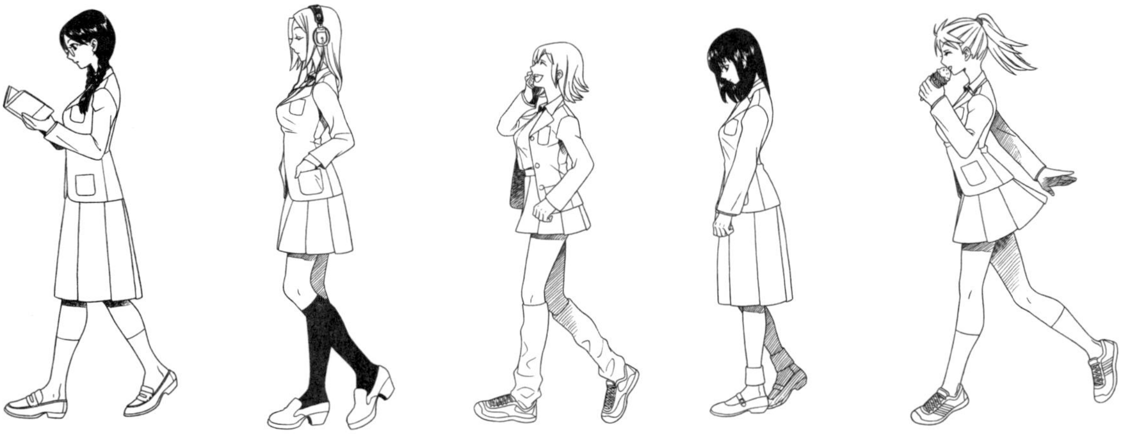

Reading

Listening to Music/Runway Model-Style

Talking on the Cell Phone

Plodding Along, Dejected

Eating, Hurrying

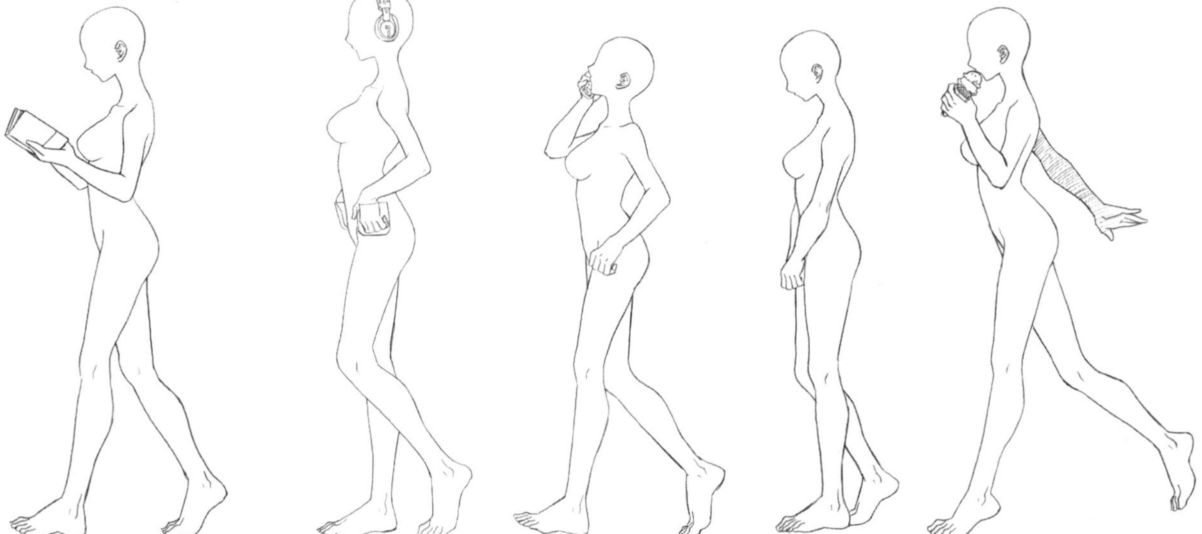

Drawing Characters Entering through Doors

Panels of characters walking through doors are used to introduce characters, as their big entrance scenes, to change scenes, etc. Such a setting serves well in breaking up monotonous scenes or unvarying storylines. Because drawing an open door is rather difficult, artists often opt to show a character standing in front of a closed door.

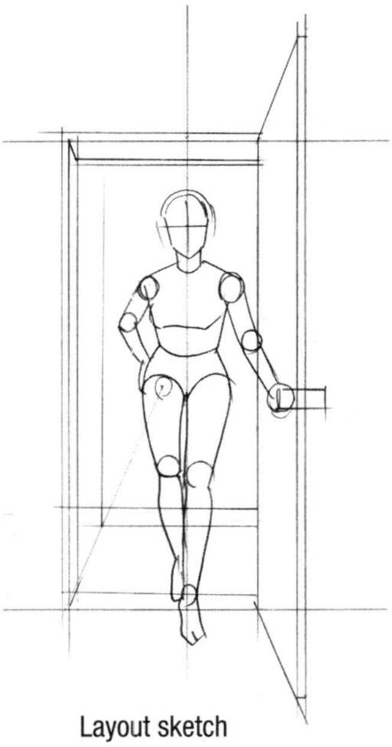

Layout sketch

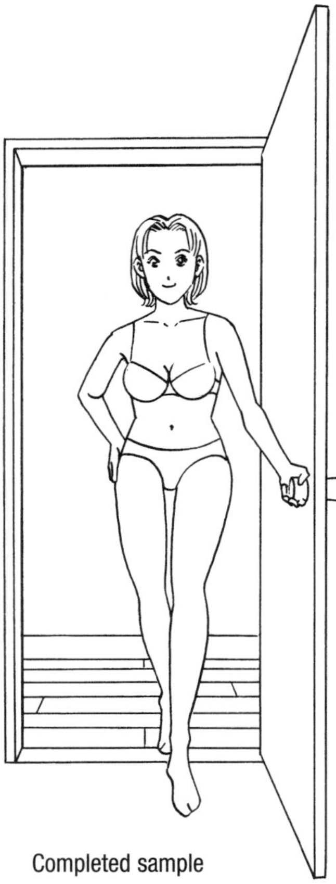

Completed sample

• Standard Door Size

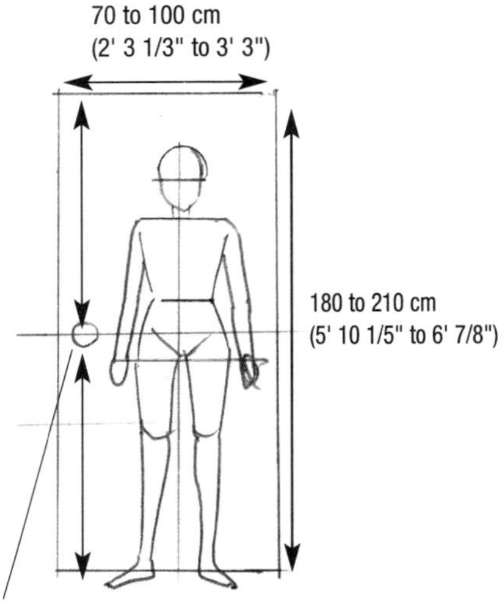

The doorknob lies midway along the door.

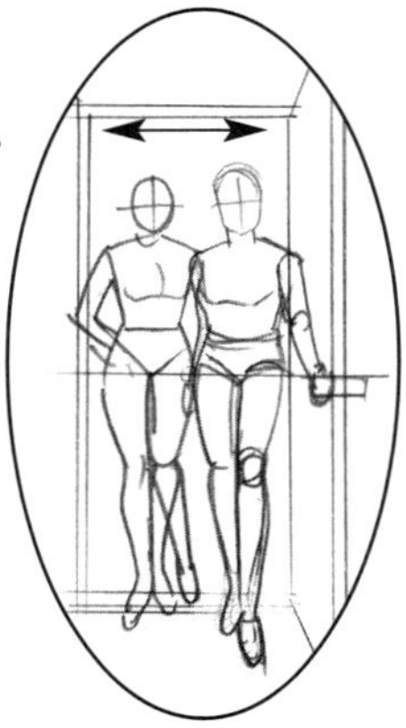

The door width should equal that of two characters side-by-side.

• Steps in Drawing a Door

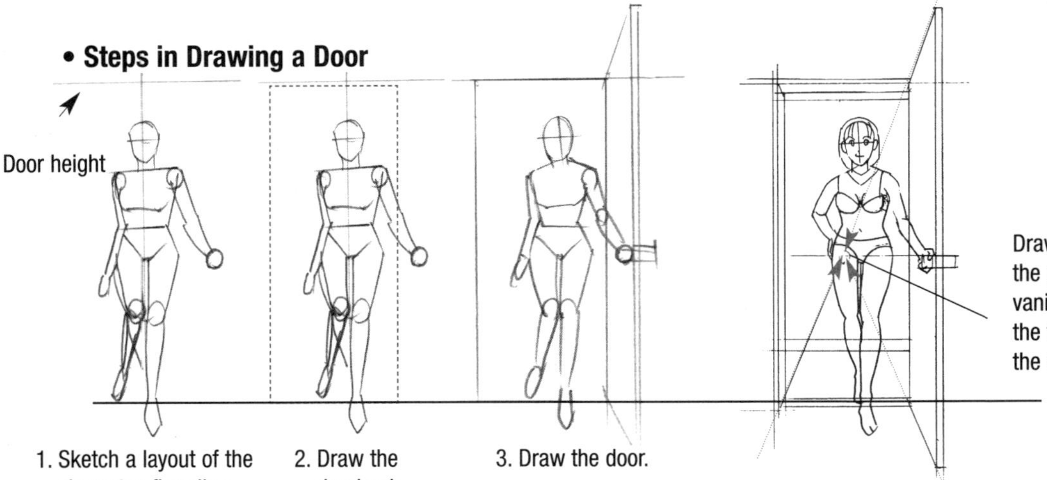

1. Sketch a layout of the character, floor line, and door height.
2. Draw the doorjamb.
3. Draw the door.

Draw the doorknob at the point where the vanishing lines for the top and bottom of the door meet.

Creeping or Sneaking through a Door

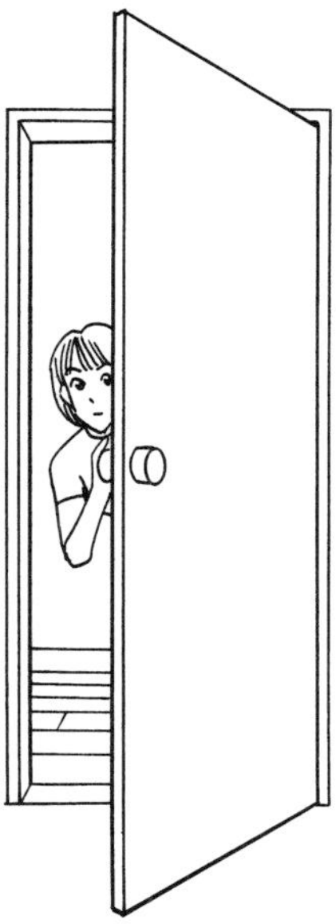

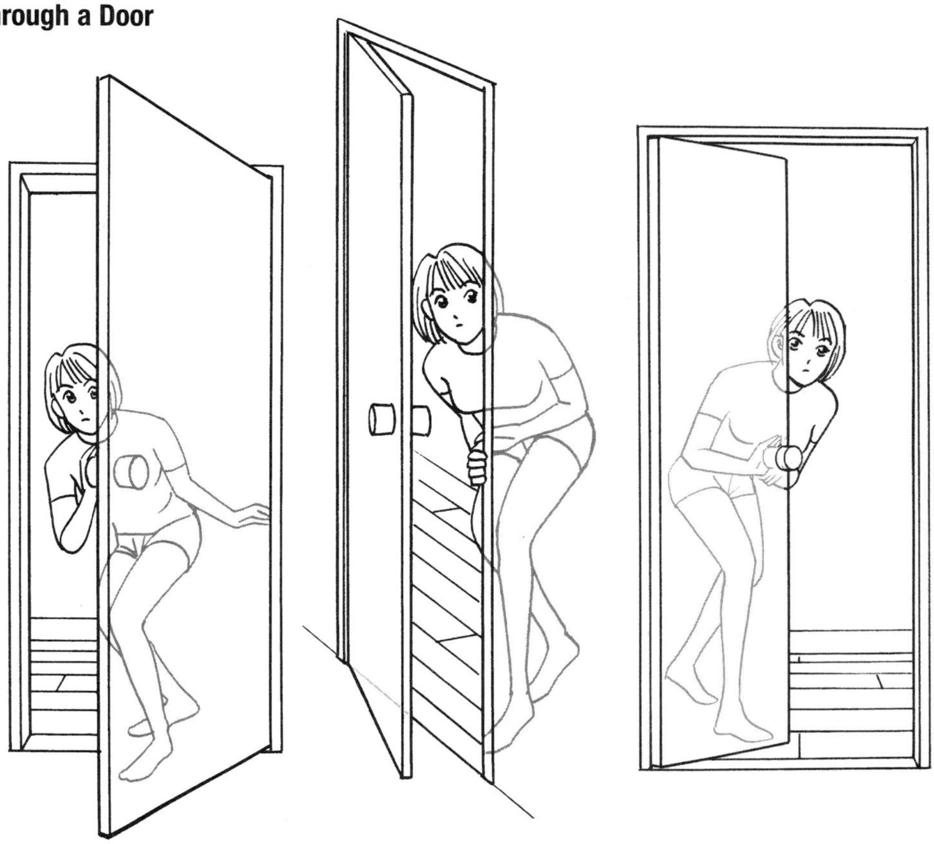

In the sketch stage, remember to jot down the remainder of the figure hidden by the door.

Bounding through a Door

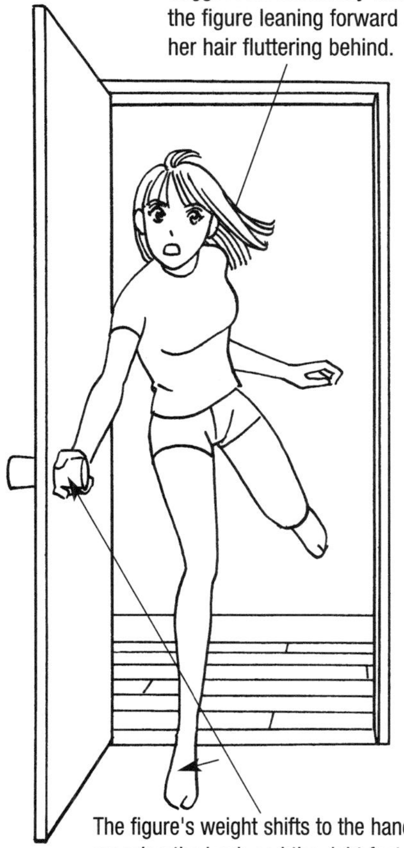

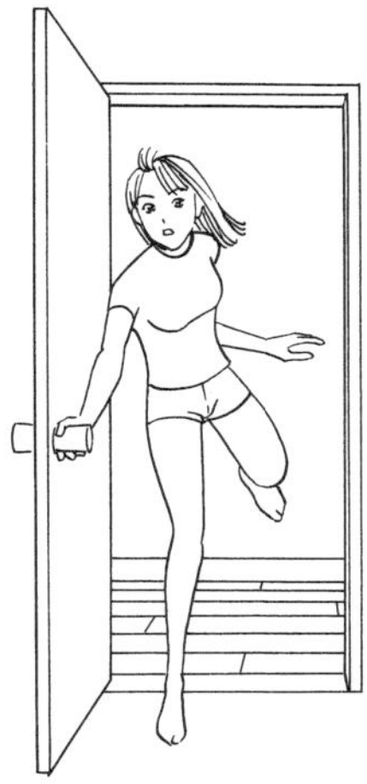

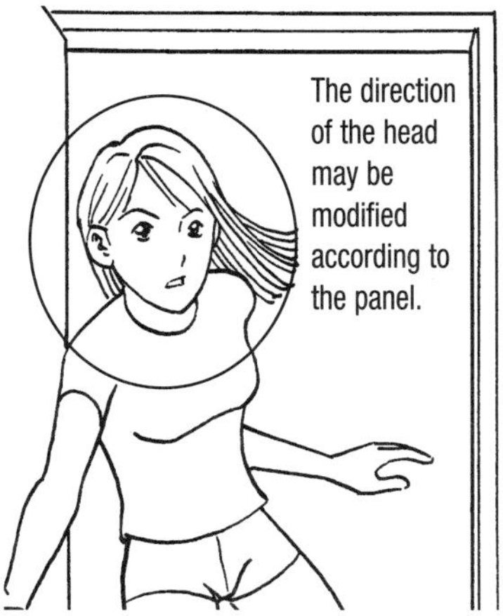

Gracefully Entering through a Door

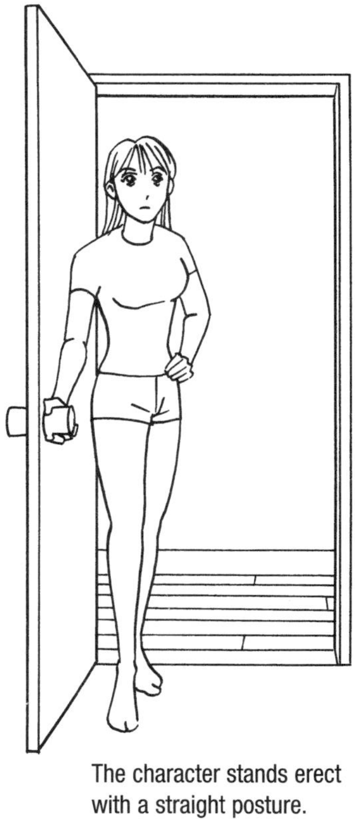

The character stands erect with a straight posture.

Portraying a Closing Door

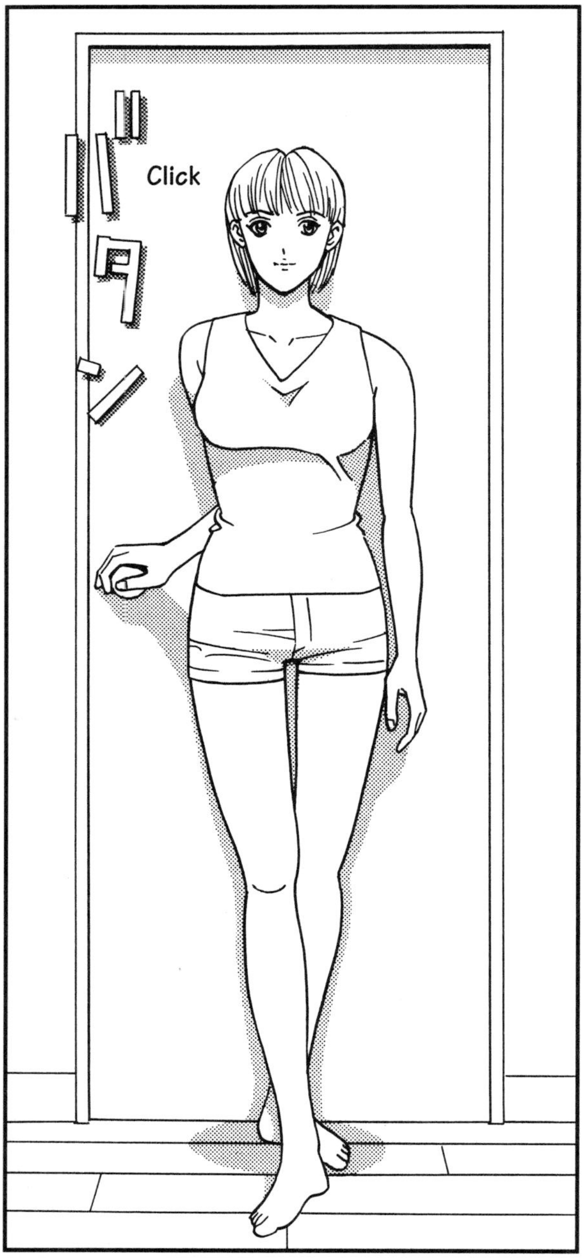

Big entrance scene

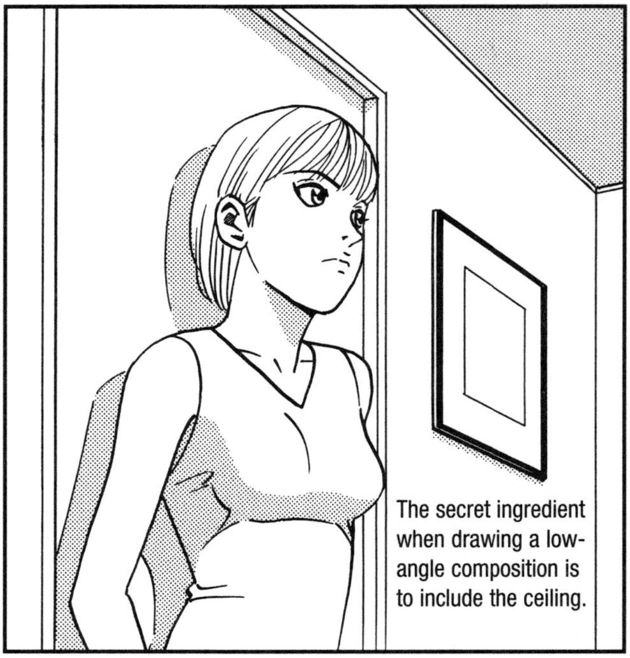

The secret ingredient when drawing a low-angle composition is to include the ceiling.

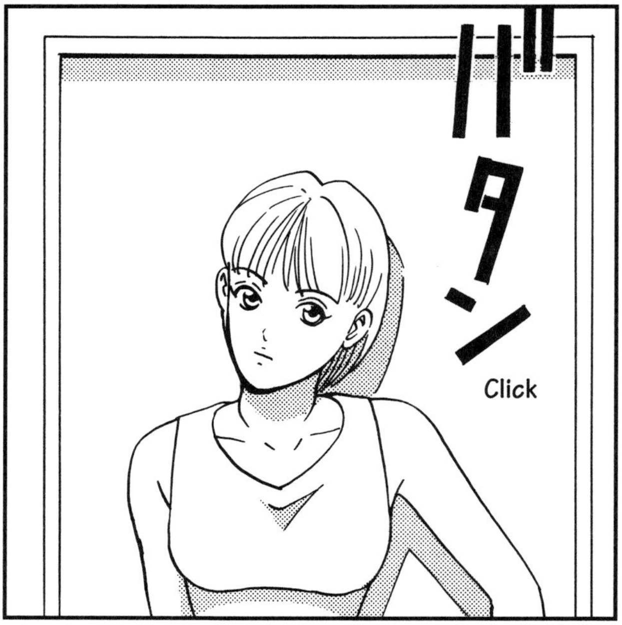

Draw the doorframe.

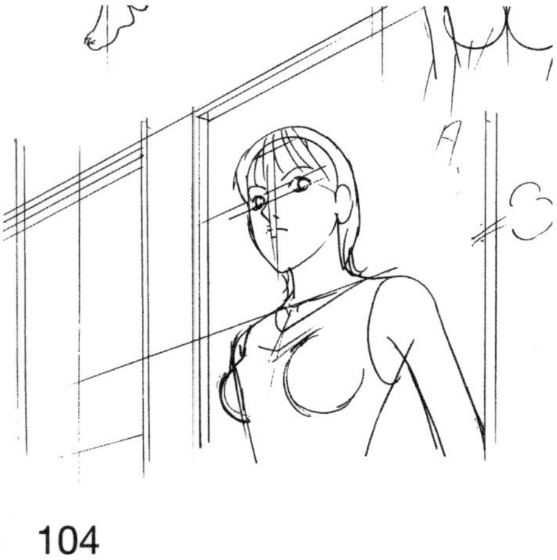

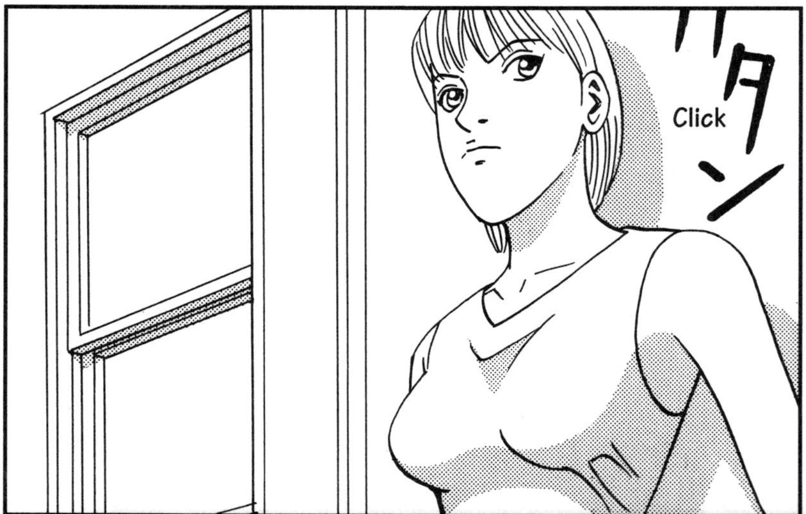

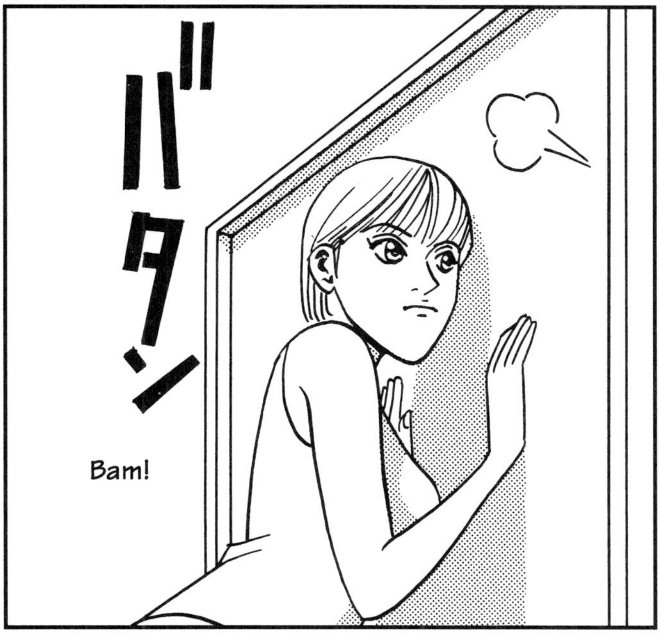

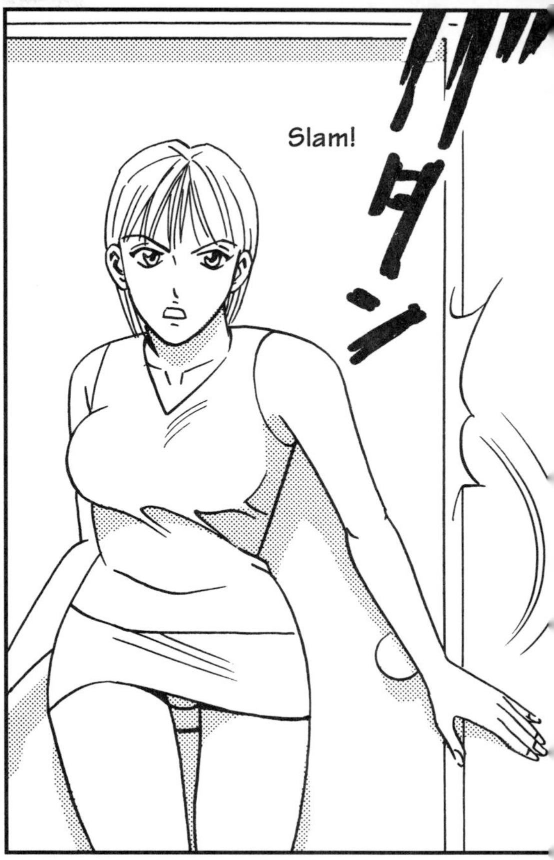

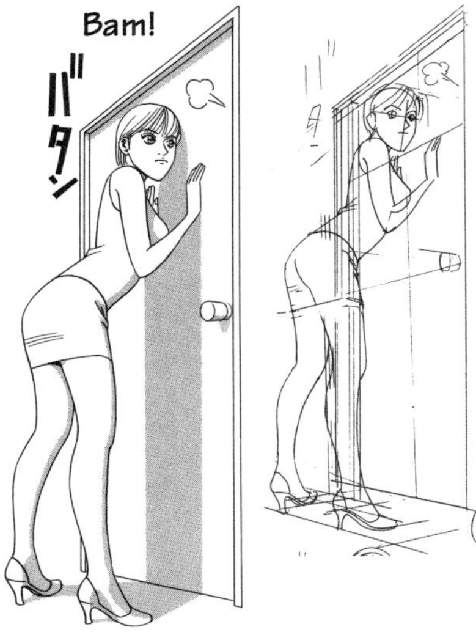

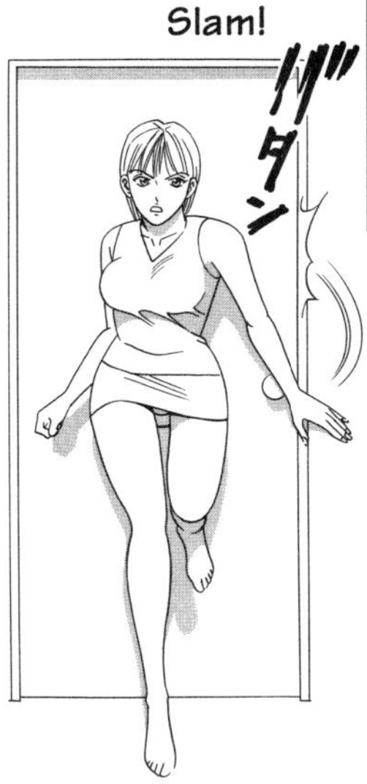

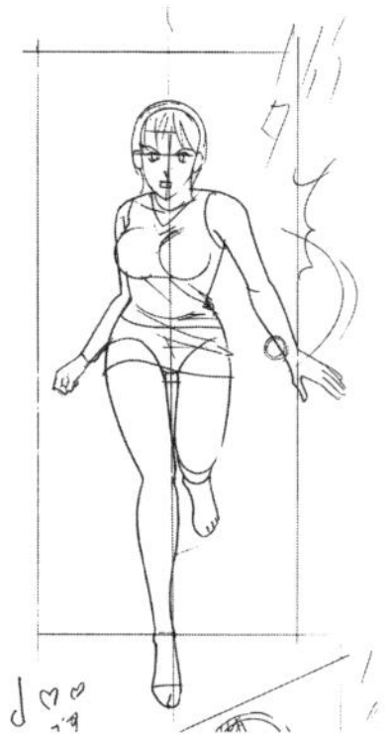

Simply drawing the door closed allows you to portray effortlessly scenes where a character is entering or has entered a room.

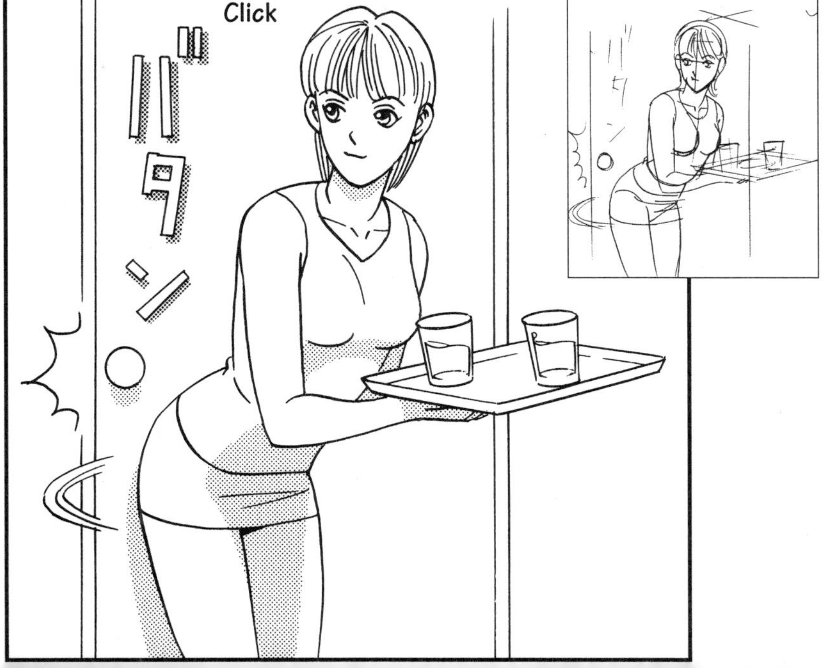

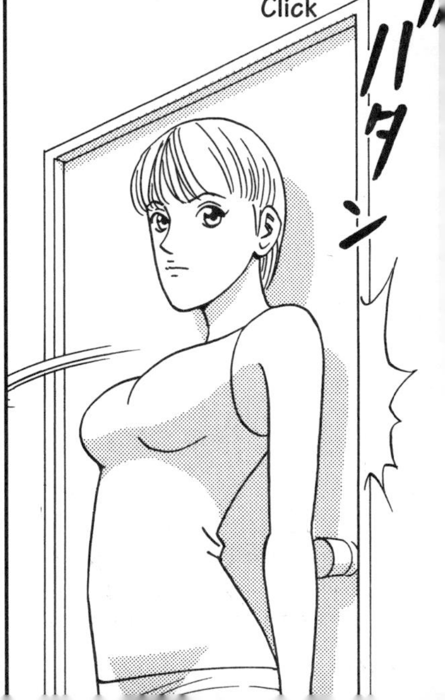

Popular Relaxed, Conversational Poses

Leaning, sitting, crouching, and other relaxed poses help portray monologue or conversation scenes. Such poses appear in a host of different scenes from school to fantasy settings.

Leaning against a Wall While Standing

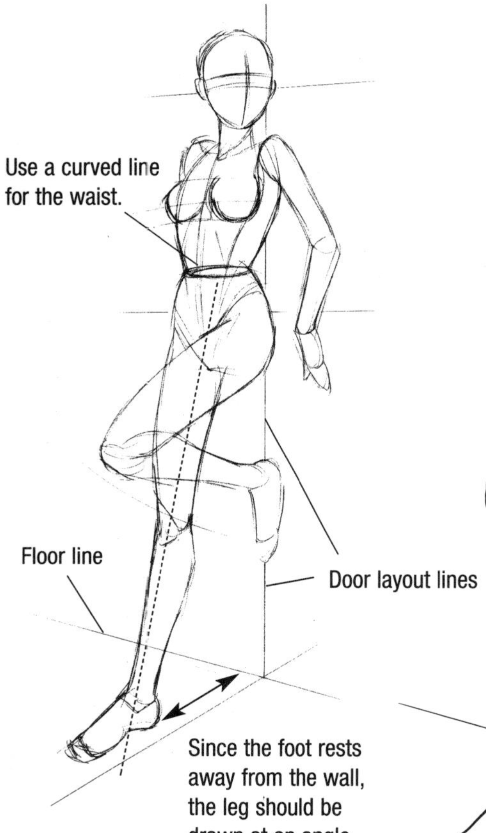

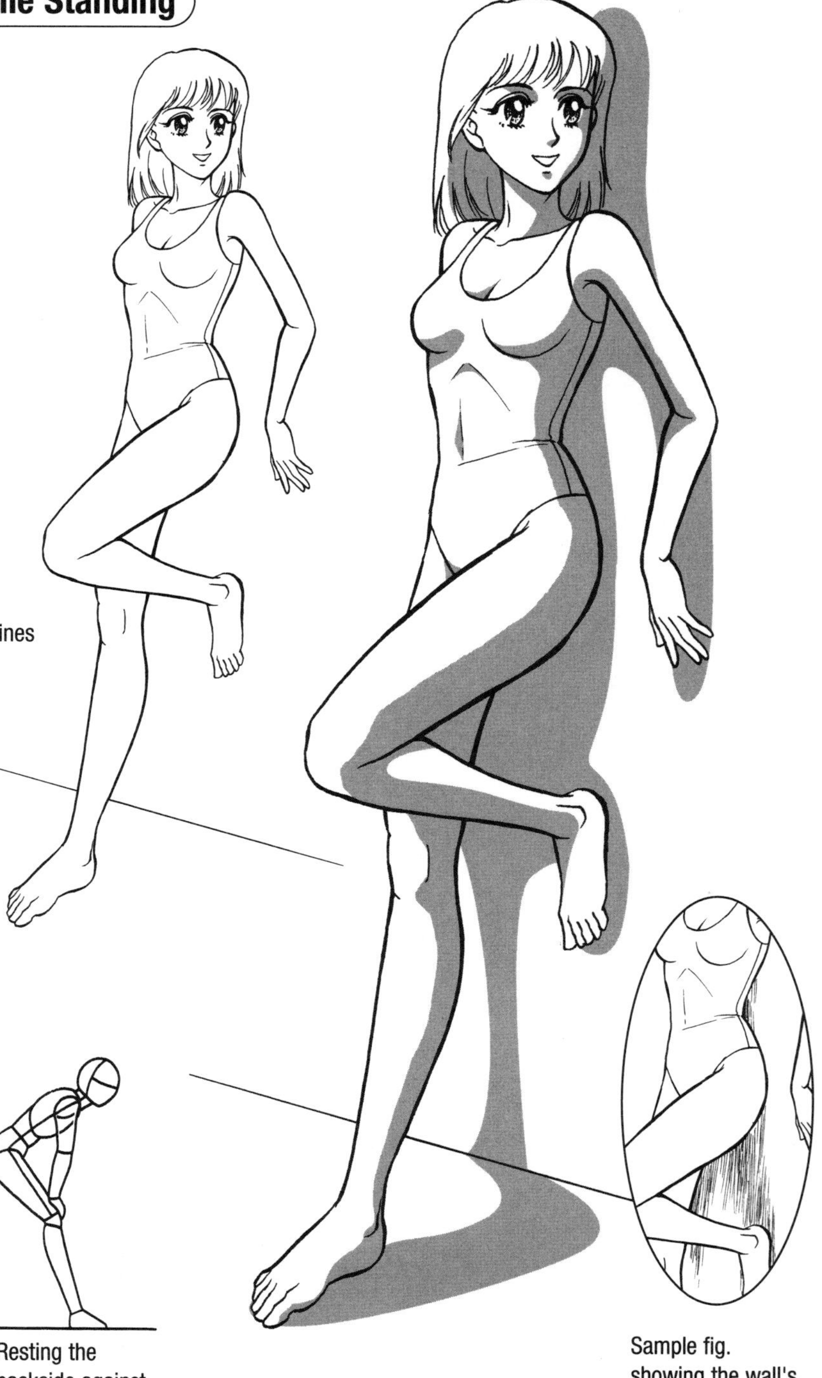

Popular Leaning Poses

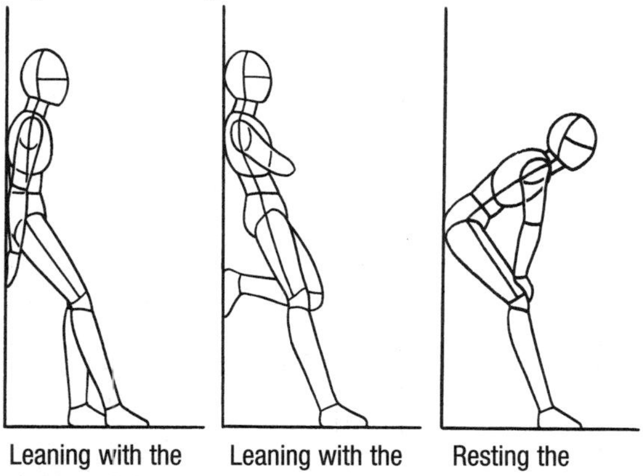

Leaning with the entire back flush against the wall

Leaning with the shoulders and shoulder blades against the wall.

Resting the backside against the wall

Sample fig. showing the wall's texture rendered in hatching.

Sample Fig.

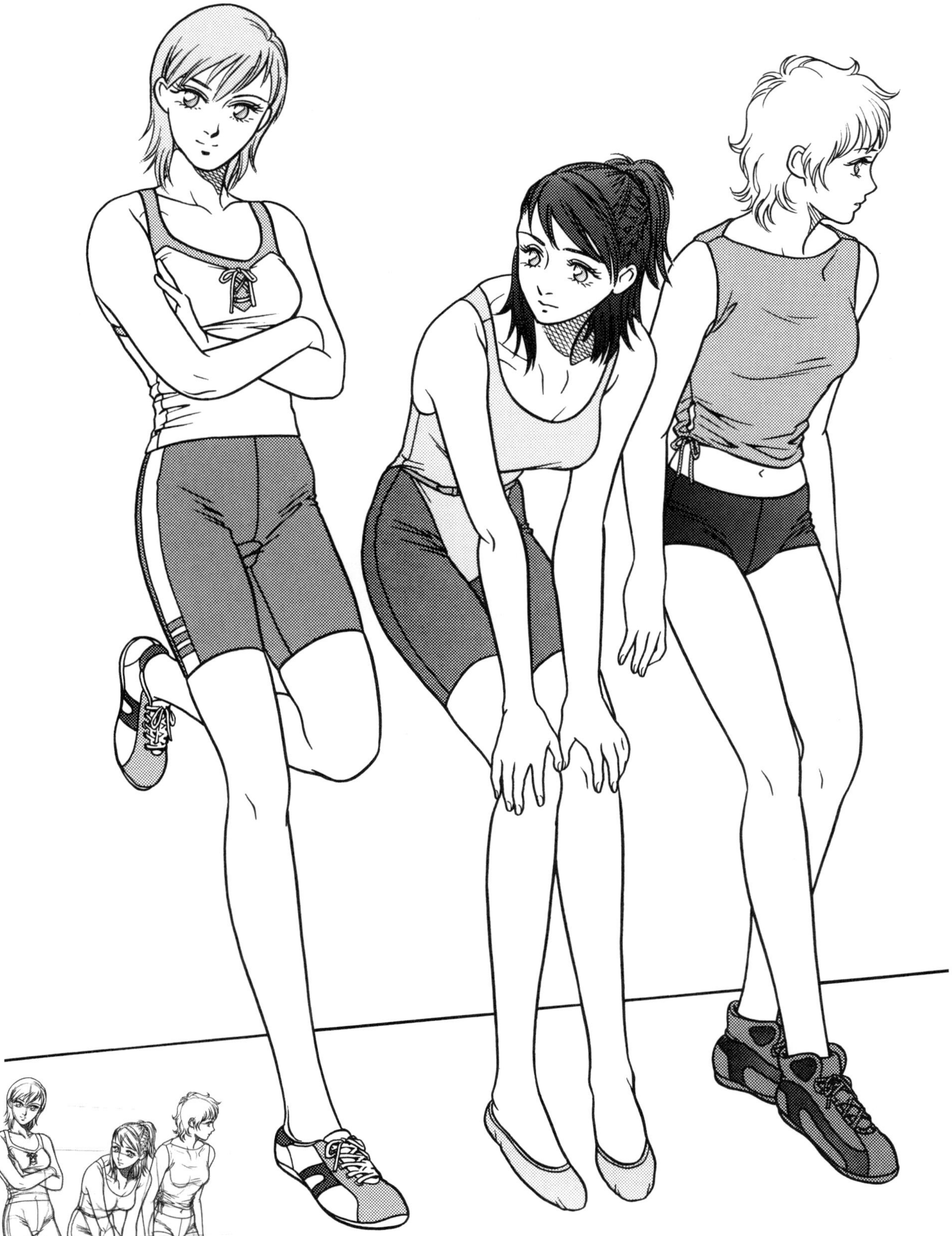

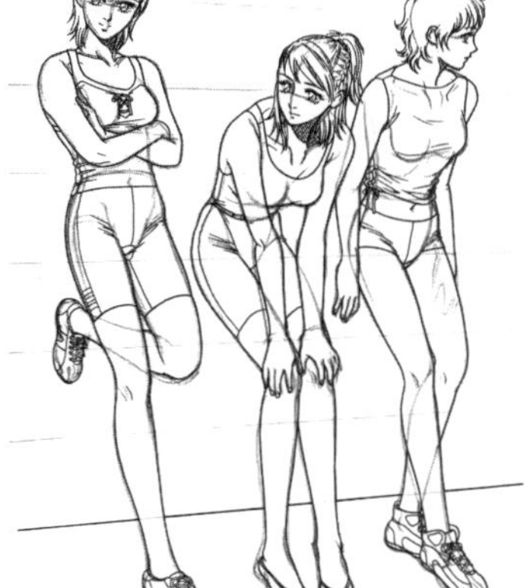

If the figures are wearing colored costumes, then there is no need to add shadows to the wall(s) or floor. (This would just make the composition cluttered and confusing.)

Sitting Near a Wall

Girls are often found gathered near a wall chatting. Artists can manipulate the mood or atmosphere of a given pose by adjusting the angle of composition. The most common seated poses are often used in monologue scenes.

Leaning against a Wall

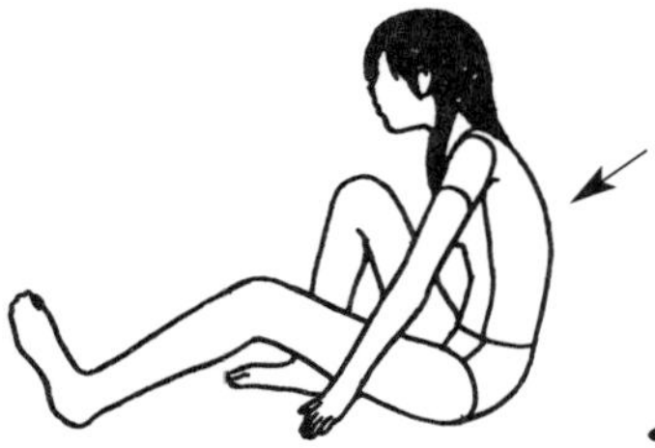
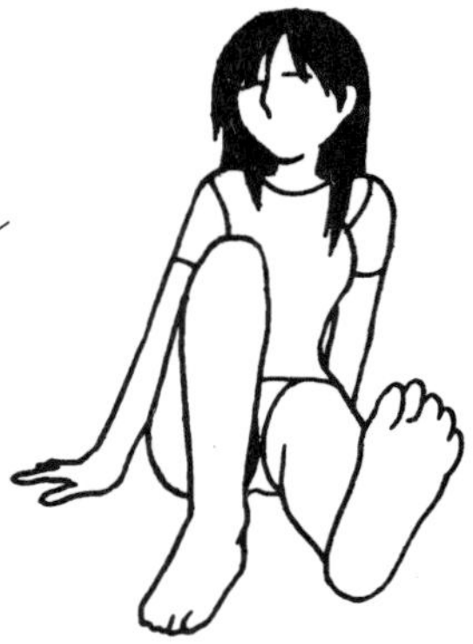
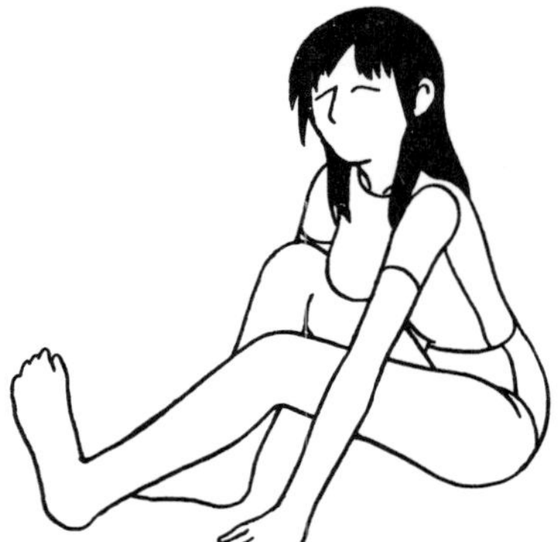

Leaning with one knee raised

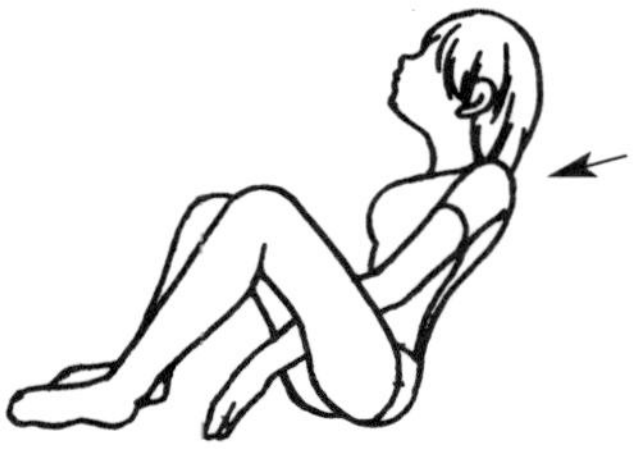
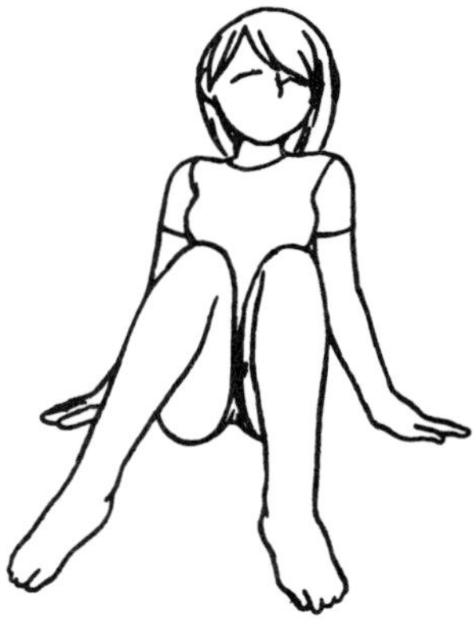
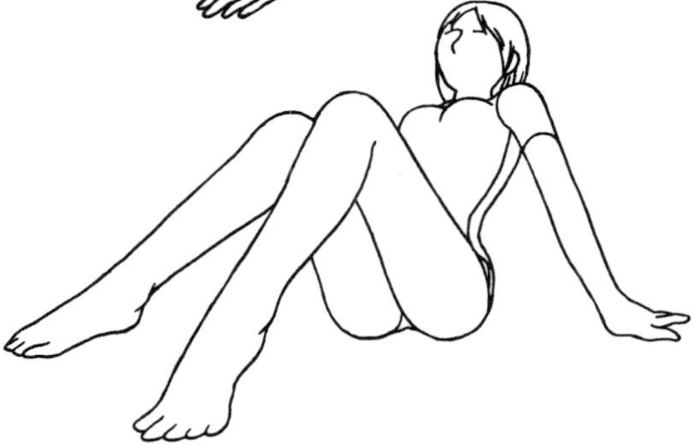

Leaning back

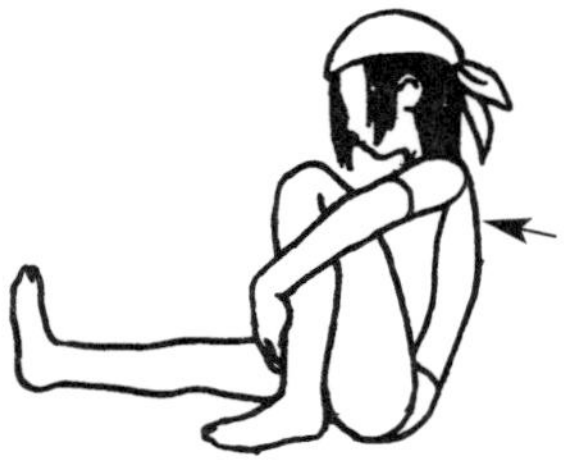
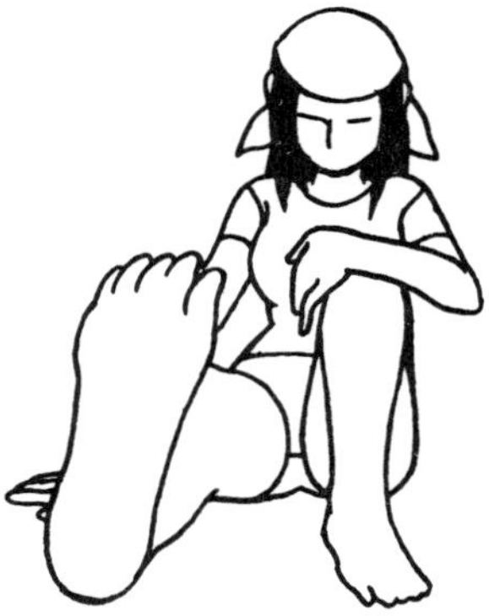
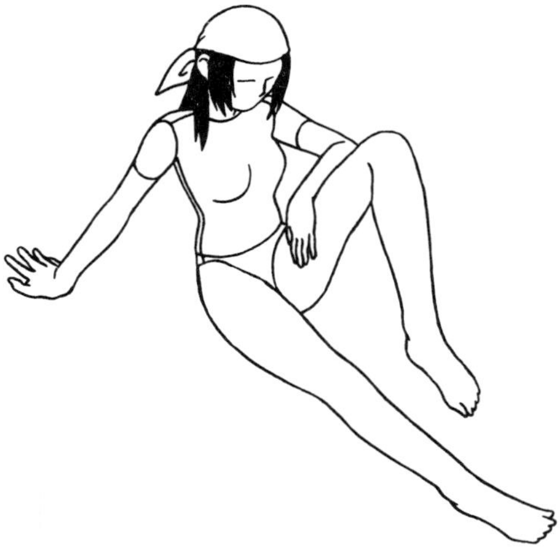

Leaning with an arm wrapped around one leg

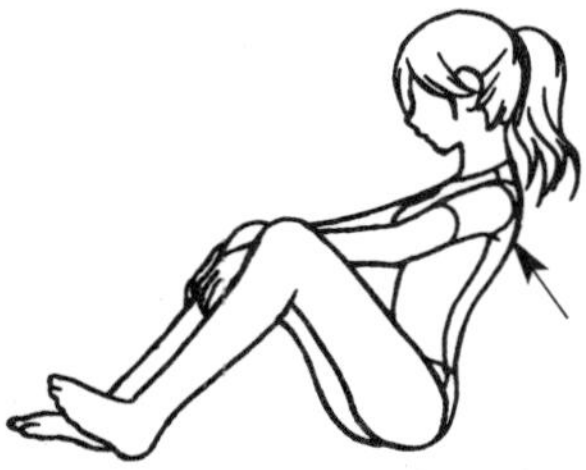
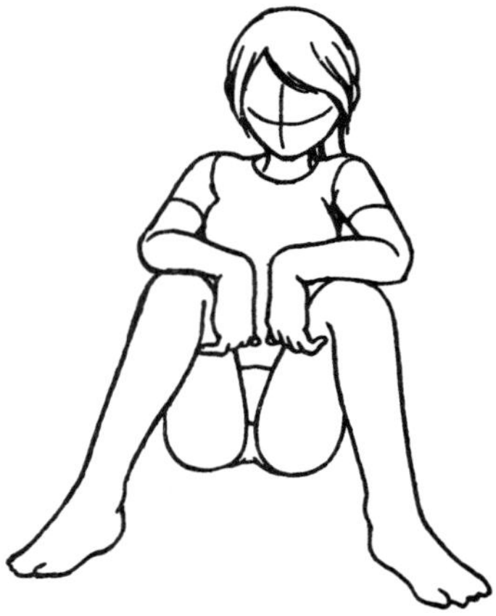
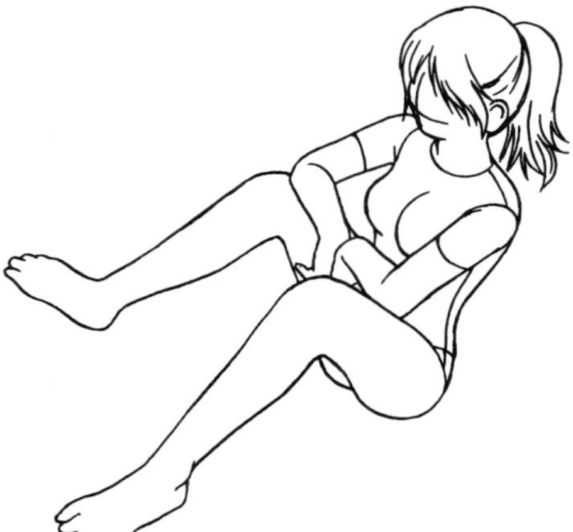

Leaning with both knees raised

Not Leaning against a Wall

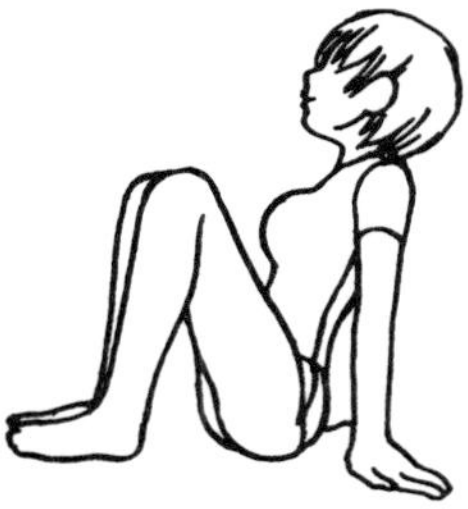

Both knees raised

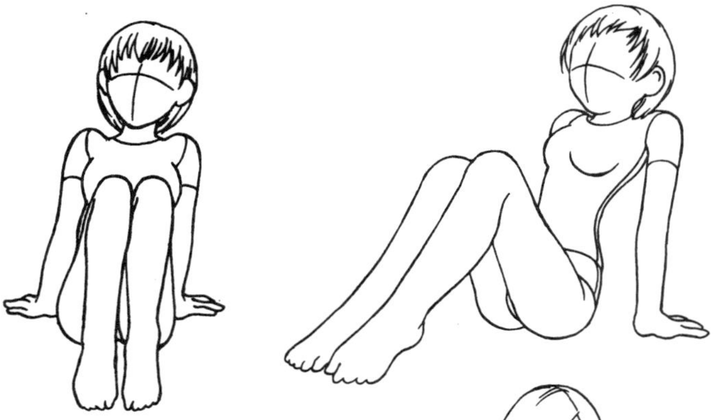

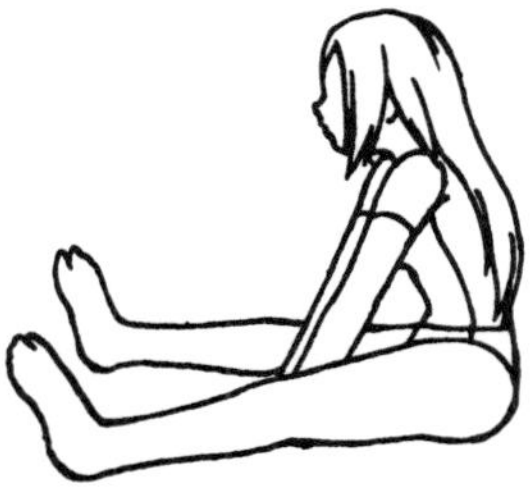

Both legs straight out

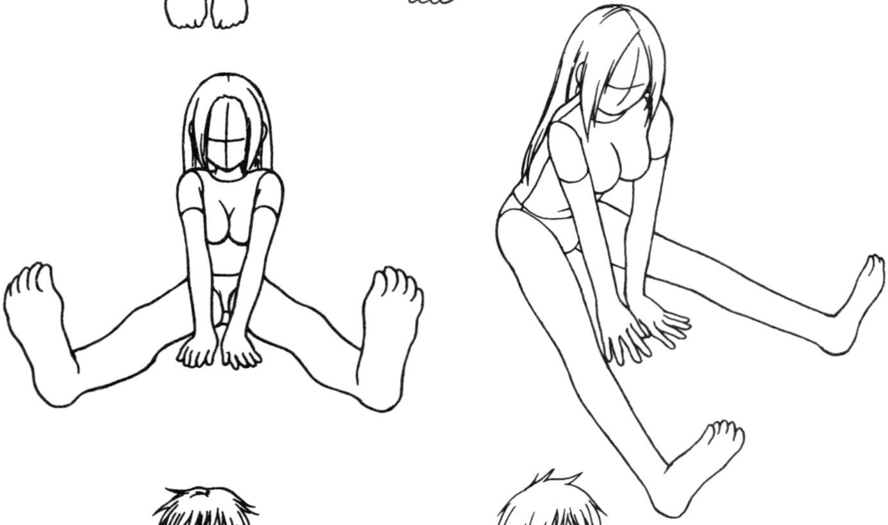

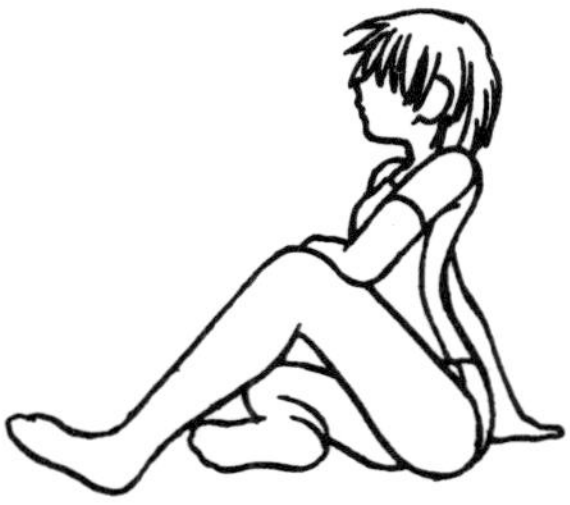

One knee raised

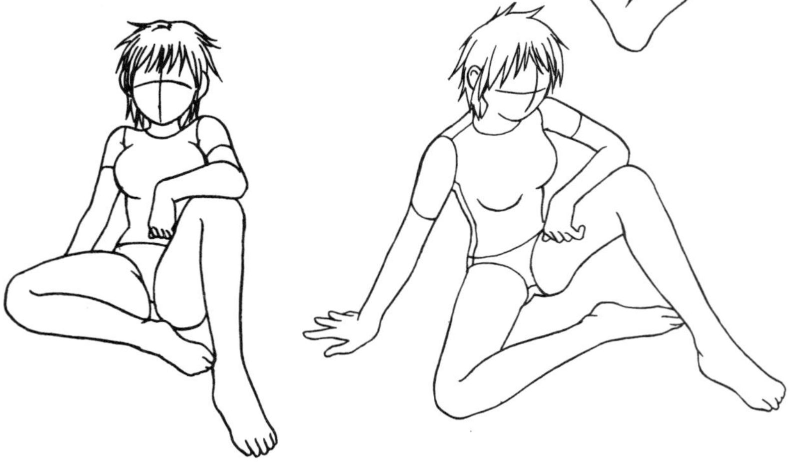

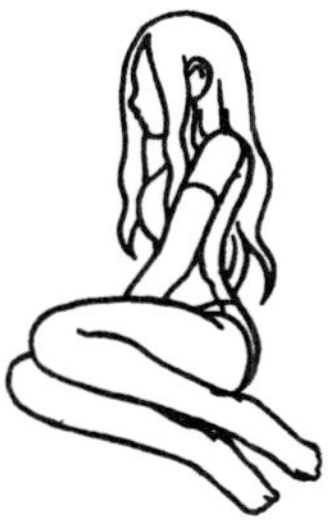

Knees held together

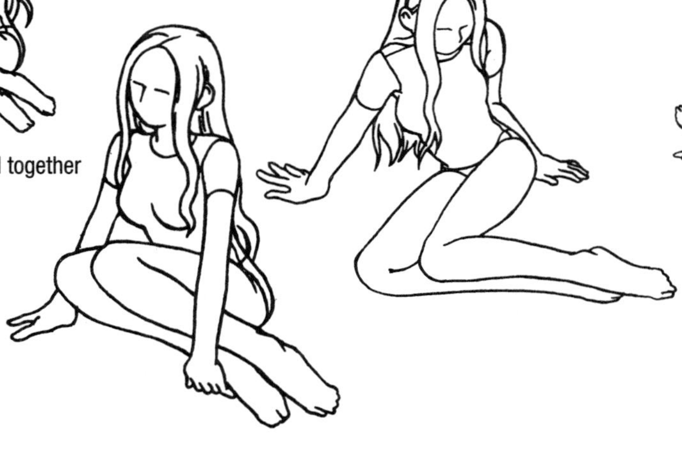

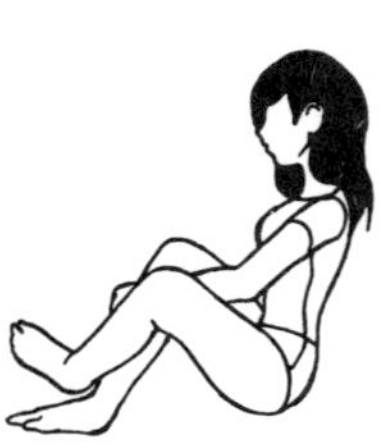

Legs crossed

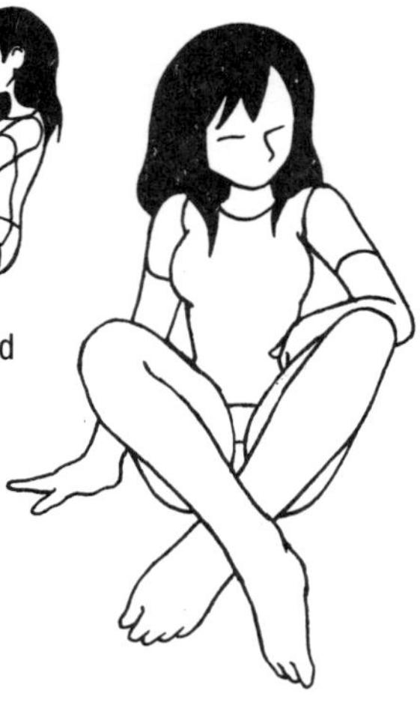

Chatting Scene: 3 to 4 Figures Sitting Near a Wall

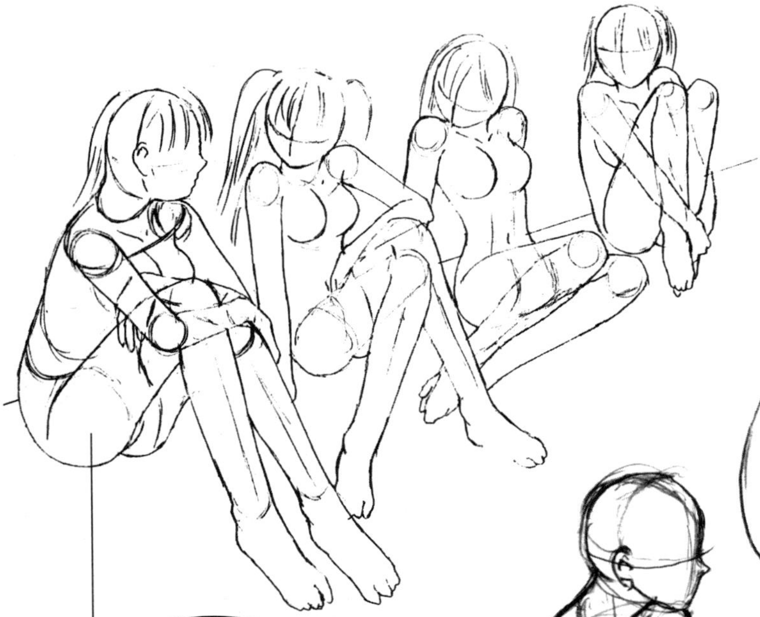

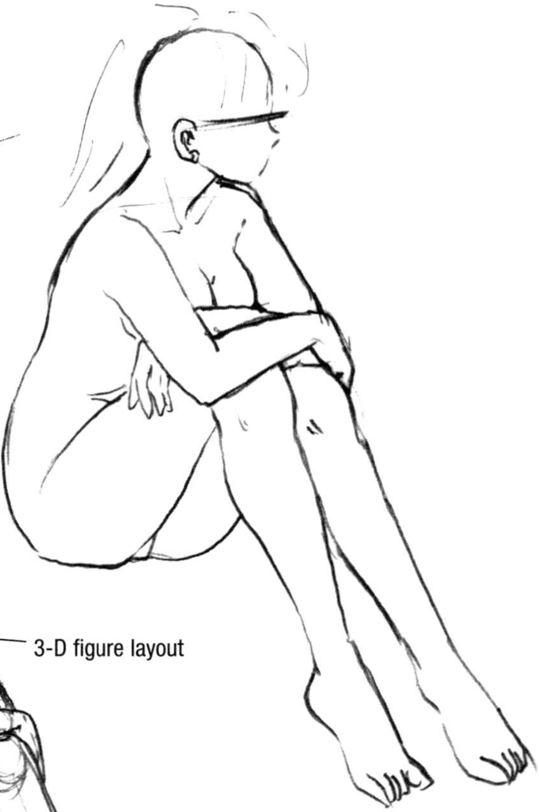

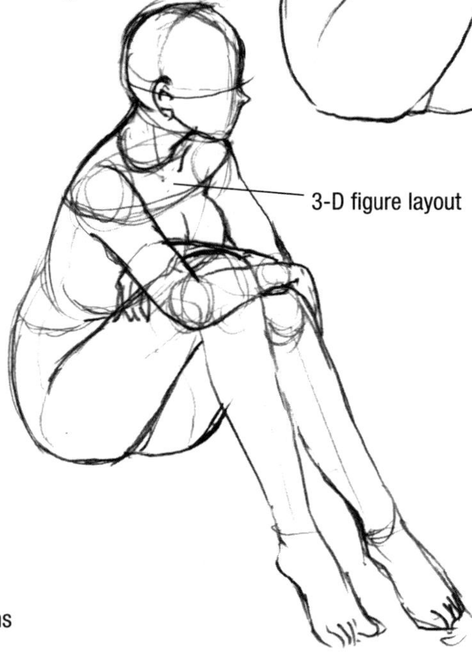

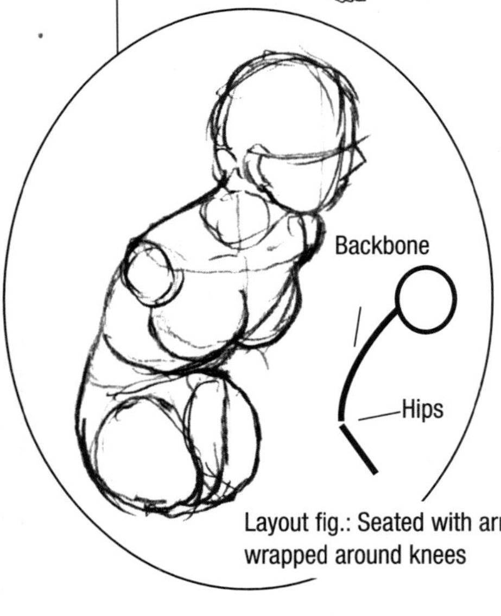

Layout fig.: Seated with arms wrapped around knees

Make the heads of the further characters smaller.

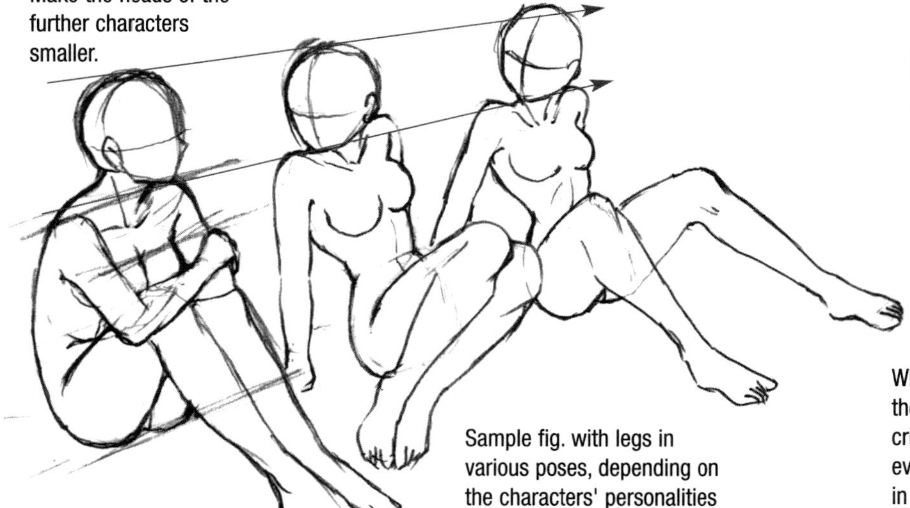

Sample fig. with legs in various poses, depending on the characters' personalities or setting.

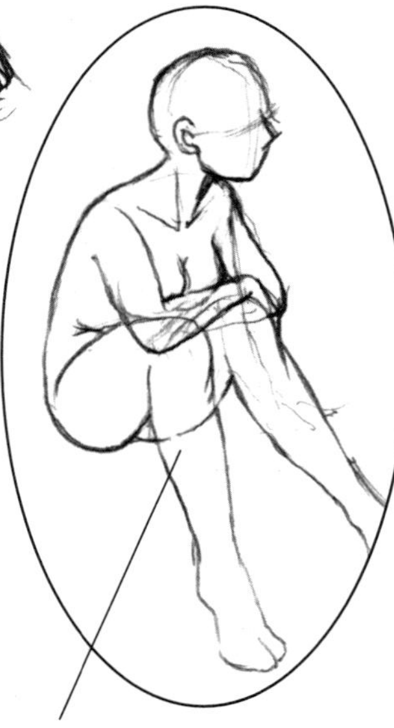

What is visible will depend on how the legs are positioned, but it is critical that you always sketch out even those parts that will be hidden in the final drawing.

Completed Sample Fig: Gym Class Uniforms

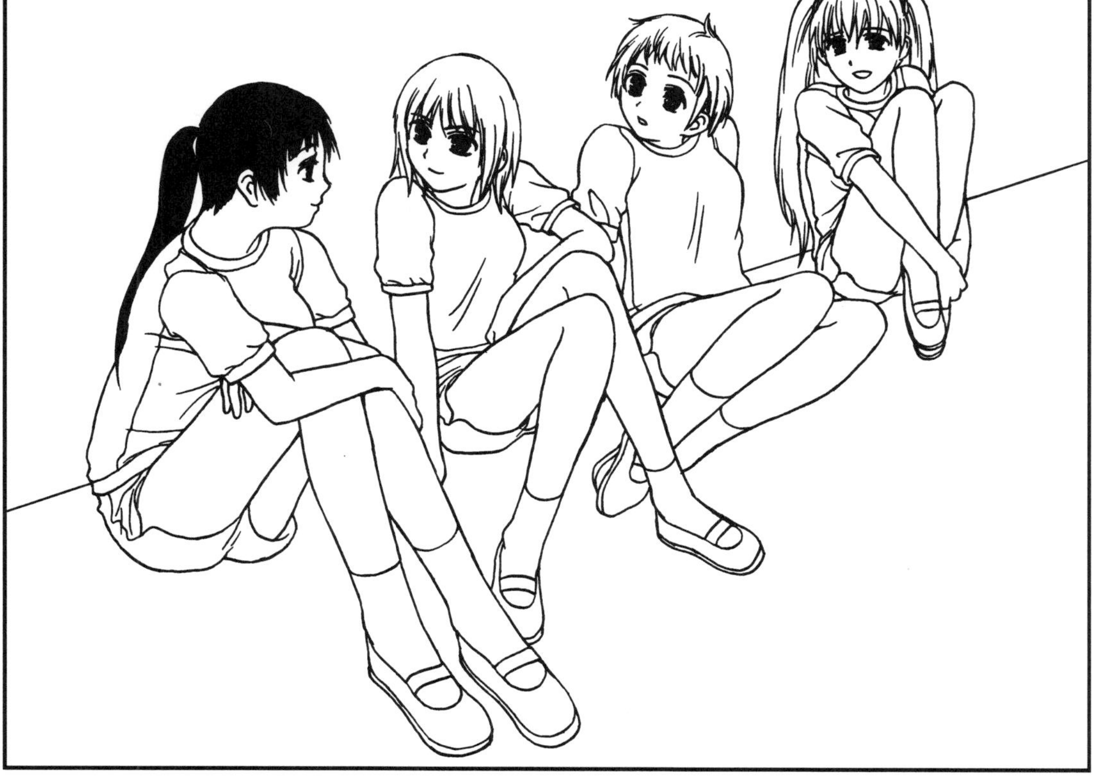

School Uniforms

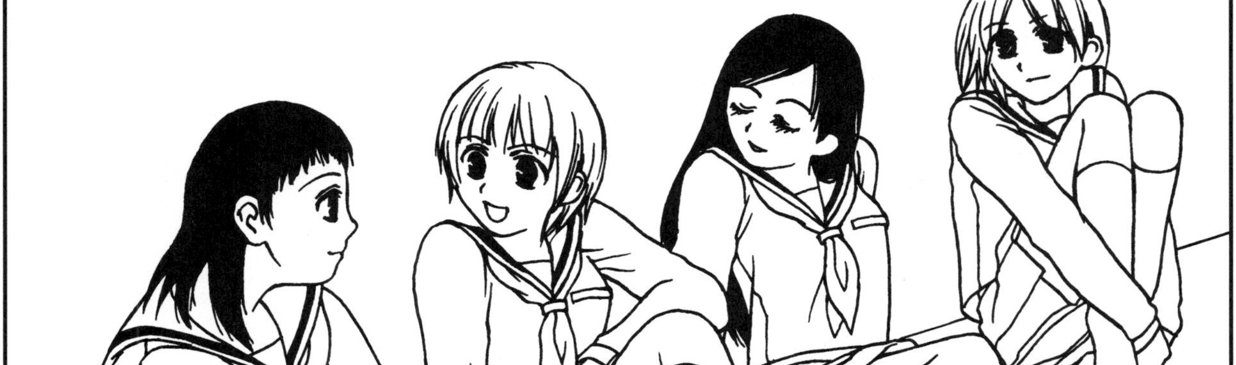

Crouching

Crouching figures may also appear in scenes of multiple characters gathered near a wall chatting.

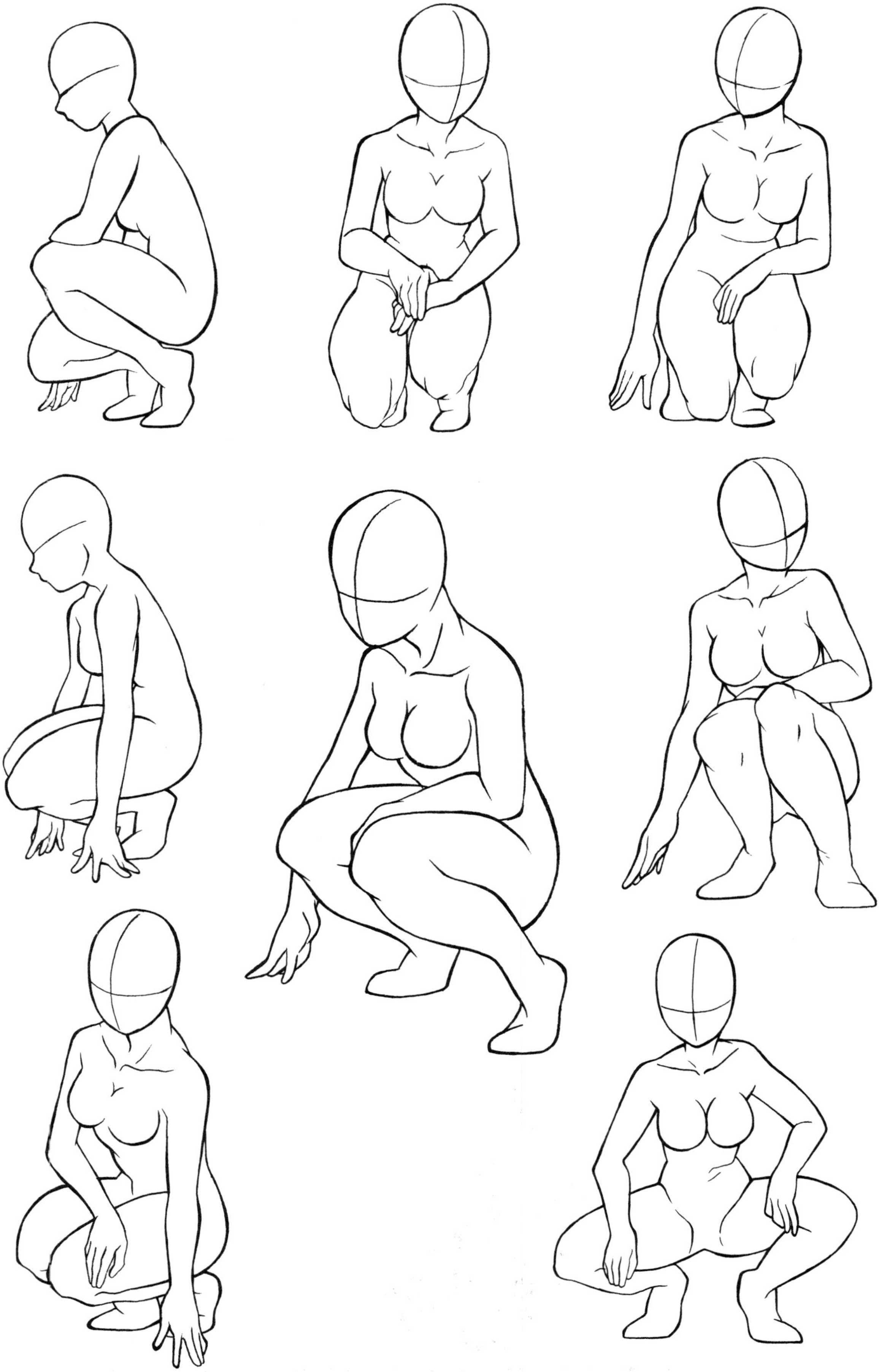

Crouching Fig. in Uniform

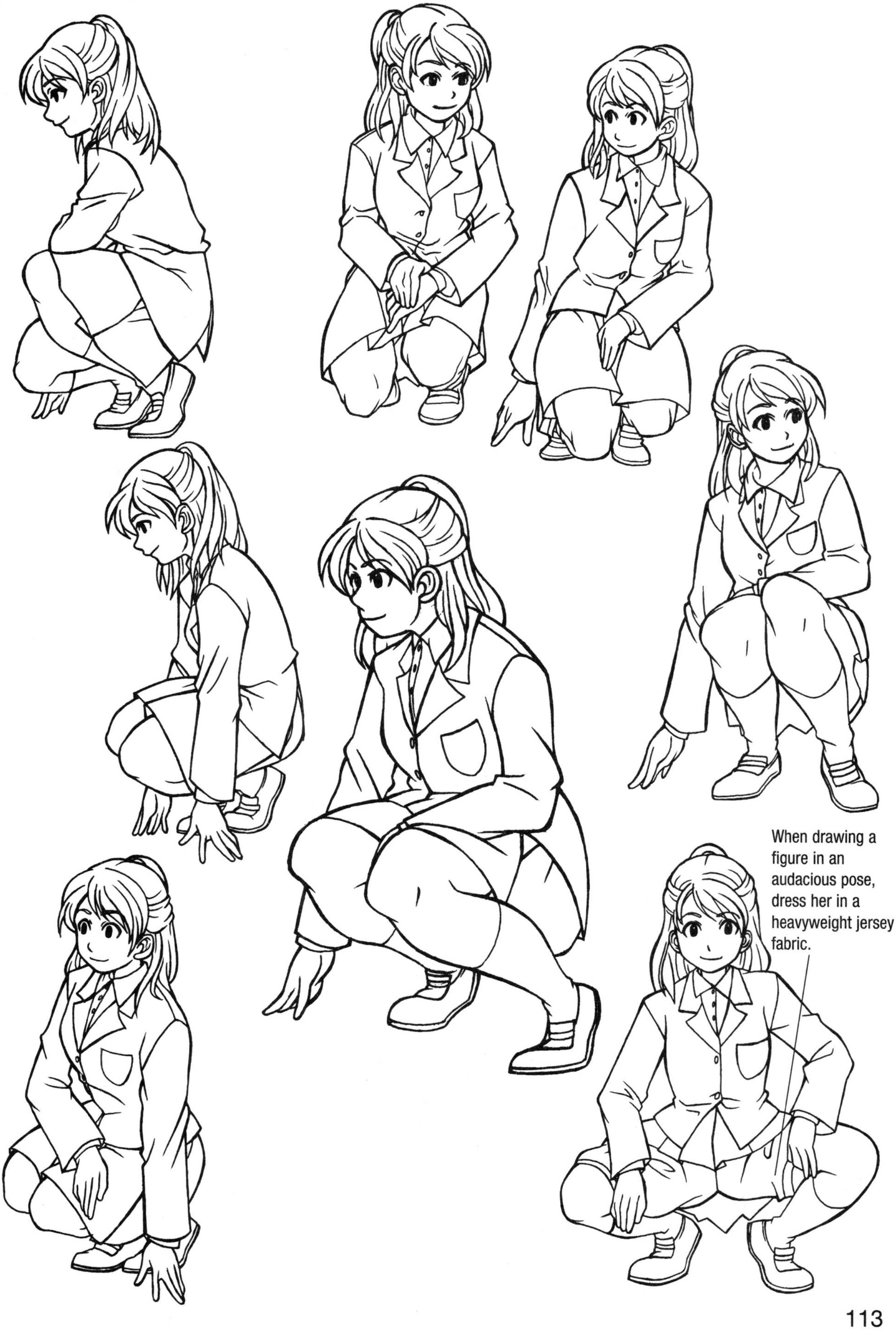

Leaning While Crouching

- **With Knees Together**

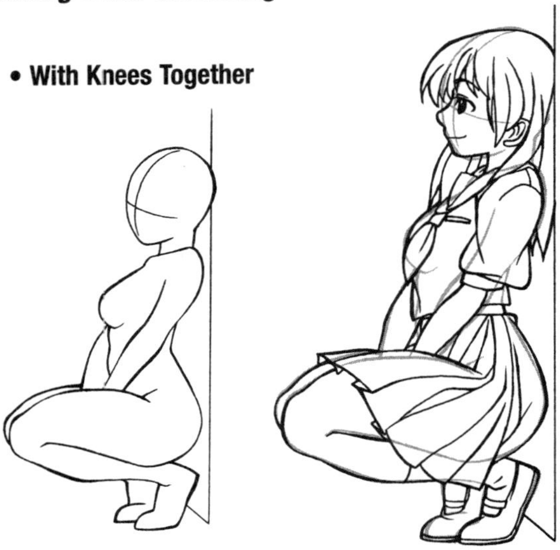

- **With Knees Apart**

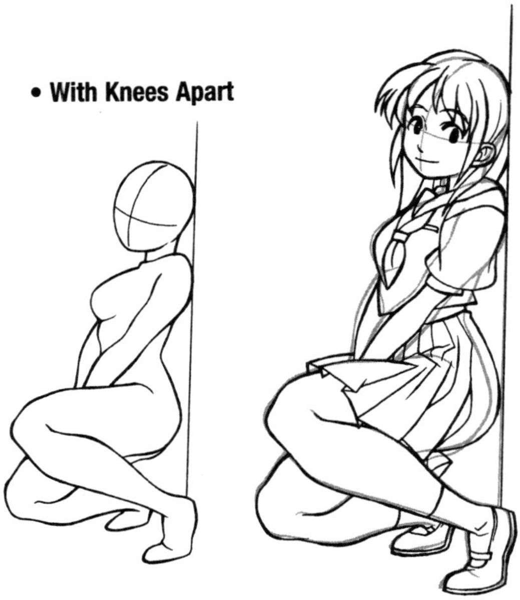

Sample Conversation Scenes

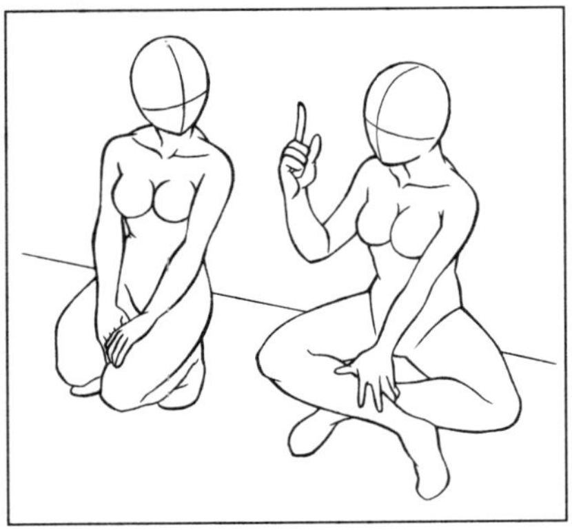

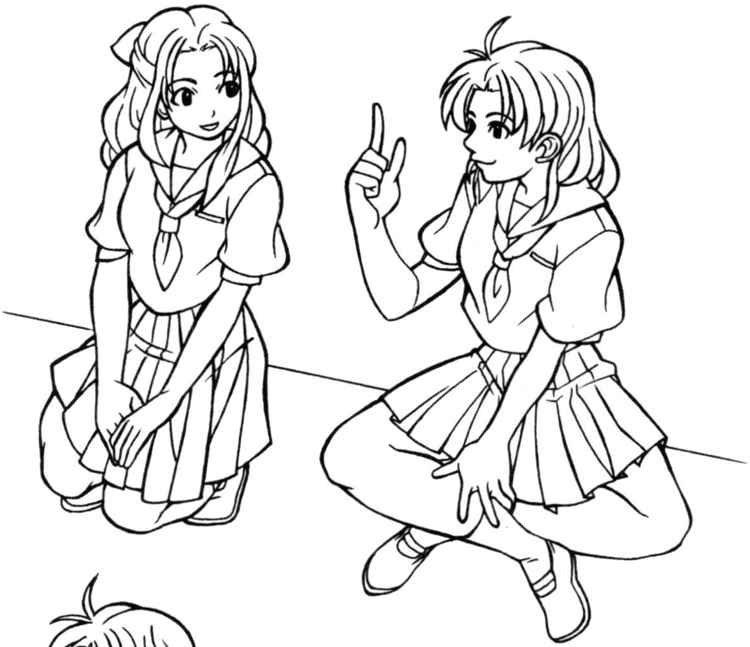

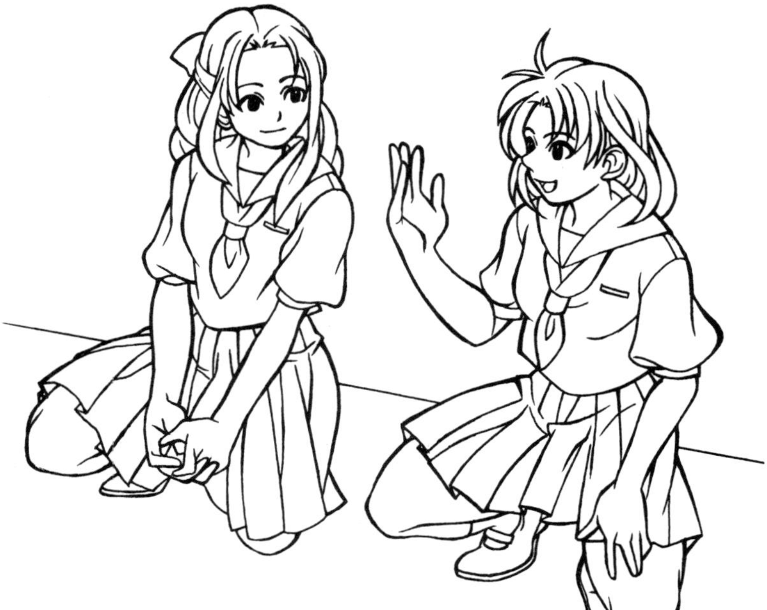

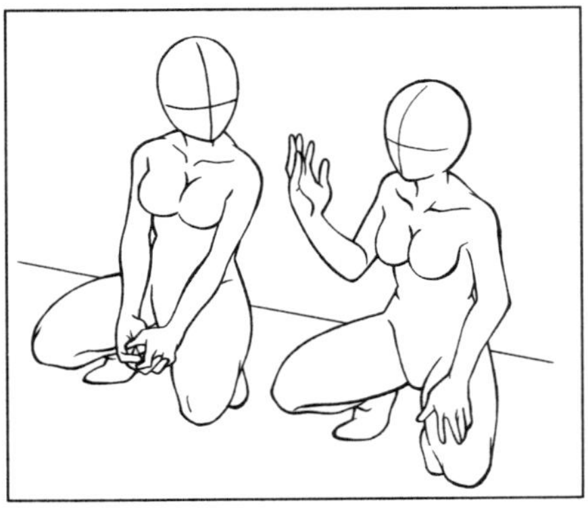

Sitting against a Wall Chatting

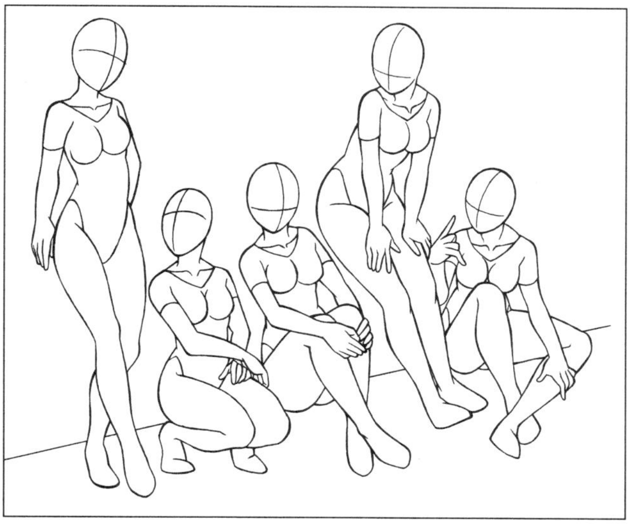

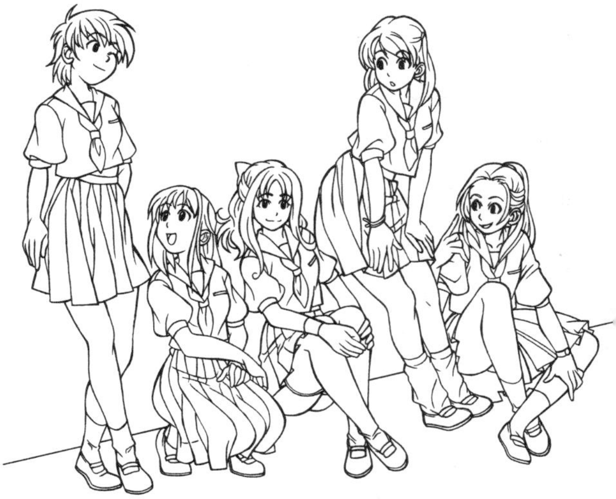

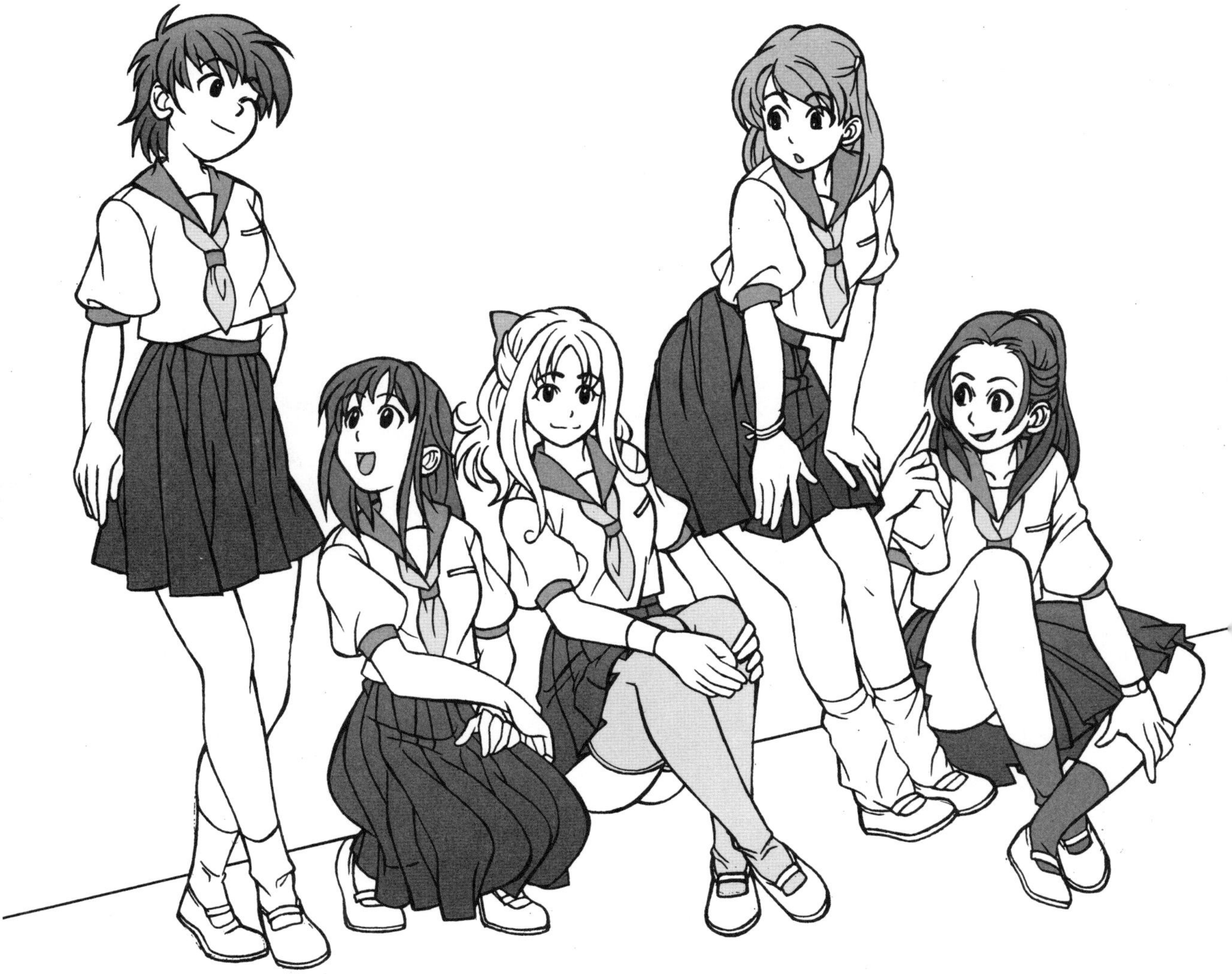

Hand Gestures in Conversation Scenes

Conversation scenes would soon become tedious if rendered solely in close-ups or bust-shots. Adding gestures not only serves to give movement to a dull scene, but also brings the character to life.

Greeting and Signaling Gestures

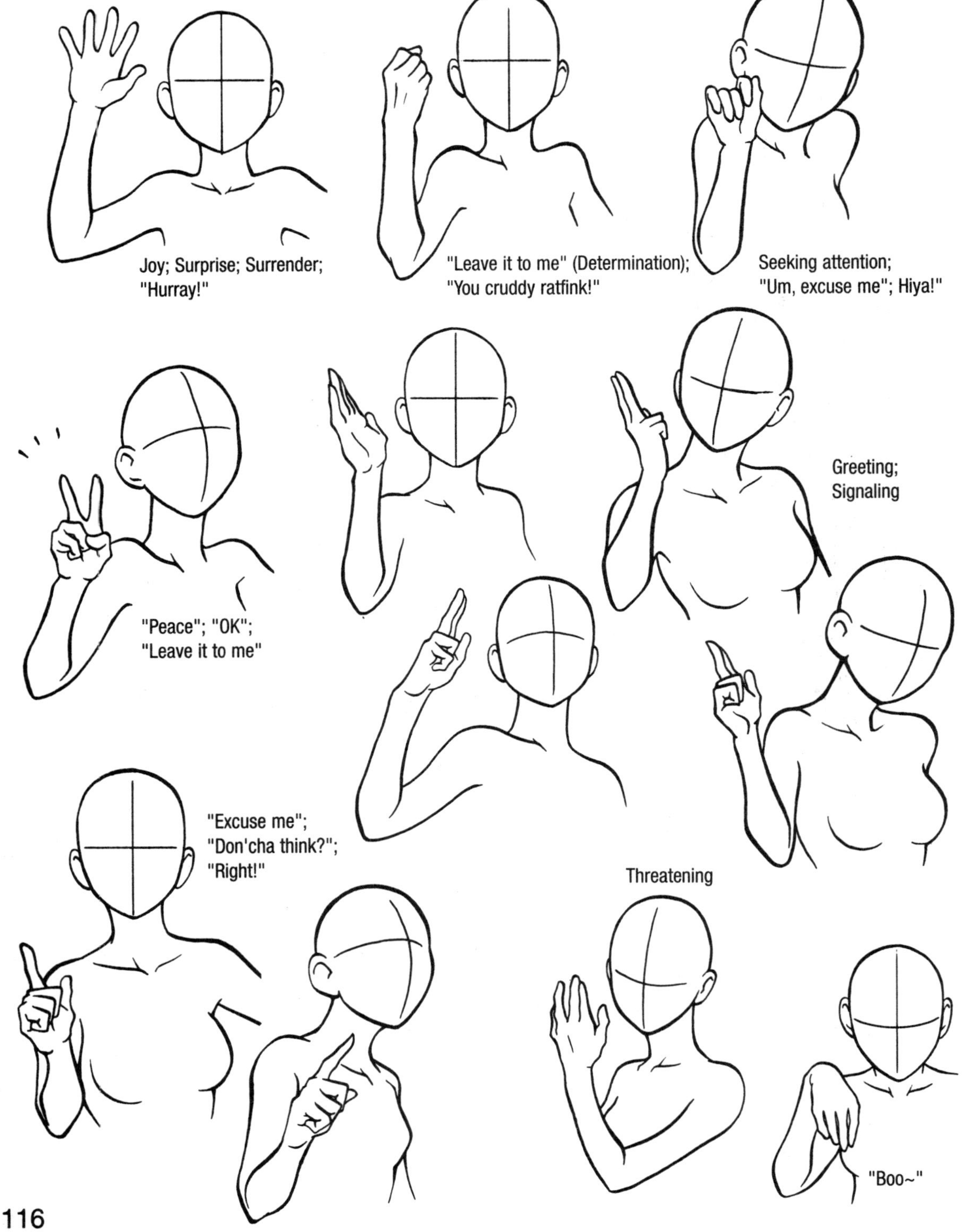

Joy; Surprise; Surrender; "Hurray!"

"Leave it to me" (Determination); "You cruddy ratfink!"

Seeking attention; "Um, excuse me"; Hiya!"

"Peace"; "OK"; "Leave it to me"

Greeting; Signaling

"Excuse me"; "Don'cha think?"; "Right!"

Threatening

"Boo~"

Being Pensive, Thinking While Resting on a Hand, Listening

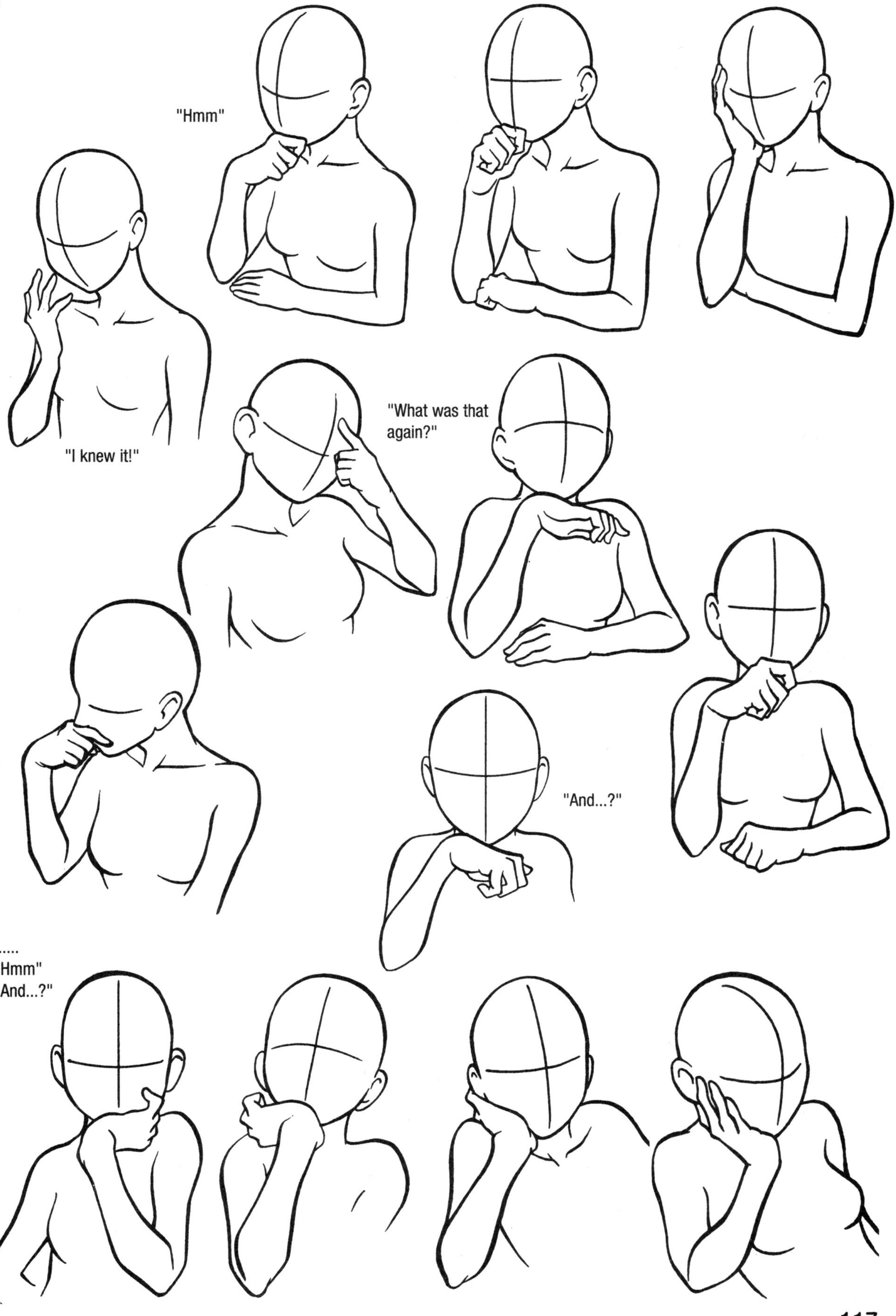

Covering the Mouth with the Hand: Surprise, Crying, Pensiveness

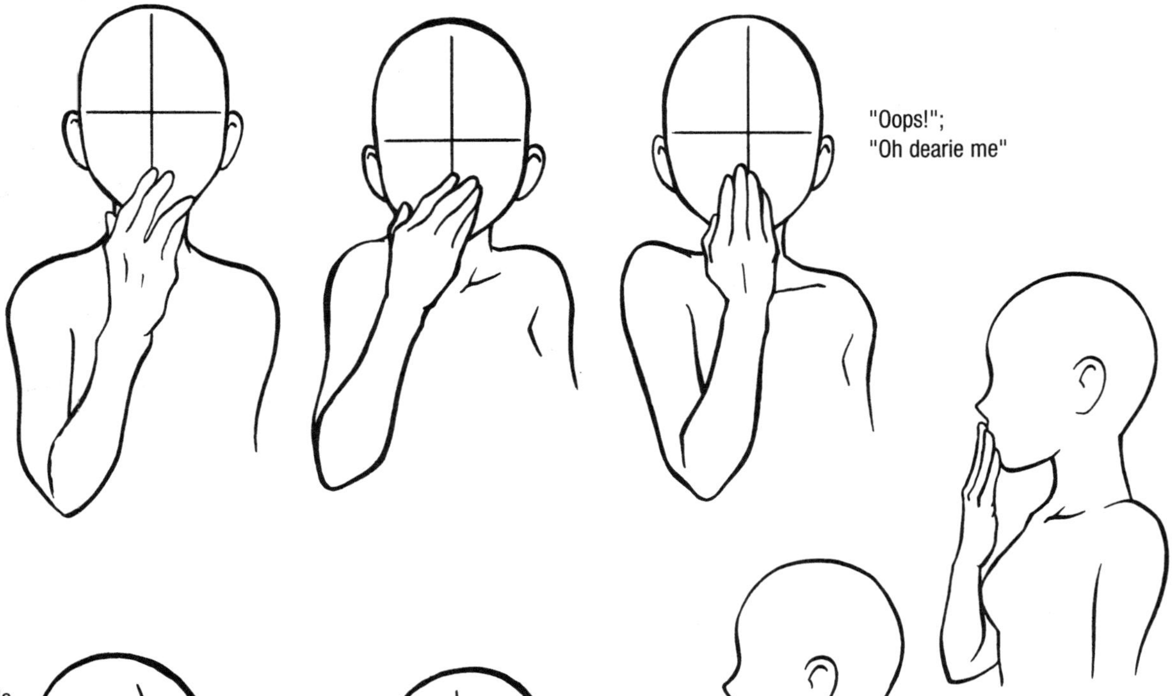

"Oops!";
"Oh dearie me"

Sniffle

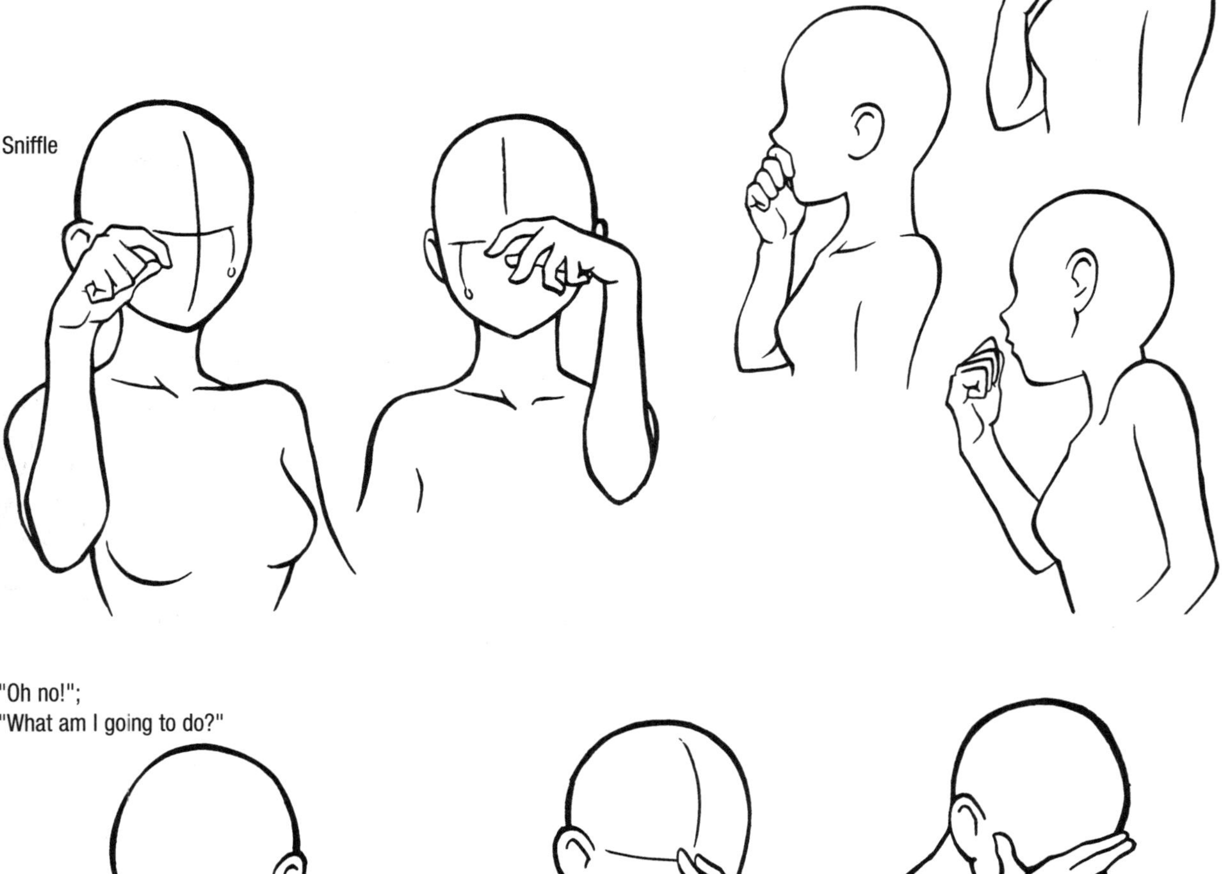

"Oh no!";
"What am I going to do?"

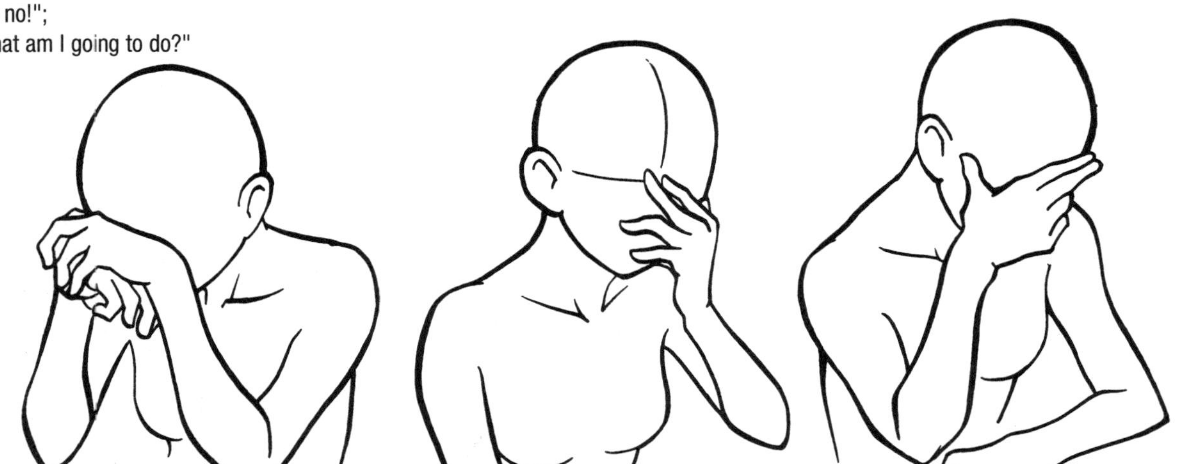

Two-Handed Gestures: Listening, Surprise, Determination, Pleading

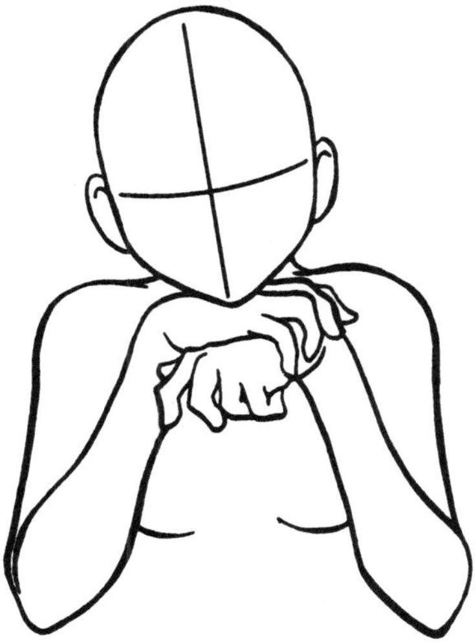

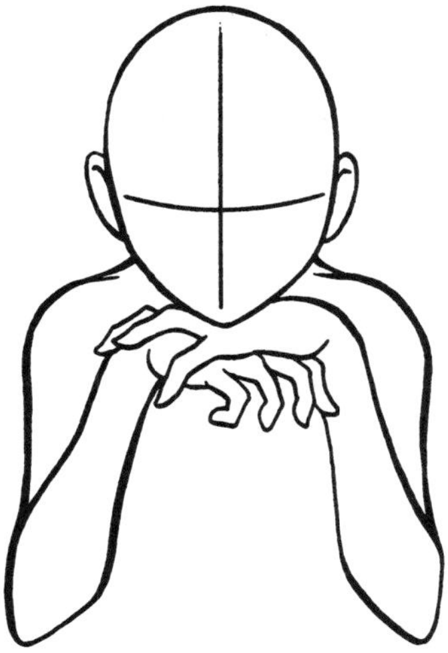

Absorbed in listening

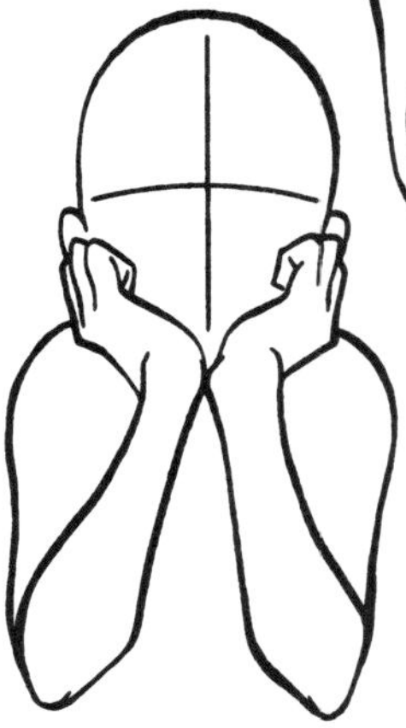

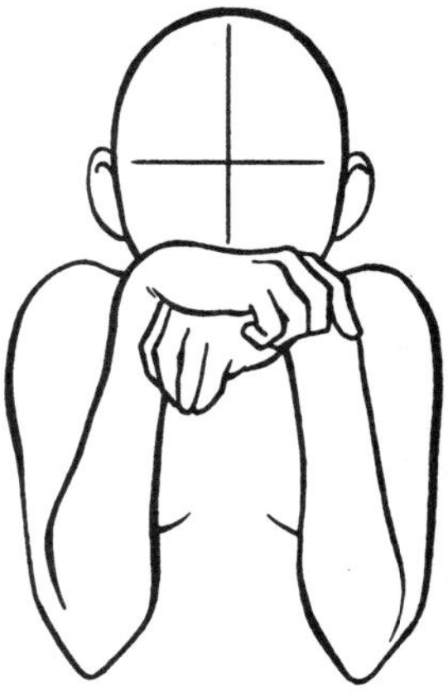

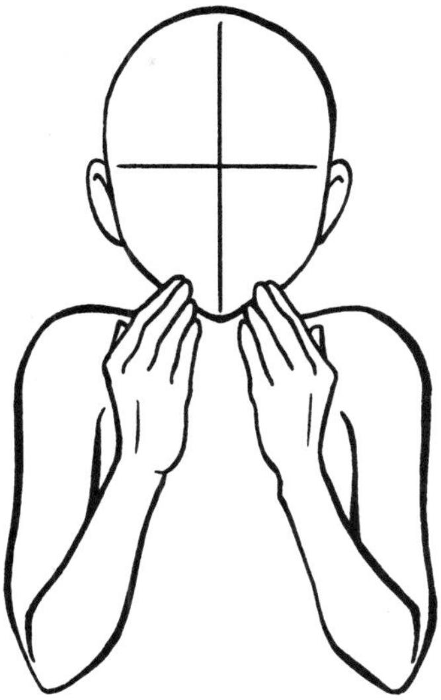

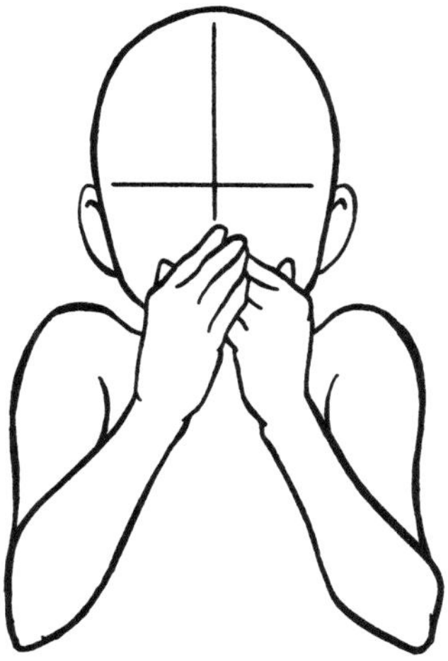

"You're kidding?"; "Unbelievable!"; "No way!"

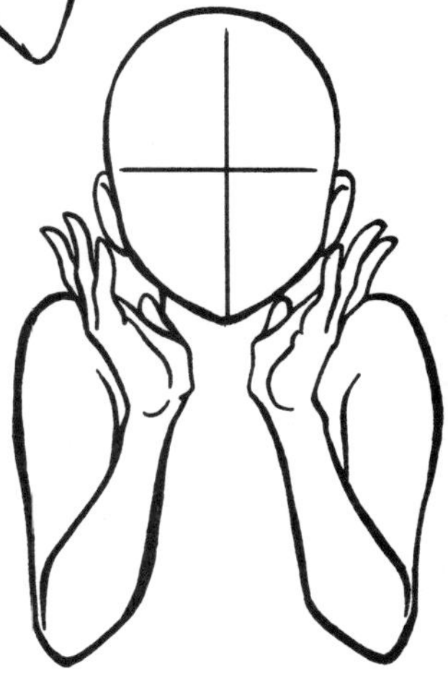

"Huh?"; "Great!"

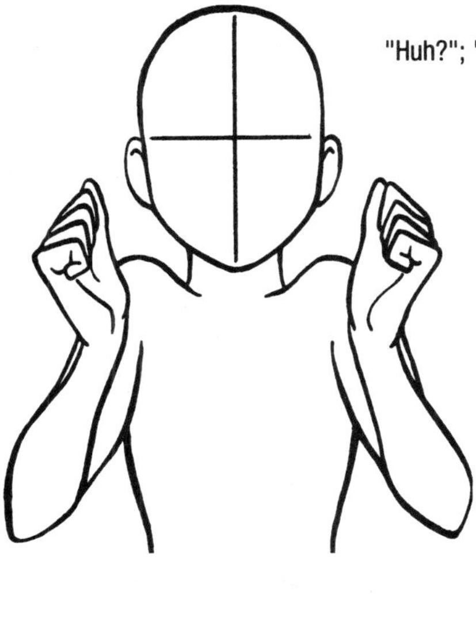

"All right!"; "Leave it to me!"; "Done!"

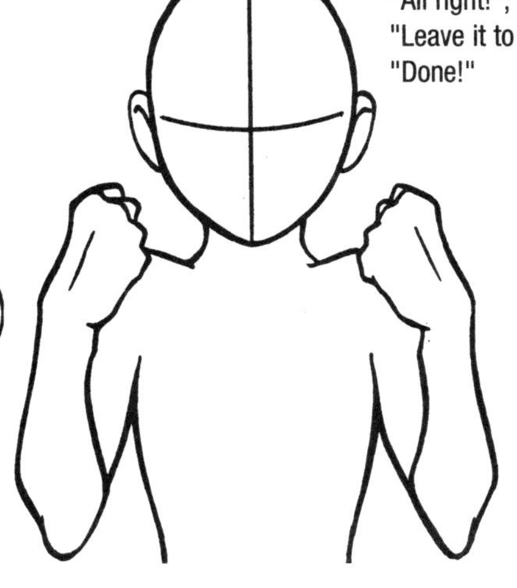

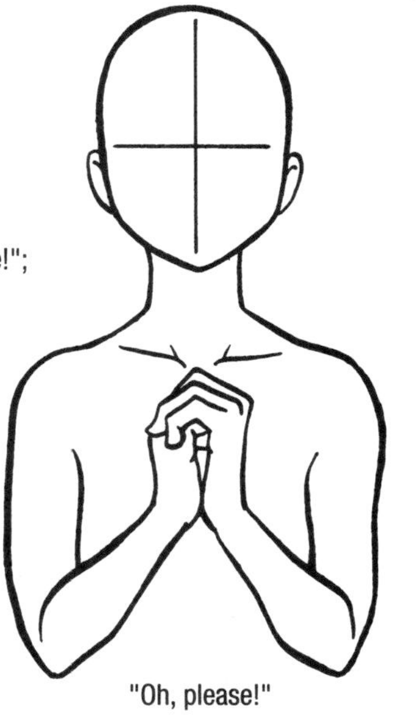

"Oh, please!"

Running, Leaping, Falling
Three Basic Action Poses

1 Breaking into a Run; Running

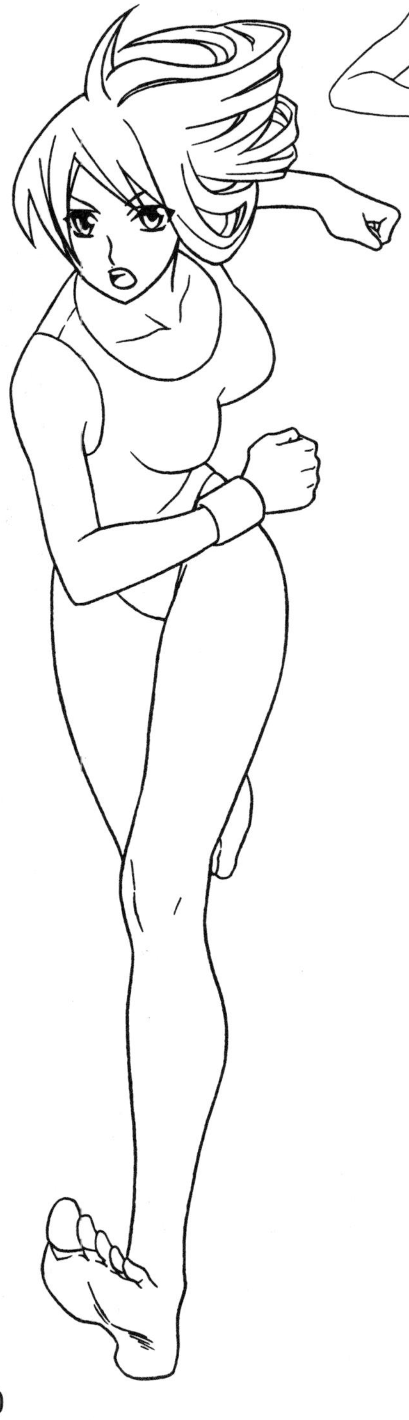

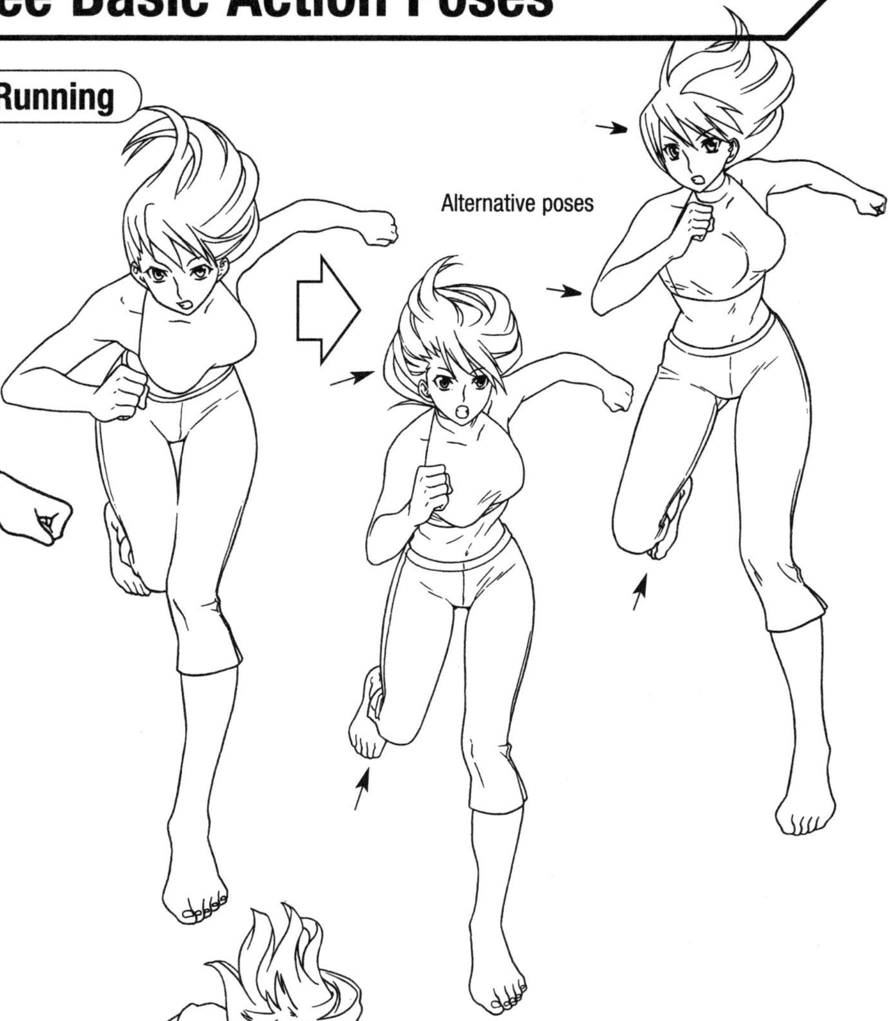

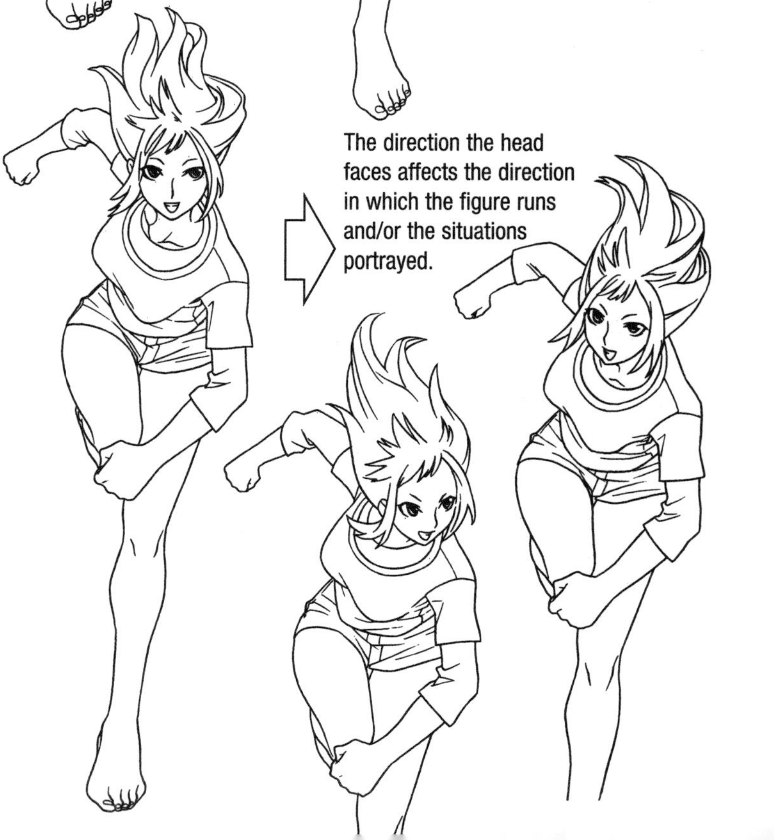

Sprinting

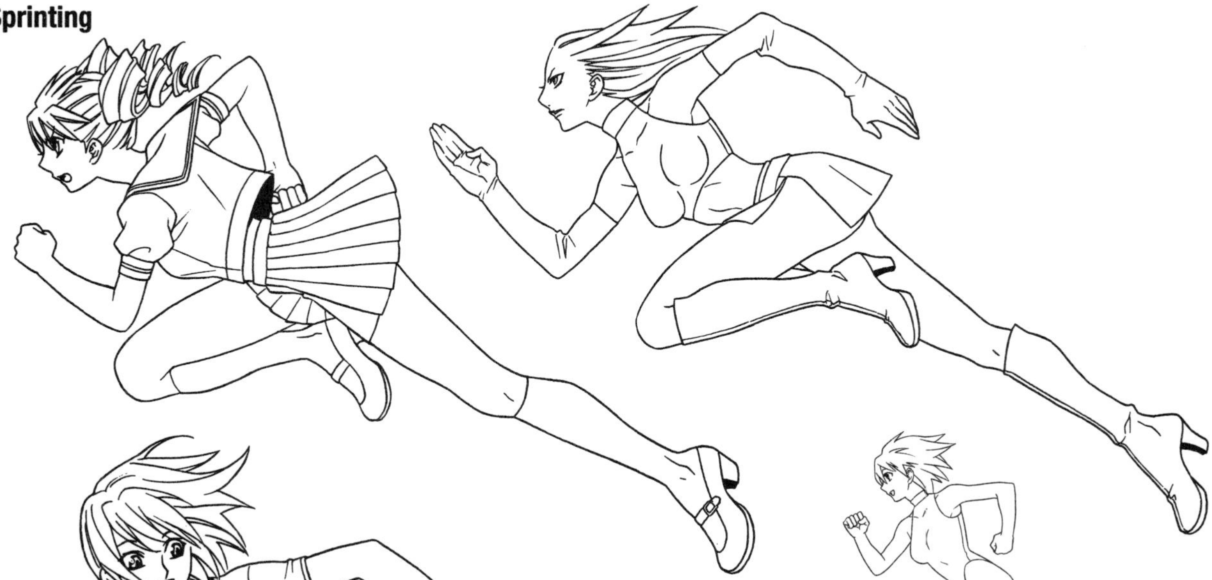

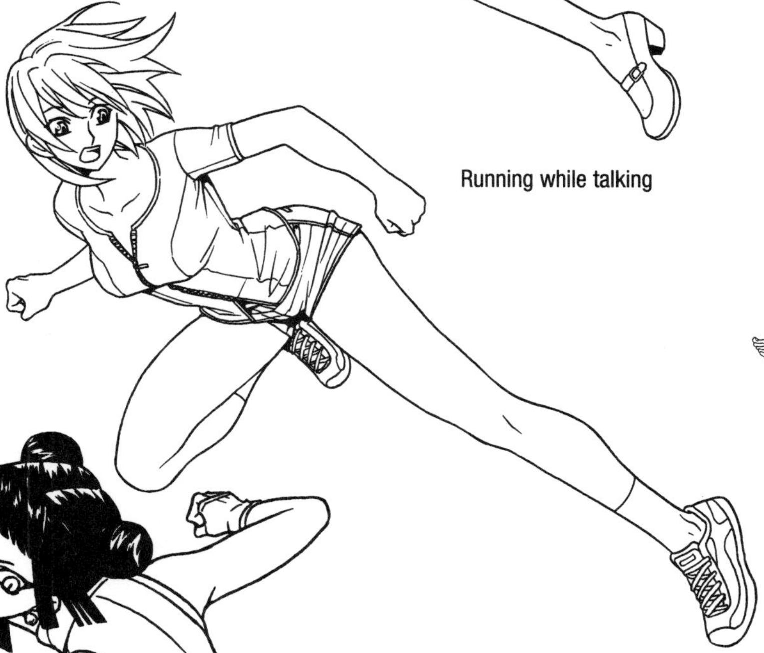

Running while talking

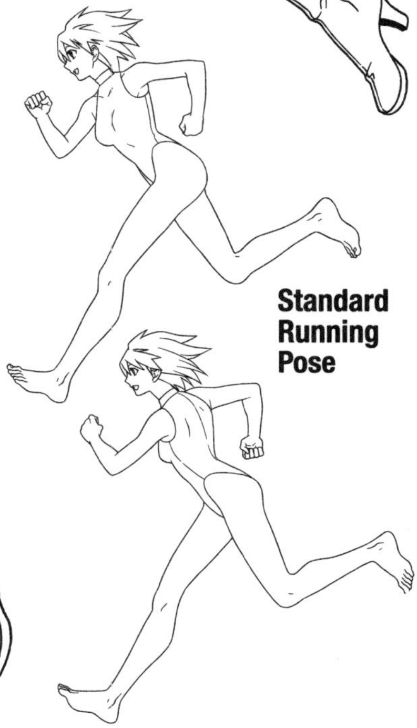

Standard Running Pose

Standard Running Pose vs. Sprinting

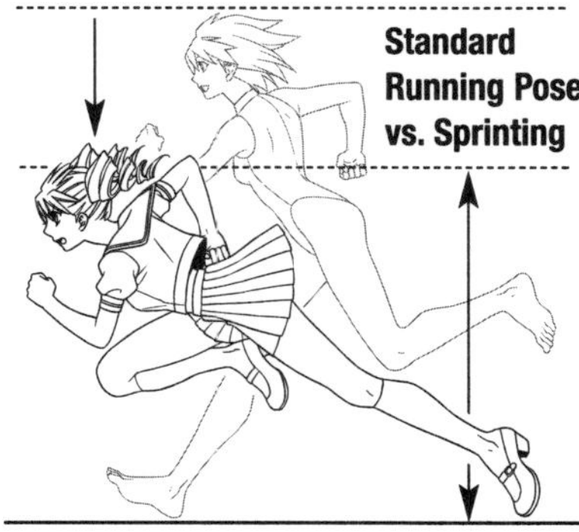

Increase the sense of speed by drawing the body leaning deeply forward to about where the waist would be in a standard running pose.

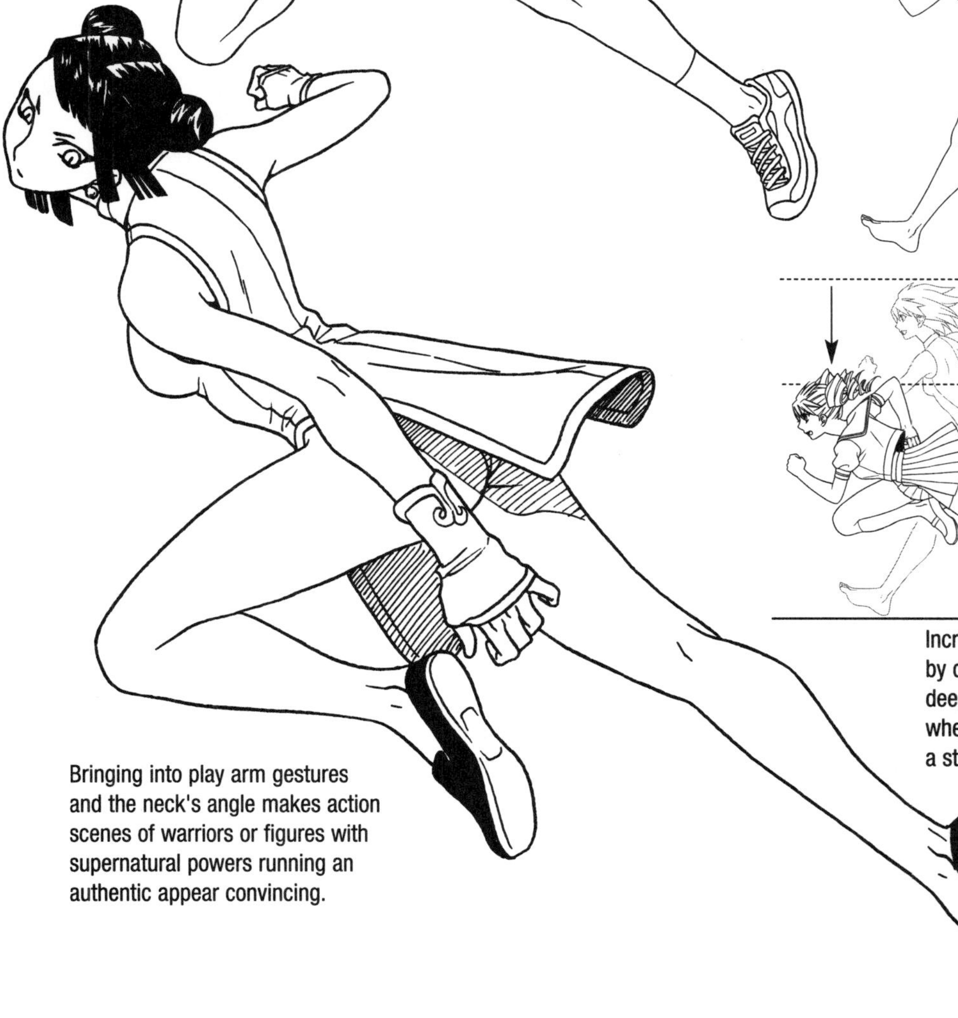

Bringing into play arm gestures and the neck's angle makes action scenes of warriors or figures with supernatural powers running an authentic appear convincing.

2 Jumping (Leaping)

I recommend low angled compositions for obtaining a sense of weightiness. Show the arms swinging any way that you prefer. Both arms may be raised above the head or swung out to the side or in front.

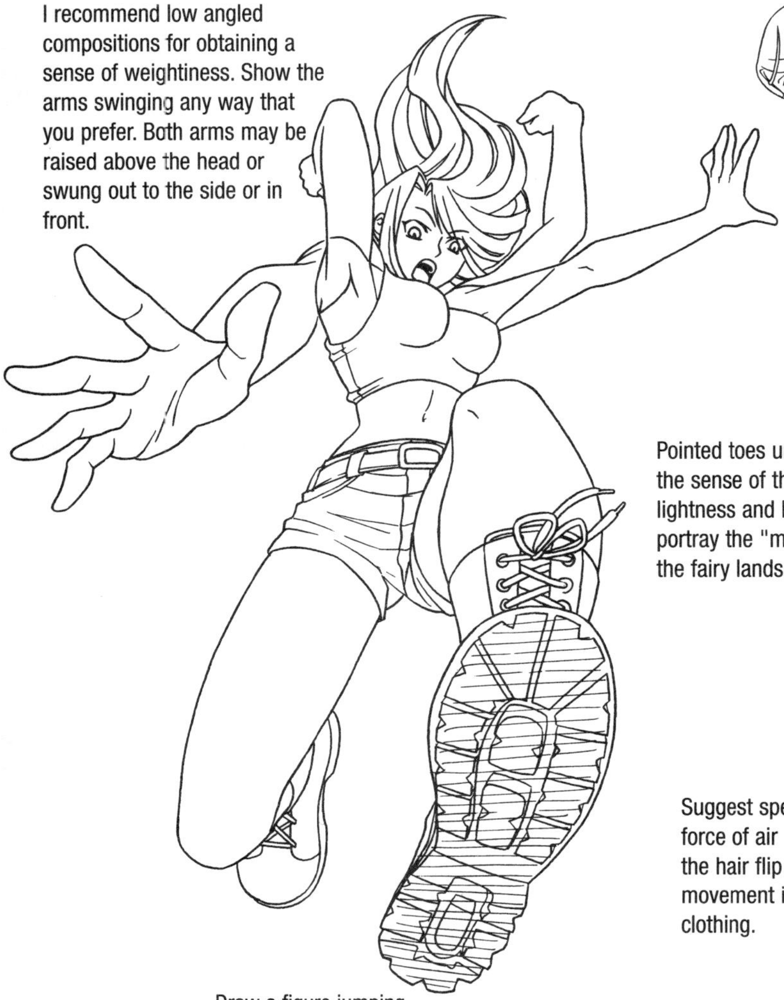

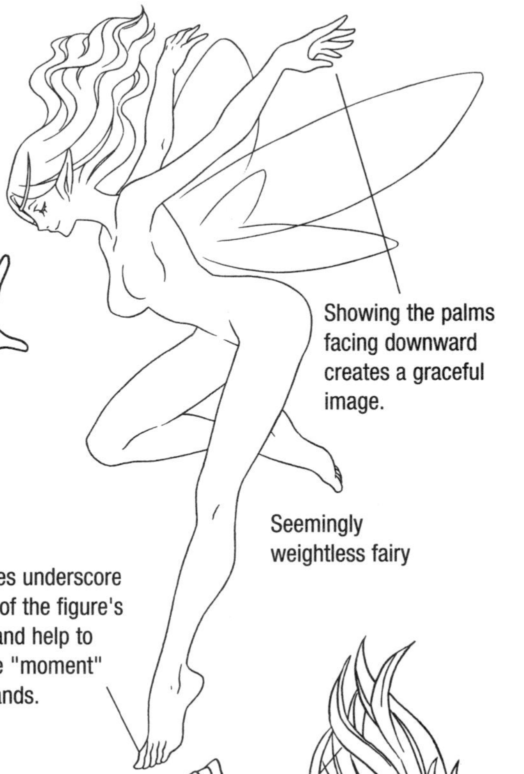

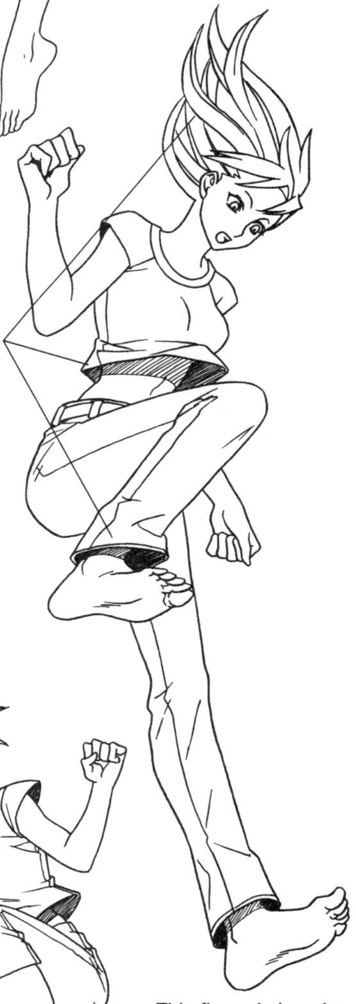

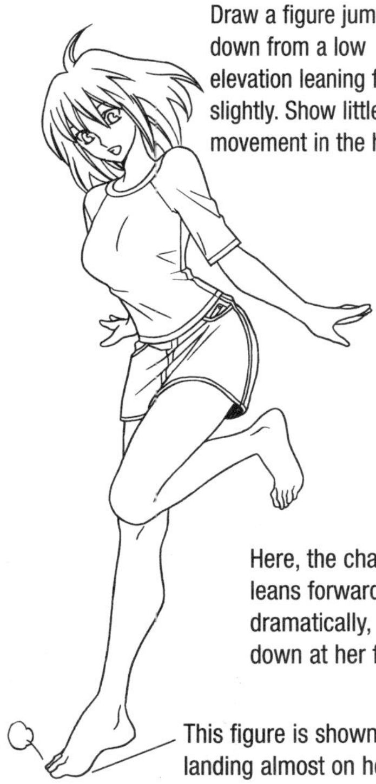

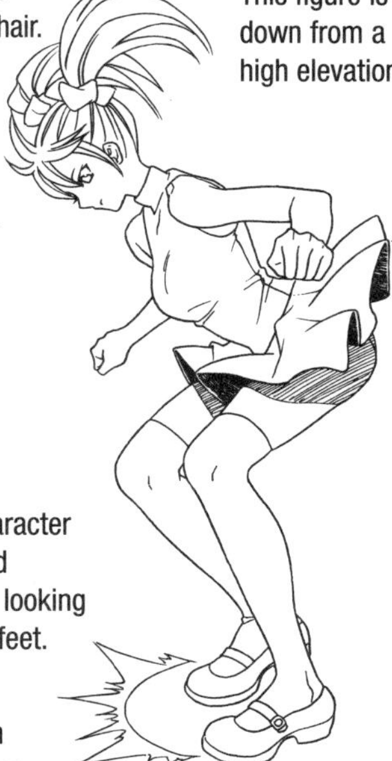

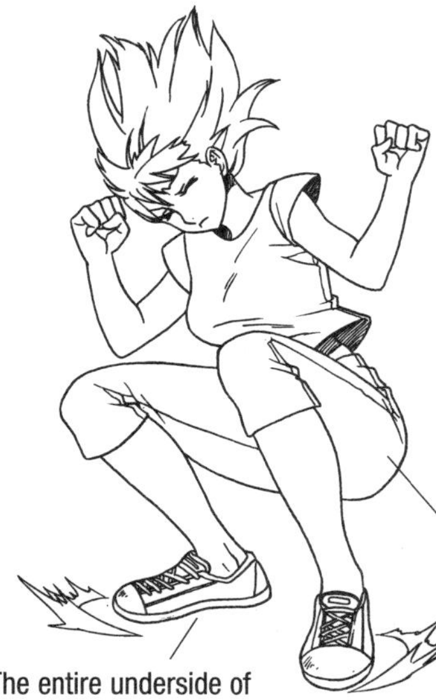

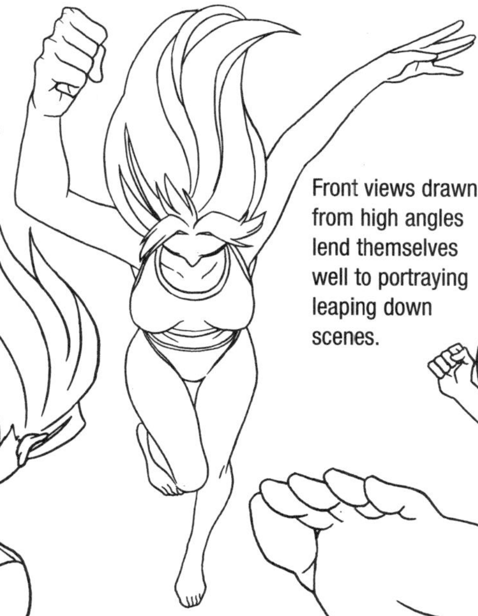

Front views drawn from high angles lend themselves well to portraying leaping down scenes.

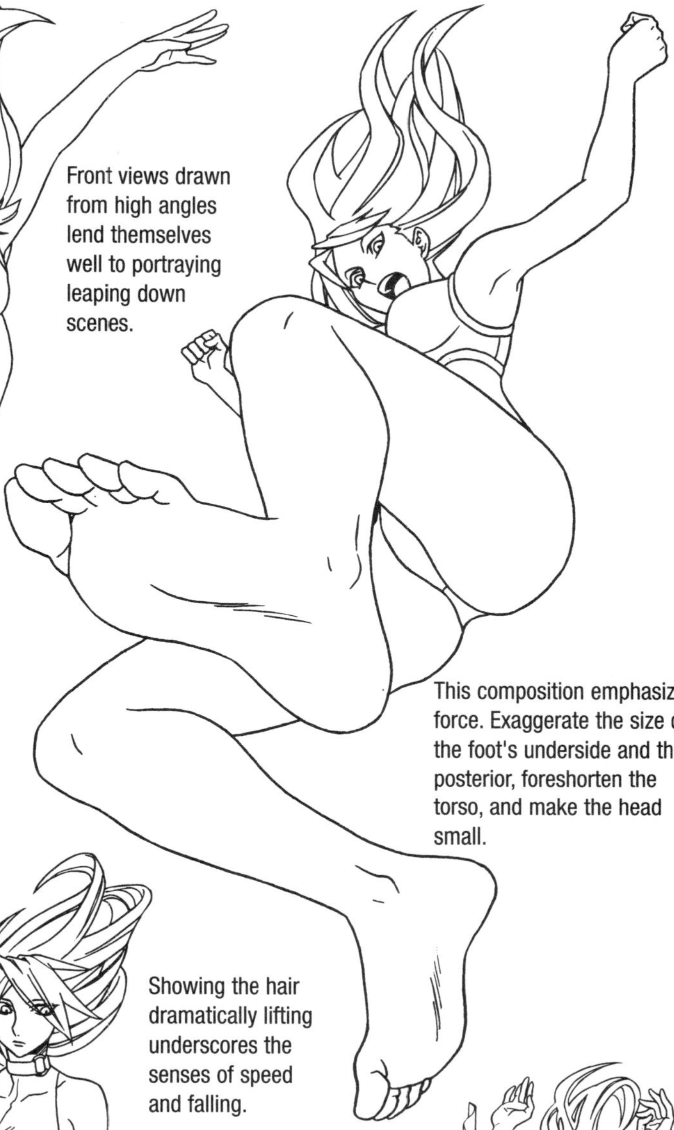

This composition emphasizes force. Exaggerate the size of the foot's underside and the posterior, foreshorten the torso, and make the head small.

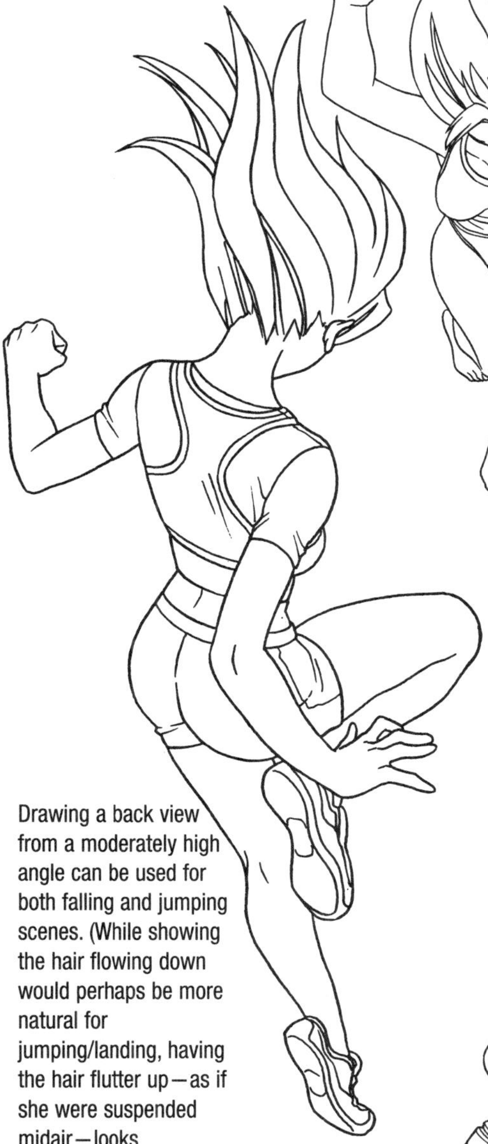

Drawing a back view from a moderately high angle can be used for both falling and jumping scenes. (While showing the hair flowing down would perhaps be more natural for jumping/landing, having the hair flutter up—as if she were suspended midair—looks spectacular.)

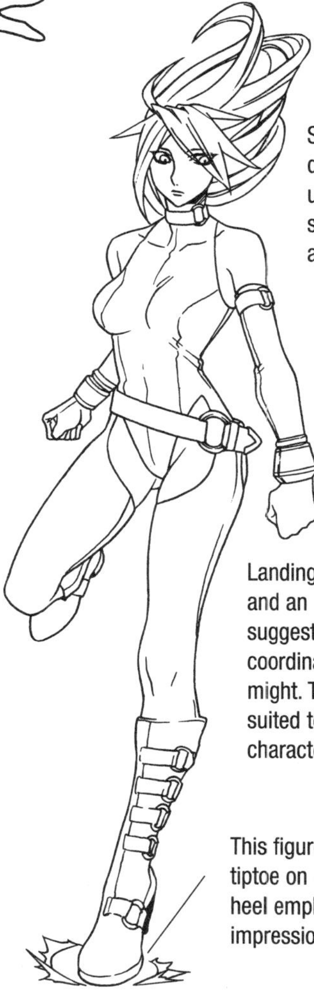

Showing the hair dramatically lifting underscores the senses of speed and falling.

Landing with fluttering hair and an erect upper body suggests developed muscle coordination and physical might. This landing pose is suited to superhuman characters.

This figure is landing on tiptoe on one foot. The raised heel emphasizes the impression of strength.

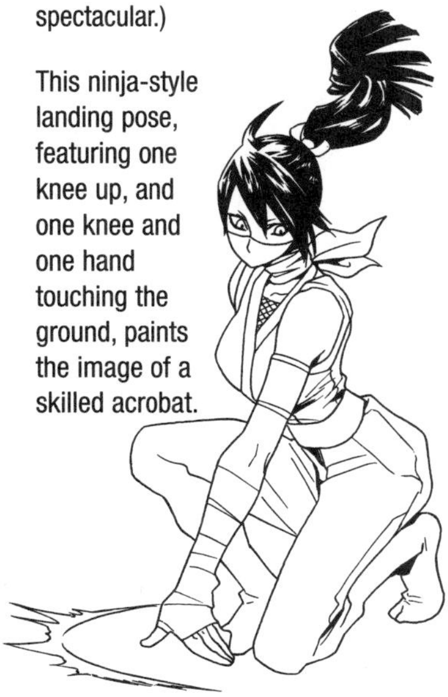

This ninja-style landing pose, featuring one knee up, and one knee and one hand touching the ground, paints the image of a skilled acrobat.

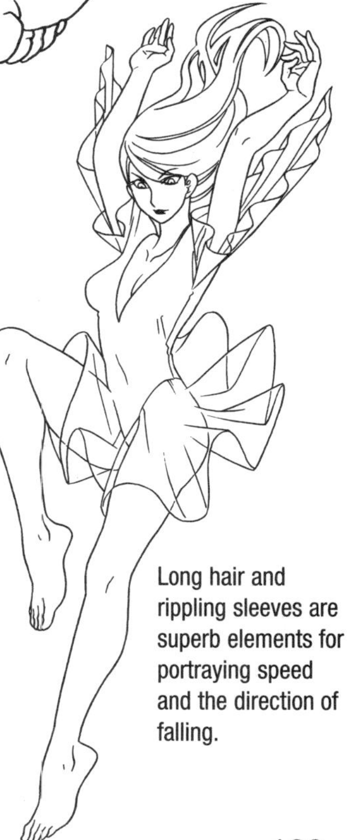

Long hair and rippling sleeves are superb elements for portraying speed and the direction of falling.

3 Falling

Stumbling

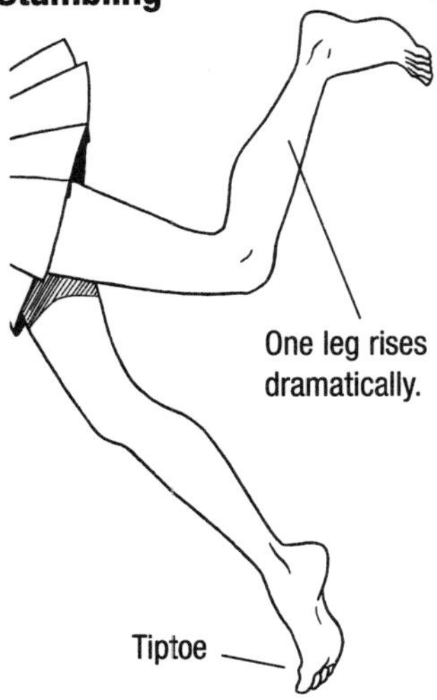

One leg rises dramatically.

Tiptoe

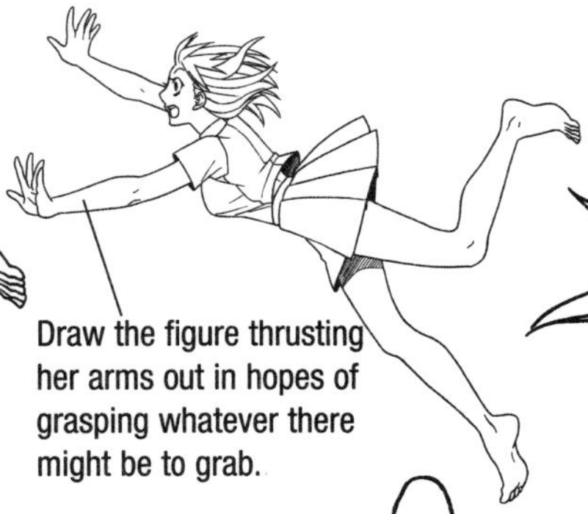

Draw the figure thrusting her arms out in hopes of grasping whatever there might be to grab.

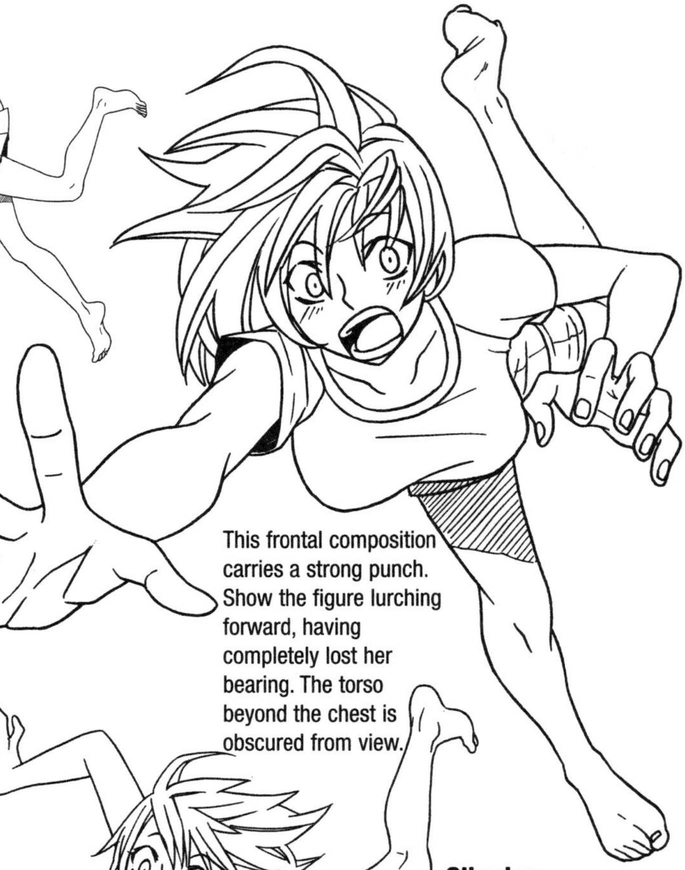

This frontal composition carries a strong punch. Show the figure lurching forward, having completely lost her bearing. The torso beyond the chest is obscured from view.

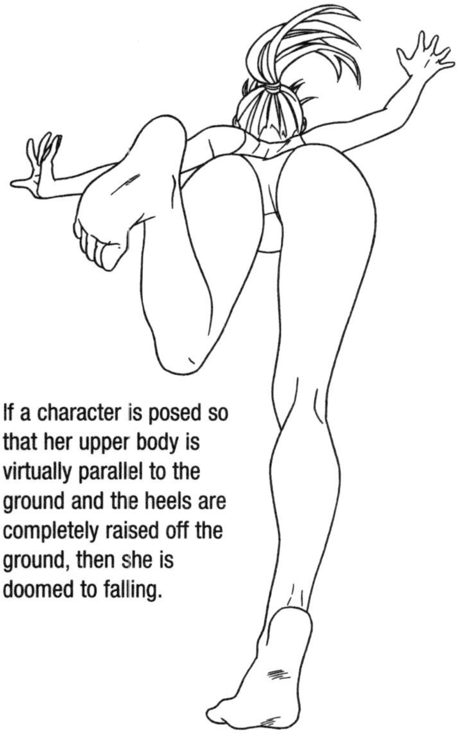

If a character is posed so that her upper body is virtually parallel to the ground and the heels are completely raised off the ground, then she is doomed to falling.

Slipping

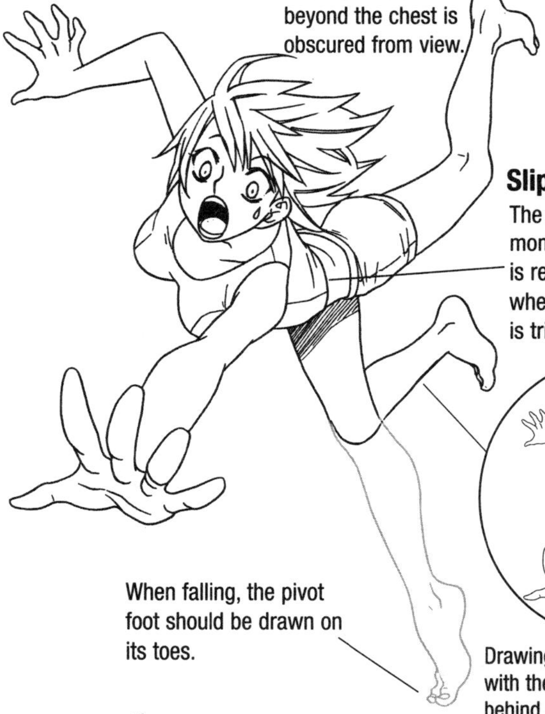

The upper body at the moment of stumbling is rendered identically whether the character is tripping or slipping.

When falling, the pivot foot should be drawn on its toes.

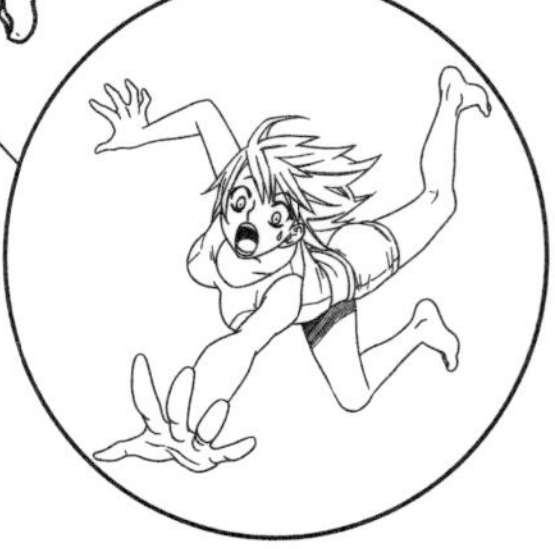

Drawing a character slipping with the pivot foot brought behind figure creates the illusion of floating in midair.

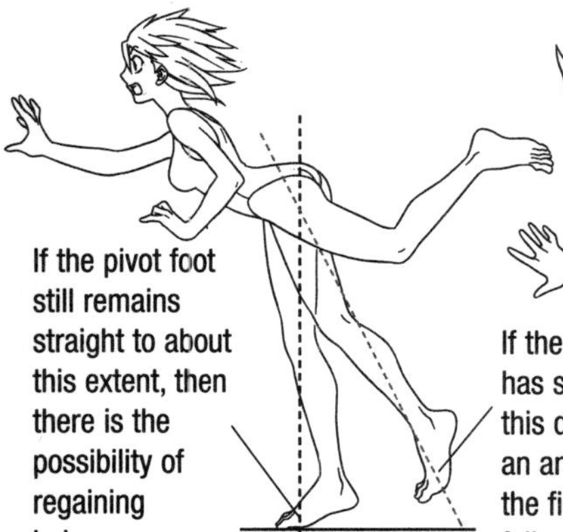

If the pivot foot still remains straight to about this extent, then there is the possibility of regaining balance.

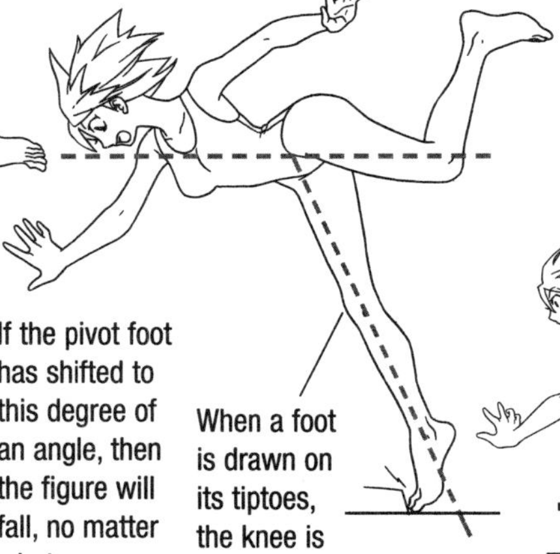

If the pivot foot has shifted to this degree of an angle, then the figure will fall, no matter what.

When a foot is drawn on its tiptoes, the knee is straight.

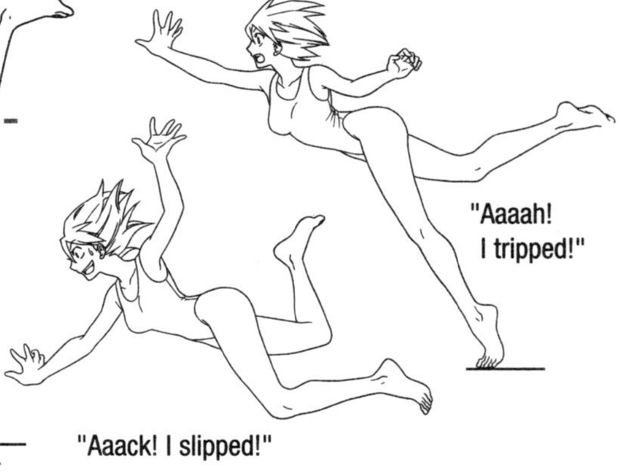

"Aaaah! I tripped!"

"Aaack! I slipped!"

Landing on the Rump

Characters are usually drawn landing on their backsides after slipping.

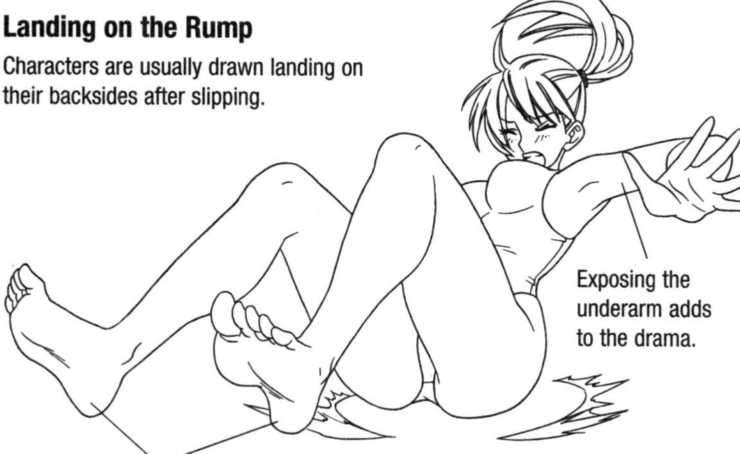

Exposing the underarm adds to the drama.

The heels are elevated.

Draw the legs flailing extravagantly upward when portraying a character running and then falling with a thud.

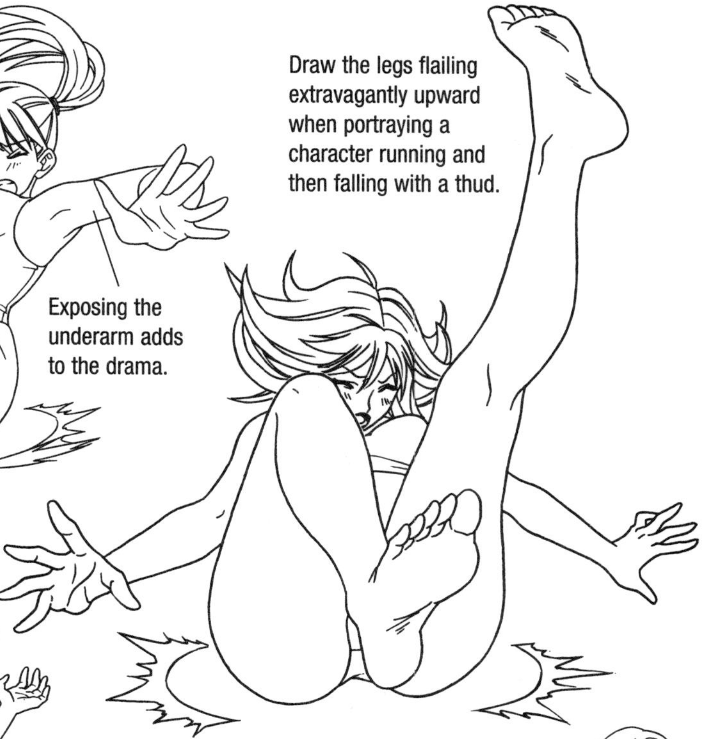

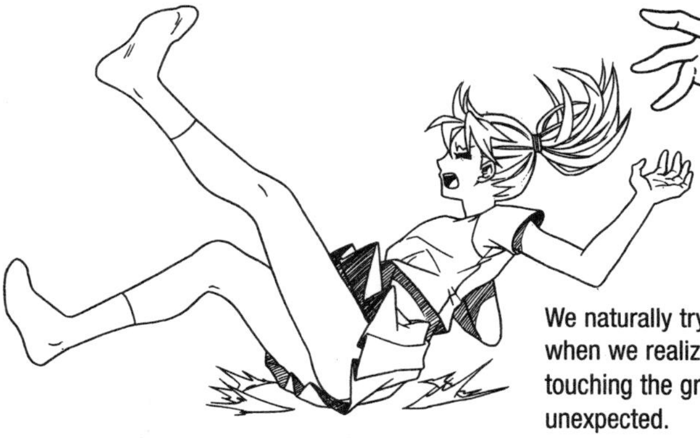

We naturally try to stop ourselves with our hands when we realize we are falling. Drawing no hand touching the ground implies that the fall was unexpected.

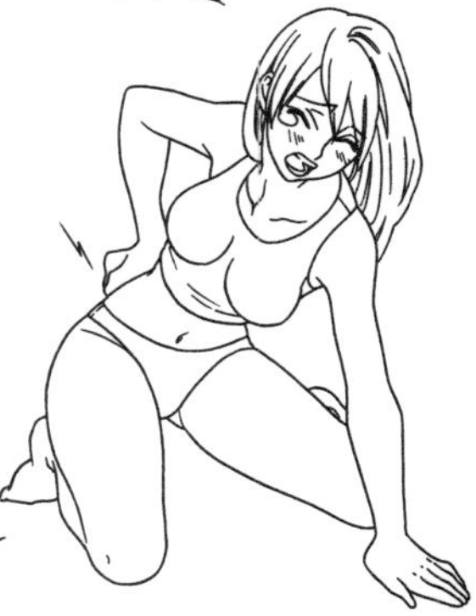

Plunging Forward

Artists often draw the character's back view from an overhead angle when drawing the entire figure.

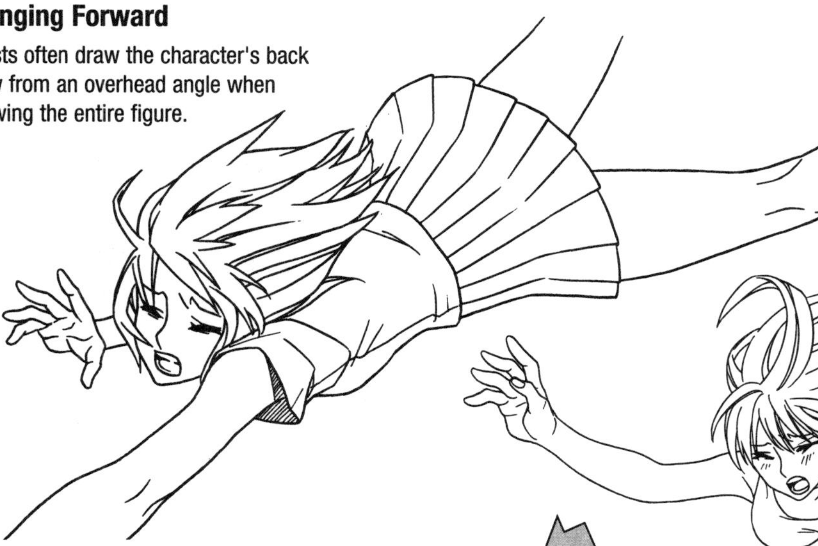

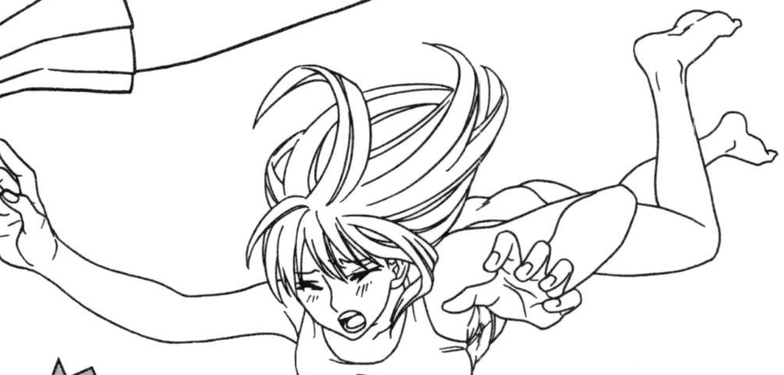

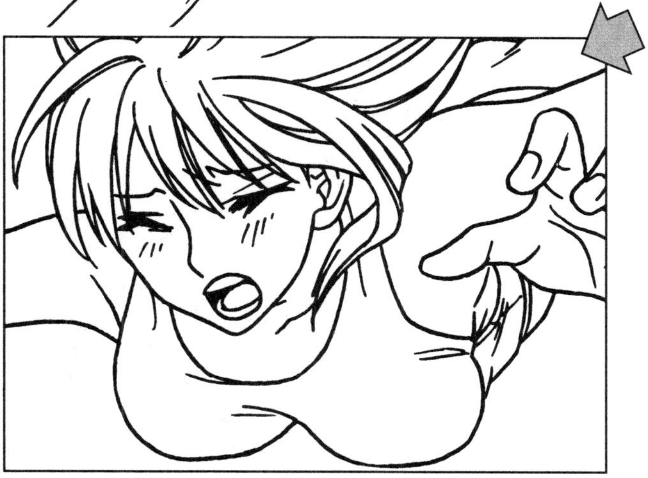

When showing the character's face, composing from a front view generates an intense mood. Cropping the composition to just the head and chest region results in an effective image.

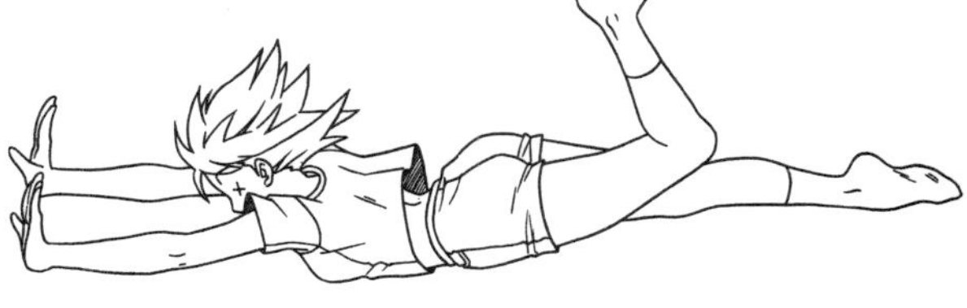

Straight-on side views tend to look humorous.

Figures and Cars

Using Facial Expressions and Body Language to Portray Driving

Driving Normally

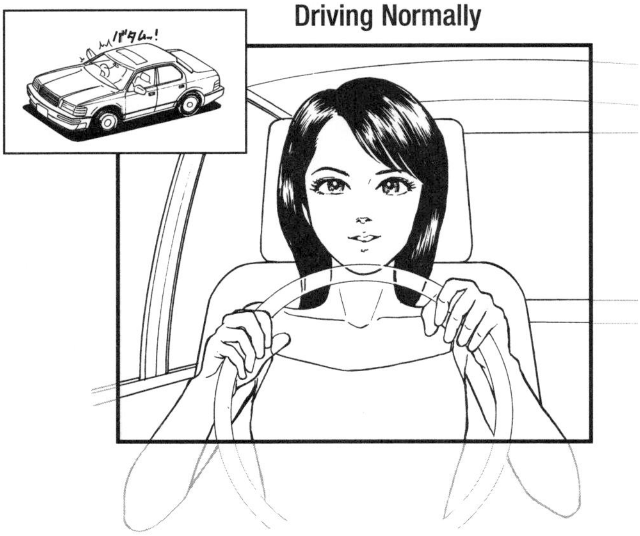

Happy; In Good Spirits

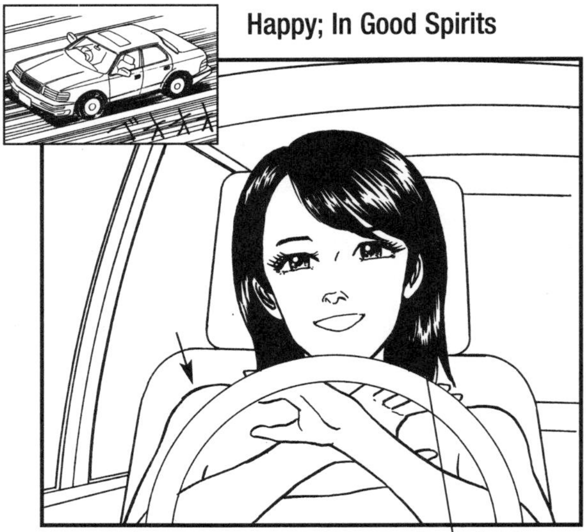

When driving normally, the shoulders are relaxed.

Tilting the head slightly indicates a pleasant mood.

Stuck in Traffic; Annoyed

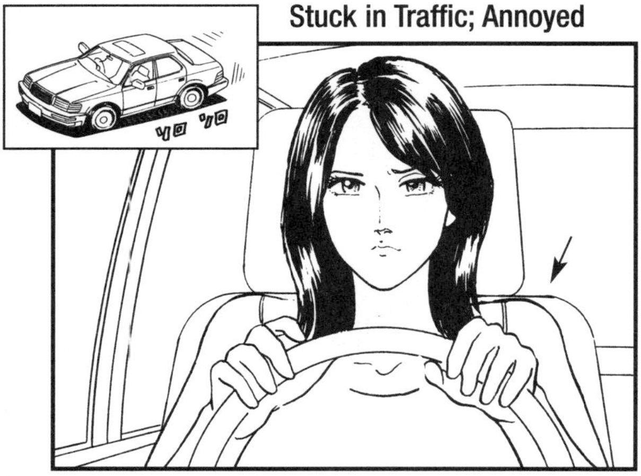

The shoulders rise when tensed.

Newbie Driver; Holding on for Dear Life

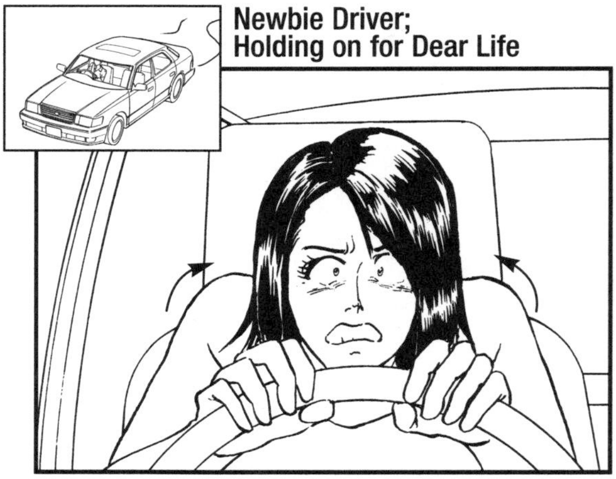

The shoulders rise from being tensed.
The character leans forward out of anxiety.

Slamming on the Brakes; Startled

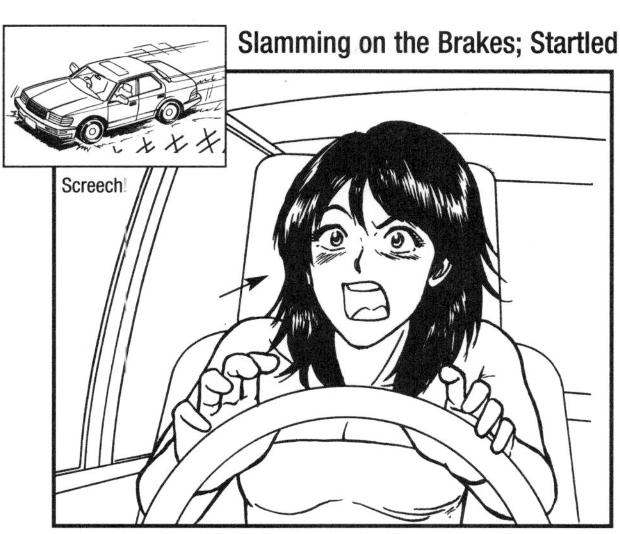

The head is thrown back slightly.

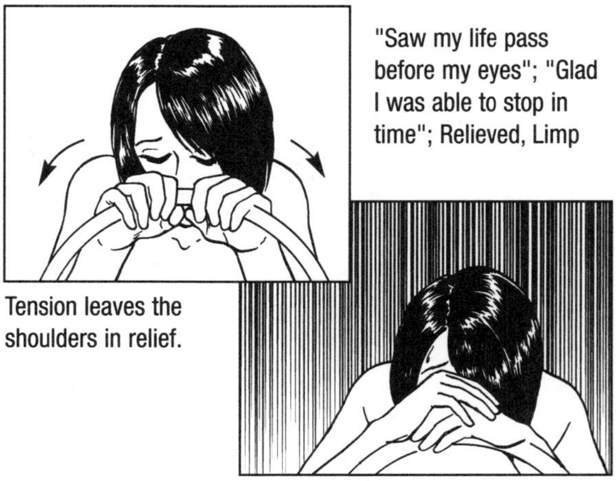

"Saw my life pass before my eyes"; "Glad I was able to stop in time"; Relieved, Limp

Tension leaves the shoulders in relief.

Graphic-sha Publishing Co., Ltd.

MANGA INSTRUCTION FROM THE MANGA MASTERS!

MORE HOW TO DRAW MANGA FROM GRAPHIC-SHA PUBLISHING

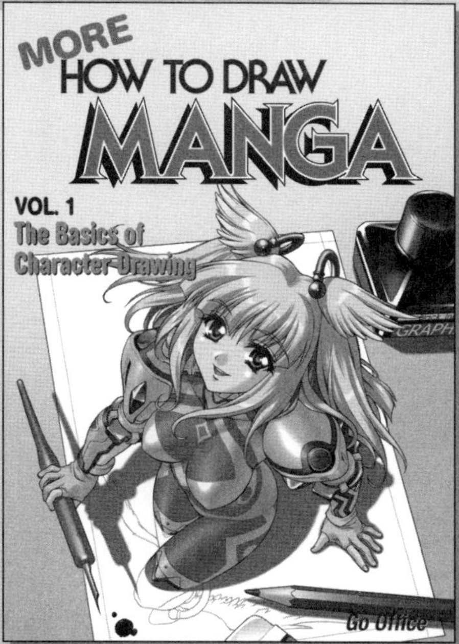

ISBN4-7661-1482-5

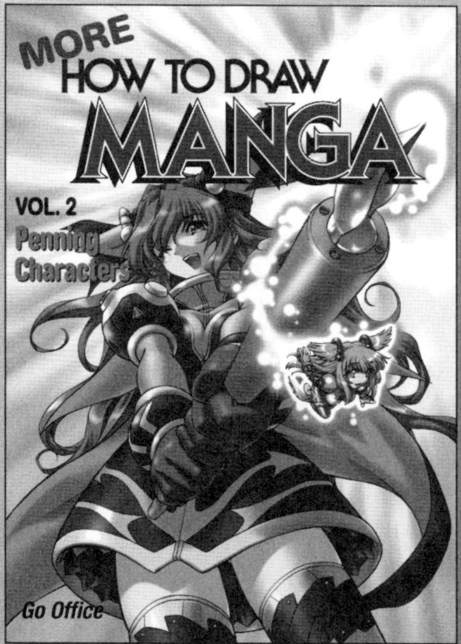

ISBN4-7661-1483-3

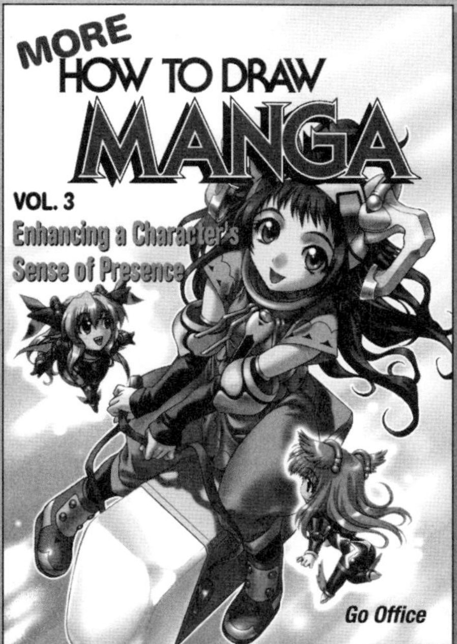

ISBN4-7661-1484-1

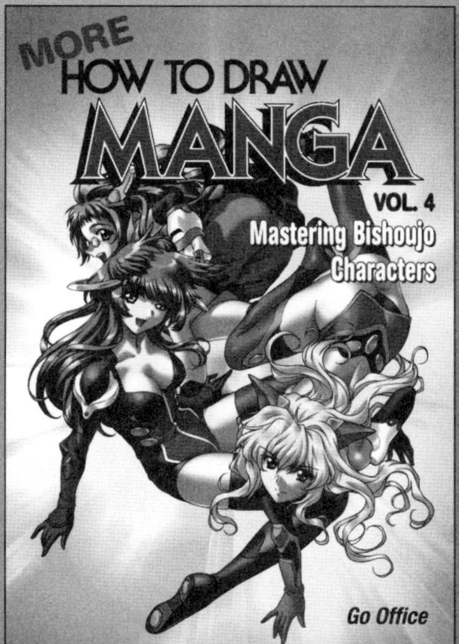

ISBN4-7661-1485-X